# Adult Behavior Therapy Casebook

# Adult Behavior Therapy Casebook

Edited by

**Cynthia G. Last**
and
**Michel Hersen**

*Nova University*
*Fort Lauderdale, Florida*

**PLENUM PRESS • NEW YORK AND LONDON**

Library of Congress Cataloging in Publication Data

Adult behavior therapy casebook / edited by Cynthia G. Last and Michel Hersen.
    p.    cm.
  Includes bibliographical references and index.
  ISBN 0-306-44451-8 (Hardbound); ISBN 0-306-44459-3 (Paperback)
  1. Behavior therapy—Case studies. I. Last, Cynthia G. II. Hersen, Michel.
  [DNLM: 1. Behavior Therapy—case studies. WM 425 A2435 1993]
RC489.B4A327 1993
616.89′142—dc20
DNLM/DLC                                                              93-6252
for Library of Congress                                                 CIP

ISBN 0-306-44451-8 (Hardbound)
ISBN 0-306-44459-3 (Paperback)

© 1994 Plenum Press, New York
A Division of Plenum Publishing Corporation
233 Spring Street, New York, N.Y.  10013

Printed in the United States of America

# Contributors

JEFF BAKER • Department of Psychiatry and Psychology Training, University of Texas Medical Branch at Galveston, Galveston, Texas 77555

J. GAYLE BECK • Department of Psychology, University of New York at Buffalo, Buffalo, New York 14260

GILLIAN BUTLER • Department of Clinical Psychology, Warneford Hospital, Headington, Oxford, United Kingdom OX3 7JX

PAUL CINCIRIPINI • Department of Psychiatry and Psychology Training, University of Texas Medical Branch at Galveston, Galveston, Texas 77555

ELLEN COSTELLO • Department of Psychiatry and Human Behavior, Brown University School of Medicine, and Department of Psychology, Butler Hospital, Providence, Rhode Island 02906

A. ECCLES • Kingston Sexual Behaviour Clinic, and Department of Psychology, Queens University, Kingston, Ontario, Canada K7L 3N6

MINDY ENGLE-FRIEDMAN • Department of Psychology, Baruch College, New York, New York 10010

EDNA B. FOA • Center for Treatment and Study of Anxiety, Medical College of Pennsylvania at Eastern Pennsylvania Psychiatric Institute, Philadelphia, Pennsylvania 19129

DAVID M. GARNER • Department of Psychiatry, Michigan State University, East Lansing, Michigan 48824-1316

RICHARD G. HEIMBERG • Center for Stress and Anxiety Disorder, State University of New York at Albany, Washington Avenue Extension, Pine West Plaza, Building 4, Albany, New York 12205

MICHEL HERSEN • Nova University, Fort Lauderdale, Florida 33314

HELLA HISS • Center for Treatment and Study of Anxiety, Medical College of Pennsylvania at Eastern Pennsylvania Psychiatric Institute, Philadelphia, Pennsylvania 19129

DEBRA A. HOPE • Department of Psychology, University of Nebraska–Lincoln, Lincoln, Nebraska 68588-0308

TERENCE M. KEANE • Boston Department of Veterans Affairs Medical Center, Boston, Massachusetts 02130

GABOR I. KEITNER • Department of Psychiatry and Human Behavior, Brown University School of Medicine, and Department of Psychology, Butler Hospital, Providence, Rhode Island 02906

BENOIT LABERGE • Centre Hospitalier de l'Université Laval, Université Laval, Sainte-Foy, Québec, Canada G1V 462

CYNTHIA G. LAST • Nova University, Fort Lauderdale, Florida 33314

BARRY M. MALETZKY • Oregon Health Sciences University, Portland, Oregon 97202

W. L. MARSHALL • Kingston Sexual Behaviour Clinic, and Department of Psychology, Queens University, Kingston, Ontario, Canada K7L 3N6

RICHARD A. MCCORMICK • Psychology Service, Cleveland Veterans Affairs Medical Center, Brecksville Division, Brecksville, Ohio 44141

F. DUDLEY MCGLYNN • Department of Psychology, Auburn University, Alabama 36849-5214

PATRICK W. MCGUFFIN • Hahnemann University, Philadelphia, Pennsylvania 19063

MARY ANN MERCIER • 2570 Oak Valley Drive, Vienna, Virginia 22181, and consultant for the Department of Psychiatry, College of Physicians and Surgeons, Columbia University, New York, New York 10027

IVAN W. MILLER • Department of Psychiatry and Human Behavior, Brown University School of Medicine, and Department of Psychology, Butler Hospital, Providence, Rhode Island 02906

RANDALL L. MORRISON • Response Analysis Corporation, 377 Wall Street, Princeton, New Jersey 08542

TIMOTHY J. O'FARRELL • Department of Psychiatry, Harvard Medical School, and Veterans Affairs Medical Center (116B), Brockton, Massachusetts 02401

PEGGY O'HARA • Department of Epidemiology and Public Health, University of Miami School of Medicine, Miami, Florida 33101

THOMAS VOPAT • Department of Hospital Dentistry, University of Missouri–Kansas City School of Dentistry, Kansas City, Missouri 64108-2795

FRANK W. WEATHERS • Boston Department of Veterans Affairs Medical Center, Boston, Massachusetts 02130

S. LLOYD WILLIAMS • Department of Psychology, Lehigh University, Bethlehem, Pennsylvania 18015

# Preface

Several years ago we edited a casebook on behavior therapy with children. The book appeared to fill a gap in the existing child literature and was quite well received. A similar gap appears to exist in the behavioral literature for adult cases, in that there are very few adult casebooks currently available. The present book was developed in order to devote an entire casebook to both standard and more innovative clinical applications of behavioral treatments to adult problems.

The book, containing 19 chapters, is divided into two parts. In the first part, in a chapter entitled Clinical Considerations, we discuss a variety of clinical issues that are of importance to designing and executing behaviorally based interventions with adults. The bulk of the book, the remaining 18 chapters, contains a variety of cases presented by our experts.

Each of the treatment cases is presented using the same format in order to increase consistency and comparability across chapters. Specific sections for each chapter are as follows: (1) Description of the Disorder, (2) Case Identification, (3) Presenting Complaints, (4) History, (5) Assessment, (6) Selection of Treatment, (7) Course of Treatment, (8) Termination, (9) Follow-up, and (10) Overall Evaluation.

Thanks are extended to our many expert contributors, without whom this book would not be possible. We also wish to acknowledge the technical support of Mrs. Kim Sterner. Finally, we thank our editor at Plenum, Eliot Werner, for his support and forbearance in the face of the inevitable delays.

CYNTHIA G. LAST
MICHEL HERSEN

*Fort Lauderdale, Florida*

# Contents

PART I

# INTRODUCTION

# CHAPTER 1

# Clinical Considerations

## CYNTHIA G. LAST and MICHEL HERSEN

If we were writing this chapter in the 1960s, our view of the clinical issues would be vastly different. Of course, when one is aware of the historical context (Hersen, 1981, 1983, 1985; Kazdin, 1978; Krasner, 1990), it becomes clear why behavior therapists in the 1960s were so strident in their assertions as to the superiority of their approach. Indeed, Hersen (1981) has referred to such "breast beating" as the historical imperative that transpires when the supremacy of the reigning theoretical position is being challenged. However, those with a sense of humor about history are quick to realize that in science the hegemony of a given theoretical position can easily give way to its finding the direction to the wastebasket of disproven approaches. But the fate of the new theoretical approach (or at least some of its less functional parts) may eventually be identical to the one that it has replaced.

In light of this, we will consider a number of statements behavior therapists were making three decades ago and see how they now appear, given our broader clinical experience over the ensuing years:

1. "Behavior therapy is an efficient short-term treatment that can be carried out in 10 to 15 sessions." There are problems and disorders where this approach is valid. However, for the greatest proportion of referrals made to behavior therapists, the disorders are complex, the symptoms are often resistive to therapeutic application, and a multilevel and multisystem approach is required over extended time periods (Hersen, 1983), with booster and maintenance sessions standard over the course of treatment. Some disorders have

CYNTHIA G. LAST and MICHEL HERSEN • Nova University, Fort Lauderdale, Florida 33314.

*Adult Behavior Therapy Casebook,* edited by Cynthia G. Last and Michel Hersen. Plenum Press, New York, 1994.

been conceptualized as chronic diseases for which the client must continuously remain in the therapeutic system (cf. Kazdin, 1987).

2. "Removal of the symptoms will lead to cure of the neurosis." To begin with, behavior therapists now deal with a far more extended range of patients, thus challenging the simplistic notion inherent in that statement. Moreover, there is increasing evidence that different etiologies (e.g., psychological, medical, drug-induced) can lead to an identical symptom picture (cf. Hersen, 1981; Hersen & Van Hasselt, 1992; Twerski, 1984). It behooves the astute behavioral assessor to understand the particular pathway to psychopathology, since the etiology will have implications for the specific therapeutic modality that will be selected.

3. "There is no basis for psychiatric diagnosis in behavioral assessment and treatment." This statement made sense with respect to *DSM-I* and *DSM-II* (the first and second editions of the American Psychiatric Association's *Diagnostic and Statistical Manual of Mental Disorders*) in that psychiatric diagnoses in the two original nosological schemes were not reliable or valid (Hersen, 1976). However, with the advent of *DSM-III* (American Psychiatric Association, 1980) and *DSM-III-R* (American Psychiatric Association, 1987) and the development of semistructured interview schedules that enhance diagnostic reliability and validity, the complementarity of behavioral assessment and psychiatric diagnoses (Hersen & Bellack, 1988) has assumed greater importance. Most important, however, is the fact that behavior therapists can no longer ignore the scientific relevance of diagnostic categorization.

4. "Motoric behavior is the focus of behavioral treatment; cognitions are not important." The proliferation of cognitive-behavioral treatment strategies that have been empirically evaluated (Ingram & Scott, 1990) has nullified the original argument and clearly supports the notion that cognitions can be not only modified directly but also operationalized so that cross-study comparisons can be made. Contemporary behavior therapists are interested in the modification of motoric, physiological, and cognitive indices of behavior. Moreover, recent work in psychoneuroimmunology suggests that biochemical indicants should be added to the list as well (Kiecolt-Glaser & Glaser, 1992).

5. "The relationship between the therapists and the client is not the critical ingredient in behavior therapy; it is the technique that brings about change." Although technique in behavior therapy may be preeminent, in the absence of a positively reinforcing therapeutic relationship patients simply *will not* carry out the many and sometimes complicated homework assignments that will be given to them by the therapist. As early as 1971 Hersen, in a somewhat obscure publication, talked about the prevalence of resistance to direction in behavior therapy. This factor is now well acknowledged, and the importance of the therapist–client relationship no longer is given short shrift.

6. "Symptom substitution is a myth proffered by psychoanalysts that has

no bearing in behavior therapy." As early as 1976 Blanchard and Hersen (both ardent behavior therapists) carefully examined the issues and, on the basis of the clinical evidence, concluded that in instances of incomplete behavioral treatment both symptom return and symptom substitution did occur.

    7. "Many behavioral techniques can be automated and administered without a therapist." This perhaps was the greatest myth perpetrated by the early behavior therapists. As already noted, the human element in behavior therapy is important. We know of no computer program that is sufficiently complex to capture the myriad techniques and resulting therapist–client interactions that take place in clinical practice.

    Perhaps the best way to summarize the changing complexion of behavior therapy as it has matured is to quote Fishman and Lubetkin (1983), two eminent behavioral therapists, on how they have been compelled to modify their own clinical practices. We should underscore that we fully concur with the position reflected in the following quote:

> As client's problems have become less circumscribed and multifaceted (this distinction may be more apparent than real—the change may be due to the way problems are currently assessed) over the decades of our practice, our own emphasis has shifted from a problem-centered, technique-oriented approach to strategies that provide our patients with more general coping capabilities. Our goals for therapy are to provide the patient with skills for exercising greater control over their presenting problems and further, to provide them with the means for both assessing and remediating problems that may arise in their future functioning. This shift in emphasis in our own treatment planning is reflected in the fact that our mean number of sessions from intake to termination has increased from approximately 22 sessions, 10 years ago, to about 50 sessions per patient currently. By way of summary, this change in the actual number of contact hours per patient can be attributed to a number of or combination of factors alluded to above: (1) the field has been modified in general, which has led practitioners to being sought out for and addressing more global problems; (2) with increased procedural sophistication in methods of assessment, practitioners are now focusing on more aspects of patients' problems and not targeting only the manifest problem; and (3) practitioners are functioning in a much more holistic way in the application of the various cognitive-behavioral approaches in a "coping skills" paradigm.

## ASSESSMENT AND DIAGNOSIS

    The hallmark of behavior therapy has always been the close, if not isomorphic, relationship between assessment and treatment (Bellack & Hersen, 1988; Hersen & Bellack, 1976, 1981). This close relationship has best been observed in the single-case design (Barlow & Hersen, 1984; Hersen 1990; Hersen & Barlow, 1976), whereby the effects of the specific treatment are discerned graphically and statistically on the targets selected for modification. Termed the "functional relationship" by those of operant persuasion, such precision of study eventuated in many refinements of our therapeutic applications.

In the preceding paragraph we have described the microanalysis used when dealing with the problems presented by our clients. And, indeed, this microanalysis has been the cornerstone of behavioral assessment from its inception. More recently however, behavioral assessors have followed a broader perspective. As noted by Hersen and Bellack (1988), they are now concerned with intellectual evaluation in addition to simply pinpointing behavioral targets (Nelson, 1980); they are more cognizant of developmental issues (Harris & Ferrari, 1983); they are aware of the multiple etiologies of presenting symptoms (Hersen & Van Hasselt, 1992); and there is increased attention to selecting multiple target foci for behavioral treatment (Kazdin, 1985). Furthermore, the biological underpinnings of behavior (Rebec & Anderson, 1986) and the medical contributions to assessment and diagnosis (Ganguli, 1983; George, 1991) are now given the credence that they fully deserve.

Given the improvements in the psychiatric system of classification, with the advent of the multiaxial system in *DSM-III* and *DSM-III-R* (American Psychiatric Association, 1980, 1987) and the attendant improvement in diagnostic reliability and validity, behavioral clinicians have not been able to ignore psychiatric diagnosis. As noted elsewhere, in looking at the complementarity of behavioral assessment and psychiatric diagnoses, behavioral assessment is conceptualized "as the *idiographic* approach within the broader *nomothetic* system encompassed by *DSM-III*. Thus, the strength of behavioral assessment is to identify specific targets (e.g., activity levels) that can be evaluated during the course of treatment . . . . On the other hand, it is the specific targets (or criteria) in a particular pattern that contribute to the diagnostic label" (Hersen & Bellack, 1988, p. 78).

Related to effective assessment is the selection of the response system that will be modified. The tripartite system of assessment (motoric, cognitive, physiological) has long been the standard approach followed by behavior therapists (Hersen, 1973). However, the nature of the particular client presentation and the setting in which he or she is seen may determine whether one, two, or three of the channels are examined. The ideal, of course, is represented in the multiple baseline case study by Van Hasselt, Hersen, Bellack, Rosenblum, and Lamparski (1979), in which motoric, physiological, and self-report information was evaluated in baseline and treatment sessions for a preadolescent multiphobic child. But, as noted by Bellack and Hersen (1985a), at times there may be a discrepancy between the theory and practice of behavior therapy. In inpatient settings and clinical research settings, where an extensive research personnel is available, it generally is possible to obtain repeated motoric observations. In these settings there is also a greater likelihood that physiological monitoring equipment will be available. Such is not the case in the consulting room or private practice setting, where there inevitably is greater reliance in the client's self-report. However, there is evidence that clients, given appropriate training, can learn to self-monitor with some degree of reliability (c.f. Hersen, 1978; Meichenbaum, 1976). And another option remains open to the private practitioner: he or she can obtain collateral information from relatives or friends of the client. In this connection, we must reiterate our prior position: "Behavioral therapy proceeds most smoothly when therapists are fully informed, thus enabling them to maximize their technical expertise" (Last & Hersen, 1985, p. 8).

## THE THERAPIST–CLIENT RELATIONSHIP

In our *Behavior Therapy Casebook* (Last & Hersen, 1985) we previously articulated the following:

> Graduate level students (in clinical psychology and psychiatry) learning how to apply behavioral strategies unfortunately are still entering the clinical setting with a good number of misconceptions as to how senior therapists operate. Some of these misperceptions, of course, can be traced to the earlier writings of behavior therapists, who underscored the technical aspects of treatment at the expense of important clinical considerations that apply to clinicians irrespective of their theoretical stance. These notions were further bolstered by the claims that under certain circumstances clinical procedures such as systematic desensitization could be applied mechanically in the absence of a therapist. (pp. 8–9)

Our objective then (and certainly now) was not to downplay the technical innovations of our behavioral colleagues over the ensuing years. Indeed, some amazing technical achievements have been published by behavior therapists in their treatment of an extremely wide range of cases (see Bellack & Hersen, 1985b, for the *Dictionary of Behavior Therapy Techniques*). However, we pose the following rhetorical question: In the absence of a warm and caring alliance between the therapist and client, will that client (1) maintain carefully detailed diaries and records; (2) self-monitor, self-evaluate, and self-reinforce outside of therapy; (3) practice a number of lengthy relaxation strategies; (4) attempt newly developed assertive responses in the natural environment; (5) follow through with the strictures of behavioral contracting; (6) attempt to decrease deviant, albeit positively reinforcing, appetitive responses; and (7) practice responses incompatible with natural desires?

Certainly, our clients at times have proven to be resistive to our best efforts (see DeVoge & Beck, 1978; Hersen, 1971; Martin & Worthington, 1982). Since the reasons for such resistance have been clearly stated by us in the past (Last & Hersen, 1985), we will not belabor the point here. Nonetheless, to put the issue at rest, the myth of the behavior therapist as being cold and mechanical (unfortunately, still perpetrated in some clinical circles) is simply not true. In at least two major clinical trials in which therapist–client behavior was precisely evaluated, behavior therapists were rated as significantly more empathic, congruent, and supportive than their nonbehavioral colleagues (cf. Greenwald, Kornblith, Hersen, Bellack, & Himmelhoch, 1981; Sloane, Staples, Cristol, Yorkston, & Whipple, 1975).

## CURRENT ISSUES

Since its inception the practice of behavior therapy has changed dramatically. In the beginning the behavioral movement considered directly observable behaviors to be the sole focus of intervention. This orientation toward treatment came in large part from the operant conditioning model, which played a profound role in the development of applied behavior analysis. During the past several decades, however, covert or private events, that is, those that are not directly observable, have become equal in status as targets for intervention within behavior therapy. In other words, both cognitions and physiological responses are now recognized as important in their own right.

The importance of cognitions in mediating maladaptive behavioral and emotional responses is now accepted by most practicing behavior therapists. This represents a dramatic shift from traditional behavior therapy in that modification of covert events was previously considered unimportant. The utility of modifying cognitions has been demonstrated for a variety of mental disorders ranging from childhood behavioral disturbances (i.e., conduct disorder, attention deficit disorder) to more internalizing emotional disorders, including both anxiety and depressive disorders. For anxiety disorders, catastrophic ideation in escalating arousal and avoidance behavior has been circumvented through various cognitive modification procedures. Depressed affect may be successfully altered through changing clients' negative cognitive distortions about themselves and their environment. Regardless of the disorder that is being treated, the goal is to modify dysfunctional patterns of thinking. However, it should be noted that even those who consider themselves to be strict cognitive therapists consider the incorporation of behavioral exposure experiences to be critical to successful application of cognitive treatments.

Physiological responses also have become a common target for behavioral intervention. Whether one is treating chronic headaches, sexual deviations, or anxiety disorders, modifying arousal patterns have proven beneficial in many cases. In all of these disorders the focus is on modifying a maladaptive arousal pattern rather than on the behavioral ramifications of that arousal. It is assumed that successful intervention in the physiological realm will have ultimate affects in changing behavior and/or cognitions.

It should be noted that even when covert events are not the primary focus of treatment, behavior therapists may monitor changes in these systems in order to determine whether they play an important role in behavior change. Also, behavior therapists may utilize cognitive or physiological change mechanisms in order to engender behavior change. For instance, the use of coping self-statements have been used quite frequently to get phobic patients to confront their feared stimuli; although the cognitive change is not seen as primary to the process of therapeutic change, it is viewed as a helpful adjunct or aid.

Another way in which behavior therapy has changed is the use of psychopharmacological intervention in combination with behavioral techniques. This combined treatment approach has been used successfully for a wide range of psychiatric disorders, including anxiety and depression as well as behavioral disturbances.

Finally, it should be noted that while behavior therapy originated with treatment at the individual level, we have increased in our sophistication so that we now treat couples, families, and groups. The widespread utility of behavioral marital therapy, behavioral family therapy, and group treatment of a variety of mental disorders attests to the success of behavioral techniques in a group format. Even when behavior therapy is administered on an individual level, significant others may be incorporated into the treatment program to increase efficacy. Perhaps one of the best examples of this is in treating school-phobic children, where both parent and teacher are viewed as integral to the successful application of a behavioral school reentry program. The utility of including a significant other in treatment was demonstrated in a study by Barlow, O'Brien, and Last (1984) in which female agoraphobics receiving behavior therapy showed greater improvement when their husbands participated in the treatment process.

## SCOPE OF THE BOOK

In the 18 clinical cases that follow, the increased sophistication of behavior therapists over the last few decades should be apparent. Considering that the last casebook that focused on adult disorders was published almost 30 years ago (Ullmann & Krasner, 1965), we felt that the time was ripe to document how behavior therapists now conceptualize, assess, and treat their clients. In order to facilitate cross-case comparisons in this book, the following format was selected for each chapter:

1. Description of the Disorder
2. Case Identification
3. Presenting Complaints
4. History

5. Assessment
6. Selection of Treatment
7. Course of Treatment
8. Termination
9. Follow-up
10. Overall Evaluation

The disorders described generally are consistent with *DSM-III-R* criteria. It should be noted that each of the authors has a unique perspective; as a group they reflect the range in behavior therapy. However, the underlying and unifying factor is their empirical approach to treating the behavioral problems displayed by their clients.

## REFERENCES

American Psychiatric Association. (1980). *Diagnostic and statistical manual of mental disorders* (3rd ed.). Washington, DC: Author.
American Psychiatric Association. (1987). *Diagnostic and statistical manual of mental disorders* (3rd ed.). Washington, DC: Author.
Barlow, D. H., & Hersen, M. (1984). *Single case experimental designs: Strategies for studying behavior change* (2nd ed.). New York: Pergamon Press.
Barlow, D. H., O'Brien, G., & Last, C. G. (1984). Complete treatment of agoraphobia. *Behavior Therapy, 15,* 41–58.
Bellack, A. S., & Hersen, M. (Eds.). (1985a). General considerations. In M. Hersen & A. S. Bellack (Eds.), *Handbook of clinical behavior therapy with adults* (pp. 3–19). New York: Plenum.
Bellack, A. S., & Hersen, M. (Eds.). (1985b). *Dictionary of behavior therapy techniques.* New York: Pergamon Press.
Bellack, A. S., & Hersen, M. (Eds.). (1988). Future directions. In A. S. Bellack & M. Hersen (Eds.), *Behavioral assessment: A practical handbook* (3rd ed., pp. 609–615). New York: Pergamon Press.
Blanchard, E. B., & Hersen, M. (1976). Behavioral treatment of hysterical neuroses: Symptom substitution and symptom return reconsidered. *Psychiatry, 39,* 118–128.
DeVoge, J. T., & Beck, S. (1978). The therapist–client relationship in behavior therapy. In M. Hersen, R. M. Eisler, & P. M. Miller (Eds.), *Progress in behavior modification* (Vol. 6, pp. 204–248). New York: Academic Press.
Fishman, S. T., & Lubetkin, B. S. (1983). Office practice of behavior therapy. In M. Hersen (Ed.), *Outpatient behavior therapy: A clinical guide* (pp. 21–44). New York: Grune & Stratton.
Ganguli, R. (1983). Medical assessment. In M. Hersen, A. E. Kazdin, & A. S. Bellack (Eds.), *The clinical psychology handbook* (pp. 455–465). New York: Pergamon Press.
George, A. (1991). Medical assessment. In M. Hersen, A. E. Kazdin, & A. S. Bellack (Eds.), *The clinical psychology handbook* (2nd ed., pp. 491–505). New York: Pergamon Press.
Greenwald, D. P., Kornblith, S. J., Hersen, M., Bellack, A. S., & Himmelhoch, J. M. (1981). Differences between social skills therapists and psychotherapists in treating depression. *Journal of Consulting and Clinical Psychology, 49,* 757–759.
Harris, S. L., & Ferrari, M. (1983). Developmental factors in child behavior therapy. *Behavior Therapy, 14,* 54–72.

Hersen, M. (1971). Resistance to direction in behavior therapy: Some comments. *Journal of Genetic Psychology, 27,* 375–378.

Hersen, M. (1973). Self-assessment of fear. *Behavior Therapy, 4,* 241–257.

Hersen, M. (1976). Historical perspectives in behavioral assessment. In M. Hersen & A. S. Bellack (Eds.), *Behavioral assessment: A practical handbook* (pp. 3–22). New York: Pergamon Press.

Hersen, M. (1978). Do behavior therapists use self-reports as major criteria? *Behavioral Analysis and Modification, 2,* 328–334.

Hersen, M. (1981). Complex problems require complex solutions. *Behavior Therapy, 12,* 15–29.

Hersen, M. (Ed.). (1983). Perspectives on the practice of outpatient behavior therapy. In M. Hersen (Ed.), *Outpatient behavior therapy: A clinical guide* (pp. 3–20). New York: Grune & Stratton.

Hersen, M. (1985). Historical overview. In M. Hersen (Ed.), *Practice of inpatient behavior therapy: A clinical guide* (pp. 3–32). New York: Grune & Stratton.

Hersen, M. (1990). Single-class experimental designs. In M. Hersen (Ed.), *International handbook of behavior modification and therapy* (2nd ed., pp. 175–212). New York: Plenum.

Hersen, M., & Barlow, D. H. (1976). *Single-case experimental designs: Strategies for studying behavior change.* New York: Pergamon Press.

Hersen, M., & Bellack, A. S. (Eds.). (1976). *Behavioral assessment: A practical handbook.* New York: Pergamon Press.

Hersen, M., & Bellack, A. S. (Eds.). (1981). *Behavioral assessment: A practical handbook* (2nd ed.). New York: Pergamon Press.

Hersen, M., & Bellack, A. S. (Eds.). (1988). Fundamental issues: *DSM-III* and behavioral assessment. In A. S. Bellack & M. Hersen (Eds.), *Behavioral Assessment: A practical handbook* (3rd ed., pp. 67–84). New York: Pergamon Press.

Hersen, M., & Van Hasselt, V. B. (1992). Behavioral assessment and treatment of anxiety in the elderly. *Clinical Psychology Review, 12,* 619–640.

Ingram, R. E., & Scott, W. D. (1990). Cognitive behavior therapy. In A. S. Bellack, M. Hersen, & A. E. Kazdin (Eds.), *International handbook of behavior modification and therapy* (2nd ed., pp. 53–66). New York: Plenum.

Kazdin, A. E. (1978). *History of behavior modification: Experimental foundations of contemporary research.* Baltimore: University Park Press.

Kazdin, A. E. (1985). Selection of target behaviors: The relationship of the treatment of focus to clinical dysfunction. *Behavioral Assessment, 7,* 33–47.

Kazdin, A. E. (1987). Treatment of antisocial behavior in children: Current status and future directions. *Psychological Bulletin, 102,* 187–203.

Kiecolt-Glaser, J. K., & Glaser, R. (1992). Psychoneuroimmunology: Can psychological interventions modulate immunity? *Journal of Consulting and Clinical Psychology, 60,* 569–575.

Krasner, L. (1990). History of behavior modification. In A. S. Bellack, M. Hersen, & A. E. Kazdin (Eds.), *International handbook of behavior modification and therapy* (2nd ed., pp. 3–26). New York: Plenum.

Last, C. G., & Hersen, M. (1985). Clinical practice of behavior therapy. In M. Hersen & C. G. Last (Eds.), *Behavior therapy casebook* (pp. 3–15). New York: Springer.

Martin, G. A., & Worthington, E. L. (1982). Behavioral homework. In M. Hersen, R. M. Eisler, & P. M. Miller (Eds.), *Progress in behavior modification* (Vol. 13, pp. 197–226). New York: Academic Press.

Meichenbaum, D. H. (1976). A cognitive-behavior modification approach to assessment. In M. Hersen & A. S. Bellack (Eds.), *Behavioral assessment: A practical handbook* (pp. 143–176). New York: Pergamon Press.

Nelson, R. O. (1980). The use of intelligence tests within behavioral assessment. *Behavioral Assessment, 2,* 417–423.

Rebec, G. V., & Anderson, G. D. (1986). Regional neuropharmacology of the anti-psychotic drugs: Implications for the dopamine hypothesis of schizophrenia. *Behavioral Assessment, 8,* 11–29.

Sloane, R. B., Staples, F. R., Cristol, A. H., Yorkston, N. J., & Whipple, K. (1975). *Psychotherapy versus behavior therapy.* Cambridge, MA: Harvard University Press.

Twerski, A. (Ed.). (1984). *Who says you're neurotic?* Englewood Cliffs, NJ: Prentice-Hall.

Ullmann, L. P., & Krasner, L. (Eds.). (1965). *Case studies in behavior modification.* New York: Holt, Rinehart & Winston.

Van Hasselt, V. B., Hersen, M., Bellack, A. S., Rosenblum, N. D., & Lamparski, D. (1979). Tripartite assessment of the effects of systematic desensitization in a multiphobic child: An experimental analysis. *Journal of Behavior Therapy and Experimental Psychiatry, 10,* 51–55.

# PART II

# CLINICAL CASES

# CHAPTER 2

# Schizophrenia

## PATRICK W. McGUFFIN
## and RANDALL L. MORRISON

## DESCRIPTION OF THE DISORDER

Schizophrenia is an extremely disabling disorder that produces a wide range of disruptive symptoms in the patient and leads to a significant loss of ability to function independently. Schizophrenia is generally first diagnosed in adolescence or young adulthood, although onset in childhood or in later adulthood does occur. The prevalence of schizophrenia in the general population is relatively low. The data on prevalence vary: findings indicate that the number of people who will be diagnosed as schizophrenic at some point in their life ranges from less than 1 in 1,000 to 1 in 100 (Karno & Norquist, 1989). This disparity in prevalence rates appears to be secondary to the various diagnostic criteria for schizophrenia that are used throughout the world (Karno & Norquist, 1989) as well as the range of symptoms that individuals display.

The diagnosis of schizophrenia is complex. The revised third edition of the *Diagnostic and Statistical Manual of Mental Disorders* (American Psychiatric Association, 1987) lists a range of symptoms from which an individual must exhibit a minimal number in order to receive a diagnosis of schizophrenia. Owing to the heterogeneity of symptoms, the illness can appear quite differently across patients.

While schizophrenia is a heterogenous disorder, there are some requisite core features. All persons who receive a diagnosis of schizophrenia must

PATRICK W. McGUFFIN • Hahnemann University, Philadelphia, Pennsylvania 19063    RANDALL L. MORRISON • Response Analysis Corporation, 377 Wall Street, Princeton, New Jersey 08542.

*Adult Behavior Therapy Casebook,* edited by Cynthia G. Last and Michel Hersen. Plenum Press, New York, 1994.

exhibit psychotic symptoms and have a deterioration in adaptive functioning (school/work functioning, self-care practices, etc.). These symptoms cannot be secondary to any organic disorder. The types of psychotic symptoms and the particular changes in adaptive functioning, however, can vary significantly between individuals.

Typical psychotic symptoms that are displayed by a patient with schizophrenia include hallucinations, delusions, and thought disorders. Auditory hallucinations are far and away the most frequent type of hallucination seen in schizophrenia. Patient's with auditory hallucinations generally report voices making statements to them, often commenting on their behavior. At times the voices are reported to give instructions or commands to the individual. The command hallucinations may tell individuals to harm themselves or others. Therefore, any interview with a patient must not only consider the presence of auditory hallucinations but also inquire as to the content of the hallucinations in order to determine if the patient or other persons are at risk.

Other types of hallucinations (olfactory, tactile, visual, etc.) may also occur, but their frequency is extremely low. When any of these other hallucinations are present, they generally coexist with auditory hallucinations. Any report of olfactory or visual hallucinations should be followed by a neurological evaluation to rule out organic factors.

Delusions represent false beliefs that develop out of a misinterpretation of environmental events. These include grandiose delusions (e.g., a patient's belief that he or she is a famous individual or has extreme powers), paranoid delusions (e.g., the belief that an individual or group of individuals is plotting to harm the patient), and delusions of reference (i.e., the belief that external events and individuals have special messages for the patient). Other types of delusions include thought insertion and thought withdrawal (delusions in which patients believe that someone is either putting thoughts into or taking thoughts out of their brain) and thought broadcasting (the belief that others can hear the patient's thoughts).

Thought disorders are disturbances in the organization or the content of an individual's thoughts. One example is "flight of ideas," whereby the patient's verbalization quickly shifts from topic to topic. While they often appear unrelated, there is a connection between the topics being discussed. Conversely, in looseness of association, patients' verbalizations switch from one unrelated topic to another, without any apparent recognition by the patients of the absence of logic in their statements. Other examples of thought disorder are perseveration and echolalia: in the former the individual repeats the same word or phrase over and over; in the latter the patient repeats those words or phrases that another person has uttered.

The aforementioned symptoms all fall under the category of positive symptoms. In addition to positive symptoms, persons with a diagnosis of schizophrenia must display decreased role functioning and may also display other negative symptoms, including social withdrawal and loss of adaptive personal and social skills, which result in an overall loss of adaptive functioning. Negative symptoms also include flat affect, attentional impairment, poverty of speech (the patient's statements to others are normal but convey very little information), increased speech latency (the patient responds to others appropriately, but an abnormally long period of time passes between the end of the other person's statement and the initiation of the patient's response), and negative motor symptoms (i.e., patients maintain bizarre postures, passively allow others to manipulate their body, or display catatonic stupor, meaning that they exhibit no response to or interaction with the external environment).

## CASE IDENTIFICATION

John, a 30-year-old male admitted to a psychiatric inpatient facility, was the third of four children of a middle-class professional couple. No evidence of psychopathology was noted in any of his immediate family members. John had graduated from high school and had attended college for a time. At the time of this admission John was living alone in an apartment, attending a therapeutic day program. He received funds from the government to cover his living expenses. His parents also provided him with money when he had exhausted his monthly government check. John saw a psychotherapist weekly on an outpatient basis, and was prescribed antipsychotic medication (fluphenazine) by a psychiatrist.

## PRESENTING COMPLAINTS

John was brought to the psychiatric emergency room by local police. His parents had called the police due to his refusal to stop banging on the front door of their house and made repeated threatening statements. The parents reported that John had been getting progressively more argumentative and disheveled over the last few weeks; they suspected that he had stopped taking his antipsychotic medication. The parents had encouraged John to make an appointment with his psychiatrist in order to have his medications evaluated, but John had refused to do so. The parents reported that John appeared to have lost weight recently, and they were concerned that he was not eating. It was learned that John had not attended his therapeutic day program for 2 weeks.

On admission, the patient was disheveled and dirty. He made repeated angry and threatening statements to the emergency room personnel, stating that his rights were being abused and that he intended to sue the hospital for malpractice. He stated that he intended to file criminal charges against anyone who gave him medication.

## HISTORY

This was John's eighth hospitalization. His first hospitalization occurred when he was 19, during his first year of college. His parents reported that he had had no significant problems either socially or academically prior to college, although they stated that he had some difficulty in new social situations and had had only two close friends throughout high school. At the time of this first hospitalization, John had been attending a small private college. He had told his parents prior to the hospitalization that he was finding the schoolwork difficult and that he often felt lonely. He was living in the dormitory, and while he made no negative comments about his roommate, he stated that he did not consider him a friend.

Immediately prior to his first hospitalization John stopped attending classes and spent most of his waking hours either lying on his bed or wandering around campus alone. In the few weeks just before his hospitalization he stopped bathing, wore the same clothes for several days in a row, and began hoarding food in his pockets and in the dorm room. He argued frequently with his roommate and others in the dormitory, accusing them of stealing from him, spying on him, and making false accusations about him to the police and the college administration. On a night when John became very loud and threatening toward others in the dormitory, campus security was called, and John was transported to the emergency room of the local general hospital, where he was admitted to the psychiatric unit.

The course of treatment during John's first hospitalization was primarily pharmacological. Following institution of antipsychotic medication, John began to recompensate and was less argumentative and threatening. His parents made several visits to the hospital and participated in counseling sessions with his social worker. After 3 weeks in the hospital, John was discharged to his parents' home. He stated that he did not want to return to college at that time as he felt embarrassed by his behavior there and felt that the stress of college life was more than he could handle.

Throughout the 11 years between his first hospitalization and the present one, John had held many semiskilled and unskilled jobs. He had also participated in therapeutic day programs. John's hospitalizations were precipitated by his becoming paranoid and threatening toward family members. He would sometimes yell threats at strangers on the street at these times as well but had never made continuous threats to strangers. These periods of paranoia and threatening behaviors generally followed his decision to discontinue his antipsychotic medication. He stated that the medication was not helping him and interfered with his ability to think clearly and interact with others. He would also state, at times, that be believed that the medications were poisonous and that his psychiatrist and parents were conspiring with the police to control his life and take away his ability to think and be successful. He would often become grandiose at these times, stating that he was a genius, that he had created all of the major technological advances of the last 20 years, and that the police–medication conspiracy was the only thing keeping from his rightful place as the world's leader.

## ASSESSMENT

Admission staff assessed John's mental status. He was hostile and refused to answer any specific questions. He volunteered that he saw no reason for his being placed in the hospital and that the police and his parents were plotting against him. John stated that the hospital staff were conspiring with the police to keep him in the hospital against his will and without justification. On the basis of his behavior on admission, parental reports, and the hospital staff's past experience with him, schizophrenia, paranoid type, was listed as the admitting diagnosis. John displayed paranoid delusions and inappropriate affect. Parental reports indicated that he had been having auditory hallucinations (although John did not respond when questioned about hallucinations). His self-care was impaired, and he had recently stopped attending his day program.

In order to better specify and quantify the patient's psychiatric symptoms, several objective symptom rating scales were administered. The Brief Psychiatric Rating Scale (Overall & Gorham, 1961), the Scale for the Assessment of Negative Symptoms (Andreason, 1982), and the Global Assessment Scale (Spitzer, Gibbon, & Endicott, 1975) are widely used and well-validated symptom measures for which considerable normative data exist. Results of these assessments indicated that John had significant impairment in functioning, hostility, suspiciousness, and some degree of apathy (poor grooming, difficulty maintaining involvement in his day program). A brief neuropsychological screening indicated no significant deficits, although John exhibited limited attention to the tasks presented to him. It has been noted that attention deficits relate to and perhaps underlie difficulty in role functioning among schizophrenic patients (Morrison & Bellack, 1984).

Given John's hostility and because of concern over impulse control, he was placed in a locked ward, where he could be closely monitored and risks of injury to him or others would be minimized. John continued displaying hostile and threatening behaviors throughout the first several days in the hospital. He was also inconsistent in his willingness to take his medication and would not initiate any self-care activities. He would not bathe or change his clothes without prompts and encouragement, and even with encouragement he would at times refuse to complete these tasks. It was felt that John's compliance with the medication regimen was imperative for his discharge from the hospital. It was also felt that his poor personal hygiene would have negative impact on his potential for successful transition back to the community and that his unwillingness to attend to hygiene was indicative of a diminished mental status.

Frequency counts were made of days in which John completed his personal hygiene tasks (showering, shaving, brushing teeth, and putting on clean clothing) in the morning without being reminded. Counts were also made of his compliance with these tasks when he was reminded. Compliance with medication was also assessed via frequency counts.

John's interpersonal functioning was also assessed. Deficits in social skills have been noted to be "critical to the etiology and persistence of the schizophrenic disorders" (Morrison & Bellack, 1984, p. 247). John's hostile behavior toward others (both persons in authority at the hospital and other patients) was clearly socially inappropriate. Other areas of concern with regard to his interpersonal skills included his difficulty in making requests of others and his limited nonverbal skills (eye contact, speech volume, etc.). In order to minimize the disruptive impact of positive symptomatology on social competence, the social skills assessment was not attempted until John had been stabilized on his medication.

There is a range of specific skill areas within the overall topic of social skills. These include, among many others, initiating and maintaining conversations, making requests, dealing with conflicts, assertiveness, initiating and maintaining intimate relationships, and job interviewing skills. The assessment of social skills was designed to evaluate overall social competence as well as several particular skills that impact on the quality of interpersonal interactions. John's assessment included measures of volume of speech (inaudible or overly loud), duration of utterances, eye contact and other nonverbal skills, and variation in skill performance in different settings. The assessment involved role-playing of specified interpersonal interactions. The role-play scenes were videotaped so that they could be reviewed and scored later. Prior to each role-play enactment, a description of each role-play scenario was provided for John. After John read the scene description, the therapist began the role-play interaction and John was expected to respond. The presence or absence of a response from John and the quality of the response were used to assess his level of social functioning. The following is an example of a typical scene, prompts, and responses:

SCENE DESCRIPTION: Your car is in the shop for repairs. Karen offers you a ride to and from work while the car is getting fixed. You are very pleased with her offer. She says:

THERAPIST: I know you won't have a car for a few days. I'll be glad to pick you up and bring you home in the evening.

JOHN: Ah. Ah, well, I'll see if I can make other arrangements first.

THERAPIST: Okay. I know I had a problem getting around the last time my car was in the garage.

JOHN: Well, if I need to I'll let you know.

The types of scenes that were presented varied so that different skills could be assessed and variation in behavior in different situations could be evaluated.

When John was first presented with a social interaction scene to practice with his therapist, he tended to offer monosyllabic responses. When scenes involved issues of interpersonal conflict, John became hostile and displayed behavior inappropriate to the content of the scene. For example, when a scene was presented in which John and the therapist were playing the roles of two people attempting to determine which of two shows to watch on television, John offered no opportunity for compromise. He was unwilling to give up any control of the television and became threatening: "Go ahead, just try and change the channel; it's my TV." Thus, findings from this assessment suggested that John needed training in how to maintain social interactions in general and that he needed to gain specific skills relative to the appropriate resolution of interpersonal conflict.

An additional area assessed in preparation for the development of John's treatment plan was family interaction. The goals of this assessment were to evaluate the family's attitudes toward the illness, to assess their interpersonal strengths, to identify specific problem behaviors that the family members tended to display, and to evaluate the level of stress within the family, as familial stress has a negative impact on the course of schizophrenia (Falloon et al., 1985). Evaluation involved an interview of John's parents; critical comments made by them regarding John were assessed. Emotional overinvolvement was also evaluated (see Strachan, 1986, for a review of family treatments used with patients with schizophrenia).

A finding of the family assessment was that many critical comments and a high level of hostility occurred between John and his father. The number of critical comments and the degree of hostility tended to escalate as John and his father continued their discussions of topics related to John's illness and hospitalization. At these times John's mother would become progressively less involved in the interaction until she ceased speaking and began looking down at the floor. Clearly, John and his father needed to develop a means for discussing emotion-laden topics without resorting to hostile tactics, since these tactics create additional conflicts rather than resolve existing ones. Additionally, John's mother needed to develop skills for maintaining active involvement in family problem solving.

Other areas of difficulty in the family included the parents' belief that John had more control over his symptoms than he actually did, that his improvement or lack thereof was primarily a function of how much effort John expended. The family assessment also showed that John's parents had difficulty setting limits on his behavior and that he had difficulty accepting limits. The parents had difficulty in being clear when they attempted to set limits on their son's behavior and generally failed to be consistent in holding to those limits. Part of their difficulty may have been secondary to their frustration and fear when John made paranoid and threatening statements (which he often did when his parents set limits). One finding from this assessment was that the parents could benefit from training in how to set appropriate limits, how to enforce them, and how to reward John's compliance with the limits; it was also clear that they needed to understand the importance of being consistent in maintaining limits.

## SELECTION OF TREATMENT

Management of John's hallucinations, delusions, and disruptive behaviors was seen as being of primary importance in the treatment plan. Given his history of positive response to antipsychotic medication, John was prescribed medication (fluphenazine), initially to be administered intramuscularly, with oral medication to be considered following diminution of his symptoms. Dosage was titrated and side effects were monitored by the ward psychiatrist. (For a discussion of neuroleptic dosage strategies and adverse reactions, see the American Medical Association's *Drug Evaluation Annual* 1991).

John's disruptive and noncompliant behaviors were seen as significant impediments to his being discharged from the hospital and his ability to be successful once discharged. His refusal to perform personal hygiene tasks and comply with his medication regimen were selected as the first behaviors to be targeted for treatment. Following improvement in these two areas, his disruptive, argumentative behavior on the ward would be addressed. A reinforcement program was developed, using John's parents and the gifts they provided as reinforcers.

It was determined that after improvement was seen in the targeted problem behaviors, the second phase of John's treatment would begin. This phase involved social skills training to address John's hostile interactions with others, his difficulty in accepting negative statements from others, his limited ability to compromise, and his tendency to avoid interactions with others. It was decided that social skills training would begin by having John practice appropriate social and conversational skills with his primary therapist and a second therapist. Two therapists were used so that they could role-play social situations for John and serve as models of appropriate social interactions. Once John showed evidence that he was able to display appropriate social skills in these sessions, he would be "graduated" to group social skills training, where he would have opportunities to practice appropriate social skills with other patients at the hospital.

In order to maintain as much contact between John and the community as possible, it was decided that he would return to his therapeutic day program as soon as he complied with his medication regimen and his personal hygiene responsibilities, and was able to maintain appropriate social control (no aggression or threats toward others) on the hospital ward. The therapeutic day program was able to provide feedback to the hospital staff regarding John's behavior, so that appropriate reinforcers could be provided to him and treatment at the hospital could be tailored to address his needs.

Behavioral family therapy was planned to start after John had begun attending his therapeutic day program and had made some initial progress in social skills training. The behavioral family therapy was designed to help John and his parents communicate with one another more effectively. Primary topics to be addressed in this area of treatment were the setting of realistic goals for John (both by John and by his parents), limit setting by his parents, improvement in communication skills between John and his parents, and the reduction of stress and tension within the family. It was planned that behavioral family therapy would begin while John was still a patient in the hospital and that it would continue following his discharge. In addition, it was decided that relevant information regarding the nature of schizophrenia (its typical symptoms, course, etc.) could be provided to the parents through the therapy sessions.

This treatment plan was intended to address the primary needs of John and his family during his hospitalization; the plan also involved continued treatment for John at the therapeutic day program once he was discharged from hospital.

## COURSE OF TREATMENT

A behavioral contract was developed to reinforce John's compliance with his medication regimen and the rules of the hospital ward. Compliance with his medication regimen was seen as imperative to John's treatment success; without medication compliance, it was seen as unlikely that John would maintain significant improvement (he had responded positively to antipsychotic medication in the past). The contract also established rewards for the elimination of hostile, threatening statements. John was unwilling to sign the contract, but his parents (who were judged to be sources of reinforcement for John) agreed to participate in the treatment plan.

The contract stated that John's parents would visit him twice a week if he was 100% compliant with his medication and his personal hygiene tasks. His parents would call the hospital every Wednesday and Saturday, prior to coming to the hospital, to obtain a report on his behavior since their last visit. If John did not meet the required criteria, his parents would talk to him on the phone and tell him that they were not going to visit him that day. They also told him why they were not going to visit him. These conversations tended to result in his screaming and cursing at his parents and threatening them. The parents were instructed to tell John that they would not remain on the phone if he continued to speak to them that way, and they were instructed to hang up if his abusive behavior continued after the warning. This aspect of the contract worked very well. While John did not reach criteria for two of the first three scheduled visits, he missed none of the following five scheduled visits.

In order to address John's hostile, threatening statements, a second reinforcement strategy was developed: John would be able to go out on a pass with his parents when they visited if he had made no hostile threatening statements in the days since their last visit. John's parents also agreed to make their gifts of spending money contingent on the absence of such statements. The amount of money John would receive from his parents during their visits would be based on the number of days without hostile threatening statements since their last visit. Money was chosen as a reinforcer for John because of its historical effectiveness with him. If money had not been available or if money had not been reinforcing to John, another reinforcer would have been chosen. In addition to the rewards John received from his parents, he was also able to receive free coffee on the ward, three times a day, contingent on the absence of the hostile, threatening statements.

Within several weeks John was generally compliant with his medication and personal hygiene. Such compliance continued throughout the remainder of his hospitalization. Additionally, he showed a significant decrease in the frequency of his hostile threatening statements. At this time John began leaving the hospital every day to attend his therapeutic day program. He was reported to be generally compliant and cooperative at this program.

Because of John's difficulty with interpersonal interactions at the hospital and his history of inappropriate social behavior just prior to his hospitalization, social skills training was initiated. In order for the training program to result in the acquisition of skills that would be of use to John in his natural environment, the social skills that were taught were chosen on the basis of their relevance to his current life situation. The treatment addressed John's ability to interact appropriately with staff and other patients at the hospital. Skills to improve such interactions were seen as being easily practiced and transferable to interpersonal interactions outside of the hospital.

After John exhibited some gains in behavior during a span of eight individual sessions, group training was initiated. At this point individual and group training sessions were each conducted twice a week (an hour for each session) for 8 weeks. The first 4 weeks of social skills training took place at the hospital, and the second 4 weeks of training took place at John's day program.

Social skills training focused on several specific skill areas. Initially, training focused on initiating and maintaining conversations. While John displayed an ability to initiate conversations, he rarely initiated conversations for a purpose other than to make negative statements about someone or to complain about the way he was being treated. Following this initial focus of training, skills relating to compromise and negotiation and to appropriately expressing negative feelings were addressed.

Social skills training began with the cotherapists describing the specific skills they were going to teach. The cotherapists then role-played scenes of conversations to highlight specific conversational skills. An example of such a conversation follows:

THERAPIST 1:   Hi, John. How are you?

THERAPIST 2:   I'm fine. How about yourself?

THERAPIST 1:   Good, thanks. This is some nasty weather we're having, isn't it?

THERAPIST 2:   Sure is. I had a really tough time getting into work today. How about you?

THERAPIST 1:   I take the train, so it didn't bother me at all, until I got off the train. I got soaked walking to the office from the station.

THERAPIST 2:   Well, I just hope the weather clears up before this weekend.

THERAPIST 1:   Me too. Well, I've got to get going. I've got to get some work done today.

THERAPIST 2:   Okay. I'll talk to you later.

THERAPIST 1:   All right. See you later.

Following the role play between the cotherapists, John would take the place of one of the therapists and repeat the same scene. As time passed, he would role-play scenes with one of the therapists without observing the cotherapists practice the scene beforehand.

A key element of social skills training is the repetition of specific skills. Practicing a single skill with immediate reinforcement of any display of the skill is necessary for skill acquisition. Patients with greater impairment generally require more repetition (Liberman, Masse, Mosk, & Wong, 1985). Social skills training involves the use of five techniques: providing instructions to the patient, role play utilizing a particular skill, feedback and reinforcement to the patient, modeling of appropriate social skills by the therapist, and repeated practice (including homework) of the social skill (Morrison & Bellack, 1984). Once John was able to exhibit basic conversational skills with the cotherapists in standard role-play scenarios, more personalized scenes were practiced.

Also at this time John began to participate in group social skills training. In these sessions, the therapists initiated conversations and role-play scenarios among the members of the group. As much as possible, the group members were allowed to direct their own conversations, with the therapist playing the role of monitor and facilitator. Whenever conversational skill deficits became obvious in the group, the therapist would stop the interaction and use the opportunity to point out the inappropriate or inadequate social behavior and to model more appropriate behavior. After modeling the appropriate behavior, the therapist would have group members practice that behavior and then go on with the interaction.

Following the start of group social skills training, family therapy was initiated. Family therapy began by providing all family members with information regarding the nature of schizophrenia, its course, and its treatment. While all family members had previously received much of this information, it was felt that it was important to discuss these topics in order to minimize the risk of misinformation negatively influencing the progress of treatment and family interactions. Discussing issues regarding John's ability to control his symptoms (with the underlying supposition that the expression of symptoms was a conscious decision on his part) produced some heated exchanges. Indeed, John accused his father of always seeing him as using his symptoms to avoid responsibilities, and his father retorted that John could work harder to follow his treatment plan. The fact that symptoms occur as part of the disorder and not as a personal choice of the patient was pointed out to both John and his father in an attempt to minimize conflict on this issue.

Following the educational session, family therapy sessions focused on communication and problem-solving skills. Family members were trained to express positive feelings, acknowledge others' positive comments, make positive requests, express negative feelings in constructive ways, and listen actively. This family expressed positive feelings only rarely, tending to make few if any comments to one another other than nonconstructive, negative comments. The family was also trained to describe problems specifically and to actively listen to each other as the problem was described. Family members were trained to generate alternatives in dealing with the problem and to develop methods for choosing among various alternatives. Finally, they were taught to express feelings openly but to avoid critical, nonconstructive feeling statements. The family was taught to hold a family meeting to discuss problems when they occurred, to consider various solutions, and to select a solution acceptable to all. The family practiced the problem-solving method in the therapy sessions, with the therapist providing help only if hostility appeared to be escalating or if members were unable to progress toward a solution to a problem being discussed, in which case the therapist would suggest possible solutions that the family could consider.

While communication and problem-solving training were the central parts of the family therapy, treatment also included behavioral interventions for specific problems, such as compliance with family rules and independent living skills. Subsequent to training all family members in the important aspects of positive communications and interactions, actual practice of these skills was begun. The following is a transcript of a portion of a family session designed to practice these skills:

THERAPIST [*to parents*]: One thing that you have said has been a problem for you has been the amount of time that John spends at your house. You should use the communication and problem-solving skills we've been practicing to address this problem, so remember to make eye contact, to be clear in what you say, and to listen to each other. In setting goals around John's visiting, be clear and consider alternate means for reaching your goals.

MOTHER: It's not that we don't want John to visit; we're just concerned that he might be overly dependent on us.

FATHER: John is too old to be spending all of this time at our house.

THERAPIST: Tell John how you feel about this, and remember to use good communication skills.

MOTHER: John, we like having you visit us at home, but we think that you might be spending too much time with us.

JOHN: If you don't want me around, I won't bother you.

THERAPIST: John, you need to listen to what your mother said. She didn't say that you shouldn't visit, just that she's concerned about how much time you're spending at home.

JOHN: Well, it sounds like she doesn't want me around.

MOTHER: That's not it, John. I just think we should reach some sort of agreement about how often you visit.

THERAPIST: Do you think that you can come up with a schedule for visits?

FATHER: How often do you want to come over, John?

JOHN: I don't know. Some days I want to come over, some days I don't.

THERAPIST: John, do you understand why your parents want to have a schedule for your visits?

JOHN: Not really.

THERAPIST [*to father*]: Could you explain this to John?

FATHER: Your mother and I worry that if you spend too much time with us, you'll be depending on us too much, and, let's face it, we're not going to be around forever. It's important that you develop friendships outside of the family.

JOHN: I've got friends. Just because I visit you doesn't mean I don't have any friends.

MOTHER: Well, that's only part of the reason we'd like some kind of plan for your visits. If you come over at any time, we might not be home or we might be planning to go out, and we don't like to disappoint you.

THERAPIST: John, it seems clear that your parents want to develop some means for organizing your visits. Are you willing to work on developing a plan with them?

JOHN: Sure, if that's what they want.

THERAPIST: Maybe several different plans could be discussed and you could all decide on a plan that was satisfactory to each of you. [to mother] What would you like to see?

MOTHER: Maybe we could schedule two days a week that John could visit every week.

FATHER: Maybe Wednesday evening and Saturday.

JOHN: What if something came up on a Tuesday or a Sunday and I needed to come over?

THERAPIST: That's a good point. How would you deal with emergencies or other variations in the schedule? Any ideas, John?

JOHN: I don't know. I guess I could call.

THERAPIST: That seems like a good idea. [to father] What do you think?

FATHER: That would be okay, as long as John didn't call every day, saying he needed to come over.

JOHN: I wouldn't do that.

THERAPIST: How about setting up a plan that John would visit on Wednesday and Saturday and could call if he needed to come over on another day and see how that works? If problems come up, you can always develop a new plan.

FATHER: That's okay with me. John?

JOHN: Sure, I'll try it.

At this point, the therapist discussed the skills that the family had used in the conversation (active listening, setting reasonable goals, negotiation). All family members were praised for their use of good communications skills and encouraged to use them whenever problems arose. Family therapy sessions continued to use this format throughout the hospitalization.

In a later session the therapist directed the family to look at specific behaviors that caused problems when John was at his parents' home, encouraging them to discuss various means for keeping the behaviors from becoming too disruptive and helping them develop specific solutions.

Family members showed clear improvement through the course of family therapy and were better able to actively listen and to discuss delicate topics without having arguments.

## TERMINATION

Following 3 months of hospitalization, John was discharged to a community group home setting. This setting was centrally located, within 20 minutes of both the hospital and the parents' home. The group home consisted of four 2-bedroom apartments within the same apartment complex. John had a roommate, another former hospital patient.

Prior to discharge from hospital, John had begun social skills training in his therapeutic day program. At discharge, John and his parents began behavioral family therapy on an outpatient basis. It was felt that both treatments should continue following termination of hospital treatment, in order to continue the work that had been done in the hospital and to address problems as they occurred. Antipsychotic medication was continued following discharge, with weekly monitoring during the first month at the group home setting and monthly thereafter.

At the time of discharge, John had been 100% compliant with his medication regimen and his personal hygiene tasks for 2 months. He had also attended his therapeutic day program consistently during that time (he had refused to attend his day program four times during the 3 months of hospitalization but had attended all scheduled days during the last month). No significant disruptive or threatening behaviors were displayed during the last 2 months of hospitalization. At times, John would become upset and argumentative when others disagreed with him or ward group decisions went against his wishes, but he was easily directed to behave more appropriately and was often able to respond to prompts to use skills that he had learned in social skills training when he became upset. This was a significant improvement over his behavior on admission, when his most appropriate behavior was to withdraw from all interpersonal interaction when upset (although more frequently he would become extremely disruptive and threatening).

## FOLLOW-UP

Follow-up was conducted 6 months after discharge. John continued to attend his therapeutic day program and to be compliant with his medication regimen. He performed his personal hygiene tasks regularly and without need for prompting by group home staff. It was reported by group home staff that John would occasionally not want to get up for his therapeutic day program but that this was neither a problem nor atypical for residents of the group home.

In his first month at the group home John reported some brief periods of anxiety. These were generally dealt with by group home staff by providing support and reassurance to John. On the few occasions when this was not successful, John would schedule an extra session with his outpatient therapist. This was successful in all but one instance. In that one instance, which occurred around the time of John's birthday, his medication dosage was increased slightly for 2 weeks. At the end of the 2 weeks the dosage was returned to its previous level without any negative results.

At follow-up, both John and his parents reported that their relationship was much improved over what it had been prior to the last hospitalization and that they were able to spend time together without significant conflicts. John's parents reported that they felt better able to set limits with him. They stated that on those occasions when John wanted to visit and they had other plans, they used skills they had learned from family therapy to minimize the conflict that had previously occurred at these times. They also stated that whenever John became upset and began to behave inappropriately, they were able to be clear and consistent in setting limits. They said that John tended to respond well to these limits and would usually gain self-control quickly.

While John continued to attend his therapeutic day program, he began to state an interest in pursuing competitive employment. His employment goals were realistic, and he was willing to work through his day program and his therapist to find a job where he would have enough support to increase the likelihood of success. At the time of follow-up, John was preparing to go on an interview for a position in a department store stockroom.

## OVERALL EVALUATION

This chapter has presented a view of various treatment modalities designed to minimize the symptoms, and the resulting disruption of functioning, presented by an individual suffering from schizophrenia.

The initial pharmacological treatment and behavioral contract were designed to address the florid symptoms and the disruptive, threatening behaviors that had precipitated the patient's hospitalization. It was felt that these symptoms and behaviors needed to be modified before the patient would be able to leave the hospital.

It was decided that other issues, in addition to decreasing psychotic symptoms and disruptive behaviors, needed to be addressed, issues that impacted on the patient's ability to function in the community and that could improve his ability to remain out of the hospital for longer periods of time. Thus, social skills training and behavioral family therapy were initiated.

Maintaining the patient on antipsychotic medication effectively controlled the floridly psychotic symptoms. Use of the behavioral contract improved the patient's compliance with his medication regimen and resulted in improved personal hygiene and a decrease in his most flagrant disruptive behaviors. The antipsychotic medication regimen also served to improve the patient's ability to benefit from social skills training and behavioral family therapy, since medication decreased internal stimuli (hallucinations) and paranoia.

Social skills training provided the patient with the opportunity to learn and practice specific skills designed to improve social interactions. Such training developed the patient's skills in initiating and maintaining conversations, being appropriately assertive, and dealing with conflict. It was felt that by improving these skills the patient would be better able to develop social supports on which he could rely in times of difficulty. Additionally, it was felt that development of these skills would decrease interpersonal conflict, which would thereby decrease the patient's stress level.

Behavioral family therapy, too, was designed to decrease the impact of stress on both the patient and his parents. This is important since studies indicate that family stress is correlated with the exacerbation of schizophrenic symptoms (Falloon et al., 1985). The family therapy provided education to family members and offered training in setting and accepting limits. Specific skills for solving family conflicts were also taught.

This treatment package appeared to benefit the patient. His disruptive behavior decreased, his compliance with rules and expectations increased, and his interactions with others improved. He was able to leave the hospital and reside in a supported group living environment.

It is important to recognize that the patient improved following implementation of an integrated treatment package. No single aspect of the treatment should be assumed to be a sufficient treatment element. The impact of a combined treatment package has been noted to be far greater than that of any individually administered treatment (Hogarty et al., 1986).

## REFERENCES

American Psychiatric Association (1987). *Diagnostic and statistical manual of mental disorders* (3rd ed., rev.). Washington, DC: Author.

American Medical Association, (1991). *Drug evaluation annual 1991.* Chicago: Author.

Andreason, N. C. (1982). Negative symptoms in schizophrenia: Definition and reliability. *Archives of General Psychiatry, 39,* 748–788.

Falloon, I. R., Boyd, J. L., McGill, C. W., Williamson, M., Razani, J., Moss, H. B., Gilderman, A. M., & Simpson, G. M. (1985). Family management in the prevention of morbidity of schizophrenia. *Archives of General Psychiatry, 42,* 887–896.

Hogarty, G. E., Anderson, C. M., Reiss, D. J., Kornblith, S. J., Greenwald, D.P., Javna, C. D., & Madonia, M. J. (1986). Family psychoeducation, social skills training, and maintenance chemotherapy in the aftercare treatment of schizophrenia. *Archives of General Psychiatry, 43,* 633–642.

Karno, M., & Norquist, G. S. (1989). Schizophrenia: Epidemiology. In H. I. Kaplan & B. J.

Sadock (Eds.), *Comprehensive textbook of psychiatry* (5th ed., pp. 699–705). Baltimore: Williams & Wilkins.

Liberman, R. P., Masse, H. K., Mosk, M. D., & Wong, S. E. (1985). Social skills training for chronic mental patients. *Hospital and Community Psychiatry, 36,* 396–403.

Morrison, R. L., & Bellack, A. S. (1984). Social skills training. In A. S. Bellack (Ed.), *Schizophrenia: Treatment, management, and rehabilitation* (pp. 247–279). Orlando: Grune & Stratton.

Overall, J. E., & Gorham, D. E. (1961). The Brief Psychiatric Rating Scale. *Psychological Reports, 10,* 799–812.

Spitzer, R. L., Gibbon, M., & Endicott, J. (1975). *The Global Assessment Scale (GAS).* New York: New York State Psychiatric Institute.

Strachan, A. M. (1986). Family intervention for the rehabilitation of schizophrenia: Toward protection and coping. *Schizophrenia Bulletin, 12,* 678–698.

# CHAPTER 3

# Major Depression

## IVAN W. MILLER, ELLEN COSTELLO, and GABOR I. KEITNER

### DESCRIPTION OF THE DISORDER

The term *depression* refers to a wide variety of phenomena, including normal sadness, mild dysphoria, and severe depression with psychotic features. While everyone has experienced periods of sadness, the diagnosis of depression as a mental health disorder requires the presence of persistent depressed mood or loss of interest and pleasure *and* the presence of other associated features. As described by *DSM-III-R*, the revised third edition of the American Psychiatric Association's *Diagnostic and Statistical Manual of Mental Disorders*, a diagnosis of major depression requires a 2-week period characterized by the aforementioned changes "most of the day, nearly every day" *and* the concurrent presence of four of the following symptoms: (1) loss of interest and pleasure, (2) significant weight loss or gain, (3) insomnia or hypersomnia, (4) psychomotor retardation or agitation, (5) fatigue or loss of energy, (6) feelings of worthlessness or guilt, (7) impaired concentration or indecisiveness, and (8) recurrent thoughts of death or suicide. While major depression has traditionally been conceptualized as an episodic disorder, more recent research has suggested that for many patients major depression is a chronic disorder that is associated with long-term dysfunction.

---

IVAN W. MILLER, ELLEN COSTELLO, and GABOR I. KEITNER • Department of Psychiatry and Human Behavior, Brown University School of Medicine, and Department of Psychology, Butler Hospital, Providence, Rhode Island 02906.

*Adult Behavior Therapy Casebook,* edited by Cynthia G. Last and Michel Hersen. Plenum Press, New York, 1994.

## Major Depression as a Serious Mental Health Problem

Major depression is one of the most common and serious mental health problems in this country. Recent estimates suggest that 10% to 25% of the population will experience an episode of depression in their lifetime, with accompanying loss of productivity. Further consequences of major depression include substantial risk for suicide, estimated to be up to 15% lifetime mortality. Recent research has documented that the loss of productivity and the functional incapacity associated with major depression are equal to or greater than those associated with chronic medical conditions.

## The Heterogeneity of Major Depression

Even with recent clarification and specification of criteria for major depression, this group of patients remains quite heterogeneous with respect to symptoms, severity, response to treatment, course of illness, and, in all probability, etiology. For example, some depressed patients may have significant interpersonal problems while others may have few interpersonal difficulties but significant cognitive distortions. Clinically, this heterogeneity means that in order to be maximally effective, treatment approaches for major depression must be flexible enough to address a wide range of problem areas.

## Effective Treatments

There are several types of treatments for major depression that have been found to be effective, including the following: (1) individual therapy (behavior therapy, cognitive therapy, interpersonal psychotherapy, etc.), (2) pharmacotherapy, and (3) marital or family therapies. While each of these treatments has been found to be more effective than no treatment at all, none has been consistently found to be more effective than the others. And no single treatment is universally effective.

## A Problem-Focused Model of Depression

Given the heterogeneity of patients with major depression and the wide range of effective treatments that are available, a major task for the clinician is determining which treatment, or combination of treatments, is best for a specific depressed patient. In our view the essence of contemporary behavioral approaches to the treatment of depression lies in an empirical, problem-oriented approach. Specific treatments are utilized to address the problems and specific foci identified by a comprehensive behavioral analysis of the patient and his or her problem areas. Thus, our approach relies heavily on a pretreatment assessment of potential problem areas and on matching specific treatments to specific patient deficits (Miller, Norman & Dow, 1988). Note that this definition does not specify the *content* of the problems. It is our view that problems in depression re multifactorial and are found not only in the behavioral realm but also in the biological and social aspects of the patient's life as well.

## CASE IDENTIFICATION AND PRESENTING COMPLAINTS

Mr. D, a 58-year-old married man, voluntarily admitted himself to a private psychiatric hospital. He reported depressed mood, disturbed sleep, weight loss, and social withdrawal. He felt inadequate, worthless, and hopeless. In addition, Mr. D reported suicidal ideation without intent to act. At the time of his admission Mr. D was unkempt and withdrawn and had psychomotor retardation. He did not maintain eye contact and had poor rapport with the interviewer. While there were no perceptual abnormalities, he complained of difficulty concentrating and of thought blocking. He attributed this most recent depression to career difficulties.

## HISTORY

### Psychiatric History

Mr. D reported that he had been depressed since age 13, when his father died. He reported being chronically dysphoric since that time, with three previous episodes of major depression, each associated with a significant suicide attempt and severe enough to require hospitalization. His first episode occurred in the mid-sixties and led to a suicide attempt by drug overdose and a subsequent hospitalization. This episode was also associated with job failure. Approximately 10 years later, Mr. D was admitted again to a psychiatric hospital because of a "nervous breakdown." Following his discharge he overdosed on a combination of tranquilizers and alcohol. He subsequently was readmitted for treatment of alcoholism and was involved in AA for 10 years. He denied alcohol use since his treatment.

In the 2 years prior to this admission Mr. D experienced significant stress. He had lost his job after 20 years with the same company, and although he intellectually attributed this to the poor state of the regional economy, he took it personally. Ten months of a futile job search convinced him that he was unemployable in his field. He then began working in sales at a time when the market was in a downturn. He was quite unsuccessful in making money from this new endeavor, and he became increasingly dysphoric. Four months prior to the current admission the patient became severely depressed again. At that time, he took an overdose of antidepressants and was found unconscious at his home. He required intubation and was transferred to a psychiatric hospital because of his suicide risk, which he was ambivalent about surviving. After discharge, he again attempted to find work but continued to be significantly depressed. When his suicidal ideation increased again, he presented himself, at his family's insistence, for admission.

Although psychotropic medications, including amitriptyline, fluoxetine, and minor tranquilizers, had been prescribed by his family physician over the years, Mr. D had not received outpatient psychotherapy except for a very brief course following his first suicide attempt and a few sessions of marital therapy at the time of his hospitalization for alcohol abuse.

## Social History

Mr. D was the youngest of three children. Both siblings "escaped" from home after his father's death, leaving him alone with a mother whom he described as "somewhat crazy" because of mood swings and constant fights with relatives. After high school Mr. D attended college and married his current wife while in his mid-twenties. This marriage has been characterized by long-standing conflict and dysfunction. The couple has three children, two of whom are away at college and one of whom lives at home.

## ASSESSMENT

Assessment lies at the heart of the problem-oriented approach to the treatment of depression. In Mr. D's case, assessment covered six major domains: (1) diagnosis, (2) depression severity, (3) suicidal risk, (4) personality, (5) cognitive dysfunction, and (6) marital and family functioning. The results of these assessments led to a comprehensive case formulation and to a treatment plan tailored to Mr. D's particular problems.

In this case we utilized formal assessment instruments in addition to clinical assessment to analyze these domains of functioning. While the quantity of assessment instruments used here may not be feasible in all clinical settings, the important point is that all of these potential problem areas need to be seriously considered and gauged. As illustrated in this case, the use of assessment instruments can augment clinical diagnosis. However, use of such instruments may not be necessary or cost-effective in all circumstances.

## Differential Diagnosis

In order to more formally assess the patient's depression and to rule out other psychiatric disorders, the Structured Clinical Interview for *DSM-III-R*, Patient Version (SCID-P) was administered. The SCID-P (Spitzer, Williams, Gibbon, & First, 1990) is a structured interview format designed to assist in making diagnoses according to the American Psychiatric Association's criteria, as set forth in *DSM-III-R*. On the SCID-P, Mr. D met criteria for a current episode of major depression and also reported three previous episodes. He also met criteria for dysthymic disorder. He did not meet diagnostic criteria for any other *DSM-III-R* disorders (except for alcohol dependence, which was in remission). Thus, Mr. D met criteria for double depression, a combination of major depression and chronic dysthymia that is particularly difficult to treat.

## Severity of Depression

To assess the severity of Mr. D's depressive symptoms, the Modified Hamilton Rating Scale for Depression (Miller, Bishop, Norman, 1985) and the Beck Depression Inventory (BDI; Beck, Ward, Mendelson, Mock, & Erbaugh, 1961) were administered. Mr. D's scores on these scales were 32 and 17, respectively, which indicates a moderate-severe level of depressive symptoms. Specifically, Mr. D reported symptoms of depressed mood; distinct quality of mood; lack of reactivity to environmental events; diurnal variation; feelings of worthlessness, helplessness and hopelessness; guilt; insomnia; decreased energy; decreased interest; and mild psychomotor retardation.

## Suicidal Ideation

Suicidal ideation was assessed with the Modified Scale for Suicidal Ideation (MSSI; Miller, Norman, Bishop, & Dow, 1986), which is a structured clinical interview and rating form designed to assess the presence and severity of suicidal ideation and intent. The MSSI, which consists of 18 questions, examines a range of issues, including the client's desire to die; the frequency, intensity, and duration of suicidal thoughts; and the patient's suicide plans, the presence of deterrents, and the strength of the client's belief in his or her competence to execute a plan. Mr. D received a score of 32 on the MSSI, which indicates the presence of high levels of suicidal ideation. While he denied being actively suicidal on this admission to the hospital, it is clinically noteworthy that Mr. D had little desire to live, with reasons for dying outweighing those for living. At the time of the initial evaluation Mr. D spontaneously made such remarks during the interview as "I'm more trouble than I'm worth" and "Suicide would end the pain, hurt, and failure." His only reason to continue living was to participate in a seasonal recreational activity that he frequently engaged in.

## Personality

While the patient tended to avoid conflict and was interpersonally rather unassertive and isolated, he did not meet *DSM-III-R* criteria for any personality disorder on the SCID-II, a structured interview that assesses personality disorders.

## Dysfunctional Cognitions

Three self-report measures were administered to Mr. D to assess his level and type of dysfunctional cognitions. These included the Dysfunctional Attitude Scale (DAS; Weissman & Beck, 1978), the Automatic Thoughts Questionnaire (ATO; Hollon & Kendall, 1980), and the Hopelessness Scale (Beck, Weissman, Lester, & Trexler, 1974). Mr. D's scores on these self-report measures prior to treatment were as follows: DAS, 177; ATQ, 108; Hopelessness Scale, 19. These results indicate a high level of dysfunctional cognitions, particularly in areas concerning self-perception and self-esteem.

## Family Functioning

Clinical family assessment indicated that in Mr. D's case marital problems and family dysfunction were long-standing. Mr. D was married to a successful career woman, whom he perceived as critical and unsupportive. He was nonassertive and noncommunicative with her. He attempted to minimize conflict by keeping his thoughts and feelings to himself. His wife was frustrated by his unwillingness to communicate and felt burdened by her financial responsibility for the family. She perceived Mr. D as fragile and avoided making demands on him for fear they would lead to another suicide attempt. She felt that he had let her down repeatedly and that she couldn't trust him to take responsibility.

Family functioning was gauged by two measures assessing the seven dimensions of the McMaster Model of Family Functioning (problem solving, communication, roles, affective responsiveness, affective involvement, behavior control, and overall family functioning). The McMaster Family Assessment Device (Epstein, Baldwin, & Bishop, 1983) is a self-report questionnaire completed by all family members, and the McMaster Clinical Rating Scale (Miller et al., in press) is a clinician-rated scale. These assessments confirmed a high level of family dysfunction in Mr. D's family and major problems in problem solving, communication, and level of involvement among family members, particularly between Mr. D and his wife. While practical details of family living were handled very well, family members had difficulty responding to each other's emotional needs, discussing their own feelings, and reaching out to one another. There was little intimacy between husband and wife.

## SELECTION OF TREATMENT

Assessment information, obtained through clinical and objective measures, led to the following case formulation and treatment plan. Mr. D had a recurrent major depressive disorder characterized by significant neurovegetative symptoms. Current assessment, as well as previous history, indicated a high level of suicide risk, requiring that his potential for suicide be tackled immediately. Mr. D was also characterized by persistent low levels of self-esteem, high levels of dysfunctional cognitions concerning vocational and interpersonal roles, and low levels of assertiveness. His social sphere was largely limited to his relationship with his wife who was often critical and unsupportive.

Given the severity and chronicity of these symptoms, as well as his family history, it seemed likely that Mr. D had an underlying biological predisposition to depression. This predisposition to depression appeared to be stimulated by his dysfunctional cognitions about himself. These dysfunctional cognitions, in turn, appeared to be exacerbated by his actual job performance and by the nature of his relationship with his wife. In other words, when faced with difficulties in his work performance, Mr. D would experience increasingly maladaptive cognitions and would become depressed; this increased depression would lead to even poorer vocational performance and thus to increased conflict and criticism from his wife. In a biologically vulnerable individual like Mr. D these factors would further intensify the dysfunctional cognitions and increase the depression, thus continuing the downward spiral into severe depression.

On the basis of this formulation it was decided that a multicomponent treatment approach would be most appropriate for this patient. First, because of the severity of his depressive symptoms, including significant neurovegetative symptoms, pharmacotherapy was indicated. Second, since the patient exhibited a high level of dysfunctional cognition and a low level of assertiveness, individual cognitive-behavioral psychotherapy was initiated. Finally, in view of the marital conflicts and their interrelationship with the patient's depression, problem-focused family treatment was also begun. Under ideal circumstances all of these treatments would be administered by a single individual; in this case there were different therapists for each treatment modality.


## COURSE OF TREATMENT

### Hospitalization

During Mr. D's 12-day hospital stay pharmacotherapy was initiated, comprehensive assessments were completed, and individual and family treatments were initiated.


### Acute Outpatient Phase

*Overview.* After discharge from the hospital, Mr. D received intensive treatment for a 6-month period, including 37 cognitive-behavioral therapy sessions, 8 medication sessions, and 16 family treatment meetings.

All therapy sessions were arranged on an as-needed frequency basis. For Mr. D, this translated into semiweekly cognitive-behavioral therapy sessions for approximately the first 2 months and weekly thereafter for the first 6 months of treatment. Initially, Mr. D came in weekly for medication management sessions, but when he stabilized and tolerated the antidepressants well, the frequency of contact was reduced. Family therapy sessions were held once every week or two, the spacing of sessions depending on the practicality of finding mutually convenient times to meet as well as on the amount of time needed to complete homework assignments. The psychiatrist, cognitive-behavioral therapist, and family therapist were all members of a clinical treatment team that met on a weekly basis to discuss the case and share information. In part, the chronicity and severity of Mr. D's problems led to a more intensive treatment schedule than usual. The frequency of both cognitive-behavioral therapy and medication maintenance sessions increased in the fourth month after discharge when Mr. D, under family pressure to get a job, again became suicidal.

*Pharmacotherapy.* Mr. D was placed on 40 milligrams of fluoxetine, which he tolerated well with no significant side effects. He remained on fluoxetine for the entire acute outpatient phase of treatment.

*Family treatment.* Although the children were involved in the assessment of family problems and in a few family meetings, marital therapy was the primary focus of treatment. Some limited gains were made. With communication training, the couple increased their communication skills and were better able to listen to one another. The therapist also recognized and identified the following transactional pattern: Mr. D would express his opinion, his wife would promptly reject it, Mr. D would withdraw, and his wife would become overly solicitous and then angry at Mr. D for not responding and would then withdraw. This pattern changed as the couple became more aware of its existence and as Mr. D took more risks in revealing himself while his wife listened without judgment. While these interventions reduced tension between them, neither spouse really trusted the other and there was little intimacy in the relationship.

Mr. D and his wife decided 5 months into treatment to terminate family therapy, saying that they had gained all they were going to from that therapeutic approach. They opted not to come back for follow-up family therapy sessions.

*Cognitive–behavioral therapy.* After being discharged from the hospital, Mr. D became more depressed and hopeless. Initial therapy sessions had three major goals: (1) building the therapeutic alliance between patient and therapist, (2) decreasing depression through behavioral interventions of activity scheduling and increased pleasurable activities, especially socialization, and (3) decreasing the patient's sense of hopelessness through cognitive interventions.

Mr. D quickly became engaged in the therapy process. He was a bright, personable individual who quickly grasped the therapeutic rationale and used it to reduce his feelings of shame and guilt. With the exception of refusing to allow the therapist to read his written work, a request he resisted because of a long history of learning difficulties, he complied with homework assignments. Mr. D accepted the compromise of writing his assignments and reading them to the therapist from a notebook kept for this purpose; because of Mr. D's avoidant traits and his tendency to mask his emotions, the therapist had to check frequently to ensure that Mr. D was saying what he thought and not just what he guessed the therapist wanted to hear. A strong therapeutic alliance was established early in therapy. Not only did this alliance facilitate management of suicidal impulses, but it provided a valuable learning experience in discussing and processing relationship issues.

These initial interventions were relatively successful in decreasing Mr. D's depression and hopelessness. However, he still continued to be very reactive to stress, particularly stresses related to vocational and marital issues. As Mr. D's depression improved, his wife began to place more pressure on him to find employment. Despite some efforts to find work, Mr. D was unable to find a job. These issues led to increasing depression and a renewal of suicidal ideation in the fourth month after discharge (BDI score, 19). These changes were addressed by increasing the frequency of sessions and by adding additional focus on changing Mr. D's belief system and on increasing his assertiveness with his wife.

As noted previously, Mr. D had a high level of dysfunctional cognitions, focusing on negative aspects of himself and his work performance. He initially made such comments as the following: "I'm no good"; "It's safer to be quiet; I can't defend myself"; "If I let things out, they'll escalate and I'll lose"; "Saying no to someone means I'm lazy or selfish"; and "There's no forgiveness." His self-statements concerning work were equally negative: "I've failed"; "I shouldn't make mistakes"; "I'm weak if I ask for help, and if they know I'm weak, they'll reject me"; and "I can't trust." This last statement referred to his perception that he had been loyal to his company for many years and had been laid off without cause. However, it also characterized his interpersonal relationships.

Spontaneously generated cognitions, recorded between therapy sessions on the Daily Record of Automatic Thoughts (Beck, Rush, Shaw, & Emery, 1979), provided the basis for Socratic questioning, scaling, and other cognitive techniques and were used to generate homework assignments to test the validity of the underlying beliefs. As therapy progressed, Mr. D was able to generate evidence for and against some of his beliefs and examine the advantages of holding these beliefs. He did particularly well in challenging his all-or-none thinking by developing continuums with behavioral anchors and placing himself at different points along the continuum. For example, he developed a scale ranging from "totally inadequate" to "totally adequate" and rated his performance as a spouse, parent, worker, breadwinner, and friend. He also noted his high and low points for each of these roles so he could see the range in which he operated. This helped break his pattern of all-or-nothing thinking. To his surprise, he discovered that some of the same evidence he used to convince himself he was inadequate could also be used to affirm his adequacy. For example, because he was laid off he could point to his work as a sign that he was a failure; at the same time, he could look at his substantial earnings over 35 years, as well as his many promotions, and see success. Similarly, he used his alcohol abuse history to support his belief that he was inadequate, but he was also able to bolster his self-esteem by noting that he had completely stopped drinking 18 years ago.

Mr. D was initially quite unassertive in general and in particular with his wife. Further assessment indicated that while he had the behavioral repertoire to be appropriately assertive, he often failed to act assertively because of his maladaptive beliefs. He was particularly fearful of criticism because he felt inadequate to defend himself.

THERAPIST:   What's the worst possible thing that would happen if you assert yourself in a conversation with your wife?

MR. D:  The fear is basically that it won't be limited to what we're discussing, it will get bigger and bigger. The bad consequences, as it turns out in thinking about it, is that it wouldn't be one bit worse than what happens anyway. [*laughs*]

THERAPIST:  That's the rational you talking.

MR. D:  Now the feelings associated with it, it's this thing of being attacked or accused.

THERAPIST:  How frequently are you attacked or accused?

MR. D:  I feel on the verge of that in an awful lot of instances, in any kind of conversation just as simple as "What did you do today?" And if I start saying what I did today, there's this fear, "Well, why didn't you do this, or why didn't you do that?"

THERAPIST:  So you're always anticipating. How often does it really happen?

MR. D:  I don't think it happens that frequently. It's the fear of it happening rather than the actual thing happening.

THERAPIST:  So you spend a good deal of your life attempting to avoid a fearful situation that occurs in fairly low frequency. Is that correct?

MR. D:  Yeah, the actual occurrence is low.

THERAPIST:  Over the course of your marriage, if you got rejected or attacked in one of these conversations, how bad was it? Could you stand it?

MR. D:  Yeah, it would certainly be worth trying. As I was saying, probably the conversation would be no worse than it is anyway.

After behavioral rehearsal of Mr. D being appropriately assertive with his wife, an experiment was designed in which Mr. D would either assert or not assert himself with his wife and would then gauge his degree of discomfort in the conversation ("I'll say how I'm feeling and what I think about things and see what happens"). Contrary to his expectations, he discovered that when he expressed his opinions his wife backed down and that his mood improved regardless of her reaction. Mr. D used these lessons to change his interactions with his children as well as his spouse. He began to believe that at least in some circumstances he could handle conflict or strong emotions.

Similar exercises were used to examine his assumptions that he was disorganized and unable to accomplish tasks. While it turned out that he had some actual deficits in this area, he was able to stop labeling himself negatively and to pinpoint specific areas of strengths and weakness. He also realized that his wife's style of problem solving differed from his and that each style had its own advantages and disadvantages. He concluded that comparing himself to others, particularly his wife, left him feeling inadequate and inferior, and he made a concerted effort to stop doing so.

While noticeable changes occurred during therapy, some areas showed minimal movement, and progress was slower with Mr. D than with less severely depressed outpatients. The patient was able to use the chronicity of the problem to battle feeling of hopelessness, telling himself that the bad periods were temporary.

## Maintenance Phase

At the completion of the acute phase of treatment 6 months following discharge from the hospital, the patient had made significant improvements in his levels of depression, suicidal ideation, and levels of dysfunctional cognitions, as indicated by the following changes on assessment measures:

|                                                | Pretreatment | After six months |
|------------------------------------------------|--------------|------------------|
| Modified Hamilton Rating Scale for Depression  | 32           | 10               |
| Beck Depression Inventory                      | 17           | 1                |
| Dysfunctional Attitude Scale                   | 177          | 84               |
| Hopelessness Scale                             | 19           | 3                |
| Modified Scale for Suicidal Ideation           | 32           | 0                |

Mr. D was functioning within a normal range on all of these measures. He attributed his success to modified biochemistry and changes in his underlying belief system. On the basis of this information, the patient and the treatment team decided to move treatment into a maintenance phase. The decision to continue in maintenance treatment in a relatively asymptomatic patient was based on the following reasoning: While the patient was clinically improved, he still appeared somewhat reactive to environment stress. Since he had not found a job and family treatment had not been completely successful, it appeared likely that the patient would continue to experience serious stress in the future. Thus, it was thought that the patient was at fairly high risk for a relapse. Similarly, while not a current suicide risk, the patient was judged to become a serious future risk in the event of a relapse. Finally, recent research evidence (Frank et al., 1990) suggests that maintenance treatments, both pharmacological and psychotherapy, are quite effective in decreasing the risk for future episodes of major depression. For these reasons, treatment was continued in a maintenance phase of reduced frequency of contacts for an additional 1-year period: Mr. D received 24 additional sessions of cognitive-behavioral therapy and 13 more medication management sessions over the subsequent 1-year period (although there were no further family therapy meetings).

During the maintenance period, Mr. D's depression generally remained at low levels. However, he had one crisis, which was precipitated by increasing conflict with his wife, that resulted in his moving out of his home. At that time he was under enormous stress and had increased suicidal thoughts. He denied any intention of acting on these thoughts. Because of his suicidal risk, he was seen once or twice a week, as needed, during this time. With this increased treatment contact, this crisis soon resolved, and Mr. D's level of depression returned to normal.

After 11 months on fluoxetine, the patient was briefly switched to 150 milligrams of imipramine in the hope that it would help his concentration and attention span. Approximately 6 weeks later, he requested a switch back to fluoxetine, on which he is currently maintained; he found no therapeutic benefit to imipramine with regard to either his depressive symptoms or his organizational skills and could not tolerate the side effects.

With the exception of the period of crisis, precipitated by conflicts with his wife, Mr. D was seen every 3 to 4 weeks during the maintenance phase, both for cognitive-behavioral therapy booster sessions and medication checks. He continued to do well, describing himself as not depressed. At the end of the 1-year maintenance phase, Mr. D's assessment scores continue to be quite low, well within the normal range.

## TERMINATION

After a 1-year maintenance period, including 8 consecutive months with normal levels of depressive symptoms, cognitive-behavioral treatment was discontinued by mutual agreement between patient and therapist. Because Mr. D had been able to form a good therapeutic relationship and make real gains in functioning and coping with his depression, he indicated that he would reenter therapy if his suicidal ideation ever returned. While many of the same stressors that led to his suicide attempt and hospitalization still exist, Mr. D perceived himself and his options very differently at termination.

## OVERALL EVALUATION

This case report illustrates several important points about treatment of depressed patients. First, it is our judgment that use of an empirical, problem-oriented perspective to assessment and treatment was critical. Initial thorough assessment led to a comprehensive case formulation and analysis that pointed the way to treatment. Second, this case illustrates the efficacy of combining biological, psychological, and social treatments. Each of the three treatments played an important role in this patient's recovery, and it seems likely that excluding any of these treatments would have resulted in a much poorer outcome. Within this context of a combined treatment plan, however, it was clear that the cognitive-behavioral intervention was the major treatment component for this patient. It is our clinical sense that the therapeutic relationship and the coping skills developed in the cognitive-behavioral treatment were truly lifesaving for this patient. The success of this cognitive-behavioral treatment for this severely depressed and suicidal man illustrates the applicability of cognitive-behavioral interventions to this patient group. Finally, this case demonstrates the importance of long-term maintenance treatments for depressed patients. The ongoing therapeutic relationship and continued pharmacotherapy helped this patient cope with a very traumatic life event (separating from his wife), which in the absence of continued treatment might have resulted in another episode of severe depression and possible suicide attempt.

## REFERENCES

Beck, A. T., Rush, A. J. Shaw, B. F., & Emery, G. (1979). *Cognitive therapy of depression.* New York: Guilford Press.

Beck, A. T., Ward, C. H., Mendelson, M., Mock, J. R., & Erbaugh, J. (1961). An inventory for measuring depression. *Archives of General Psychiatry, 4,* 561–571.

Beck, A. T., Weissman, A., Lester, D., & Trexler, L. (1974). The measurement of pessimism: The Hopelessness Scale. *Journal of Consulting and Clinical Psychology, 42,* 861–865.

Epstein, N., Baldwin, L., & Bishop, D. (1983). The McMaster Family Assessment Device. *Journal of Mental and Family Therapy, 9,* 171–180.

Frank, E., Kupfer, D., Perel, J., Cornes, C., Jarrett, D., Mallinger, A., Thase, M., McEachran, A., & Grochocinski, V. (1990). Three-year outcome for maintenance therapy in recurrent depression. *Archives of General Psychiatry, 47,* 1093–1099.

Hollon, S. D., & Kendall, P. C. (1980). Cognitive self-statements in depression: Development of an Automatic Thoughts Questionnaire. *Cognitive Therapy and Research, 4,* 383–395.

Miller, I. W., Bishop, S. B., & Norman, W. H. (1985). The Modified Hamilton Depression Rating Scale: Reliability and validity. *Psychiatric Research, 14,* 131–142.

Miller, I., Kabacoff, R., Epstein, N., Bishop, D., Keitner, G., Baldwin, L., & Van der Spuy, H. (in press). The development of a clinical rating scale for the McMaster Model of Family Functioning. *Family Process.*

Miller, I. W., Norman, W. H., Bishop, S. B., & Dow, M. G. (1986). The Modified Scale for Suicidal Ideation: Reliability and validity. *Journal of Consulting and Clinical Psychology, 54,* 724–725.

Miller, I. W., Norman, W. H., & Dow, M. G. (1988). Depression. In E. Blechman & K. Brownell (Eds.), *Handbook of behavioral medicine for women* (pp. 362–385). New York: Pergamon Press.

Spitzer, R. L., Williams, J. B., Gibbon, M., & First, M. B. (1990). *Structured Clinical Interview for DSM-III-R.* Washington, DC: American Psychiatric Press.

Weissman, A., & Beck, A. T. (1978, November). *Development and validation of the Dysfunctional Attitude Scale (DAS).* Paper presented at the meeting of the Association for the Advancement of Behavior Therapy, Chicago.

# CHAPTER 4

# Dysthymic Disorder

## MARY ANN MERCIER

## DESCRIPTION OF THE DISORDER

### Historical Background

*Dysthymic disorder* was included as a new diagnostic category in the Affective Disorders section when the American Psychiatric Association introduced the third edition of its *Diagnostic and Statistical Manual of Mental Disorders (DSM-III)* in 1980. This was controversial since in *DSM-II* chronic states of depression were listed as *cyclothymic personality* or *depressive neurosis* within the Personality Disorders and Neuroses sections. Persistent low-grade depressive symptoms of insidious onset are difficult to differentiate from personality structure (see Kocsis & Frances, 1987, for a historical review). The inclusion of *dysthymic disorder* in the Affective Disorders section of *DSM-III* (called *dysthymia* in the Mood Disorders section of *DSM-III-R*) represents an important shift in the conceptualization of chronic mood states.

The current criteria for dysthymia in *DSM-III-R* are the following:

1. Depressed mood that is present more time than it is not for at least 2 years
2. No asymptomatic periods lasting for more than 2 months
3. No major depressive episode during the first 2 years of the depression

MARY ANN MERCIER • 2570 Oak Valley Drive, Vienna, Virginia 22181, and consultant for the Department of Psychiatry, College of Physicians and Surgeons, Columbia University, New York, New York 10027.

*Adult Behavior Therapy Casebook,* edited by Cynthia G. Last and Michel Hersen. Plenum Press, New York, 1994.

4. Presence of at least two depression symptoms (loss of appetite or overeating, insomnia or hypersomnia, fatigue, low self-esteem, poor concentration or difficulty making decisions, hopelessness)
5. No history of mania or hypomania; no evidence of an organic factor; and not superimposed on a chronic psychotic disorder
6. In addition, dysthymia may be either primary (i.e., not related to a preexisting condition) or secondary and of early (before 21 years) or late onset.

## Incidence of Dysthymia

According to Weissman, Leaf, Bruce and Florio (1988), who conducted an epidemiological study of dysthymia in five communities using *DSM-III* criteria, the disorder affects approximately 3% of the adult population and is more common in women, unmarried persons, and young people with low incomes.

## Relationship of Dysthymia with Other Disorders

Klein, Taylor, Dickstein, and Harding (1988) studied primary early-onset dysthymia. The dysthymics had a high rate (59%) of comorbid major depression. In addition, those with a superimposed major depression were more likely to have higher rates of melancholia and personality disorders, greater impairment, and substance abuse. Family histories of affective disorders in the dysthymics were common (84%).

Weissman et al. (1988) also found a high comorbidity with major depression (39%), as well as with anxiety disorders (46%) and substance abuse (30%). In fact, only 25% to 30% of their cases of dysthymia occurred in the absence of other psychiatric disorders.

## Treatment Approaches

Traditionally, chronic depressions have been treated with psychotherapy, but recent studies suggest that dysthymics may also respond to antidepressant medication (Kocsis et al., 1988; Stewart et al., 1989). Follow-up data on the persistence of gains with continuation of antidepressants or once medication is withdrawn are not available.

## CASE IDENTIFICATION

Unlike other disorders that often present in their pure state, pure dysthymia is more the exception than the rule. Therefore, one must consider whether to select an example of pure dysthymia or a case that is more representative of dysthymia as it is found in the general clinical population. I have elected to do the latter.

This is a case of a 33-year-old married woman who lived with her husband and three children (two boys, ages 11 and 6, and one girl, also age 6) in an urban area and owned her own business. Jane, the eldest of four children, had two brothers and one sister. Both of her parents were still living, and she had frequent contact with her family. Her husband's family also lived in the same community.

Jane reported that as a child she had few friends, often isolated herself from others, and spent much time alone in her room. However, at other times, she was more outgoing. She was an attractive woman who graduated from high school, married, and had her first child when she was 21 years old. She stayed at home with her children for several years. She started her own business approximately 1½ years prior to seeking treatment.

## PRESENTING COMPLAINTS

Jane did not have a chief presenting complaint, but she said she was having trouble running her business. She had started the business while she was being treated for depression and panic disorder with phenelzine, a mono-amine oxidase inhibitor antidepressant medication. She stopped the medicine 4 months prior to seeking help, and since that time had been less productive.

Upon further questioning, Jane revealed that she had felt "down in the dumps" at least 75% of the time for as long as she could remember, dating back to her early childhood years. She usually had at least one good day a week but complained of feeling very tired, withdrawn, and pessimistic on the other days. She frequently overslept and had trouble concentrating but was able to enjoy some activities even when depressed. In addition, Jane reported having frequent spontaneous panic attacks and admitted to some phobic avoidance. She also said that she had been frequently bingeing, felt out of control around food, and at times would fast for as long as 3 days to counteract the bingeing.

## HISTORY

### Depression

Although Jane had described feeling down for most of her life, there were two instances in which she described herself as being more persistently depressed. These depressive episodes occurred at ages 21 and 27, after the birth of her son and then the birth of her fraternal twins. At these times she experienced weight gain, insomnia (no early morning awakening but, rather, initial insomnia), agitation, feelings of worthlessness, loss of interest in activities, and impaired concentration. However, she was still able to enjoy some activities and could be cheered up by positive events. She described these postpartum depressions as similar to being in a state of mourning.

During the 14 months that Jane took phenelzine she felt much better. However, it was also during this time that she started her own business, became involved in many other new activities, had unusually creative ideas, was excessively talkative and extremely productive, had a markedly decreased need for sleep, and felt grandiose. In other words, she became hypomanic while on phenelzine.

## Substance Abuse

Jane also described various episodes of drug use over several years. From ages 17 to 26 she used marijuana heavily, along with amphetamines from ages 18 to 20; she used cocaine from ages 26 to 30. She stopped using cocaine because she was depressed and had started having panic attacks. She had not used any of these drugs within 2 years of her evaluation.

## Anxiety Disorder

When Jane stopped using cocaine, her panic attacks nevertheless continued, at least weekly, except while she was on phenelzine. Her symptoms included choking sensations, chest pains, palpitations, feeling faint, abdominal upset, feelings of depersonalization, paresthesia, flushes, chills, trembling, and fear of dying. These symptoms returned after discontinuation of phenelzine.

Both Jane's mother and sister had panic attacks and her mother may have also been depressed. Jane was also phobic of snakes, spiders, and mice. Her fear appeared to be excessive and irrational—even to her.

Jane's anxiety worsened after her older son became critically ill. Although he survived with no aftereffects, Jane constantly feared a recurrence of his illness, especially a fatal recurrence.

## Eating Disorders

Jane's difficulty with food dated to her days of amphetamine use, when she lost 20 pounds but thought she should lose more. However, she did not lose her periods, nor did she lose 25% of her body weight. At intake, she was maintaining her weight despite bingeing, by not eating for several days. She never resorted to vomiting.

## ASSESSMENT

The Structured Clinical Interview for *DSM-III* (SCID) and the Structured Clinical Interview for *DSM-III-R* Personality Disorders (SCID-II) were used to assess Axis I and II, respectively. Two clinician-rated measures were also used: Hamilton Rating Scale for Depression (Ham-D) and Clinical Global Impression (McGlashen, 1973).

A batter of self-report inventories was also used and included the following: Beck Depression Inventory (BDI) (Beck, Word, Mendelsohn, Mock, & Erbaugh, 1961); Social Adjustment Scale (Weissman & Bothwell, 1976), which assess social functioning; Hopelessness Scale (Beck, Weissman, Lester, & Trexler, 1974), which is a measure of pessimism and a predictor of suicide risk; Dysfunctional Attitude Scale (DAS; Weissman & Beck, 1978), an instrument designed to tap underlying beliefs and attitudes believed to be associated with depression; Hollon and Kendall's (1980) Automatic Thoughts Questionnaire (ATQ), which measures the frequency and type of negative self-statements; and the Self-Control Scale (Rosenbaum, 1980), designed to measure coping resources.

## Results of Assessment with SCID and SCID-II

Jane's depression was rated on the SCID as lifelong and without a preexisting major depressive disorder. Because she had never been without depressive symptoms for more than a month, except while taking phenelzine, the course of Jane's illness was considered to be chronic but intermittent. Her dysthymia was both primary and of early onset.

Jane did not meet *DSM-III-R* criteria for current major depression, although her postpartum depressions did meet criteria. These past episodes were recurrent but not melancholic. Jane had numerous symptoms of hypomania while on phenelzine. Because her symptoms were felt to be drug-induced, she was not considered to have spontaneous hypomania. She did, however, meet criteria for substance abuse with marijuana, amphetamines, and cocaine. She was most likely trying to self-medicate.

In terms of anxiety disorders, Jane acknowledged having at least four spontaneous panic attacks within a 4-week period preceding assessment with at least four symptoms, all of which developed within 10 minutes and existed in the absence of any organic factor. These attacks began at age 29. Concurrent with the development of panic was the serious illness of her older son.

The amount of phobic avoidance associated with her panic was rated as limited or mild. Jane's fears of mice, spiders, and snakes also met criteria for simple animal phobia, which was lifelong.

Jane met criteria for bulimia nervosa; these criteria include recurrent binges, a sense of lacking control over eating behavior, fasting, and at least two binges per week for at least 3 months.

In summary, Jane met criteria for the following diagnoses: primary, early onset dysthymia; a major depression that is recurrent, without melancholia, and in remission; cannabis, amphetamine, and cocaine abuse, in remission; simple phobia; panic disorder with limited phobic avoidance; and bulimia. Jane did not meet criteria for any personality disorder on the SCID-II.

## Clinician-Rated Measures

At evaluation, Jane's Ham-D score was 13. Although this depression score seems low, she did not receive points for her oversleeping or overeating. On the Clinical Global Impression scale, the level of her symptomatology was rated as mild.

## Self-Rated Measures

Jane's scores on all the self-rated measures suggested a moderate level of depression. Particularly striking were her excessive feelings of guilt and her loss of interest in and lack of satisfaction from activities. Her score on the Hopelessness Scale (10) approximated that seen in patients with a recurrent depression.

Jane's pattern of responses on the Dysfunctional Attitude Scale, a measure of beliefs and attitudes, suggested that the most difficult areas for her were needing the approval of others to feel good about herself and excessive perfectionism. Her strengths were in the areas of autonomy and achievement. Her most frequent negative self-statements, according to her score on the ATQ, reflected her need for change in her life. Her self-concept and self-esteem appeared minimally impaired; nor did she appear to feel helpless. However, the Self-Control Scale score (–23) suggested that she did not have much experience with coping strategies and that she might benefit from learning such strategies.

Jane's level of social functioning was impaired in her work, social and leisure activities, and in her roles as a wife and a parent. She reported spending time alone watching TV and feeling lonely, bored, and uncomfortable. When she did get together with her parents and siblings, she usually was not able to talk about her feelings, and she often felt that they had let her down.

Although she was able to complete her work around the house, she felt bored with most of her daily activities. She felt unable to complete all of her work for her business.

## SELECTION OF TREATMENT

Jane had never been in any kind of psychotherapy in all the years that she had been depressed, except for a support group she attended while on medication. She did not see her depression as unusual, which is common for dysthymics, until she experienced her postpartum depressions (and when she discontinued phenelzine).

Jane and I met at the clinic where she had previously been treated with phenelzine. She was referred to me by the psychiatrist she consulted after her depression returned. He recommended phenelzine as the treatment of choice, inasmuch as Jane had been successfully treated with that antidepressant in the past, but she declined medication and requested a nonpharmacologic treatment.

I suggested a course of cognitive therapy. I explained to her the basic ideas of cognitive therapy, including the importance of the completion of self-help assignments. She agreed to 16 weeks of cognitive therapy, after which she and I, along with the referring psychiatrist, would reevaluate her treatment needs.

## COURSE OF TREATMENT

### Overview

The protocol for the 16-week cognitive therapy outlined in *Cognitive Therapy of Depression* (Beck, Rush, Shaw, & Emery, 1979) was modified because of Jane's anxiety and panic. The 16-week course of cognitive therapy can be subdivided into three main sections: (1) the development of a problem list to guide treatment; (2) the implementation of behavioral and cognitive strategies, including the collection of behavioral data to determine baseline levels of activity and interest, the introduction to the client of the relationship between cognition and emotion, activity planning to increase pleasure, and the teaching of rational responding (cognitive restructuring); and (3) relapse prevention.

Bibliotherapy was used throughout treatment to explain cognitive therapy and common thinking patterns associated with depression.

## Problem List

Jane reported five main problems: a pervasive sense of guilt, lack of productivity, lack of assertiveness, a loss of interest in activities, and anxiety whenever her older son appeared ill.

## Behavioral and Cognitive Strategies

Jane's first two self-help assignments were to read *Feeling Good: The New Mood Therapy* (Burns, 1980) and to complete a weekly activity schedule. The latter required an hour-by-hour account of her activities, with ratings of pleasure and mastery (on scales of 0 to 10) for each activity. We reviewed the activity schedules for the preceding 2 weeks:

THERAPIST:  It really looks to me like you are a very busy woman, yet you believe you aren't very productive. What do you see when you look at this? [*hands Jane the activity schedule*]

JANE:  When I see it written down, I do see that I'm busy and am not wasting time like I thought I was. But I'm not getting everything done that I want to.

THERAPIST:  Is that because you are unproductive?

JANE:  I don't know. When I was on medicine I could do so much—but I know that I was doing too much then. Of course, I do have more to do now that I started my business.

THERAPIST:  If it were true that you have more to do now than before you started your business, what conclusions would you draw about your productivity?

JANE:  Well, . . . that I am trying to do too much and maybe I cannot do it all because there is too much to do.

THERAPIST:  What evidence do you have that this thought is true?

At this point Jane told me about how her friends and family had been urging her to hire someone to help her with her business. By the end of the session she decided she would follow through on hiring part-time help.

This was an important discussion, as it was the first time that Jane began to question her beliefs. She had assumed that if she thought something was true, it must be true and that there could be no other explanation. It was after this discussion that we began to integrate the behavioral components of the treatment with the cognitive. Jane was asked to "catch" her thoughts when she experienced a mood shift and to then ask herself two questions about each thought: What is the evidence for and against the thought? Are there any other explanations?

Jane's reports that she did not get much pleasure appeared to be due more to her failure to engage in pleasurable activities than to anhedonia. Once she hired part-time help, Jane agreed to spend 4 hours a week engaging in activities she enjoyed, such as swimming.

By the fourth week, Jane's son appeared to be sick again. Whenever he complained of a headache, she would experience excessive anxiety because she feared he would again become critically ill. We therefore addressed her anxiety. She had learned progressive muscle relaxation in her support group but had experienced relaxation-induced panic attacks. To the relaxation protocol we simply added the instruction that she wiggle her fingers whenever she feared losing control so that she would know that she was in control. She was to practice this daily. In addition, she agreed to write down her thoughts whenever she felt fearful about her son's health, including the evidence for and against her beliefs in these thoughts. A review of the thoughts about her son revealed two problems: her prediction of a serious disease and her belief that her son's illness was God's punishment of her. She rated her anxiety as much lower after she gave her son Tylenol and saw him improve, and also after writing her thoughts down.

THERAPIST: Why was it important for you to write these thoughts down?

JANE: When I saw my thoughts in black and white, I knew that I was trying to predict the future and saw that I judge myself on things that I have no control over.

THERAPIST: What do you mean?

JANE: Well, children get sick. If one of my kids gets sick, it shouldn't be my fault if I have taken care of them. And I do.

THERAPIST: Were you assuming that since you felt guilty, that you must *be* guilty?

JANE: Yeah, I was . . . that's emotional reasoning, isn't it?

THERAPIST: Yes. In anxiety, people tend to think if they feel a certain way, then that

Table 1
Automatic Thoughts and Rational Responses Regarding Son's Illness

| Automatic thoughts | Rational responses |
| --- | --- |
| 1. Oh God, he's sick again and he will get worse. Maybe this time he will die. | 1. His symptoms are the same as his brother's and sister's. They each have the flu. If he has the flu, he will also be better with Tylenol. (She had given him Tylenol and he did improve.) |
| 2. If he dies it will be my fault. God will be punishing me. | 2. If God had wanted to punish me, he would have taken my son before. Anyway, I believe in a loving God, not a punishing one. Anyway, I am a good mother and a good wife. |
| 3. It's happening again. | 3. His symptoms are totally different from last time. |

means it must be true, rather than looking at the facts. Also there is a tendency to predict the future—negatively, of course. [*laughter*]

Although Jane and I had worked on rational responding together in session, this was the first time that she had used it on her own.

Over the next couple of weeks, Jane and I developed a plan for what to do when her son became ill in the future, a plan that included reading over her list of rational responses and practicing relaxation. Basic to the success of this plan was Jane's need to understand that her initial anxiety could be used as a cue to cope rather than to panic. We used the ACT formula developed by Emery and Campbell (1986), which entails: (A) accepting the current reality ("I will be anxious when my children tell me they are sick"), (C) choosing what you want (to decrease time spent in distress), and (T) taking action to create what you want (using coping strategies and calling the doctor, when appropriate).

By our ninth week Jane was regularly engaging in pleasurable activities, was using a thought record to write down her automatic thoughts and rational responses whenever she felt bad, and was using the ACT formula to deal with anxiety situations. Her BDI and HAM-D scores were greatly reduced (see Figure 1).

## Relapse Prevention

At this point we began to carry out relapse-prevention work because Jane was concerned about the coming of winter, especially since her pleasurable activities were outdoor ones and her children were more likely to be sick in winter. After identifying her most vulnerable situations, we developed coping strategies for each using the tools she had already learned (rational responding to negative automatic thoughts, relaxation, ACT, and distraction). We also turned our attention from her automatic thoughts to her underlying belief system, which maintained that she had to be perfect or something horrible would happen. We identified the basis for this belief and challenged its accuracy.

Over the next few weeks Jane became more assertive and sure of herself. She no longer apologized for her anxiety. This was made easier by the fact that she was learning to do things in spite of her anxiety (such as riding in a submerged submarine!). She talked back to thoughts of inappropriate guilt, especially her tendency to hold herself responsible for how others felt. Her eating normalized without our focusing on it specifically.

At the twelfth week of treatment Jane's fears about rejection were still prominent. Unfortunately, a situation arose at the holiday season in which she was rejected by her father. Through careful planning, which included starting

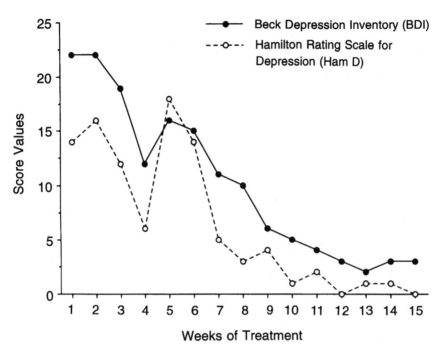

Figure 4-1. Jane's BDI and Ham-D scores by weeks of treatment.

new family holiday traditions and arranging to visit those family members she most wanted to see, Jane was able to deal with the situation without any return of her symptoms.

By the end of 15 weeks the referring psychiatrist stated: "This woman is entirely symptom free in all areas." The accuracy of this observation was reflected in Jane's test scores on the self-report inventories.

## TERMINATION

We essentially began to work on termination from the beginning of treatment since cognitive therapy is designed to teach clients to become their own therapist. Each time we examined how Jane had used her rational responses to get through a difficult situation, I emphasized what she had done and how she had done it, so that she would know how to cope the next time it occurred. I certainly expected a woman with a lifelong history of depression to have some down hours or days, but my plan was to teach Jane how to identify her depression or anxiety the moment they started and to put a plan into motion that would decrease the likelihood of their increasing.

We did not decrease the frequency of our sessions prior to termination of the weekly therapy, but we did plan follow-up sessions. We spent our last regular session summarizing what Jane had learned from therapy, how she felt about being in therapy, how I had felt working with someone as motivated as she was, and what issues remained for her to work on by herself in the following months. She agreed to call prior to our first follow-up session if she became depressed for more than a few days.

## FOLLOW-UP

Jane attended follow-up sessions at 1, 2, 4, and 6 months. At the first follow-up session she described how she had handled another sensitive issue regarding rejection. At the second follow-up she said she had felt lethargic a couple of times but had simply forced herself to get busy doing something and had felt immediately better. She also described being able to "ride out" her anxiety, which reduced it (i.e., since she no longer got scared about being anxious, her anxiety dissipated more quickly). She had also made the decision to sell her business, and her family supported that decision.

At the 4-month follow-up Jane reported two episodes in which she had been able to handle her children being sick. She had sold her business and had felt sad and "shaky" for a few days, but this seemed completely appropriate both to me and to her. By our 6-month follow-up Jane was still doing well. We discussed the changes in her life since she had sold her business. We formally terminated all treatment at this time.

Three years later Jane still is euthymic and without panic despite several serious family crises. Although she occasionally becomes anxious and worries about the future, she does not spend time ruminating. Rather, she seeks solutions to her problems. She is able to enjoy working, her family, and her spare time interests. She is confident that she will stay well because of her automatic application of cognitive therapy strategies. I share her optimism.

## OVERALL EVALUATION

Jane was a typical dysthymic in that she had past episodes of major depression, comorbid anxiety disorders, and a past history of substance abuse. In addition, her dysthymia was both primary and of early onset. In fact, she had reported a lifelong depression and before successful treatment, first with phenelzine and later with cognitive therapy, had never been asymptomatic for more than a month.

Biological psychiatrists often consider a positive medication response as an indicator of a biological disorder. Jane had responded to phenelzine, her hypomania not withstanding. Thus, biological psychiatrists would be unlikely to consider psychotherapy for a patient like Jane.

In addition, this patient's chronic lifelong depression, not to mention her panic attacks, phobias, substance abuse, and an eating disorder, might have seemed too ingrained and multifaceted to most therapists for them to consider her likely to benefit from a few months of psychotherapy. Nonetheless, it is clear that she benefited dramatically from a 16-week course of cognitive therapy. Even more compelling is her maintenance of a nondepressed, nonanxious state for 3 years following termination of therapy.

### ACKNOWLEDGMENT

I wish to acknowledge the assistance of Jonathon W. Stewart, M.D., Department of Psychiatry, College of Physicians and Surgeons of Columbia University, whose comments were helpful in the preparation of this chapter. Thanks also to Mary Guardino, Director of Freedom From Fear, for her assistance.

## REFERENCES

Beck, A. T., Rush, A. J., Shaw, B. F., & Emery, G. (1979). *Cognitive therapy of depression.* New York: Guilford Press.

Beck, A. T., Ward, C. H., Mendelsohn, M., Mock, J., & Erbaugh, J. (1961). An inventory for measuring depression. *Archives of General Psychiatry, 4,* 561–571.

Beck, A. T., Weissman, A., Lester, D., & Trexler, L. (1974). The measurement of pessimism: The Hopelessness Scale. *Journal of Consulting and Clinical Psychology, 42,* 861–865.

Burns, D. D. (1980). *Feeling good: The new mood therapy.* New York: Morrow.

Emery, G., & Campbell, J. (1986). *Rapid relief from emotional disorders.* New York: Rawson.

Hollon, S. D., & Kendall, P. C. (1980). Cognitive self-statements in depression: Development of an Automatic Thoughts Questionnaire. *Cognitive Therapy and Research, 4,* 383–395.

Klein, D. N., Taylor, E. B., Dickstein, S., & Harding, K. (1988). Primary early-onset dysthymia: Comparison with primary nonbipolar nonchronic major depression on demographic, clinical, familial, personality, and socioenvironmental characteristics and short-term outcome. *Journal of Abnormal Psychology, 97,* 387–398.

Kocsis, J. H., & Frances, A. J. (1987). A critical discussion of *DSM-III* dysthymic disorder. *American Journal of Psychiatry, 144,* 1534–1542.

Kocsis, J. H., Frances, A., Mann, J. J., Sweeny, J., Voss, C., Mason, B., & Brown, R. P. (1988). Imipramine for treatment of chronic depression. *Archives of General Psychiatry, 45,* 253–257.

McGlashen, T. (1973). *The documentation of clinical psychotropic drug trial.* Rockville, MD: National Institute of Mental Health.

Rosenbaum, M. (1980). A schedule for assessing self-control behaviors: Preliminary findings. *Behavior Therapy, 11,* 109–121.

Stewart, J. W., McGrath, P. J., Quitkin, F. M., Harrison, W., Markowitz, J., Wager, S., & Liebowitz, M. R. (1989). Relevance of *DSM-III* depressive subtype and chronicity of antidepressant efficacy in atypical depression. *Archives of General Psychiatry, 46,* 1080–1087.

Weissman, A., & Beck, A. T. (1978, November). *The dysfunctional attitude scale: A validation study.* Paper presented at the meeting of the Association for the Advancement of Behavior Therapy, Chicago.

Weissman, M. M., & Bothwell, S. (1976). Assessment of social adjustment by patient self-report. *Archives of General Psychiatry, 33,* 1111–1115.

Weissman, M. M., Leaf, P. J., Bruce, M. L., & Florio, L. (1988). The epidemiology of dysthymia in five communities: Rates, risks, comorbidity, and treatment. *American Journal of Psychiatry, 145,* 815–819.

# CHAPTER 5

# Alcohol Dependence and Abuse

## TIMOTHY J. O'FARRELL

### DESCRIPTION OF THE DISORDER

The most frequently used and most widely accepted clinical description of alcoholism is contained in the revision of the third edition of *Diagnostic and Statistical Manual of Mental Disorders (DSM-III-R),* published by the American Psychiatric Association (1987). In *DSM-III-R* the term *alcoholism* is no longer used. *Alcohol dependence* and *alcohol abuse* are the two diagnostic categories used to describe serious problems with alcohol; they are classified under the general heading of Psychoactive Substance Use Disorders, a rubric that includes problems with other drugs as well.

### Alcohol Dependence

The essential feature of alcohol dependence, as described in *DSM-III-R,* is "a cluster of cognitive, behavioral, and physiological symptoms that indicate that the person has impaired control of [their alcohol intake] and continues [to drink] despite adverse consequences" (p. 166). According to *DSM-III-R,* at

TIMOTHY J. O'FARRELL • Department of Psychiatry, Harvard Medical School, and Veterans Affairs Medical Center (116B), Brockton, Massachusetts 02401.

*Adult Behavior Therapy Casebook,* edited by Cynthia G. Last and Michel Hersen. Plenum Press, New York, 1994.

least three of the following nine symptoms must be present for the diagnosis of alcohol dependence[1]:

1. The person finds that when he or she ... [drinks], it is often in larger amounts or over a longer period than originally intended. For example, the person may decide to take only one drink of alcohol, but after taking this first drink, continues to drink until severely intoxicated.

2. The person recognizes that the [alcohol] use is excessive, and has attempted to reduce or control it, but has been unable to do so (as long as [alcohol] is available). In other instances the person may want to reduce or control his or her drinking, but has never actually made an effort to do so.

3. A great deal of time is spent in activities necessary to procure [alcohol, drinking] it, or recovering from its effects. In mild cases the person may spend several hours a day [drinking], but continue to be involved in other activities. In severe cases, virtually all of the user's daily activities revolve around obtaining, using, and recuperating from the effects of [alcohol].

4. The person may suffer intoxication or withdrawal symptoms when he or she is expected to fulfill major role obligations (work, school, homemaking). For example, the person may be intoxicated when working outside the home or when expected to take care of his or her children. In addition, the person may be intoxicated or have withdrawal symptoms in situations in which [alcohol] use is physically hazardous, such as driving a car or operating machinery.

5. Important social, occupational, or recreational activities are given up or reduced because of [drinking]. The person may withdraw from family activities and hobbies in order to spend more time with [heavy-drinking] friends, or to [drink] in private.

6. With heavy and prolonged alcohol use, a variety of social, psychological, and physical problems occur, and are exacerbated by continued [drinking]. Despite having one or more of these problems (and recognizing that [drinking] causes or exacerbates them), the person continues to [drink].

7. Significant tolerance, a markedly diminished effect with continued use of the same amount of [alcohol], occurs. The person will then [drink greatly increased amounts of alcohol] in order to achieve intoxication or the desired effect ....

8. With continued [heavy drinking] ... withdrawal symptoms [e.g., tremors, nausea, sweating] develop when the person stops or reduces [the amount of drinking] ....

9. After developing unpleasant withdrawal symptoms, the person begins [drinking alcohol] in order to relieve or avoid those symptoms. This typically involves [drinking] throughout the day, beginning soon after awakening. (pp. 166–167)

For the diagnosis of alcohol dependence some of these nine symptoms must have persisted for at least a month or must have occurred repeatedly over a longer period of time (p. 168).

---

[1] The quotations from *DSM-III-R* that describe the criteria for the diagnoses of alcohol dependence and alcohol abuse have been changed in one small way: the words *alcohol* or *drinking* have been inserted in places referred to in *DSM-III-R* by the words *substance use* or *use of the substance*. This was done to make the criteria specific to problems with alcohol. *DSM-III-R* states diagnostic criteria in general terms for all psychoactive substances.

A final point is that in *DSM-III-R* alcohol dependence is viewed as having different degrees of severity. *DSM-III-R* includes guidelines for mild, moderate, and severe dependence and for dependence in partial or full remission.

## Alcohol Abuse

In *DSM-III-R* alcohol abuse is defined as

> a residual category for noting maladaptive patterns of [alcohol] use that have never met the criteria for [alcohol dependence]. The maladaptive pattern of use is indicated by either (1) continued [drinking] despite knowledge of having a persistent or recurrent social, occupational, psychological, or physical problem that is caused or exacerbated by [drinking] or (2) recurrent [drinking] in situations when use is physically hazardous (e.g., driving while intoxicated). The diagnosis is made only if some symptoms of the disturbance have persisted for at least one month or have occurred repeatedly over a longer period of time. (p. 169)

## CASE IDENTIFICATION

Mr. V was a 45-year-old unemployed white male engineer. He was the father of six children, ages 13 to 21. The patient had been separated from his wife for 5 months at the time of his admission to the medical service of a large Veterans Administration hospital.

## PRESENTING COMPLAINTS

Mr. V's complaints at the time of admission (taken from the admitting summary) were difficulty sleeping, tenseness, depression, chest pains, and excessive alcohol use of from 1 to 2 quarts of rum daily for 4½ months prior to admission. Because of the chest pains and a history of two serious heart attacks and two other episodes of severe chest pain requiring hospitalization in the previous 12 years, the patient was admitted to the medical service for detoxification from alcohol and close monitoring of his cardiac status.

## HISTORY

### Events Leading to Hospitalization

The events immediately leading to Mr. V's hospitalization were the following: (1) his oldest son had a court hearing following an arrest for theft; (2) he and his wife had argued about the son's difficulties; (3) he had returned to the family home and destroyed several articles of his wife's clothing, in response to which the wife had initiated a court petition for legal separation; and (4) he had experienced thoughts of suicide, including an idea of purchasing a gun for this purpose.


## Earlier History

Mr. V began drinking at age 15 at parties during high school but did not feel it was a problem then or later during military service and college. His drinking started to increase around age 30, when his work as an engineer began to involve increased drinking with clients and associates. At age 36, when the patient had his first heart attack, his physician advised him to stop drinking, a warning that went unheeded. During the next 6 years he suffered more cardiac problems and suffered from a ruptured disk that required a spinal fusion. Drinking continued to increase. Despite the extensive history of heavy drinking, both Mr. V and his wife dated the onset of what they considered a drinking problem to the period when the patient, at age 42 and after suffering the aforementioned health problems, lost his job owing to a company reorganization; this was also the time when his oldest son was arrested. Mr. V's drinking escalated to a quart or more per day of rum. On occasion he became verbally abusive and threatening to his wife, especially when they argued about the oldest son's problems or Mr. V's excessive drinking.

Approximately 18 months prior to the present hospital admission, the patient again suffered serious chest pain. When his physician diagnosed possible alcoholic cardiomyopathy, the patient entered a 7-day detoxification program. He did not drink and attended Alcoholics Anonymous sporadically for 6 weeks after this first alcoholism treatment; however, he then resumed drinking after an argument with his wife. The patient found a new job and resumed heavy drinking. Approximately 14 months prior to the present admission, patient and wife were arguing frequently. After an incident in which the patient became extremely abusive and threatening, the couple separated—just prior to their 25th wedding anniversary—and remained living apart for 2 months. Six months after their reconciliation and approximately 5 months prior to the present admission, Mr. V quit his job after his boss told him he should get help for his drinking problem. The couple again separated. The patient continued to drink daily, and the quantity increased to 2 quarts of rum on many days. Mr. V became increasingly depressed and was very unhappy and dissatisfied with the separation from his wife and children. When his wife refused to let him visit her and the children over the New Year holiday because he was drinking heavily, he inflicted a superficial gash in his wrist with a razor blade and called his wife to ask her to contact the police. For 2 months after this, he remained separated from his wife and family, worked at a new job, and continued drinking very heavily, until the events (described earlier) that immediately preceded his admission to the hospital.

## ASSESSMENT

Results of the various assessment procedures conducted were consistent with the aforementioned history. Medical testing and evaluation revealed elevated liver enzymes, without liver pathology, and evidence of coronary artery disease complicated by alcoholic cardiomyopathy. In terms of drinking behavior, the patient's responses to the Time-Line drinking interview (O'Farrell & Langenbucher, 1988) showed that he had spent 80% of the days in the previous year drinking. When drinking, Mr. V was a daily drinker, consuming rum and Coke in quantities from 1 to 2 quarts of rum daily. He had experienced blackouts and severe shakes and sweats when trying to stop drinking on his own. On the Michigan Alcoholism Screening Test (MAST) he received a score of 47, indicating multiple and serious consequences from alcohol abuse. A diagnostic interview was conducted by a psychiatrist in response to the patient's complaints of depression, sleep disturbance, and suicidal ideation and his request for antidepressant medication. The psychiatrist concluded that alcohol dependence was the primary diagnosis and that the patient's depression and other complaints were caused by the alcohol problem and did not indicate an affective disorder for which an antidepressant would be helpful. In addition, an obsessive–compulsive personality disorder was suggested as a possible secondary diagnosis. Finally, an evaluation of the marital relationship was conducted, the results of which are presented here in the description of the marital therapy sessions.

The assessment and history material indicated a number of antecedents that had been associated with Mr. V's alcohol consumption. For each antecedent the short-term consequence of drinking had brought some temporary improvement, but the longer-term consequences had been the creation or exacerbation of serious life problems. The following analysis was presented to Mr. V, and he concurred with this formulation of factors involved in his drinking:

1. He was a rigid, perfectionist individual who experienced considerable anxiety and both mental and physical (muscular) tension in response to daily life events. Alcohol helped temporarily to relieve such tension. In particular, after his first episode of chest pain he became quite alarmed whenever he experienced muscular tension, fearing that this might lead to another heart attack. Alcohol relieved the tension and his fears about a heart attack in the

short run, but it exacerbated his cardiac problem leading to alcoholic cardio-myopathy in the long run.

2. Business-related social drinking with clients and associates was customary in his work and seemed to help these relationships initially. As time went on, he developed a reputation as a heavy drinker, which he reluctantly admitted may have contributed to his loss of two jobs. Drinking helped relieve his distress over this job instability but cost him his current job, when he had to enter the hospital for alcoholism treatment.

3. Marital conflict clearly contributed to the drinking, which brought temporary escape from the feelings of frustration, anger, and loss associated with these conflicts. In fact, he felt that his marital and family problems were the most important contributors to his drinking problem. Eventually, drinking led to increasingly more frequent and severe abusive and destructive outbursts at his wife, outbursts that led to police intervention, marital separation, and finally a court petition for a hearing for legal separation that would, most likely, eventuate in divorce.

4. The losses experienced led to feelings of depression, sadness, and guilt, which were at first relieved by, and later seriously increased by, the alcohol. The patient had made one suicidal gesture when intoxicated, and serious suicidal ideas continued to frighten him when he was abstinent.

5. He had drunk in sufficiently large quantities so that he had become physically dependent on alcohol. Some of his drinking was done to decrease discomfort associated with falling blood alcohol levels (i.e., to ward off with-drawal symptoms).

## SELECTION OF TREATMENT

After being successfully detoxified from alcohol and completing repeated testing to insure that his cardiac condition was stable, the patient entered a 4-week inpatient alcoholism treatment program. The inpatient treatment was followed by outpatient aftercare treatment to maintain the gains achieved during the intensive inpatient treatment.

## COURSE OF TREATMENT

### Inpatient Treatment

Mr. V's inpatient alcoholism treatment (O'Farrell & Langenbucher, 1987) consisted of (1) alcohol education, (2) individual and group behavioral therapy to clarify his decision about drinking and to provide alternative behaviors to use to deal with problems, (3) marital counseling, (4) Antabuse, and (5) planning for aftercare. Vocational assistance was offered since Mr. V was unemployed, but he declined, saying he did not need this (and he was correct: he had located some promising job leads by the time of discharge and started work a few weeks later).

*Alcohol education.* The patient attended a comprehensive alcohol education program and chose four aspects of the material that were particularly meaningful to him to discuss with his therapist. Because he had been a medical technician in the military, the medical consequences of excessive alcohol use interested the patient. The potentially life-threatening effects of alcohol to his heart and the potential of eventual liver damage if he continued excessive drinking proved very important to him. The effects of alcohol on mood and affective state was a second area he found particularly relevant. Educational material about alcohol's immediate positive and delayed deleterious effects and about the elevated risk of suicide among middle-aged, divorced male alcoholics was discussed at length by the patient. A third area of interest to Mr. V was alcoholism and marriage, specifically, the effect of marital conflict on drinking and common stages in a wife's reaction to her husband's alcoholism. In relation to the latter, the patient was impressed by the information that the greater the alcohol-related marital stressors (especially verbal and physical abuse and job/financial instability), the more likely the marriage would end in divorce. Finally, the educational material on Antabuse led to a request by the patient to start this drug immediately. Antabuse (disulfiram), a drug that produces extreme nausea and sickness when the person taking it ingests alcohol, is widely used in alcoholism treatment as a deterrent to drinking.

*Individual and group behavior therapy.* The discussions of educational material and the review of the assessment and history information resulted in the decision matrix about drinking presented in Table 1. The decision matrix, taken from the work of Marlatt and Gordon (1985), was used to aid the patient in clarifying his reasons for not drinking and to increase his commitment to abstinence. The overall goal of the decision matrix process was to have the patient consider all possible outcomes of the decision to drink or not in as complete, specific, and emotionally meaningful a form as possible and to enable him to share this decision making with the therapist.

The patient said he felt that unless he stopped drinking he could not solve any of the life problems facing him and that drinking would only make them much worse. He very much wanted to regain his wife and family and provide a stable life for his children and, secondarily, to restore his professional reputation. To him, Antabuse seemed like the one way he might manage to remain abstinent, but he was almost refused a prescription. The prescribing physician

Table 1
Decision Matrix for Stopping Drinking

| | Immediate consequences | | Delayed consequences | |
|---|---|---|---|---|
| | Positive | Negative | Positive | Negative |
| To continue or resume drinking | Relieve depression<br><br>Escape negative feelings about marriage<br><br>Relieve tension and fear of impending chest pain<br><br>Ease initial conversation with clients<br><br>Help forget job problems<br><br>Ward off withdrawal symptoms | Verbal/physical abuse to wife<br><br>Decreased awarness of "real" chest pain<br><br>Impaired judgment in negotiations with clients | Continued gratification | More depressed; Suicidal urges/acts<br><br>Divorce<br><br>Increased cardiac problems; death<br><br>Harm to professional reputation<br><br>Job loss<br><br>Continued addiction to alcohol |
| To stop drinking or remain abstinent | Talk better with wife<br><br>Approval of wife and children<br><br>Feel better physically<br><br>Feel less depressed<br><br>Alert with clients<br><br>Improved sense of self-worth | Initial tension with clients<br><br>Difficulty not drinking when angry at wife | Chance of keeping wife and family<br><br>Better cardiac functioning<br><br>Keep job<br><br>Rebuild reputation<br><br>Avoid committing suicide | Denial of gratification (becomes less intense) |

was concerned that if the patient drank on Antabuse the reaction would kill him and that Antabuse might have cardiac side effects that could be dangerous in this patient's case. A cardiology consultation ruled out the side effects as a concern. The patient insisted that he understood the seriousness of an Antabuse reaction for him. He indicated further that continued drinking also was life threatening for him. After Mr. V offered to sign a statement relieving the physician of responsibility for any negative consequences from Antabuse, he received the prescription (a week before discharge).

The behavioral therapy group in which the patient participated during his inpatient stay consisted of fifteen 90-minute sessions devoted to (1) relaxation training; (2) acquisition of problem-solving skills as an alternative to drinking in problem situations; (3) training, through behavioral rehearsal, in assertiveness and drink refusal; and (4) instruction in self-control skills, including use of a contract with a significant other to maintain Antabuse ingestion. Since the patient's individual therapist was also a cotherapist in the group, group material of particular relevance was discussed in individual therapy sessions to determine how it applied to specific situations in the patient's life. Relaxation to cope with anxiety and tension and the use of problem solving to think through alternative ways to deal with work and other situations that frequently caused the patient considerable worry and distress both proved helpful. After the concept was introduced in the group, drink refusal training for work-related social situations was the focus in individual sessions of repeated role playing of specific past and likely future situations. Finally, the patient indicated strong interest in negotiating an Antabuse contract with his wife (however, the therapist did not encourage this because it appeared for most of the inpatient stay that Mr. V would not be medically cleared for Antabuse).

*Marital therapy.* While Mr. V was still an inpatient, six marital sessions were conducted with him and his wife. At the first session both husband and wife indicated that they were willing to try marital therapy to see whether their relationship could be improved enough to justify keeping their marriage intact. Mr. V then insisted he wanted to return home to live after discharge while they continued for a "trial period" together. Mrs. V refused, saying she was not ready to have the patient back home. She needed time to get over her bitterness about her husband's recent destructive behavior and to feel more secure that she could trust him not to drink. She also indicated that the marital separation had been very difficult for her financially and emotionally and that having to make a decision about the future of their relationship was overwhelming. At the end of the first couple session, it was agreed to meet for additional couple sessions (1) to evaluate briefly what needed to be changed in their relationship in addition to the husband's drinking, (2) to explore ways they could make weekend visits pleasant times for each other in order to provide an incentive for further reconciliation, and (3) to start communication training so the couple could discuss constructively the difficult issues they would face if they went back to living together. In addition, it was agreed that they would not discuss past negative events or whether Mr. V would return home to live.

Treatment sessions were spent in planning weekend visits. The couple was assigned homework of engaging in an enjoyable recreational activity together. They also agreed to record any behavior of their partner that they found pleasing and to set aside 4 hours of "caring time" to do something special for the other. These assignments were reviewed after each weekend visit and used as the vehicle for practicing communication skills of listening and expressing feelings directly. Both spouses reported positive reactions to the couple sessions. Nonetheless, at the start of the session held a week prior to the scheduled hospital discharge, Mrs. V was still quite reluctant to have her husband return home (Mr. V had arranged for another place to stay). During this session Mr. V announced that his request for Antabuse had been granted. He proposed an Antabuse contract in which his wife would observe his Antabuse ingestion each day if he returned to live at home on discharge. He also indicated that he expected to start a new job within a few weeks and emphasized the financial benefits of not having to maintain two households. The patient also stressed that he planned to attend weekly outpatient aftercare counseling sessions once he was discharged from the hospital and that he wanted to continue marital therapy sessions. After hearing this plan, Mrs. V agreed that the patient could return home to live but indicated that she was not interested in additional couples sessions at that time. She wanted to get their lives stabilized financially and needed to observe continued abstinence on her husband's part before investing further in the marital relationship.

## Outpatient and Aftercare Treatment

Aftercare proceeded as planned, and the wife met periodically with the patient and outpatient counselor so that compliance with the Antabuse contract could be monitored. Four months after Mr. V's hospital discharge, the couple entered a behavioral marital therapy (BMT) couples group, the format of which is described in detail elsewhere (O'Farrell, 1993).

Mr. and Mrs. V attended ten weekly 2-hour group therapy sessions. Three other couples, all with newly sober alcoholic husbands, also participated in the couples group sessions. A male and female cotherapist team led all group sessions. In the BMT group the therapists used extensive behavioral rehearsal of new communication skills, specific weekly homework assignments, written behavior change agreements, and other BMT techniques (to be described) to help couples change specific behaviors during the group session and at home. The general goals of the BMT group were to promote sobriety for the alcoholic and recovery of the marriage through increased positive activities and better communication.

*Promoting sobriety.* The Antabuse contract, monitoring urges to drink, and planning to prevent relapse were the three methods used to promote sobriety. Mr. and Mrs. V had negotiated an Antabuse contract (O'Farrell & Bayog, 1986) when Mr. V left the hospital, and they continued it through the end of the BMT group. In the Antabuse contract, Mr. V agreed to take Antabuse daily at a time when his wife could be present to observe him. Both agreed to thank the other for participating in this contract, because it brought peace of mind to Mrs. V and positive reinforcement for sobriety for Mr. V. Compliance with the contract was reviewed at the start of each BMT group meeting. The couple missed carrying out the Antabuse contract on only two occasions during the 10 weeks of the group (both when Mr. V was gone overnight on business).

At the start of each group meeting, Mr. V and the other alcoholics in the group completed a form on which they recorded any urges or thoughts of drinking that they had experienced during the previous week. They recorded the day, time, and circumstances surrounding the urge to drink and how strong the urge had been on a 1 ("weak") to 10 ("very strong") scale. Figure 1 is a graph of urges to drink reported by Mr. V at each of the 10 BMT group sessions. Through many of the early group meetings, Mr. V reported thoughts of drinking, which were of moderate to high intensity. Two types of situations accompanied Mr. V's thoughts of drinking: (1) business-related social functions when he was somewhat tense or in a positive, convivial mood and (2) occasions when he was alone and in a dysphoric mood after thinking about some of the unresolved problems in his life. Mr. V seemed to benefit from discussing these thoughts of drinking in the group. Learning that others had similar experiences and having the therapists point out that he had successfully coped with the urges were helpful. The therapists' suggestions that he try actively to distract himself with other thoughts and activities when confronted by the thought of drinking proved particularly appealing to Mr. V, who liked the prospect of actively controlling his urges to drink. As depicted in Figure 1, Mr. V reported no further urges to drink after the sixth group session.

During the last two group sessions, some time was spent discussing factors that might precipitate renewed drinking and what plans the alcoholics and their partners could make to prevent relapse. Mr. and Mrs. V decided to continue the Antabuse contract for an additional year after the end of the BMT group. They had both been pleased with the beneficial effects that the contract had produced in terms of both Mr. V's sobriety and Mrs. V's willingness to

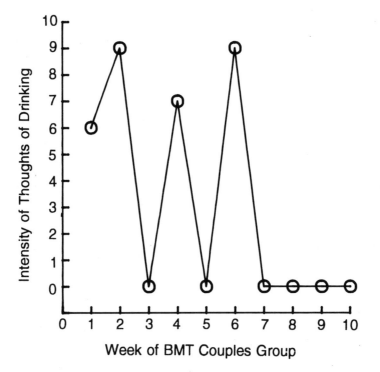

Figure 5-1. Thoughts of drinking for each week of 10-week BMT couples group (intensity ratings: 0 = no thoughts of drinking; 1 = weak thoughts of drinking; 10 = very strong thoughts of drinking).

reinvest in the marriage. Continuing the contract was something both of them decided to do to prevent relapse.

*Increasing positive couple and family activities.* Two methods were used in the BMT group to increase a couple's positive joint activities: Shared Rewarding Activities and Catch Your Spouse Doing Something Nice. The first method began with a homework activity after the second group session in which Mr. and Mrs. V separately listed shared rewarding activities (SRAs) they might like to carry out with each other—either alone, with their children, or with other adults. When they reported their SRA lists in the next session, the therapists pointed out that a number of activities appeared on both partners' lists. Planning an SRA was the next assignment, and SRA plans were finalized in the next group session, with help from the therapists and group members, as needed. Similar SRA assignments were given weekly thereafter, with one spouse responsible for planning an activity and the other spouse having veto power. The planning role was alternated weekly to show that taking turns is one simple way to resolve conflicts about recreation and also about many other issues. Mr. and Mrs. V had stopped doing fun activities together because in the past Mr. V had so frequently sought enjoyment only in alcohol-involved situations and had embarrassed his wife when he drank too much. Further, as their marital relationship deteriorated over the years, Mr. and Mrs. V had spent less and less time engaging in activities together. The first few SRAs they planned in the group were relatively brief and nonthreatening. The first SRA they carried out was having pizza together at a local pizza parlor. As they progressed during the group, the couple gradually tried longer and more meaningful activities—going out to dinner to a nice restaurant, entertaining another couple at home. By the end of the group sessions, they had spent a weekend away together.

Catch Your Spouse Doing Something Nice had as its goal an increase in the frequency with which spouses noticed, acknowledged, and initiated pleasing behaviors on a daily basis. Pleasing behaviors were defined as "behaviors that your spouse does that you appreciate." Homework required each spouse to write down one pleasing behavior performed by the partner each day. This procedure was designed to compete with the spouses' tendency to ignore positive behaviors and focus on negative ones. Mr. V had difficulty with this procedure initially. He recorded pleasing behavior on only 2 days during the first week the assignment was given. He had trouble noticing pleasing behaviors because he overlooked small daily behaviors (e.g., his wife preparing meals) and instead tried to find special, out-of-the-ordinary behaviors. After considerable discussion about the dangers of taking your partner for granted and after observing other group members doing the assignment completely, Mr. V began to notice a variety of pleasing behaviors performed by his wife.

Next, a communication session to practice acknowledging behaviors introduced ways that spouses could reinforce what they wanted more of and start opening their hearts to each other. The group leaders modeled these behaviors, noting the importance of eye contact, smiling, a sincere and pleasant tone of voice, and totally positive content. Then each spouse practiced acknowledging the two best pleasing behaviors from the daily list they had recorded during the prior week. Although somewhat difficult for Mr. and Mrs. V, repeated role-playing with extensive prompting, coaching, and modeling (especially by other group members) succeeded in getting them to acknowledge genuinely the behaviors they had appreciated. A 2-to-5-minute daily communication session was assigned for further practice in acknowledging pleasing behaviors at home.

Both spouses indicated that this exercise, especially the daily acknowledging of pleasing behaviors at home, contributed a great deal to a more positive relationship. The weekly ratings of overall happiness graphed over the

10 weeks of the BMT group and presented as part of Figure 2 show a gradual increase in the couple's happiness with their relationship.

   *Teaching communication and negotiation skills.* Therapists used instructions, modeling, prompting, behavioral rehearsal, and feedback in teaching the communication skills of listening and expressing feelings directly; they also promoted the use of planned communication sessions. Training started with nonproblem areas that were positive or neutral and moved to problem areas and charged issues only after each skill had been practiced on less threatening

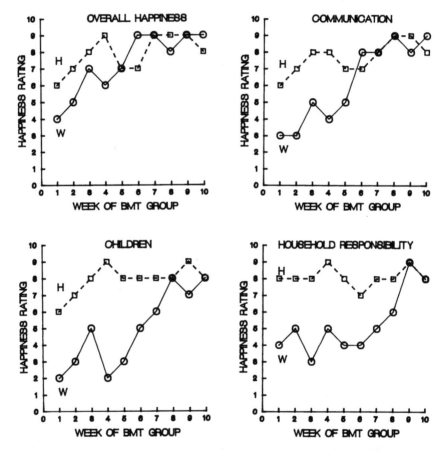

Figure 5-2. Weekly marital happiness ratings for Mr. and Mrs. V during a 10-week BMT couples group on four parameters: Overall Happiness with Relationship, Communication, Children, and Household Responsibilities. Scores are from the Marital Happiness Scale (Azrin, Naster, & Jones, 1973), which was administered weekly (1 = completely unhappy; 10 = completely happy; H = husband, W = wife).

topics. The benefits of the training in communication can be seen in graphic form in Figure 2 in the gradual increase over time in satisfaction with communication reported by Mr. and Mrs. V.

Once a base of communication and renewed goodwill in the relationship started to solidify, training in negotiation skills was undertaken to help the couple obtain agreements for specific changes each wanted from the other. Learning to translate vague relationship complaints into positive specific requests and to negotiate and compromise is necessary if the couple is going to make realistic behavior change agreements. Mr. and Mrs. V spent considerable time in the group and at home discussing and negotiating two issues that were major problems owing to the wife's unhappiness with the husband's behavior. The first issue concerned disagreements about their adolescent children, especially one of their daughters. For example, the daughter would ask permission for various activities from Mr. V after being refused by Mrs. V and he would give her the permission she requested. The second concerned a variety of household tasks that Mr. V kept promising to accomplish but kept failing to follow through to completion. A series of agreements concerning these two issues was negotiated and successfully carried out. Figure 2 displays the increased satisfaction regarding children and household responsibilities that occurred as a result of these agreements.

## TERMINATION

At the end of the BMT couples group, ongoing regular treatment sessions were terminated. Quarterly checkup sessions to monitor progress were scheduled at this time. When Mr. and Mrs. V ended formal treatment, it had been 10 months since Mr. V's last drink prior to his hospital admission. Table 2 presents scores on marital and emotional adjustment tests given before and after their participation in the BMT couples group. On the Locke-Wallace Marital Adjustment Test (MAT: Locke & Wallace, 1959) both spouses scored well into the unhappily married range, with the wife's score being extremely low. After the BMT group, both spouses had improved on the MAT, with the husband scoring in the nondistressed range while the wife, although showing improvement, still received a score indicating some marital unhappiness. On the Marital Status Inventory (Weiss & Cerreto, 1980), which indicates thoughts and actions toward divorce, the wife scored high at pretest, indicating considerable concerns about possible separation and divorce; the husband at pretest also showed some similar concerns, although to a lesser degree. At posttest, neither spouse reported any concerns about possible separation or divorce. Scores on the Areas of Change Questionnaire (Margolin, Talovic, & Weinstein, 1983), which measures unresolved conflicts

Table 2
Marital and Emotional Adjustment Test Scores for Husband and Wife
Before and After Participating in a BMT Couples Group

| Test | Before | After |
|------|--------|-------|
| Marital adjustment | | |
| Marital Adjustment Test (Husband) | 69[a] | 105[b] |
| Marital Adjustment Test (Wife) | 26[a] | 73[a] |
| Marital Status Inventory (Husband) | 3[a] | 0[b] |
| Marital Status Inventory (Wife) | 11[a] | 0[b] |
| Areas of Change Questionnaire (Couple) | 22[a] | 4[b] |
| Emotional adjustment | | |
| MAACL[c] (Husband) | | |
| Anxiety | 13[d] | 0[e] |
| Depression | 28[d] | 7[e] |
| Hostility | 14[d] | 2[e] |
| MAACL[c] (Wife) | | |
| Anxiety | 15[d] | 7[e] |
| Depression | 21[d] | 10[e] |
| Hostility | 6[e] | 7[e] |

[a]Score is in range of unhappily married couples.
[b]Score is in range of nondistressed couples.
[c]MAACL is the Multiple Affect Adjective checklist (Zuckerman & Lubin, 1965).
[d]MAACL score indicates a moderately severe or very severe level of emotional distress.
[e]MAACL score indicates a mild degree of or little or no emotional distress.

about desired relationship change, were in the severely distressed range at pretest and were reduced by posttest into the range for happy couples. Further improvements in marital adjustment were indicated by the fact that frequency of sexual intercourse increased from less than once a month at pretest to once a week at posttest. Emotional adjustment was measured with the anxiety, depression, and hostility subscales of the Multiple Affect Adjective Checklist (MAACL; Zuckerman & Lubin, 1965). Mr. V scored in the moderately severe to very severe emotional distress range for these three MAACL subscales at pretest and in the normal range at posttest. The depression score is noteworthy in that it was the most highly elevated at pretest. Recall that Mr. V's depressive feelings about drinking and marital problems had been a concern during his inpatient stay. The MAACL depression score at posttest was in the normal range after 10 months of sobriety and an improved marital relationship. Mrs. V scored in the range of moderately severe emotional distress for the anxiety and depression MAACL subscales at pretest; by posttest she had improved into the normal range on depression and was in the mildly distressed range for anxiety.

The condition of Mr. V and his wife upon termination of treatment can be summarized as follows: Mr. V had been sober for 10 months. Both he and his wife reported a much more positive and less conflicted marital relationship. They also reported much less emotional distress.

## FOLLOW-UP

Five years after hospital discharge, the patient remained continuously abstinent, was employed, and had stable cardiac functioning. The couple's marriage had stabilized, and no separations had occurred. Mr. and Mrs. V have returned for further couples therapy sessions when these were needed to deal with major life stressors and unresolved relationship issues.

## OVERALL EVALUATION

This chapter presents the successful behavioral treatment of a case of alcohol dependence. A multimodal, broad-spectrum behavioral approach was used to treat the patient's alcoholism. Long-term sobriety and improvement in other areas (cardiac, occupational, emotional, and marital) that had been linked to the patient's alcohol problems are concrete objective indicators of successful treatment outcome.

The patient's high degree of motivation for change certainly was an important ingredient in the success of the treatments used. He had lost his job, seriously risked his health, considered suicide, and nearly lost his family when he entered the hospital for detoxification, all because of his drinking. Inpatient treatment bolstered his desire for change and increased his motivation by providing specific methods he could use to cope with his drinking and other problems. Outpatient marital treatment reinforced sobriety directly through the Antabuse contract and indirectly by reducing marital conflicts which had been a threat to continued sobriety.

The multifaceted program described in this case is typical of current behavioral therapy for alcoholism. The interested reader is referred to the recent handbook by Hester and Miller (1989) for more information on current methods for treating alcoholism.

## REFERENCES

American Psychiatric Association. (1987). *Diagnostic and statistical manual of mental disorders* (3rd ed. rev.). Washington, DC: Author.

Azrin, N. H., Naster, B. J., & Jones, R. (1973). Reciprocity counseling: A rapid learning-based procedure for marital counseling. *Behaviour Research and Therapy, 11,* 365–382.

Hester, R. K., & Miller, W. R. (Eds.), (1989). *Handbook of alcoholism treatment approaches: Effective alternatives.* New York: Pergamon Press.

Locke, H. J., & Wallace, K. M. (1959). Short marital adjustment and prediction tests: Their reliability and validity. *Journal of Marriage and Family Living, 21,* 251–255.

Margolin, G., Talovic, S., & Weinstein, C. D. (1983). Areas of Change Questionnaire: A practical approach to marital assessment. *Journal of Consulting and Clinical Psychology, 51,* 920–931.

Marlatt, G. A., & Gordon, J. R. (Eds.), (1985). *Relapse prevention: Maintenance strategies in the treatment of addictive behaviors.* New York: Guilford.

O'Farrell, T. J. (1993). A behavioral marital therapy couples group program for alcoholics and their spouses. In T. J. O'Farrell (Ed.), *Marital and family therapy in alcoholism treatment* (pp. 170–209). New York: Guilford Press.

O'Farrell, T. J., & Bayog, R. D. (1986). Antabuse contracts for married alcoholics and their spouses: A method to insure Antabuse taking and decrease conflict about alcohol. *Journal of Substance Abuse Treatment, 3,* 1–8.

O'Farrell, T. J., & Langenbucher, J. (1987). Inpatient treatment of alcoholism: A behavioral approach. *Journal of Substance Abuse Treatment, 4,* 215–231.

O'Farrell, T. J., & Langenbucher, J. (1988). Time-line drinking interview. In M. Hersen & A. Bellack (Eds.), *Dictionary of behavioral assessment techniques* (pp. 477–479). New York: Pergamon Press.

Weiss, R. L., & Cerreto, M. C. (1980). The Marital Status Inventory: Development of a measure of dissolution potential. *American Journal of Family Therapy, 8,* 80–85.

Zuckerman, M., & Lubin, B. (1965). *Manual for the Multiple Affect Adjective Checklist.* San Diego, CA: Educational Testing Service.

# CHAPTER 6

# Nicotine Dependence

## PEGGY O'HARA

### DESCRIPTION OF THE DISORDER

The nicotine dependence disorder, as classified by the *DSM-III-R* (American Psychiatric Association, 1987) is most commonly associated with cigarette smoke. For most smokers the dependence disorder begins in late adolescence or in early adult life. In the United States adult population approximately one-third use tobacco, with the prevalence greater among males than females. However, the fastest growing group of cigarette users is female adolescents (USDHHS, 1990).

As smokers become more aware of the numerous health risks associated with smoking, many are attempting to quit. This process usually involves several quit attempts. Of the current smokers (according to a 1987 National Health Interview Survey [NHIS] survey), only 19% have never tried to quit. When a dependent smoker does attempt to give up smoking, it is likely that nicotine withdrawal symptoms will develop.

The primary criterion for defining drug dependence includes a highly controlled or compulsive use of the substance driven by strong, often irresistible urges that persist despite a desire or repeated attempts to quit its use. In order to distinguish dependence from a strong habitual behavior, it must be demonstrated that the drug with psychoactive effects on the brain enters the bloodstream. In addition, the psychoactive ingredient must be shown to func-

PEGGY O'HARA • Department of Epidemiology and Public Health, University of Miami School of Medicine, Miami, Florida 33101.

*Adult Behavior Therapy Casebook,* edited by Cynthia G. Last and Michel Hersen. Plenum Press, New York, 1994.

tion as a reinforcer that directly strengthens behavior leading to further ingestion of the drug (USDHHS, 1988).

According to *DSM-III-R* criteria, nicotine dependence involves continuous tobacco use for at least 1 month with (1) unsuccessful attempts to stop or
reduce tobacco use on a permanent basis or (2) attempts to stop smoking that
lead to development of tobacco withdrawal or (3) the presence of a physical
disorder that the individual knows is exacerbated by continued smoking. The
tobacco dependence disorder diagnosis is given to individuals only when they
are seeking professional help to quit smoking or when tobacco use is seriously
affecting their health.

Dependent smokers who have smoked cigarettes on a long-term basis
usually find quitting cigarettes difficult. Within 2 hours of abstinence, changes
in performance and mood can be experienced owing to the syndrome. Craving
reaches a peak in 24 hours and continues, as abstinence is maintained, on and
off for a period of several days to several weeks. The primary features of the
syndrome include craving for tobacco, irritability, anxiety, difficulty concentrating, restlessness, headache, drowsiness, and gastrointestinal disturbances.
According to *DSM-III-R* guidelines, the tobacco withdrawal syndrome is diagnosed if four or more of these symptoms are experienced. Recent studies show
that symptoms generally are diminished greatly after 1 month, with the exception of weight gain, hunger, and craving. Those three symptoms may still be
experienced for as long as 6 months after quitting smoking (Hughes, Gust,
Skoog, Keenan & Fenwick, 1991).

## CASE IDENTIFICATION

The identified client in this case is a 49-year-old male smoker who works
full-time as a fire fighter and holds a part-time job as a carpenter (Mr. A).
Seven years ago while on the job as a fire fighter Mr. A's breathing apparatus
fell apart, which resulted in his taking in superheated breaths. He shows a
rapid decline in pulmonary function as demonstrated by pulmonary function
testing. Quitting smoking may slow the lung function decline as well as
provide increased energy for this patient. At one point, immediately after the
accident, a physician informed the client that he could not smoke again. The
client asked a friend to leave a cigarette for him in the hospital; when he tried
to smoke, he could not tolerate it. He quit smoking for 14 to 15 months. Three
years after resuming smoking, out of concern for his health his coworkers,
friends, and wife, understanding how destructive smoking is to this man, urged
him to stop smoking. (His wife was a former smoker herself and was able to
quit smoking without too much difficulty.)

I was working with the fire department on a cardiovascular risk reduction program, developing a smoking cessation program for fire fighters. While I was on a site visit to the station, one of the fire fighters informed me that our identified client was interested in talking with me about receiving help in quitting smoking. I met him, we talked briefly, and at that time I asked a few questions to establish his readiness to quit smoking. He stated that he would like to think about the timing of quitting, since he had a brother-in-law who was planning to quit at the same time and he thought that it would be helpful if they quit together. I gave him the option to contact me when he felt ready to schedule a program. Within 2 weeks he called to discuss a quit date and treatment plans.

## PRESENTING COMPLAINTS

During an assessment visit I determined the client's presenting complaints through a series of questions. The following questions about respiratory and illness symptoms, taken from the American Thoracic Society (ATS) questionnaire, were asked (the client's responses appear to the right of each question):

| Cough | |
| --- | --- |
| Question | Answer |
| 1. Do you usually have a cough? | Yes |
| 2. Do you usually cough at all on getting up? | Yes |
| As much as 4–6 times, 4 days a week? | Yes |
| 3. Do you usually cough at all during the rest of the day or at night? | Yes |
| **Phlegm** | |
| 4. Do you usually bring up phlegm from your chest? | Yes |
| 5. Do you bring up phlegm at all on getting up or first thing in the morning? | Yes |
| 6. Do you usually bring up phlegm at all during the rest of the day or at night? | Yes |
| **Wheezing** | |
| 7. Does your chest ever sound wheezy or whistling when you have a cold? | Yes |
| Occasionally apart from a cold? | Yes |
| **Shortness of Breath** | |
| 8. Are you troubled by shortness of breath when walking fast on level ground or walking up a slight hill? | Yes |
| **Chest Illness** | |
| 9. During the last year have you had any chest illnesses? | Yes |
| 10. Did the illnesses keep you off work, indoors at home, or in bed? | Yes |
| 11. How many illnesses with increased phlegm did you have in the past year? | Two |

From the initial interview it appeared that the client had respiratory symptoms related to his cigarette habit. However, he did not yet seem to suffer impairment in his job, nor did he have to limit activities because of his habit.

## HISTORY

Mr. A initiated his smoking habit at the age of 17 years and within a year was a regular pack-a-day smoker. For approximately 20 years he expressed a desire to quit smoking. When he began treatment with me, he was smoking one pack a day of Marlboro cigarettes. He felt that he was addicted to cigarettes, that they were "in the system," and that even though he continued to smoke cigarettes they were not really enjoyable anymore. He understood the effects of smoking to his health and disliked the fact that cigarettes were contributing to a decline in his respiratory functioning. In fact, when he first came to see me, it was only in the evenings that he thought about smoking, and even at that time he would think, "I'll quit tomorrow."

The client indicated that he was ready to give up the smoking habit despite the fact that he knew it could be difficult. He recalled from past quitting experiences that stopping was the "hardest thing" he ever had to do. When he was abstinent for 14 to 15 months, he was not aware of changes in lifestyle habits except for an increase in appetite and eating. He reported snacking and a resulting weight gain of approximately 30 pounds.

## ASSESSMENT

At the initial assessment visit degree of tobacco dependence was assessed. The diagnostic criteria for nicotine dependence *(DSM-III-R)* include the following:

A. Continuous use of tobacco for at least one month and, +

B. At least one of the following:

    (1) serious attempts to stop or significantly reduce the amount of tobacco use on a permanent basis have been unsuccessful

    (2) attempts to stop smoking have led to the development of tobacco withdrawal

    (3) the individual continues to use tobacco despite a serious physical disorder that he or she knows is exacerbated by tobacco use

Additional questions in this assessment visit revealed Mr. A's past experience with physician advice to quit smoking, the degree of support or encouragement he expected from friends, family, and coworkers, and the degree of his dependence on nicotine, as can be seen from the following transcript excerpts:

### Physician Advice

THERAPIST:  Have you ever been advised by a physician to stop smoking?

MR. A:  Yes, many times.

THERAPIST:  Why did the physician advise you to quit smoking?

MR. A:  After the accident I was told that I was never to smoke another cigarette.

### Support

THERAPIST:  Do you expect help or encouragement in quitting smoking from your spouse, family, or friends?

MR. A:  Yes, I expect help from a lot of people—my wife and the guys I work with at the station.

THERAPIST:  Does your wife smoke, or has she ever smoked cigarettes?

MR. A:  She used to smoke, but two years ago she had back surgery and when she went into the hospital she quit smoking cold turkey and hasn't smoked since.

### Dependence Questions

THERAPIST:  Do you smoke more during the first two hours of the day than during any other two-hour period?

MR. A:  I smoke very little in the morning. Most of the cigarettes I smoke are in late afternoon or evening.

THERAPIST:  Of the cigarettes you smoke in a day, which cigarettes are most important?

MR. A:  The ones I smoke at my part-time work when I am busy are the ones I enjoy the most. At the firehouse I am restricted and can't smoke in lots of areas anymore so it isn't so much a problem there.

THERAPIST:  Do you smoke if you are so ill that you are in bed most of the day?

MR. A:  Yes, I smoke even when I don't feel well, although I usually cut down on the numbers I smoke.

## Assessing Readiness to Quit Smoking

Prochaska and DiClemente (1984) identified distinct stages that can be used as a systematic guide for helping people progress through the process of changing their smoking habit. In the precontemplation stage, the smoker is not seriously thinking about changing or is unaware of having a problem that requires a change in behavior. In the contemplation stage there is awareness that a personal problem does exist and some distress associated with admitting that something significant in one's life is not okay. For the smoker in contemplation there is serious thought about changing but no commitment to change the behavior. It is in the action stage, that is, when the smoker is willing to commit to changes in behavior and environmental conditions, that the behavioral changes occur. Responses to the following three basic questions indicate the client's current phase in the process of changing the smoking habit:

1. Have you been thinking about your smoking recently? (If the response is yes, the client is in the precontemplation phase.)
2. Is quitting smoking something you would consider? (If the response is yes, the client is in the contemplation phase.)
3. Are you ready to set a date for quitting smoking in the next couple of weeks? (If the response is yes, the client is in the action phase.)

In this case Mr. A responded that he had been thinking about quitting smoking. When he was asked the third question, he stated that he believed he could quit smoking within the next month. Once it was established that Mr. A was in the action stage, it was important to determine if a quit attempt was feasible at that time. Questions were asked about the following topics:

- Previous cessation experiences (e.g., nicotine gum use, withdrawal problems)
- Previous relapse experiences
- Past or present significant psychological problems, alcohol use, substance use
- Current level of stress and behavioral and coping strategies that were used in prior quitting attempts
- The amount of smoking encountered at work and at home

Mr. A indicated that he had previously tried to use nicotine chewing gum (Nicorette), which he had obtained from a coworker but without instruction in its proper use, and that it had not been successful for him. The withdrawal symptoms he experienced when he gave up cigarettes "cold turkey" were severe and included anxiety, craving, difficulty concentrating, impatience, and irritability. The symptoms decreased in severity after several months but never really disappeared entirely.

The primary coping strategy Mr. A used in the prior quit attempt was substituting food for cigarettes. The relapse experience occurred during a period of personal stress after a divorce. Mr. A reported that during a period of depression and anxiety he was with friends in a bar and just decided that "it wouldn't matter" if he smoked. He had a couple of drinks, cigarettes were on the table, and he just picked one up. No one he was with even tried to discourage him from smoking. Within 2 or 3 days, he was back to a regular smoking habit.

At the time of the assessment interview the client had already learned that he was capable of quitting smoking. He wanted to try quitting again and believed that if he could remain abstinent for a 1-month period, he would not go back to cigarettes.

## SELECTION OF TREATMENT

His past withdrawal experiences indicated that Mr. A was nicotine dependent, as did his answers to questions on the Nicotine Dependence Questionnaire (Fagerstrom, 1982). Since he had the symptom of intense craving with a reliance on oral substitution to minimize the craving, he was considered a good candidate for treatment based on the use of nicotine gum. (When behavioral intervention programs include nicotine gum, abstinence rates increase; when nicotine gum is combined with regular follow-up visits, sustained abstinence increases over the long term as well as the short term (Killen, Maccoby, & Taylor, 1984)). This client's lack of either cognitive or behavioral coping strategies in the past suggested that frequent contact with and support by the therapist during the initial week of quitting, so that the therapist could teach and then monitor the use of these skills, should be a part of the treatment plan.

Self-help quitting techniques, including self-control activities, knowledge and skill acquisition, and attempts to increase self-efficacy, are important for clients to use at home. In addition, there are printed materials for those who support clients in their abstinence effort, which include descriptions of behaviors that are helpful to clients as well as those that are a hindrance to their quitting smoking. These materials are given out and reviewed (Strecher & Rimer, 1987).

It was decided that telephone contact for follow-up would be a component of the intervention with this client, since frequent contact was considered necessary and the distance he had to travel for visits and difficulties with his work schedule made frequent direct contact impossible. When withdrawal symptoms are severe, initial contacts with the client are on a daily basis for the first 72 hours and are less frequent thereafter. The treatment schedule is negotiated with the client. Intensive and frequent intervention contacts occur during the initial week of quitting; weekly contacts are made during the maintenance phase; and contact is made with the client every other week, for relapse prevention activities, in the following 2 months. A 6-month follow-up visit and a 1-year follow-up visit are scheduled as well.

## COURSE OF TREATMENT

Initial quitting is achieved by the target quit day approach. Mr. A's preparation for quit day includes the following activities: (1) getting a prescription for nicotine gum and purchasing one box to have available on that date, (2) beginning to change the daily smoking routine in order to gain some feeling of mastery and control over the habit, (3) making a list of the reasons for wanting to quit smoking and a list of the reasons for wanting to continue smoking, (4) obtaining a baseline weight in order to monitor any weight change that may take place over the next few months. The self-help material includes a checklist of these various activities. The material is reviewed with the client at the preparation visit. Finally, once a quit day is negotiated, an appointment is scheduled for that date.

## Session 1: Quit Week

In the first 48 hours of withdrawal the symptoms are at their peak of severity. Effective coping strategies to prevent urges to smoke and to reduce the severity of urges include substitution, changing the order of events previously associated with smoking, and stimulus control activities, such as, removal of cigarettes, matches, and other smoking reminders. For nicotine gum to be effective, the first piece should be chewed immediately following the client's last cigarette, with a recommended dose of 8 to 12 pieces per day.

On the first day after quitting, during a mid-afternoon appointment, the client reaches a difficult period of nicotine deprivation. In the dialogue below, the therapist and client discuss ways to manage the first evening without cigarettes.

THERAPIST: At this point, how comfortable are you not smoking—let's say on a scale of one to ten, with ten being high discomfort?

MR. A: I haven't had a cigarette since last night at bedtime, I feel pretty good right now, so I'd say about a two and one half.

THERAPIST: When you have a craving or urge for a cigarette, what are you doing that is helpful to you?

MR. A: Right now, the gum seems to be helping a lot. I took one piece at eight-thirty A.M. and another piece at eleven. I'm also staying real busy. Seems to be going pretty well right now.

THERAPIST: You've indicated that after dinner is a time that you enjoyed smoking the most. What plans do you have for this evening when the meal is finished?

MR. A: I may go out for a walk after dinner. I'll use gum if the cravings are bad.

THERAPIST: Continue to remove any cigarettes and matches you may have left around in pockets, desk drawers, or in other rooms of the house. Leaving the smoking paraphernalia around can sometimes trigger a craving or an urge for a cigarette. At this point if you can stay away from other smokers, so you don't have to see them light up, you will be more comfortable.

During the first hours of quitting smoking there is an excitement, almost a euphoria, in making the change from being a smoker to being a nonsmoker. This can take clients through the first day without using many behavioral strategies, but it is important to prepare them for coping once the initial euphoria ends. For this client it was important to review the proper use of the nicotine gum. He was using this pharmacological aid as his major coping strategy, but he was not using enough of it to receive the full benefit of its use. Breathing exercises are also helpful to reduce the tension that occurs with the cravings; they take the form of "smokeless inhalation" and should be practiced in this early treatment session.

Later in quit week, usually after 72 hours of abstinence, the ex-smoker begins to experience tiredness, some depression, and frustration with the continued difficulty of withdrawal. Daily contact with the therapist and other support persons appears to be crucial to clients in maintaining their ability to continue abstinence.

## Session 2: Quit Week

As Mr. A came into the office on Day 3, he exhibited tiredness, a lack of sleep, and a general dissatisfaction with the treatment plan.

THERAPIST: Well, it's now the third day since your quit day. Have you had any cigarettes or puffs of cigarettes since we last met?

MR. A: No, not a one.

THERAPIST: What is your current situation with urges and cravings to smoke?

MR. A: I am really irritable; stress is a real problem for me.

THERAPIST: How is it affecting you—at home, at work?

MR. A: Work is really tough. I haven't been at the fire station—[I'm] on 24 hours, off 48 hours—and when I went out to my other job I found I had really bad cravings. It was impossible to concentrate.

THERAPIST: How did you manage to get through the morning?

MR. A: I didn't. I had to get in my truck and leave. I went home and took a nap. That helped.

THERAPIST: Are you using Nicorette?

MR. A: Not much. I cut down to just a quarter of a piece. Any more than that is really hard on the stomach.

THERAPIST: Review how you're using the gum. Are you chewing, then swallowing? If you are, the nicotine is going right to the stomach and will cause side effects. Think of the gum as a lozenge that is briefly chewed to release nicotine and then parked at the side of the cheek. That way the nicotine is absorbed through the lining of the cheek and can get into the system faster.

Now, let's talk about the stress you are experiencing at work. Before you get there you can plan ahead with some strategies that may be effective for you. First, have Nicorette on hand, take water to drink—perhaps a toothpick or straw to chew on. Remind yourself to practice the breathing exercises when you have an urge to smoke. Short walks may also help since a change of scenery can break the association that you may be making with concentrating on the task and having a cigarette in hand. These techniques are on the checklist in your manual, here. I'll call you at the end of the next day you're on the construction job to see how it has gone for you. We'll go over the checklist then.

## Session 3: Maintenance

The following transcript excerpt is from a session that took place with the client during his second week of abstinence from cigarettes. During quit week he had used very few coping strategies, and the self-help materials were used more by his spouse than by the client himself. It appeared that the nicotine gum was being used minimally and that distraction was the major coping skill being used by the client.

THERAPIST:  It is now one full week since you've stopped smoking. How comfortable are you as a nonsmoker?

MR. A:  I feel good now. I think I can make it. Yesterday I went to my other job and didn't have any problems while I was there. I took the gum with me but didn't use it. The gum still causes some stomach problems.

THERAPIST:  What kinds of things are you doing that are helpful to you?

MR. A:  I am snacking a little more, keeping busy, but really don't need to do too much. I feel pretty good actually.

THERAPIST:  That's probably working for you right now, but we want to prepare you for times when there are trouble spots ahead. You want to have a repertoire of things that you know will work for you during periods of stress or when you are tempted to smoke.

MR. A:  I know that if I can make it for two weeks that I won't go back to cigarettes again. You know, my brother-in-law quit about the same time I did, and he's really struggling. Of course, his wife still smokes, so that makes it tougher for him.

THERAPIST:  If you are seeing him this weekend, take the self-help workbook along and look over the suggestions for coping with stress of quitting. You have tried the deep breathing, or smokeless inhalation, technique. Have you given thought to changing your exercise habits as a way of relieving tension and anxiety from quitting and even maintaining body weight this time?

MR. A:  Yeah, at the station we work out some on the stationary bike and I try to walk some at home but I really haven't been too regular at it.

## Session 4: Relapse Prevention

Severe withdrawal symptoms often precipitate early relapse (during the first 48 hours). However, as abstinence continues, the major approach of treatment is to view the smoking behavior as a problem in self-control or self-management. The focus is not on the client's personal traits or the pathology of the disorder but on coping skills and high-risk incidents that may lead to relapse (Marlatt & Gordon, 1980).

The following excerpt is from a telephone conversation with Mr. A that took place after maintaining abstinence for 3 weeks.

MR. A: I was doing so well. Then the last two days the cravings have been driving me crazy. I can't use that gum, it's too upsetting to my stomach. They [cravings] just don't go away.

THERAPIST: Sounds like you've been having kind of a rough week. Why don't you come in for an appointment today or tomorrow?

MR. A: I'm pretty busy at work, but I'll call if I can get off early.

[These comments suggested that the client was discouraged and was perhaps heading for relapse. Often, clients who make such comments do not call for another appointment and are ready to discontinue treatment.]

THERAPIST: Look, it's not unusual that you are discouraged by the fact that you were pretty comfortable last week and then find this a difficult period with regard to cravings. As your length of abstinence increases you'll find that time between urges is longer, but when they do occur urges to smoke can be just as severe as they were initially. At this time your use of coping skills will determine how the week will go. In your last quitting experience you learned that alcohol contributed to a relapse back to smoking. Alcohol use seems to be something we should consider about now. Maybe we ought to talk about that.

Since he had not been successful in producing coping responses in the past, this was a good time to review past relapse experiences with this client and determine how to head off a repeat of that situation. Scheduling a future appointment to maintain contact was important at this time.

## Session 5: Relapse

The client failed to call to schedule an appointment. After leaving a message for him to call back, which went unanswered, the therapist phoned the client a week later:

THERAPIST: Have you smoked any cigarettes since we last spoke?

MR. A: Yes, it just didn't get any better for me, so I had a couple of cigarettes a few days ago.

THERAPIST: Are you now smoking regularly?

MR. A: Yes, just a couple a day since. I just can't seem to go without having any. It just never got any better for me.

Despite the anxiety and cravings for cigarettes that this client experienced, he did not continue the use of the nicotine gum, which might have helped to minimize the symptoms. The client never really acknowledged that a relapse crisis was near. He chose not to keep his appointment or to acknowledge that a coping response of some kind, either behavioral or cognitive, was called for in this circumstance. Now that he once again has an established pattern of smoking, even though the number of cigarettes per day is less, it is unlikely that the client will establish another quit day and begin the process again.

The following questions should be asked of the smoker who was able to establish abstinence for a time and who then returned to smoking: Where were you when the slip occurred? What activity were you engaged in at the time of the slip? Were you with a smoker? These questions begin the debriefing of the relapse crisis and elicit information about the nature of the crisis. A discussion should take place concerning the events precipitating the crisis so that the client is able to locate specific factors that led to the crisis. The attempts at coping are then explored very carefully: What thoughts or actions were considered? The final step of debriefing explores the reactions of the client and others to the relapse: What feelings were there after the event took place? In summarizing the relapse event for the client it is important to convey the sense that relapse is part of the process of learning to quit smoking. Debriefing of the relapse crisis in this manner is crucial to the next quit attempt. Finally, the client's motivation for continuing treatment and attempting to gain abstinence is again explored.

## TERMINATION

Treatment may be terminated at the request of the client after a relapse back to smoking has occurred. For the client who had quit smoking for a period of more than a week and then relapsed, it is important to determine the current level of motivation for continuing in the action stage of the process. The following dialogue took place when the client in this case returned to the therapist at a 3 month follow-up visit.

THERAPIST:  Well, you've made an attempt at quitting that shows you could manage the initial stage of the process. In that stage you used Nicorette and distraction techniques to help you cope with the withdrawal symptoms. You walked away from situations when the urges to smoke were especially severe. In the third week you were becoming fairly comfortable without cigarettes.

MR. A:  Yeah, I was in good shape and thought I had this licked but then it really hit me again.

THERAPIST:  In the fifth week of quitting a relapse crisis appeared that called for more coping responses. When you decide to set a new quit date and begin the process again, we need to be aware of the specific cues that triggered those urges to smoke.

MR. A:   I got too tired, I guess. I just didn't want to work that hard and be that miserable anymore.

THERAPIST:   Maybe you need to consider staying with Nicorette for a longer period of time while you are working on some specific strategies for coping. But look, five weeks is a long time to stay off cigarettes. That should be an encouragement when you decide to try again.

MR. A:   You're right. I never thought I would be able to quit for that long. Now just isn't a good time for me to quit again. I haven't been feeling real well—tired, and a lot is going on at work.

The client called a few weeks after the final contact to request self-help materials for a neighbor. He said that he would call again in a few months when he was ready to select a quit date.

For the ex-smoker who has maintained abstinence for a 2-month period, who experiences minimal withdrawal discomfort, and who does not have problems with weight gain or other side effects of cessation, follow-up visits are arranged on a 3-month, 6-month and 1-year visit schedule. The client may be vulnerable to relapse for as long as 1 to 2 years after quitting. Once the goal of long-term abstinence is achieved and both the client and therapist agree that the client can survive a relapse crisis, the self-management program is considered to be successful, even though the client may still experience occasional urges and desires to smoke.

## FOLLOW-UP

In the treatment of nicotine dependence disorder, nicotine chewing gum may be an effective adjunct to the behavioral treatment program for many clients. At the 3-month visit, tapering the amount of gum used may be directed by the client. In the event the client does not taper or resists tapering his use of the gum, an assessment of gum use is made at this time in order to evaluate the situations where gum is used, the number of pieces used daily, and any dependency that might be developing on the gum.

At the final 1-year visit both client and therapist may view this anniversary of the beginning of abstinence as a special event. The visit not only marks 1 year of abstinence but discontinuance of all nicotine gum use as well. Discussion centers around changes in the client's other health behaviors, such as diet, weight management, and physical activity. The benefits of quitting smoking are a focus of the meeting, and because there are still some high-risk situations the ex-smoker may encounter, the danger of having "just one" is discussed.

## OVERALL EVALUATION

For smokers, such as the client in this case, cigarettes have come to serve many functions. They may suppress appetite, aid in concentration, reduce boredom, increase arousal, serve as a break between tasks, or act as a reward for a job or task that is completed. Clients have legitimate needs that need to be addressed in order to substitute more functional ways of meeting such needs than smoking.

In the early stages of quitting, short-term coping measures are used as substitutes for the cigarettes in order to minimize the cravings. Nicotine gum, snacking, leaving the scene of an urge, and avoiding people who smoke are temporary measures, not long-term coping responses.

In the later stages of treatment the focus shifts to lifestyle changes, to exercise, relaxation techniques, food substitutes, and efforts to restructure the social environment. Changes in these areas are the responses that appear to be effective in maintaining abstinence and preventing relapse.

Nicotine-dependent smokers tend to be heavy smokers with a long-term dependence on the drug. Many enter treatment, slip, then relapse for one or more cycles before reaching the final nonsmoking status. The client in this case has now relapsed for a second quitting attempt. He has pulmonary function decline, which will further decline as he continues to smoke. For him, a debriefing session is crucial in order to discuss the relapse and the types of antecedent activities that occurred prior to the relapse. A critical part of maintaining abstinence is the ability to recover from such relapse events. A great portion of the treatment and follow-up effort must be directed toward the difficulties that arise during the maintenance phase. Anticipating high-risk situations and experience practicing coping responses will be helpful to the client in this case in his next attempt at quitting.

Side effects that occur from smoking cessation, particularly weight gain and an increased stress level, require continued treatment for many recent ex-smokers. It may not be possible or advisable to continue treatment for sufficient periods of time to make many of the desirable smoking-related changes. Group programs and printed materials or aids, such as video- and audiotapes, are resources that the client may wish to pursue.

## REFERENCES

American Psychiatric Association. (1987). *Diagnostic and statistical manual of mental disorders* (3rd ed., rev.). Washington, DC: Author.

Fagerstrom, K. (1982). A comparison of psychological and pharmacological treatment in smoking cessation. *Journal of Behavioral Medicine, 5,* 343–351.

Hughes, J. R., Gust, S. W., Skoog, K., Keenan, R. M., Fenwick, J. W. (1991). Symptoms of tobacco withdrawal. *Archives of General Psychiatry, 48,* 52–59.

Killen, J. D., Maccoby, N., Taylor, C. B. (1984). Nicotine gum and self-regulation in smoking relapse prevention. *Behavior Therapy, 15,* 234–238.

Marlatt, A. & Gordon, J. (1980). Determinants of relapse: Implications for the maintenance of behavior change. In P. Davidson & S. Davidson (Eds.), *Behavioral medicine: Changing health lifestyles* (pp. 438–445). New York: Brunner/Mazel.

Prochaska, J., & DiClemente, C. (1984). *The theoretical approach: Crossing the traditional boundaries of therapy.* Homewood, IL: Dow Jones/Irwin.

Strecher, V. J., & Rimer, B. (1987). *Freedom from smoking for you and your family.* New York: American Lung Association.

U.S. Department of Health and Human Services. (1988). The health consequences of smoking: Nicotine Addiction (DHHS Publication No. CDC 88–8406). Washington, DC: U.S. Government Printing Office.

U.S. Department of Health and Human Services. (1990). *The health benefits of smoking cessation* (DHHS Publication No. CDC 90–8416). Washington, DC: U.S. Government Printing Office.

# CHAPTER 7

# Somatization Disorder

## JEFF BAKER and PAUL CINCIRIPINI

### DESCRIPTION OF THE DISORDER

Somatization disorder is difficult to recognize. It is associated with the presence of multiple physical symptoms, but usually there is no obvious physical or psychological disorder present. However, there are certain psychological factors in the patient profile that are important to the development of somatic disorders and that are not attributable to any apparent organic condition (Knapp, 1985). The confusion resulting from an attempt to separate physical and psychological factors in the etiology of the disorder is a common problem for many practitioners when making their preliminary assessment. In fact, the lack of a clear relationship between the physical and psychological domains may be one of the early warning signs that a somatization disorder may be present. Many times referrals are from family practitioners looking for a psychological basis for what the patient has been presenting as a physical problem. The physician may see the patient as difficult, a frequent consulter, and/or a chronic complainer (Rasmussen and Avant, 1989; Robinson and Granfield, 1986; Rittlemeyer, 1985).

Patients who are referred for psychological evaluation with the suspicion that their somatic symptoms may have a psychological basis usually fall into one of two groups: those who present with somatic symptoms that mimic known organic problems but in whom none can be found and those who are preoccupied with the possibility of having serious physical problems and in

JEFF BAKER and PAUL CINCIRIPINI • Department of Psychiatry and Psychology Training, University of Texas Medical Branch at Galveston, Galveston, Texas 77555.

*Adult Behavior Therapy Casebook,* edited by Cynthia G. Last and Michel Hersen. Plenum Press, New York, 1994.

whom, again, no physical disorder is clearly identifiable. Physicians may identify these patients with the perjorative label of "hysteric" and mental health specialists may identify them as individuals with a personality disorder and poor impulse control. The symptom is their major presenting complaint, and their history will reveal repeated visits with medical consultants.

Somatization disorder can be described as a chronic, persistent, and, many times, lifelong disorder in which the current presenting problem is only one of a continuous series of constant physical complaints by the patient. Patients usually have a long history of seeking medical advice for their physical complaints. By Diagnostic and Statistical Manual of Mental Disorders (DSM-III-R) criteria (American Psychiatric Association, 1987), these patients' complaints invariably involve the following types of symptoms: conversion or pseudoneurologic symptoms (e.g., paralysis, blindness), gastrointestinal discomfort (e.g., abdominal pain), female reproductive difficulties (e.g., painful menstruation), psychosexual problems (e.g., sexual indifference), pain (e.g., back pain), and cardiopulmonary symptoms (e.g., dizziness).

Somatization disorder is not a common condition in the population at large. Prevalence rates (deGruy, Columbia, and Dickinson, 1987; Lichstein, 1986; Gordon, 1987) indicate a range of occurrence from 0.2 to 2 percent among females. The disorder is rarely diagnosed in males. However, the disorder is prevalent enough to be a common, almost everyday, diagnosis among patients seeking assistance from family practitioners (Kaplan, Lipkin, and Gordon, 1988). In fact, there are some estimates that psychosomatic complaints may be responsible for 25% or more of patient visits to primary care physicians (Katon, 1985; Gordon, 1987).

Somatization disorder has been observed in 10% to 20% of first-degree female biologic relatives of females with somatization disorder. The male relatives show an increased incidence of antisocial personality disorder and psychoactive substance use disorders. Physicians may sometimes become frustrated with such patients and refuse to treat their symptoms, feeling that they are wasting the patients' time and money. Most often this results in patients' consulting with numerous physicians, in repeated and varied contacts in both inpatient and outpatient treatment settings, and even in unnecessary surgery.

Anxiety and depressed mood are also commonly associated with the disorder. The depressive symptoms may manifest themselves in the form of suicidal ideation, suicidal threats, and actual attempts. Disruption of the patient's interpersonal relationships is also a commonly associated feature. Family and friends have difficulty dealing with the patient's constant preoccupation with ill health. This sometimes leads the patient to withdraw from interpersonal relationships, thus exacerbating anxious and depressive feelings. The health care provider may also feel emotionally drained or frustrated with these patients who are in need of emotional support but whose complaints and behavior focus on the physical domain and thus makes the referral for psychological evaluation, having failed to identify organicity or successfully implement conventional medical treatment.

To properly identify a patient with somatization disorder one needs to rule out three specific but rare disorders: somatic delusion, conversion, and malingering. There are two other additional disorders that are also rare but frequently overlap with somatization disorder. These must also be ruled out: somatoform pain disorder and hypochondriasis.

Hypochondriasis is the preoccupation with the fear of having, or the belief that one has, a serious disease, cognitions based on the person's interpretation of physical signs or sensations as evidence of physical illness. However, the belief is not of delusional intensity, as in somatic delusion, where the belief system represents a radical departure from reality. Hypochondriacs can acknowledge the possibility that their fear or belief that they have a serious disease is unfounded. Each of these disorders is frequently confused with the others and a thorough history and review of systems can assist in identifying the rare somatization disorder.

## CASE IDENTIFICATION AND PRESENTING COMPLAINTS

The client was a 26-year-old married female who had a 1-year history of chronic joint pain as well as persistent muscle fatigue with soreness in the neck and shoulder areas. The joint pain was described as a throbbing and pulsating pain in both wrists and both knees. The pain was characterized by the client as "an uncontrollable searing pain" that affected her ability to engage in any physical activity. The joint pain was continuous throughout the day but would increase in intensity for periods of 15 minutes to several hours until the client received medication or went to sleep. Thus, at the time of treatment the pain was interfering with her daily physical and mental activities. Even minimal activity was limited. When the joint pain subsided, the client would begin to participate in some activities but at a severely reduced level—activities such as physical exercise, nonphysical recreational activities, and, many times, writing, standing, or sitting.

The client also expressed a loss of sexual desire due to the persistent pain. Other presenting concerns included a loss of social interactions, due to the time she spent secluded and in pain, and a decrease in the amount of time she spent studying and attending class with her classmates. The client also reported "undue anxiety" and a depressed mood, the latter as a result of having to "deal with the constant pain" and the inability to maintain lasting friendships. Other symptoms noted as significant by the patient included shortness of breath, not associated with exertion and sporadic palpitations.

## HISTORY

The client had a history of joint pain since the age of 11. The pain was originally associated with a broken wrist, which occurred when she fell off her bicycle. There was a normal recovery period of several months and a moderate amount of pain associated with the healing process. The pain began to reappear a few weeks after the cast was removed; physical exam and X-rays indicated that the wrist had healed. However, the wrist pain continued to wax and wane throughout the client's life. Within a year of the injury the pain seemed to "spread" from her left wrist to her right wrist, and within a few years she began reporting pain in her knees. There was no association between the pain and changes in the weather, menses, or other developmental stresses.

The client experienced pain on a persistent basis but had identified some environmental precursors that apparently related to an increase or decrease in the pain. When referred for treatment, she had recently experienced an exacerbation of the symptoms. She had noted that the pain increased during psychologically stressful events. She described herself as a person with a high need for achievement and compulsive tendencies for perfection. Academically, she consistently placed in the top 25% of her class. She was enrolled in a physician's assistant health care training program, which she described as "high stress" and stated that she had worked very hard to accomplish the goal of being admitted to professional school. She was concerned that her latest outbreak of pain was causing her to fall behind in her studies. Her joint pains had been off and on for the past 15 years but during the last 6 months they had increased to "an almost unbearable level." Previously, she had reported chronic but mild throbbing pain.

The client also reported feelings of generalized anxiety. She related the anxiety to her desire to remain competitive in her professional academic training program. The anxiety reportedly took the form of heart palpitations at unusual times (e.g., while falling asleep, walking into class, or talking with friends). The client could not attribute the palpitations to a specific cause. She also reported gastrointestinal symptoms, including nausea and abdominal pain. She reported that she easily became emotionally upset, for example, when her schedule was disrupted or when requests were made of her that were not part of her routine schedule. Her depressed mood, she reported, had also been of a chronic duration; it seemed to occur in conjunction with the social isolation and withdrawal from friends during pain episodes. The client reported having few friends and no consistent family support. She described herself as having been overprotected as a child and treated as frail by her parents. The client had no previous history of antidepressant medication use, but she had recently been recommended for Prozac, which she declined. She reported no suicidal ideation, threats, or attempts. There was also no history of depression within the biological family.

In addition to her joint pain the client also had a lengthy history of muscle soreness in the shoulder and neck areas, which resulted in chronic fatigue. The pain was generally noticeable at all times, and she had not been able to relieve the symptoms through physical therapy or muscle relaxants. This pain was of considerably less concern to her than the joint pain, but she did report that it also contributed to a reduction of her physical activities in childhood.

No organic pathology in this client had been noted by the referring physician. The patient had been treated with diazepam (Valium), Tylenol with codeine, and aspirin—all without significant relief. She stated that she had been self-referring herself to emergency rooms for treatment when the pain got too severe. They would treat her with limited oral narcotic analgesics, but she was not using such medication on a consistent basis at the time of treatment. She expressed reluctance to participate in any long-term pharmacological treatment. She had no previous history of any other injuries, nor did she report substantial alcohol use.

## ASSESSMENT

It was first necessary to rule out the presence of any physical disorder that might be associated with the type of pain experienced by the patient. Physical exam, X-ray, and serology were negative for multiple sclerosis, systemic lupus erythematosus, infection, and arthritis.

Since it is possible for panic disorder to coexist with somatization disorder, both diagnoses may be made when the occurrence of physical symptoms is not limited to panic attacks. One should also rule out factitious disorder, where the person has a sense of controlling the production of the symptoms. In the case of this client, both of these diagnoses were ruled out by interview.

Other information regarding the patient was obtained using the Minnesota Multiphasic Personality Inventory-2 (MMPI-2), Fundamental Interpersonal Relations Orientation-Behavior (FIRO-B), and a Life History Questionnaire (LHQ). The Life History Questionnaire is a self-report instrument that can be used to obtain information regarding the patient's physical, social, and psychological history. In addition to the major symptoms described earlier, the patient also admitted to the following items on the LHQ symptom checklist: headaches, dizziness, fainting spells, fatigue, insomnia, tension, tremors, inability to relax, shyness, difficulty in making decisions, feelings of inferiority, memory problems, difficulty in making friends, concentration problems, and inability to have a good time. The MMPI-2 revealed elevations with the scores above 65 on Scales 1 (Hypochondriasis) and 2 (Depression), indicating excessive concern over bodily functions and increased fatigue, reduced energy, and a depressed mood. The FIRO-B indicated that the client had a very high need for control of others, a low need of control from others, a high need for affection from others, and a low need to be with others.

A self-monitoring diary was also used to track the client's awareness of the pain, the time of occurrence, the events that immediately preceded the pain, and the thoughts she was having just prior to the pain.

## SELECTION OF TREATMENT

The method of intervention selected was cognitive behavior therapy combined with relaxation training using biofeedback. Weekly 1-hour psychotherapy sessions were scheduled to assess and train the client in cognitive behavior interventions. In addition, the client participated in a course of relaxation training through taped instruction and biofeedback. This treatment regimen was aimed at reducing the stress response that may have triggered the onset of increased joint pain. Auditory biofeedback was used to increase digital skin temperature while the client listened to the relaxation tape. The increasing skin temperature indicated that the client was progressively relaxing. An additional goal of therapy for the client was to learn to use relaxation skills in anticipation of the presentation of an environmental stressor.

## COURSE OF TREATMENT

The client was seen for a total of eighteen 1-hour individual psychotherapy sessions (three to four sessions per month) over a 6-month period, during which time cognitive behavior therapy was the primary modality of treatment. Twenty additional sessions of relaxation/biofeedback training were also conducted over the same period. The following paragraphs present a brief synopsis of several of the individual psychotherapy sessions:

### Session 1

The client was interviewed and given preliminary assessments; these identified her goal to reduce the amount of pain felt in her joints. A brief history was taken and homework was given to complete the Life History Form, the FIRO-B, and the MMPI-2. The FIRO-B questionnaire requests the responder to identify behaviors in regard to (1) moving toward persons and moving away from persons, (2) dominance over others and dominance from others, and (3) need to give affection and desire for affection from others. The profile provides information regarding the specific behaviors that the client engages in when wanting to be with others.

## Session 3

The Life History Questionnaire was reviewed. The MMPI-2 and the FIRO-B had been completed and were also reviewed with the client at this time. Her goals were restated in behavioral and cognitive terms as follows: to be able to concentrate longer on studies and engage in more activities, to be able to engage in pleasurable activities, to become more tolerant and reasonable in her expectations for performance, to reduce the amount of perceived stress in her life and improve the quality of her interpersonal relationships. A course of treatment was then outlined with the client. Biofeedback training was also explained and discussed. Some of the dialogue from the third treatment session follows:

THERAPIST: At this point we have put together the data gathered in your interviews and additional information gathered through the questionnaires you have completed. Since your physician has ruled out any organic concerns, it appears there is a psychosomatic component to your complaint. If you would like to pursue a therapy program that employs the use of thought restructuring and relaxation training, there is a strong possibility it could have some impact on your symptoms.

CLIENT: I am terribly miserable with this pain and would be willing to try something different. I have tried medications with little more than short-term effectiveness. If the program is something I am eligible for, I would like to give it a try. I think there is a relationship between my joint pain and my daily stress, but I can't seem to sort it out. At this point I am willing to try anything that is more proactive rather than reactive.

THERAPIST: Overall, there is a sense of stress and almost panic in your life. You have identified a connection between your joint pain and stress. You also seem to have a need to be at the top of your class and seem to put undue pressure on yourself to achieve. Are there times when you feel you have to control everything?

CLIENT: I work very had at keeping my life in control. I wouldn't say it is out of control, but that is one of my full-time jobs . . . that is, to keep it in control.

THERAPIST: Have you ever associated your control needs with your stress and/or pain? What kind of things do you say to yourself about how you are doing in school, or in your relationships?

CLIENT: I am somewhat of a control freak, but I don't see the relationship between that and my pain. I am very hard on myself, I tell myself that I have to be perfect all the time. I don't seem to be able to let up. I'm afraid of making a mistake, and I put a lot of pressure on myself. When I am under pressure or am feeling a lot of stress, I have a tendency to work harder and try to get the stress to go away. I sometimes will work out by swimming for hours at a time. This seems to help me relax. If I catch myself talking to myself, it always seems to have a negative tone. I feel I have to whip myself into shape by being overly critical. This seems to provide me with additional motivation to get my work done.

THERAPIST:   What kinds of statements do you find yourself saying?

CLIENT:   Sometimes, when I've caught myself, I say things like uh . . . "Get going, you have to do better"; "You are lazy, you need to get your act together"; "Your just too much of a lazy bum." I also say stuff like "You're no good, you are going to flunk out"; "You're going to have to face your parents and your friends"; "Everyone is better than you; you have to work twice as hard as anyone just to get average grades; why don't you just quit?"

THERAPIST:   Does this work for you? Does this get you back on track?

CLIENT:   Sort of. It seems to motivate me to work harder both mentally and physically. It doesn't always work but I've done this for many years and it seems to give me the kick in the butt I need.

THERAPIST:   Do you remember any feelings associated with these thoughts?

CLIENT:   Well, sometimes the pain is aggravated, and sometimes I feel sort of sad that I can't do any better.

THERAPIST:   Does the sadness follow the self-talk or does it follow the physical pain?

CLIENT:   It seems to be aggravated by both, but I've never paid much attention to any association.

THERAPIST:   I have a new strategy for you. How about if you try to let go of some of the control, just to the point where you begin to feel uncomfortable? What I mean is to change some of your self-talk and see if your need for control is associated with the pain.

CLIENT:   I don't know, my control is my safety net.

THERAPIST:   Tell me more about what you experience when you're not in control.

CLIENT:   I begin to experience some overwhelming feelings. You know, anxiety-like feelings. My heart races, I feel sweaty.

THERAPIST:   Describe a situation where you feel out of control.

CLIENT:   I'm beginning to study for a test, and all of a sudden I feel slightly panicky. I want to close the book, but I can't. I have to study to make the grade to stay in school. I start to feel the pressure mount, and it's as if I'm surrounded by unfriendly feelings.

THERAPIST:   What do you do then?

CLIENT:   I jump back in and try to ignore the feelings.

THERAPIST:   Can you remember what you are saying to yourself?

CLIENT:   I usually think negative thoughts. Something like, "I don't want to deal with this now. It always makes me feel depressed. Why can't I concentrate on this material? It seems silly I can't get this straight!"

THERAPIST:   The next time that happens, how do you think you could rephrase or change some of those thoughts to break the previous pattern?

CLIENT:   You mean, talk to myself, give myself a pep talk?

THERAPIST:  Sort of. Change your thought patterns . . . the ones that haven't been working for you. Restructure them in a way that might be more helpful. When you find yourself using negative self-talk, substitute more positive phrases and attempt to let go of some of your need to control.

CLIENT:  Oh, sort of like changing tapes. Maybe, if I focused more on positive dialogue.

THERAPIST:  Yes, how might something like that be stated the next time you are feeling like that and using negative self-talk?

CLIENT:  I have to come out of this! I am not supposed to feel this way!

THERAPIST:  Well, that's still kind of negative. Can you restate it positively?

CLIENT:  I can deal with this. These are natural feelings of anxiety. I can prepare myself in the usual way and come out of this as usual with a good grade.

THERAPIST:  You have restated it in more positive terms. You might try this the next time you identify some of the early warning signs. The feelings of anxiety, the palpitations—all of those are indicators that you are physiologically responding to what you are telling yourself or what you are thinking.

## Session 6

In Session 6 the Biofeedback training was started in order to give the client a better idea of what a relaxed state is and how it feels to be in one. A temperature probe connected to her hand and the Thought Technology digital sensor read-out device were used to indicate skin temperature. The basic premise concerning the relationship between the relaxation response and body temperature was explained to the client. Specific instructions were given on the use of the biofeedback instruments in the stress laboratory and on starting a program of listening to relaxation tapes that assist in teaching and measuring the relaxation response. The client was given a log to track her temperature and feelings of relaxation (tension rating) before and after use of the relaxation tape.

Discussion also focused around the application of the relaxation exercises as soon as the client recognized the onset of increased joint pain. She was given specific instructions on identifying the actions, behaviors, thoughts, and feelings prior to the onset of increased pain and recording them in a diary that also identified the date and time.

## Session 7

In Session 7 the client was asked about her reactions to the biofeedback and relaxation training sessions. At this point in time she had had four independent biofeedback sessions. Moderate progress had been observed, with an average baseline (after 15 minutes) temperature of 79.8°F and an average ending temperature of 81.6°F (after 30 minutes). The client reported in her log that she identified relaxed feelings and had practiced the deep breathing and muscle relaxation exercises outside of the biofeedback sessions. She also reported a reduction in the pain but was not sure what to associate it with; she speculated that it was due to her undivided attention to the problem. The client reported the joint pain to be of a less severe quality.

## Session 9

The results of the assessment instruments were again mentioned to the client to reiterate her goals of (1) reducing pain, (2) reducing those cognitions that were resulting in physiological activation, and (3) learning a relaxation response which is incompatible with anxiety through biofeedback.

## Session 14

During the 14th session additional areas of conflict were explored with the client, namely her interpersonal relationships. Cognitive restructuring was also applied to assist her in reframing her self-thoughts and to help her gain a better understanding of her interpersonal skills. The FIRO-B was also interpreted to provide some behavioral guidelines for the client in social situations. Her low need to be with others, high need for dominance over them, and a high need for affection presented a conflict between her needs for affection and social reinforcement and the skills needed to seek people out. In other words, the client was cognitively expecting affection from others and her self-talk reflected her disappointment in others when they avoided her. This led to her avoiding being with them. It was clarified that her low need to be with others was possibly keeping others away. She was instructed in developing new self-talk that took into account the relationship between her high need for affection and her need to learn new strategies for developing close, personal relationships, for example, how to spend time with others in recreational as well as nonrecreational times.

## Session 16

In Session 16 there was continued cognitive restructuring to assist the client in developing interpersonal relationships. Also at this time the biofeedback program was progressing with an average baseline temperature of 81°F and an ending average temperature of 83.2°F. Again, the client identified and recorded her feelings during the week making specific connections between her stress and the increasing perceived joint pain. A significant reduction in pain in all of her joints was reported for this week.

The client was instructed on identifying stress symptoms and the relationship between a stress response and her joint pain. Emphasis was placed on her learning to utilize her newfound relaxation response skills as early as possible whenever she recognized an increase in stress in her environment. She was told to begin identifying situations that were usually stressful for her by reviewing her diary (e.g., tests and study periods, spending recreational time with others) and to employ the stress reduction technique she had learned from the tapes to try and initiate the relaxation response whenever she became aware that she was in a potentially stressful situation.

## Session 18

This 18th meeting was the final individual psychotherapy session with the client. She reported no pain during the past month but stated she had used the breathing and relaxation responses to address what she felt was potential stress. The beginning average temperature for the biofeedback sessions this month was 79.3°F and the ending average temperature was 85.9°F. Instruction was also given in this session regarding the continued use of the breathing and relaxation responses she had learned from the cassette recording on self relaxation training to her everyday life.

## TERMINATION

Sessions 17 and 18 were termination sessions and included giving the client information about the possibility of follow-up sessions. She was instructed to return if she found that she was not making the progress she had planned.

## FOLLOW-UP

At a 3-month follow-up the client reported that she had not experienced any significant return of pain (although some pain was present at times) and she reported no use of self-medication. Her relationships with her classmates had improved and she was feeling more a part of the training program she was enrolled in. However, family relationships were still strained.

At a 6-month follow-up, the client reported that she had not experienced any extended periods of pain in which she needed medication. In general, she reported feeling somewhat pleased with her progress in her academic program, as well as with her few (but quality) relationships with members of her class. She stated that this was the first 6-month pain-free period in about 2 years.

## OVERALL EVALUATION

The overall treatment program used with this client seemed to address the symptoms of pain in her joints. By the time of her follow-up sessions she no longer experienced extended periods of pain and was relatively pain free. The treatment program could have been reduced, but because of her academic time-schedule, the program was extended over a 6-month period. Joint pain is an ideal treatment issue for the interventions chosen. The client had tried another intervention (i.e., medication), which had not worked, and organicity had been ruled out. There was a relationship between perceived stress and poor coping mechanisms, which the client had not been aware of, and her cognitions were negative to the point where they may have exacerbated her condition. The client was able to learn and employ cognitive restructuring and stress reduction techniques, the combination of which dramatically reduced her symptoms.

## REFERENCES

American Psychiatric Association. (1987). *Diagnostic and statistical manual of mental disorders* (3rd ed. rev.). Washington, DC: Author.

deGruy, F., Columbia, L., & Dickinson, P. (1987). Somatization disorder in a family practice. *Journal of Family Practice, 21,* 257–258.

Gordon, G. H. (1987). Treating somatizing patients. *Western Journal of Medicine, 147,* 88–91.

Kaplan, C., Lipkin, M., & Gordon, G. H. (1988). Somatization in primary care: Patients with unexplained and vexing medical complaints. *Journal of General Internal Medicine, 3,* 177–190.

Katon, W. (1985). Somatization in primary care [Editorial]. *Journal of Family Practice, 21,* 257–258.

Knapp, P. H. (1985). Current theoretical concepts in psychosomatic medicine. In H. I. Kaplan & B. J. Sadock (Eds.), *Comprehensive testbook of psychiatry* (4th ed., pp. 1113–1121). Baltimore: Williams & Wilkins.

Lichstein, P. R. (1986). Caring for the patient with multiple somatic complaints. *Southern Medical Journal, 79,* 310–314.

Rasmussen, R. H., & Avant, R. F. (1989). Somatization disorder in family practice. *American Family Physician, 40*(2), 206–214.

Rittlemeyer, L. F. (1985). Coping with the chronic complainer. *American Family Physician, 31*(2), 211–215.

Robinson, J. O., & Granfield, A. J. (1986). The frequent consulter in primary medical care. *Journal of Psychosomatic Res, 30,* 589–600.

# CHAPTER 8

# Panic Disorder with Agoraphobia

## S. LLOYD WILLIAMS and BENOIT LABERGE

### DESCRIPTION OF THE DISORDER

People who suffer from panic disorder with agoraphobia (PDA) present a complex condition consisting of two partly independent problems: agoraphobia and panic attacks. The PDA diagnosis is a recent addition to the American Psychiatric Association's (1987) *Diagnostic and Statistical Manual of Mental Disorders (DSM-III-R)*, and it is given to people who have a history of both panic and agoraphobia. Many PDA clients present with both problems, but in some clients the agoraphobia is the predominant presenting problem, because the panic attacks often remit while the agoraphobia persists. Even when panic has not occurred recently, many PDA clients attribute their agoraphobic behavior to a desire to avoid the risk of panic. The present case illustrates treatment of a client who experienced both agoraphobia and panic attacks.

Agoraphobia refers to fear and avoidance of various situations and activities in the community. Activities typically avoided include, among others, driving, shopping, walking along the street, using public transportation, being far from home, crossing bridges, and being in audiences, restaurants, high places, and elevators. The various phobias occur in highly idiosyncratic constellations from one agoraphobic person to another. Some agoraphobic people

S. LLOYD WILLIAMS • Department of Psychology, Lehigh University, Bethlehem, Pennsylvania 18015    BENOIT LABERGE • Centre Hospitalier de l'Université Laval, Université Laval, Sainte-Foy, Québec, Canada G1V 462.

*Adult Behavior Therapy Casebook,* edited by Cynthia G. Last and Michel Hersen. Plenum Press, New York, 1994.

are completely housebound. More often, they are able to leave home but only to a restricted range of activities, and under limited circumstances. They often function better if they are accompanied by a trusted companion or if the setting is familiar, whereas they tend to do less well if the activity involves a long time commitment, crowds, or apparent physical or psychological confinement. In some phobic areas clients might be truly disabled, that is, unable to do the activity even when they try, whereas in other areas they can force themselves to function while enduring high anxiety (Williams, 1985). The agoraphobic behavior usually starts following a "spontaneous" panic attack or a series of them. Such an attack is a sudden, unexpected rush of intense fear and autonomic and other physiological reactions and is associated with strange sensations and catastrophic thoughts of losing control, humiliating oneself, dying, or going crazy. Clients often attribute their avoidance to fear of having such a panic attack; they especially desire to prevent panic, or at least to avoid being in a situation in which panic would render them helpless and vulnerable to physical or psychosocial calamity.

The diagnosis of panic disorder in DSM-III-R is based on several criteria. First, the individual must have a history of spontaneous panic attacks, that is, of unexpected attacks occurring even when the person was not trying to engage in a frightening activity. Second, the client must have a history of either multiple attacks in a short period (four in 4 weeks) or an attack that was followed by a month of persistent apprehension of having another attack. Third, for an attack to qualify as panic, the person must report experiencing four or more of the following 13 kinds of reactions: shortness of breath or smothering sensations; dizziness, unsteady feelings, or faintness; heart palpitations or accelerated heart rate; trembling or shaking; sweating; choking; nausea or abdominal distress; depersonalization or derealization; numbness or tingling sensations; flushes or chills; chest pain or discomfort; fear of dying; and fear of going crazy or doing something uncontrolled. Fourth, at least four of these reactions must have occurred suddenly, with their intensity increasing soon (within 10 minutes) after the beginning of the attack.

Of course, the preceding definition of panic and of panic disorder is somewhat arbitrary, and the diagnosis and criteria will likely change in future diagnostic manuals, just as they have markedly in recent ones. These diagnostic minutiae are not as important as the general phenomenon of a history of intense fear attacks with current multiple phobias of community activities.

Other problems that commonly plague PDA clients include generalized anxiety and high anticipatory anxiety in advance of a date on which they must do something they fear (e.g., attend a wedding). Yet other clients remain relatively unstressed as long as they resolutely maintain their pattern of avoidance. Clients often have other phobias (especially social phobias) and depression, and some have problems with hypochondriasis or substance abuse (usually alcohol or minor tranquilizers).

The following case history illustrates some characteristics of panic disorder with agoraphobia. It also describes the assessment and treatment of a representative case.

## CASE IDENTIFICATION

Mary was a 28-year-old white housewife who sought treatment for her increasing inability to function away from home and her attacks of "light-headedness." Her common-law husband of 9 years, Bill, was a 31-year-old former auto mechanic who was disabled by a heart condition. She and Bill had two sons, ages 7 and 5. They lived in an apartment in a moderately large city.

## PRESENTING COMPLAINTS

Mary stated that she had almost completely lost her ability to function independently away from home and was limited to the area within a mile of her house. This was partly because the distance per se was scary and partly because of her severe driving and bridge phobias. Mary explained that she feared getting light-headed, panicking, and not being able to go back home. If Bill or her sister Lori accompanied her, she could function somewhat better. But even then she would not go farther than a few miles from home or cross a moderately large bridge unless she was sedated ("zonked" as she put it) with alprazolam (Xanax), which she took "as needed." Mary could not ride buses even near her home.

Mary also had problems shopping and some social fears: She could go to nearby small stores if they were not crowded, but big stores were out of the question, even when she was accompanied. She was unable to tolerate social events away from home, especially if many strangers were present. Mary and Bill and the children attended church services at a nearby Baptist church, but this was increasingly a torture for her. She required that they arrive early enough to be assured of a seat in the last row. On one recent occasion they arrived late; Mary had to force herself to sit several rows forward but did so only with great difficulty and distress, fearing that she would panic, lose control, and humiliate herself.

At the time Mary sought treatment, her panic attacks had become more frequent. She reported that she now experienced panic two or three times a week. Sometimes these occurred at night when she was sleeping. The attacks seemed to occur almost randomly, both at night and during the day. It seemed to make little difference what she was doing, although she tried to control them by lying down much of the day. She reported that the Xanax no longer helped very much.

The church episode led Mary to renew her long-abandoned attempt to get help. She called a local hot line and was referred to our university-based agoraphobia/panic research program.

## HISTORY

Mary's fears began when she was 20, soon after the birth of her first child. She had driven to get a few items in a supermarket, and once in the store she began to feel "light-headed and weird." She continued trying to shop but soon experienced a cascade of autonomic reactions: her heart pounded and raced, she sweated profusely, her arms and face tingled, her breathing quickened, and, worst of all, she felt faint and light-headed and had the terrible feeling that she was about to lose her mind. She rushed out of the supermarket and to her car; after taking some deep breaths she forced herself to start driving home. On the way she became so concerned about the aversive feelings in her body that she stopped to telephone Bill and asked him to come and take her to a hospital. The psychiatry resident there, concluding that she had had a panic attack, prescribed Xanax.

After this episode Mary was at first hesitant to leave home at all and did not try to drive. Later she gave driving another try but found it stressful. She developed a pattern in which she drove only on quiet streets, only with a companion, and only when and where it was possible for her to stop the car and let the other person take over the driving, if necessary. Gradually, the shopping, audience, bridge, and social fears developed, all of which surrounded activities that Mary believed might provoke panic, a panic with which she would have difficulty coping and from which it would be difficult to make a controlled, graceful exit.

The avoidance seemed to work at first. Mary rarely experienced panic, except occasionally at night. She stayed at home taking care of her baby, and Bill assumed responsibility for most tasks away from home. The birth of her second child at age 22, though stressful for Mary, did little to change her routine or her phobic condition. However, when the second child was a few months old, Bill experienced chest pains and learned that he had a heart condition. Because his condition necessitated their living on government disability benefits until he could get a more sedentary job, Bill became depressed and guilty and had trouble doing his usual domestic duties.

This threat to their financial security and domestic equilibrium, coming as it did at a time when she could not take a job both because of her agoraphobia and because she felt she had to care for the children herself, depressed and distressed Mary. Soon she began to experience panic attacks at home, where she thought she was the safest and there was nothing to fear. This reinforced her belief that she was weird and probably going crazy. Mary was confronted with a multitude of stressors. She worried about whether she was going crazy, whether her husband's depression would improve, whether their financial situation would improve, and whether they would be able to take proper care of their kids. Mary's phobias became worse.

## ASSESSMENT

Mary's panic- and phobia-related behaviors, thoughts, and emotional arousal were assessed by interview, questionnaires, self-monitoring, and direct observation in the natural environment. She initially was administered the Anxiety Disorders Interview Schedule-Revised (ADIS-R; DiNardo et al., 1985), a structured interview for anxiety disorders. This surveyed her phobias, explored her panic and her generalized anxiety, and checked for obsessions and compulsions. Mary described a fairly typical pattern of panic attacks and agoraphobia with some social phobic problems and generalized anxiety.

Mary also completed the Beck Depression Inventory (Beck, 1978), scoring 18 on the 0–63 scale, which indicated mild-moderate depression; Mary and the interviewer both judged her depression and generalized anxiety to be largely secondary to her phobias and panic. She did not have obsessions, compulsions, substance abuse, or other notable psychological problems. The remainder of the assessment procedure then concentrated on a more detailed evaluation of the agoraphobia and panic. Mary was given questionnaires about these latter problems to take home and bring to the second session.

### Assessment of Agoraphobia

A cognitive-behavioral evaluation of Mary's agoraphobia was conducted using an approach described by Williams (1985). The goal was to obtain from Mary specific details about each phobia-related problem area, especially her range of behavioral functioning and her self-efficacy and vulnerability to anxiety in that area. Because a primary goal of treatment would be to increase her self-efficacy and performance capabilities, the assessment closely examined her level of disability, that is, her functional limits even when trying to do as much as she could, as well as her routine behavior patterns in daily living.

To obtain Mary's ratings of self-efficacy for various tasks, the therapist asked her to complete a set of Self-Efficacy Scales for Agoraphobia (Kinney & Williams, 1988; Williams, 1985). On these scales, Mary rated the confidence with which she, alone and accompanied, could do each of a range of tasks within various phobic problem areas (e.g., crossing bridges, driving, riding elevators). She rated each task on a confidence scale ranging from 0 (cannot do) to 100 (certain). Mary also indicated how anxious she thought she would become doing the same tasks. She rated her anticipated anxiety using an anxiety scale ranging from 0 (not afraid, tense, or anxious) to 10 (extremely afraid, very tense, and anxious). Mary had very low self-efficacy and high anticipated anxiety for the majority of the tasks, but she was confident in some areas (e.g., riding elevators).

Over the next three sessions, four of Mary's high-priority problem areas were behaviorally evaluated to determine how much she could do walking, shopping, driving, and crossing bridges. While trying the tasks, Mary also rated her anxiety. The therapist explained the importance to Mary of putting her self-appraisals to a reality test, the more so because she had not tried in a long time to do most of the things she feared. Agoraphobic people sometimes badly misappraise their disability and may see themselves as more disabled and vulnerable to anxiety than they actually are. Thus, an initial behavioral evaluation identifies clearly the areas of special difficulty that will be the major focus of early treatment efforts.

The therapist took Mary to the various phobic settings and asked her to attempt, alone, the tasks that she was not entirely confident she could do, progressing from easier to harder tasks in the test hierarchy until she could not do a task. The score for each area is the percent of tasks in the hierarchy the person is able to do. (For details of behavioral testing procedures with agoraphobics, see Williams, 1985, and Kinney & Williams, 1988). After an initial failure, the therapist asked Mary to try another time or two to see whether she could rapidly increase her performance, as people sometimes do. Thus, the behavioral testing with Mary also involved some brief therapeutic practice.

On the test of walking on busy streets, Mary initially walked three blocks of the 10-block test route (30% performance), with an anxiety rating of 8 on the 0–10 scale. Two attempts later she was up to seven blocks (70% performance) and rated her anxiety only 6; she was very pleased by this rapid therapeutic progress. In the supermarket test Mary could not even go out of sight of the entrance (6% performance), and two more tries yielded no gain in performance and only a slight decline in anxiety, from 9 to 8. It seemed that this phobia would be tougher to treat than the walking phobia.

Mary's driving phobia also proved severe and refractory. Although she drove 10 blocks on a quiet residential street with high anxiety (8), she could drive only two blocks along the next route, a minor thoroughfare, and with maximum anxiety (10). On her second attempt to drive the minor thoroughfare she travelled the same distance (representing 18% test performance) and remained maximally anxious. She was not tested on major thoroughfares or freeways, which she considered far more fearsome. In contrast, Mary walked alone across a long, high bridge over a river (100% performance), and with only moderate anxiety (4). She then drove alone over this bridge with only similar anxiety. It seemed that her bridge phobia would be easily treated.

This initial behavioral evaluation of several high priority areas had already benefited Mary by showing her that she could in some areas cope better than she had thought. Her audience phobia and bus phobia would be behaviorally tested later as treatment progressed.

## Assessment of Panic Attacks

The therapist evaluated Mary's panic attacks by exploring the frequency and pattern of panic, the circumstances in which panic occurred, and, perhaps most important, the specific behavioral, cognitive, emotional, and physiological reactions experienced during panic. The defining features of panic include certain particular autonomic stress reactions and catastrophic thoughts, but in practice people report a much wider variety of such sensations and reactions. It seems clear that the panic phenomenon is due in part to exaggerated perceptions of danger, including catastrophic interpretations of bodily sensations (Barlow & Cerny, 1988; Clark, 1986). Moreover, according to the social cognitive analysis (Bandura, 1988; Williams, 1990), it is not just the physiological arousal and thoughts of danger per se but people's perceived inability to prevent, moderate, or terminate such reactions and their inability to control their behavior when faced with such reactions that are the major contributors to panic and to its capacity to impair functioning. Therefore, the therapist explored not only Mary's various sensations and thoughts but also her perceptions of inefficacy, vulnerability, and lack of control.

The therapist asked Mary to describe in detail the sequence of reactions that unfolds in a typical panic episode. Mary reported that she would usually first feel "light-headed and weird" and that her eyes would not focus right; then she would feel afraid and think, "There's something wrong with me." Her heart would pound and race, and she would break out into a sweat. Then her arms and face would tingle, and her breathing would quicken. As the attack reached peak intensity, the light-headedness would return even stronger than before and she would think, "I'm going to pass out" and/or "I'm going out of my mind." She would then initiate self-protective activities, including escape maneuvers such as scanning for an exit and starting toward it, and such defensive activities as sitting down, grabbing on to something for support, pulling off the road if driving, and popping a tranquilizer.

The second step in assessing panic attacks is to identify factors in the panic scenario that could contribute to the occurrence of most of the client's characteristic reactions. In Mary's case, these factors include being apprehensive about an attack; telling herself she cannot stop it; standing in a defensive position and staring at the floor while trying to compose herself, a response leading to blurred vision and light-headedness; labeling these reactions and the accompanying rush of fear as weird; perceiving herself as unable to handle the fear, a perception leading to an increase in stress hormones, which cause the heart to pound and race; trying to calm herself by taking deep breaths but overdoing it and ending up hyperventilating, which increases light-headedness, sweating, and tingling in the extremities; interpreting the light-headedness as a sign of imminent fainting; believing her loss of control over her feelings and perceptions means that she is losing her mind; and thinking her only hope is to escape, hold on, or take a pill.

Mary also completed a questionnaire on which she rated her self-efficacy to control her panic attacks when she is alone, without tranquilizers or other self-protective devices, and in each of the following three conditions: when she feels certain bodily sensations, when she thinks of certain feared consequences, and when she is engaging in various community activities. This self-efficacy measure identifies the client's perceived vulnerabilities; the same measure is later used to help the therapist determine whether the panic management techniques being practiced are imparting to the client a sense of mastery or whether a different approach must be tried.

Additional measures gathered on a continuous basis during the treatment program included daily records of Mary's excursions from home, her anxiety both at home and away, and her panic attacks. Mary also recorded her compliance with cognitive/behavioral homework assignments.

## SELECTION OF TREATMENT

Mary presented a picture of severe agoraphobia and frequent panic attacks. The treatments for these two problems are partly independent but complementary. Mary was treated for both problems concurrently since improvements in either can facilitate gains in the other.

## Agoraphobia Treatment Conception

The heart of phobia treatment is the therapeutic performance of phobia-related activities, often called "in vivo exposure." In particular, we applied a guided mastery approach to performance treatment (Williams, 1990), an approach based on the conception that treatments work by raising clients' sense of self-efficacy for coping effectively and for controlling scary trains of thought. The therapist's role is to foster performance successes that build a sense of cognitive and behavioral mastery. Present space limitations do not permit much systematic detail about the guided mastery approach (for a detailed account of this approach in treating agoraphobia, see Williams, 1990).

Three major strategies of guided mastery were used with Mary. First, the therapist applied a repertoire of techniques designed to help her do tasks she otherwise would have found difficult or impossible. These techniques included the therapist performing therapeutic tasks jointly with Mary, helping her graduate the treatment tasks and set proximal performance goals, modeling therapeutic tasks, and others (Williams, 1990). Second, once Mary could do a given activity, the therapist guided her to improve her performance, for example, by increasing the flexibility and proficiency of her efforts and by eliminating the self-restrictions, awkwardness, or defensive rituals ("crutches") that limit growth in self-efficacy. Third, to foster independence of functioning and an unconditional sense of mastery, the therapist provided Mary only as much assistance as was needed to promote progress; once progress was restored, he quickly faded out the assistance and arranged for Mary to have independent success experiences. He also tried to empower Mary to conduct her own therapy.

Because Mary's driving and shopping phobias were severe and refractory, the therapist began by spending several sessions with Mary in the community, helping her drive and shop. For her other phobias Mary initially received homework assignments only, that is, tasks to carry out on her own between sessions.

## Panic Treatment Conception

The guided mastery approach for panic is to foster in clients a sense of control over the various component responses of panic and confidence in their ability to dismiss irrational, panic-provoking thoughts, exercise behavioral control, and cope effectively despite panic. Mary was taught techniques to modify her various reactions, including the neurological/perceptual (light-headedness and blurred vision), the cardiological (heart racing and pounding), the autonomic (sweating), the respiratory (hyperventilation), and the cognitive (thoughts that she would faint or go crazy). One strategy was to deliberately induce panic attacks to give Mary the opportunity to apply various control techniques until she could build a strong sense of self-efficacy. There are various means of inducing panic attacks without special equipment or drugs; these include, among others, hyperventilation, physical exertion, spinning on a chair, and mental imagery. Of course, it is important to be sure that the person has no medical problems that would be aggravated by induced panic attacks. The procedure Mary used to induce panic attacks was to stand up quickly, stare at the floor, and hyperventilate through forced breathing. In order to vary the intensity of the simulated panic attacks, the duration and number of repetitions of hyperventilation trials were gradually increased.

It is preferable that clients suffering from panic attacks receive psychological treatment without medication so that they can attribute their successes to their own coping capacities. However, since Mary was partially dependent on Xanax, the therapist felt that she would have difficulty in suddenly discontinuing its use. Therefore, he encouraged Mary to take Xanax before treatment or homework sessions in the beginning and then, as treatment progressed, to try to minimize her use of it. He explained to her that true mastery of fears would require that she soon fully withdraw from the medication.

## COURSE OF TREATMENT

Mary's treatment program initially involved frequent sessions (twice a week, with each session lasting 2 or more hours). Later in the program, as she made significant progress, the sessions became less frequent and shorter in duration. The therapist explained to Mary that it was advantageous to have frequent meetings and that it was also important for her to work on her own between the sessions with him. He explained that she would have to invest time and hard work, that the program would otherwise be of little benefit to her. Bill was included in the treatment program from the outset so that he could assist Mary with field mastery tasks and be a source of knowledgeable support for her. Although he had not always been as understanding and supportive as he should have been, he genuinely wanted Mary to recover, and he was willing to learn how to help. In Mary's early sessions most of the panic management therapy took place in the office whereas most of the phobia treatment was conducted in the field, with Mary, Bill, and the therapist going out to community sites together.

Although for convenience we will describe the agoraphobia therapy separately from the panic management therapy, the reader should bear in mind that therapy for the two problems took place in parallel throughout the program, with alternating sessions of each kind of treatment, in order to attack Mary's problems simultaneously on a broad front.

### Agoraphobia Treatment

The first field therapy session was devoted to driving. The therapist drove Mary in her car, and Bill drove in his car, to a nearby minor thoroughfare with traffic lights. The following dialogue illustrates the treatment rational and several of the specific guided mastery techniques that were used to help Mary learn to cope with heavy traffic, traffic lights, and busy intersections:

THERAPIST: Let me remind you of what we are trying to do here. The best way to regain your confidence and get rid of your scary thoughts and panicky feelings about driving is to show yourself that you can manage these activities. At first we will work on easier tasks, and as you succeed in these you should gain the confidence you need to help you tackle and master harder tasks. It is important that you persist in trying, that you do as much as you can at any time, and that you try to increase what you do. Remember, too, that nothing harmful can happen to you; the worst is just feeling unpleasant but temporary anxiety. I'll suggest some things for you to do, and I will ask you about your reactions and what you find difficult, so together we can figure out the next step. What do you think?

MARY: Well, it sounds nice, but I can't believe it will really work.

THERAPIST: Well, let's just get started and see how it goes. The other day in the test you drove only two blocks on this street by yourself. Do you think you could drive farther if Bill and I rode with you?

MARY: That would help, but I still don't think I could go very far.

THERAPIST: Okay, we'll get in. Try to drive to Moreno Avenue, ten blocks away. We'll just be quiet so you can concentrate on the driving. [Mary was able to drive about six blocks, through two traffic lights at minor intersections, but pulled over just before a major intersection.]

MARY: I just can't try to go through that light. It stays red too long.

THERAPIST: What if we wait here until the light turns green, then go? Do you think you could do that?

MARY: Well, maybe, if you're sure I'll hit it green. But it's scary.

THERAPIST: Well, if you think maybe you can, then you probably can. Also, I notice that you're holding on to the steering wheel for dear life and you are leaning way forward with your shoulders up around your ears. It is important that you learn that you don't have to do that. You can do better and feel better if you just loosen your grip, drop your shoulders, and lean back comfortably. I always tell people, "Act normal even if inside you feel like hell." Okay, as soon as those cars finish turning left, the light will turn green for us, so start now. It will be green by the time you get there.

MARY: [a few moments later] I made it! I had quite a rush there for a second in the intersection.

THERAPIST: Great! You looked much better with your posture driving through the intersection. How anxious did you get, on the zero-to-ten scale?

MARY: About seven, but just for a moment, not too bad.

THERAPIST: Do you feel more confident about it now? How confident are you that you could do it again with us from zero to one hundred?

MARY: Better, maybe forty or fifty.

THERAPIST: Good. What about if Bill and I were to get out and stand on the corner while you go through the light by yourself? And we meet you on the other side. What do you think of that? Can you try it?

MARY: As long as you stay where I can see you, I'll give it a try. Don't go anywhere.

THERAPIST: Okay, we'll be right over there. Just wait till some of those cars have turned left, then go.

Next Mary deliberately caught the light red for a few seconds before it turned green; then she timed it so that she would have to wait for the full duration of the red light. Because she felt much more confident about coping with intersections, she then practiced driving distances along the route; soon she drove alone a distance of about 12 blocks, a task she performed with an anxiety level of 7. The therapist then suggested going to a larger, busier street. Mary at first objected because she was still anxious when driving on the minor thoroughfare, but the therapist explained that the best way to thoroughly overcome her anxiety about this route was to tackle a major boulevard, which would make the present route seem like "a piece of cake."

Mary initially had near-zero confidence that she could drive alone on the major thoroughfare, so the therapist suggested having Bill follow in his car directly behind her the first time she tried to drive six blocks and back. This went well, and the next time Bill followed her after a delay of 30 seconds. Mary then felt some confidence (40 on the 100-point scale) for driving eight blocks alone. She tried this and succeeded, with an anxiety level of only 4. She was quite pleased but also very tired.

In the next two field therapy sessions Mary worked on driving freeways, which went a little more slowly. She first practiced entering and then immediately leaving the freeway at a four-way cloverleaf interchange, with the therapist and Bill in the car. After using delayed following and other performance aids, Mary was able by the end of the third driving session to drive four exits by herself on a freeway, changing lanes and passing cars.

Therapist-directed field therapy then switched to grocery shopping. The general strategy was similar to driving, but for this phobia Mary made much slower progress and with much more difficulty along the way. Since her first and biggest panic attack was in a grocery store, she felt particularly inefficacious and vulnerable in this area. The initial treatment site, a large supermarket, proved too intimidating for Mary, so treatment proceeded by working up from smaller and medium-sized stores. At each site Bill initially accompanied Mary as she walked through the store; then she did it alone. The focus then changed to selecting items and purchasing them.

Because Mary and Bill were apt pupils who fairly quickly grasped the general principles of treatment, the therapist increasingly asked them to collaborate with each other in deciding on the next performance task. Nonetheless, there were setbacks and rough spots along the way, which required the therapist to remain active in suggesting ways to assist Mary. His empathic but firm encouragement to continue was also required. He had to explain to Mary and Bill the importance of continuing after setbacks. "It is actually better to work on days when you are not feeling your best," he told them, "because then you learn that you can manage even when things aren't ideal."

Six 2-hour sessions were required for Mary to be able to purchase ten items in a large supermarket, and this was only when no more than two people were ahead of her in line. This was somewhat slow progress, but it was not too discouraging to Mary because she was making many gains in other areas with her homework. Homework assignments were discussed with Mary and Bill at least briefly prior to going out for field therapy. With Mary's increasing mastery, later performance mastery treatment was conducted via homework alone. The therapist started each of these sessions by reviewing the last homework assignment and ended the session by assigning new homework; he used a form on which he wrote the assignment on the left and left room on the right for Mary to make notes about what she actually did and how anxious she became. As with the field therapy tasks, homework tasks were decided collaboratively but with increasing reliance on Mary to do the planning, with Bill serving as a potential helper and the therapist as an adviser. Throughout the program, care was taken to select tasks at a low but not zero level of self-efficacy, that is, challenging enough that doing them would give Mary a feeling of success but not so challenging that she was likely to fail. The assignments were quite specific as to particular activities, settings, and other relevant contextual factors. Moreover, the assignments were made as definite appointments, with date and time, that Mary and Bill would keep as if they were therapy appointments.

## Panic Mastery Therapy

Mary's typical panic scenario and reactions indicated that she had to learn certain behavioral and cognitive techniques to reduce her panic reactions. By hyperventilation panic-induction practice, she acquired techniques to control her panic attacks and learned that she could cope effectively even if panic should occur.

During panic sessions Mary would rehearse the following behavioral and cognitive techniques to control panic: visual scanning, which prevented her from staring at the floor when she was anxious; the Valsalva maneuver, which slowed down her heart rate and thus prevented the pounding and racing sensations in her thoracic cage (with this technique clients inhale; then close their mouth, pinch their nose, and press their tongue against the roof of the buccal cavity until their eardrums pop; and then breathe normally); slow controlled breathing to avoid hyperventilation; and walking around without holding on to furniture or the walls to test out whether she would faint or fall over. Cognitive techniques were also part of Mary's coping arsenal and included reinterpreting her panic episode in factual rather then catastrophic terms, diverting attention from panic sensations, and giving herslf a short mental status exam to test whether she was really going crazy. Once Mary learned each coping skill, the therapist asked her to integrate it into her field mastery experiences and to practice it whenever she experienced reactions associated with a panic attack. The following dialogue illustrates a panic induction session.

THERAPIST: Now that you have some coping skills to short-circuit a panic, I would like you to hyperventilate as you did the other day; when you feel some panicky sensations, raise your hand and start coping.

MARY: Okay, I'm ready.

THERAPIST: Now, what do you do first?

MARY: I feel light-headed. First, slowly scan my environment and don't stare at the floor. Second, I will slow down by breathing since hyperventilation is known to make people feel light-headed.

THERAPIST: Okay, are you still feeling light-headed?

MARY: No, but my heart is pounding and bothering me so I will slow it down using the Valsalva maneuver.

THERAPIST: How is your heartbeat now?

MARY: Better, slower.

THERAPIST: Okay, what else is bothering you?

MARY: I still think I might faint.

THERAPIST: What could you do to gain control over that thought?

MARY: Well, I could use my coping statement, for example, "I never fainted after about nine hundred panic attacks; to faint you need a decrease in blood pressure, and when you are anxious you usually have an increase in blood pressure; therefore, I am quite unlikely to faint now."

THERAPIST: Are you still bothered by the thought that you could faint?

MARY: Well, to a lesser extent than a few minutes ago, but I must admit I am still afraid I could faint.

THERAPIST: Okay, what else could you do about that?

MARY: I don't know.

THERAPIST: What about testing out your balance directly?

MARY: Right, I forgot. Maybe I should stand up and walk around.

[Mary stands up and takes a few steps while holding on to the desk.]

THERAPIST: What about now? Are you still afraid you could faint?

MARY: I don't seem to be wobbly or fainting right now, but it's hard to just get rid of the thought like that. But I do feel some doubt about fainting.

THERAPIST: Good. Try letting go of the desk, and just let your arms hang naturally by your side as you walk back and forth. That's it. Now try to stand on one foot. Okay, now the other foot. Okay, now what do you think about fainting?

MARY: Well, right now I'm pretty sure I won't but, then, the anxiety is dropping. I'm not sure what I'll think when I'm scared again.

THERAPIST: Well, this is a good start. Perhaps it will take a little more practice for you to be fully sure that you are in control and won't faint. You don't have to master everything at once.

In a later session Mary and the therapist continued to work on the fainting, with Mary walking briskly and doing balancing exercises while experiencing high autonomic arousal:

THERAPIST: You feel your heart pound, so what do you think about fainting now?

MARY: I'm sure I won't faint, but there is another thought creeping up. I'm afraid I could become crazy.

THERAPIST: What could you do to convince yourself that you are not becoming crazy?

MARY: Well, I could administer myself a mental status exam.

THERAPIST: Yes!

MARY: Okay, I'm Mary; today is Tuesday, October the fifth, 1991; I live in Bethlehem, Pennsylvania. I guess I must not be crazy, though I feel weird.

THERAPIST: Perhaps you should ask whether it is weird or just an unpleasant sensation that will go away.

MARY: You're right; it's not really weird like crazy, just unpleasant.

Mary practiced these and other kinds of exercises with the therapist, at home with Bill, and then when she was alone. She also was applying panic management strategies when coping with previously avoided activities in the community. After 5 weeks she stopped having panic attacks. Now it was necessary to more systematically withdraw the Xanax medication since continuing it threatened to interfere with the maximum development of Mary's self-efficacy. Mary had already tapered off considerably, taking only one or two pills per week, and she now felt able to abstain completely.

## TERMINATION

By the end of the 10-week treatment program for agoraphobia and panic attack, Mary was panic free and much less phobic and had not taken Xanax in over a month. She still had some difficulties in church and with social gatherings, but she had made enough progress that she felt able to continue progressing on her own. Her depression and generalized anxiety had lessened, although they had not entirely disappeared, and there were still very real worries about finances and Bill's health. However, Mary now felt able to consider working outside the home, especially since her mother had agreed to look after the children while Mary worked, at least until they could afford child care services. It was agreed that there would be three follow-up sessions, at approximately 2 months, 6 months, and 1 year, to check on progress and perhaps provide some booster therapy, if needed. The therapist encouraged Mary to call at any time in the interim if any questions, concerns, or problems arose.

## FOLLOW-UP

During follow-up sessions the therapist and Mary reviewed her responses to the various questionnaries described earlier, which indicated that her progress had been maintained (certain measures indicated that her performance had even improved). Relapse prevention was covered during the follow-up sessions. Mary had to figure out how she might relapse and what she could do to prevent it. The key element was to realize that on certain days she might feel more apprehensive and feel an urge to avoid certain activities and that on those days she must treat these urges as thoughts to be tested, not as reality to be adjusted to, and must deliberately challenge herself then more than at any other time.

Mary remained panic free throughout follow-up. Her audience and social fears were considerably reduced, so that now she regularly sat fairly far forward in church with no more than occasional mild anxiety. She no longer experienced any problem driving, and territorial limitations had almost disappeared, except for anticipatory apprehension prior to trips requiring more than about 2 hours of driving. Her Beck Depression Inventory (Beck, 1978) score had dropped to a low level of 8. By the 1-year follow-up Mary had taken a part-time job in a restaurant, and Bill had also started working, and liked his job as a clerk in an auto parts store. Now Mary and Bill shared equally in the shopping and running of errands away from home. The anxiety-related problems had begun to fade into the background.

## OVERALL EVALUATION

Mary's case was typical of PDA in most respects. The positive outcome was typical with respect to panic; in most cases even frequent, severe panic attacks can be permanently eliminated by psychosocial treatment of the kind used with Mary (Barlow & Cerny, 1988). The outcome with respect to the agoraphobia was perhaps a little better than the average case, although not markedly unrepresentative. People who, like Mary, start treatment with severely disabling phobias, that is, people who cannot do much in some behavioral pretests, present difficult cases; for such cases the guided mastery approach seems particularly appropriate inasmuch as these clients need more than just a therapist urging them to go out and conquer their fears. Rather, therapists must accompany such clients into the community environment to actively intervene on the spot, that is, precisely where clients must master their fears (Williams, 1990). With the many clients who are more avoidant than disabled, (i.e., who can do things when they try but who tend to routinely avoid), an exclusively homework-based program can sometimes be sufficient. Mary's progress was helped by her diligence in carrying out homework assignments, which not all clients show, and by her spouse's support and cooperativeness, which is by no means a universal feature.

## REFERENCES

American Psychiatric Association. (1987). *Diagnostic and statistical manual of mental disorders* (3rd ed., rev.). Washington, DC: Author.

Bandura, A. (1988). Self-efficacy conception of anxiety. *Anxiety Research, 1,* 77–98.

Barlow, D. H., & Cerny, J. A. (1988). *Psychological treatment of panic.* New York: Guilford Press.

Beck, A. T. (1978). *Beck Depression Inventory: Suggestions for use.* Philadelphia, PA: Center for Cognitive Therapy.

Clark, D. M. (1986). A cognitive approach to panic. *Behaviour Research and Therapy, 24,* 461–470.

DiNardo, P. A., Barlow, D. H., Cerny, J., Vermilyea, B. B., Vermilyea, J. A., Himadi, W., & Waddell, M. (1985). *Anxiety Disorders Interview Schedule-Revised (ADIS-R).* Albany, NY: Phobia and Anxiety Disorders Clinic, State University of New York at Albany.

Kinney, P. J., & Williams, S. L. (1988). Accuracy of fear inventories and self-efficacy scales in predicting agoraphobic behavior. *Behaviour Research and Therapy, 26,* 513–518.

Williams, S. L. (1985). On the nature and measurement of agoraphobia. *Progress in Behavior Modification, 19,* 109–144.

Williams, S. L. (1990). Guided mastery treatment of agoraphobia: Beyond stimulus exposure. *Progress in Behavior Modification, 26,* 89–121.

# CHAPTER 9

# Social Phobia

DEBRA A. HOPE and RICHARD G. HEIMBERG

## DESCRIPTION OF THE DISORDER

Social phobia is defined by the revised third edition of *Diagnostic and Statistical Manual of Mental Disorders* (*DSM-III-R;* American Psychiatric Association, 1987) as excessive, irrational fear of situations in which the person expects to be scrutinized by others and somehow humiliated or embarrassed. Social phobic situations include conversing, eating, drinking, or writing while being observed, using public restrooms; and public speaking. Despite indications in DSM-III (American Psychiatric Association, 1980) that social phobia is believed to be unlikely to represent severe impairment, both research and clinical experience have indicated that it may have a significant adverse impact on social and occupational functioning. The extent of role impairment may depend on the severity and generalization of fear and avoidance and on the presence of secondary diagnoses such as substance abuse or depression.

Although some social phobics fear only one situation, there is growing consensus that this is a relatively uncommon presentation. More frequently, multiple situations generate anxiety, and in fact *DSM-III-R* specifies a subtype called *generalized social phobia* (fear of most social situations). Recently, Holt, Heimberg, Hope, and Liebowitz (1992) completed an analysis of the situations feared by social phobics and found that nearly everyone in the

DEBRA A. HOPE • Department of Psychology, University of Nebraska-Lincoln, Lincoln, Nebraska 68588-0308    RICHARD G. HEIMBERG • Center for Stress and Anxiety Disorders, State University of New York at Albany, Washington Avenue Extension, Pine West Plaza, Building 4, Albany, New York 12205.

*Adult Behavior Therapy Casebook,* edited by Cynthia G. Last and Michel Hersen. Plenum Press, New York, 1994.

sample feared formal interactions such as public speaking. Many subjects also reported fears in informal interactions (e.g., initiating conversations, calling strangers on the telephone, and attending parties), with assertiveness and performing under observation being less commonly feared. These data highlight the need to sample a broad range of situations when assessing this population.

Social phobics typically experience physiological arousal in anticipation of or during exposure to feared situations. For some, this arousal escalates to panic. However, social phobics and panic-disordered individuals differ in that the latter fear the symptoms themselves as indicators of impending doom whereas the former fear others will see the symptoms and evaluate them negatively. In some cases, including the one to be discussed in this chapter, a specific symptom becomes the focus of the individual's fear.

Epidemiological research suggests that social phobia is quite prevalent, occurring in approximately 2% of the population in a 6-month period (Myers *et al.*, 1984). Comorbidity studies indicate that it is a common secondary problem in individuals seeking treatment for other anxiety disorders and depression. Social phobia is equally prevalent in men and women. (For a more complete review of the psychopathology of social phobia, see Turner and Beidel, 1989.)

## CASE IDENTIFICATION

The case to be described involves a 25-year-old Caucasian man (referred to here as E) who sought treatment from the Social Phobia Program at the State University of New York at Albany Center for Stress and Anxiety Disorders in response to public service announcements describing cognitive–behavioral treatment offered through the project.

## PRESENTING COMPLAINTS

E sought treatment for fear and avoidance of any situation in which he perceived himself to be the center of attention, including any extended conversation, attending and participating in meetings, eating and writing while being observed, public speaking, talking one-on-one to authority figures, and unexpectedly encountering an acquaintance. In each situation he feared that he would humiliate himself by uncontrollable sweating. He believed others would perceive him as weird and inferior if they noticed perspiration on his forehead or upper lip. (Unlike most social phobics who fear writing under observation, E had only minor fears that his hand would shake; rather, he was concerned that his self-consciousness about being observed would trigger perspiration.) These fears occurred only in what he perceived to be upper-class stores, such as small clothing shops specializing in designer labels. He feared eating in public because of the extended close proximity to others and particularly because eating a heavy or spicy meal increased the likelihood that he would begin to perspire. E believed that the propensity to perspire heavily was a family characteristic and that other members of his family would also have visible perspiration in these situations but would be unconcerned by it.

E developed elaborate coping strategies to handle his anxiety. He believed that if he exercised vigorously before entering a feared situation, he was less likely to perspire excessively. Therefore, he instigated an extensive exercise routine consisting of swimming, running, and weight lifting. He usually exercised in the morning before work to cope with the many anxiety-provoking situations that arose in that setting. He also avoided drinking coffee or tea immediately before or during a meeting or other interaction since he believed this increased his perspiration. He always carried a handkerchief with which to wipe his brow, and he used it frequently.

## HISTORY

At the time he sought treatment E was separated from his wife of 4 years, with divorce proceedings pending. He had developed another relationship with possible marriage plans. In the 2 years since graduating from college with a bachelor's degree in computer science, E had worked as a programmer in a state agency.

E had been somewhat fearful of negative evaluation since childhood. However, it was not until his midsummer wedding 4 years previously that he became excessively concerned about perspiring and his fear began to interfere with his social and occupational functioning. He stated that he had felt forced into the wedding and remembered feeling trapped during the ceremony. He was uncomfortable with his wife's family because they were from a much higher social class than that of his own family. During the ceremony he began sweating profusely, and several individuals commented on his visibly damp face. Since then he feared any situation in which others might have an opportunity to observe unexplained perspiration.

Approximately 2 years after onset of his social phobia, E sought treatment from a psychoanalyst. Although E felt that he had acquired a better understanding of himself, he had seen little symptom reduction during the first 18 months of analysis. At that point the analyst prescribed Xanax (0.5 milligrams twice a day) and encouraged E to begin entering feared situations. E disliked taking the medication but used it on an as-needed basis. He saw some limited improvement as a result of self-initiated exposure to feared situations. He terminated treatment, with the analyst just prior to pursuing the present treatment.

## ASSESSMENT

As part of general clinical procedure, E was interviewed with the Anxiety Disorders Interview Schedule-Revised (DiNardo & Barlow, 1988), and received a primary *DSM-III-R* diagnosis of social phobia, which was judged to be of moderate severity. E also completed a fear and avoidance hierarchy, self-report questionnaires, and an individualized behavioral test. The latter consisted of a 4-minute reenactment of a highly feared situation. For E the behavioral test involved unexpectedly encountering a high school classmate whom he had not seen since graduation and making conversation. A male research assistant enacted the role of the classmate.

Pretreatment scores on the most clinically relevant items from the assessment battery are presented in Table 1. E showed moderately high impairment on the Social Avoidance and Distress Scale (SADS; Watson & Friend, 1969) and on the Fear of Negative Evaluation Scale (FNE; Watson & Friend, 1969). As is sometimes the case with social phobics, there was less anxiety during the behavioral test (E's peak anxiety was 60 on the 0–100 scale) than the client anticipated he would feel in an *in vivo* situation. However, despite only moderate anxiety, E rated his performance as relatively poor, with a 40 on the 0–100 scale (higher ratings indicate better performance). The five most feared situations on E's fear and avoidance hierarchy are presented in the lower half of Table 1.

During the initial interviews and the first few therapy sessions, it became apparent that three major considerations were important in predicting how

Table 1
Pretreatment Measures for E

| Measure | Score |
|---|---|
| Social Avoidance and Distress Scale | 20 |
| Fear of Negative Evaluation Scale | 19 |
| Peak anxiety during behavioral test | 60 |
| Self-rated performance in behavioral test | 40 |

| Fear-and-avoidance hierarchy | Fear | Avoidance |
|---|---|---|
| 1. Dinner with strangers or people of a higher social status | 90 | 100 |
| 2. Formal presentation | 90 | 80 |
| 3. Parties (do not know everyone) | 83 | 90 |
| 4. Dinner with friends or equal-status acquaintances | 65 | 75 |
| 5. Meetings at work with more than one person | 50 | 62 |

*Note.* For all measures except the self-rated performance in the behavioral test (where higher ratings on the 0–100 scale indicate better performance), higher numbers indicate greater distress or avoidance. The minimum score on all measures is 0. Maximum scores are as follows: Social Avoidance and Distress Scale, 28; Fear of Negative Evaluation Scale, 30; all other measures, 100.

fearful E would become in a given situation (Hope, 1993): (1) whether or not E was the center of attention, (2) the social status of others present, and (3) whether the activity engaged in was likely to increase his body temperature. Any situation in which E perceived the other individuals present to be higher in social status than he was increased his anxiety. Included in this category were his supervisors at work and salesclerks in upscale stores. E appeared to hold the irrational belief that others might discover he did not belong in the situation with them. As noted earlier, anxiety in these situations was compounded if E had to be the center of attention and/or do something that increased the likelihood he would perspire. E's beliefs about the significance of perspiration were clarified further during treatment.

## SELECTION AND COURSE OF TREATMENT

E was treated with five other social phobics by the first author and a male cotherapist using the Cognitive Behavioral Group Treatment (CBGT) protocol described by Heimberg (1990). Previous research has supported the efficacy of the treatment (e.g., Heimberg et al., 1990). CBGT consists of three components: cognitive restructuring, role-played exposures within the sessions, and homework for *in vivo* exposure. Sessions 1 and 2 are devoted to building cohesion and teaching basic cognitive skills. Cognitive training begins with identifying the negative, irrational cognitions (automatic thoughts) group members experience in anxiety-provoking situations. Then, using procedures adapted from Burns (1980), group members classify the type of logical error evident in the thought (e.g., all-or-nothing thinking or "fortune-telling"). Finally, they practice challenging the thought using a series of questions known as "dispute handles" (e.g., "Do I know for certain that X will happen?"; Sank & Shaffer, 1984). In the remaining sessions clients take turns completing role-played exposures, with cognitive restructuring before, during, and after. Homework initially consists of practice in the cognitive skills. Later in treatment group members are instructed to enter increasingly more difficult situations. CBGT groups meet for 12 weekly 2-hour sessions, with a portion of the final session devoted to preparing for the future and saying good-bye.

### Sessions 1–4

E was an active participant during cognitive skills training. He easily made the transition from the insight-oriented model of his previous therapist to the more active cognitive model. Many clients who have become overly focused on a specific symptom have difficulty accepting the notion that their problem lies in their concern about the symptom rather than in the symptom itself. However, since E believed his brother also perspired heavily but was unconcerned about it, he was able to consider that his self-consciousness about the perspiration was the source of his fears. He was highly motivated and began to apply the cognitive skills in naturally occurring situations prior to specific instructions from the therapists to do so.

In Session 3 and 4, other group members completed role-played exposures. E actively supported those efforts and served as an audience member for one public speaking exposure.

*Exposure #1.* E's first in-session exposure occurred in Session 5. Experience from the assessment and observation of E within the group suggested that he would likely discount the social-evaluative threat in role-played exposures and would consequently experience minimal anxiety. Therefore, the therapists decided to use a more threatening situation that would be typical for a first exposure. The situation involved E's giving a brief talk about himself to the group and including such things as education, employment, hobbies, and marital status. Given that this was his first exposure, he was allowed to sit; however, the chair was positioned close enough to the other group members so that they could see whether he perspired. The following is an excerpt of the cognitive restructuring that occurred prior to the exposure.[1]

THERAPIST:   So as you think about being the center of attention and giving a talk to the group, what kinds of thoughts go through your mind?

E:   I'll get anxious and start sweating.

THERAPIST:   Good. Let's break that into two thoughts. "I'll get anxious" and "I'll sweat." What happens if you start sweating?

E:   Everyone will see it and know I'm nervous.

THERAPIST:   Where is it that people would notice the perspiration?

E:   Mostly on my forehead and upper lip.

THERAPIST:   Okay. Why would it be a problem if someone noticed you were anxious?

E:   Oh, they would think something is wrong with me, like I'm weird or inferior or something.

THERAPIST:   So they would think you were inferior. Can you explain that a little more?

E:   They will think I am not as good as they are, maybe not a worthwhile person.

In this brief dialogue, a chain of four automatic thoughts had been identified: *"I'll sweat"; "They'll see me sweat"; "They'll know I'm anxious";* and *"They'll think I'm inferior."* This progression of cognitions revealed that sweating was a problem for E because he felt it would be interpreted by

---

[1] Although both therapists and all group members typically participate in cognitive restructuring, the dialogue has been streamlined to include only one therapist and the target client in order to simplify the presentation.

others as a sign of inferiority. With the group's help, E was able to categorize these thoughts as examples of mind reading (drawing conclusions about what another person is thinking without adequate evidence) and "mental filter" (allowing a single negative detail to cloud one's entire vision of oneself; Burns, 1980).

Next, using targeted questions and input from the rest of the group, the therapist encouraged E to acknowledge that perspiration was not always indicative of anxiety and that anxiety did not indicate inferiority:

THERAPIST: So it sounds like we have a kind of chain reaction. Sweating equals anxiety equals inferiority. When people see you sweat, they will conclude you are inferior.

E: That sounds right.

THERAPIST: Okay. Let's step back and take a look at that. Using your dispute handles, can you see any way to question whether sweating equals anxiety?

E: Well, does sweating necessarily equal anxiety?

THERAPIST: Good. And how would you answer that question?

E: Well, for me it does.

THERAPIST: You never sweat at a time when you are not anxious?

E: Well, I sweat when I work out.

Other group members were able to contribute the observations that people are likely to sweat any time they are too warm or if they are coming down with or are recovering from an illness. The therapist helped E see that anxiety was only one trigger for perspiration, thus addressing the first part of E's chain of automatic thoughts. Next, the therapist addressed the link between anxiety and inferiority in a similar manner. E and the group members were able to acknowledge that public speaking makes most people feel anxious. Rather than seeing him as inferior, people may respond with admiration at his courage in facing his fears or with empathy since they experience similar anxiety. This discussion led to the following rational responses for E to use to cope with his anxiety during the exposure:

*"Sweating does not necessarily equal anxiety"* and *"Anxiety does not necessarily equal being inferior."* The goal for the exposure was for E to continue performing until the therapists instructed him to stop.

E spoke for 6 minutes, with anxiety ratings on the 0–100 Subjective Units of Discomfort Scale (SUDS) taken at 1-minute intervals. He reported SUDS of 10, 15, 15, 20, 25, 15, and 15. Even taking into account that E tended to use only the lower end of the scale for ratings, he reported only mild anxiety during the exposure. However, despite the mild anxiety, he indicated that his most feared symptom, perspiration, had been a problem. In order to demonstrate how E overestimated the amount he perspired, the therapists made a rating (from 0 to 100) on the level of perspiration they had observed in E and had each group member, including E himself, make a rating. Group members then revealed their ratings, with E reporting his rating last. As might be expected, E's rating was high (85) but everyone else had ratings below 30, averaging about 20. These ratings provided dramatic evidence to E that even if he did perspire, others would not necessarily notice (and, consequently, would not conclude that he was anxious or inferior).

Given that E's experience of anxiety in the group situation was significantly lower than in similar *in vivo* situations, E's homework for *in vivo* exposure did not involve public speaking. Rather, he was instructed to practice using his cognitive coping skills in a moderately fearful situation of browsing in a small shop that specialized in men's suits. He agreed to avoid exercising before completing his homework. At the subsequent session E reported successful completion of this assignment with only moderate anxiety.

*Exposure #2.* Although the first role-played exposure had been useful in eliciting and rebutting E's automatic thoughts, there was some possibility that he would discount the experience since he had failed to experience more than mild anxiety. At the previous session E had agreed to avoid coping with his anxiety by exercising before group sessions. The therapists then had the challenge of designing role-played exposures that would elicit anxiety levels more comparable to those he experienced in his daily life.

E's next role-played exposure was scheduled for Session 7. The therapists had requested that he bring in a prepared speech for this exposure. His task was to deliver the speech to the group while standing. Again he set the goal of staying in the situation until it was terminated by the therapists. In addition to the automatic thoughts described earlier, E also reported a new thought he had discovered during his homework exposures: *"When my face feels warm, I know I am sweating."* On the basis of his previous experience in the group (including the group ratings of his perspiration), E was able to acknowledge that flushing was not as good a predictor of *visible* perspiration as he had previously believed. The cognitive work completed to date was summarized in the following rational responses, which he was to use during the public speaking role-played exposure: *"Sweating does not equal inferiority";* *"Perspiration doesn't show as much as I think it does";* and *"Flushing does not equal sweating."*

E's SUDS ratings for the 6-minute exposure peaked at 10 on the 0–100 scale. Discussion subsequent to the exposure revealed that this lack of anxiety in one of his most feared situations was attributable to two factors: First, since the rest of the group knew about his anxiety and he felt accepted by them, he was less concerned about their opinions of him than he would be in other situations. Secondly, using his rational responses further decreased his fear.

Given his success in group and on homework assignments, E was ready to attempt a situation near the top of his hierarchy for homework from Session 7. He agreed to call an old friend he had not seen in a couple of years and go to dinner or brunch. Due to a schedule conflict with his friend, E was only able to make the phone call during that week but actually went to brunch the following weekend with moderate but manageable anxiety.

*Exposure #3.* During previous cognitive restructuring sessions with E the therapists had begun to suspect that E's concern about others perceiving him as inferior was not that they would mistakenly judge him as inferior but that they would find out something he "knew" to be true. It appeared that E believed that his perspiration revealed that somehow he was less worthwhile than other people. However, he had never articulated this thought. Therefore, the therapists decided to explore this issue during the cognitive restructuring prior to the third exposure:

THERAPIST: E, you have told us before that you are concerned about perspiring because you believe that people will think you are inferior.
[*E nods in agreement.*]
THERAPIST: Could you tell us a little more about what you are afraid they will think.
E: They'll think that I am not as together as I look. Like maybe I am flawed or not as good as they are.
THERAPIST: And if someone thought that, would they be right?
E: [*pause*] Well, most people don't get anxious and worry about the stuff I worry about.
THERAPIST: So you think they would be right.
E: I guess so.
THERAPIST: Let's go back to the chain of thoughts we have been working with: "If I sweat, others will see I'm anxious and *find out* I'm inferior." Not *"Think* I'm inferior," right?
E: Well, if I look at it logically, I know I am just as good as those people who make me nervous. But I guess you are right.
THERAPIST: Okay. Let's step back and look at this new thought, "I'm inferior." Which cognitive distortion is that?

E and the rest of the group were able to identify the thought as an example of all-or-nothing thinking. As was true for many of the individuals treated in this program, E believed he had to be perfect to be acceptable. The therapists helped him address this perfectionism by listing various aspects of himself that were part of his self-identity. These included being a computer programmer, a partner in a romantic relationship, an athlete, and someone who sweats when he gets anxious. E was able to acknowledge that he felt reasonably positive about himself in every aspect except his anxiety. He then placed each of these aspects of himself in a pie chart, giving the appropriate percentage to each. The resulting chart indicated that the anxiety only occupied 5% of his self-concept. This resulted in two new rational responses: *"I don't have to be 100% perfect"* and *"I like 95% of myself."*

Since E had become quite comfortable with the group members, role players from outside the group were incorporated into the next two exposures. Both situations involved a conversation with an individual whom he had just met at a party and whose social status E perceived to be higher than his own. In the first exposure the second author role-played himself, a clinical psychologist and university professor. In the second a graduate student in her mid-thirties role-played an attorney trained at an Ivy League institution.

E's goal for the third exposure was to continue to participate in the conversation even if he felt himself sweating. His initial SUDS immediately after being introduced to the role player was 60, higher than he had previously reported in a within-session role-play situation. Over the course of the 6-minute exposure, the ratings steadily reduced to 30 (60, 50, 50, 45, 40, 40, 30). As per therapist instruction, the role player commented on E's damp brow during the third minute.

In the discussion following the exposure, E began for the first time to separate his symptom (sweating) from who he was as a person. He spontaneously stated, "Sweating has nothing to do with what kind of person I am." This statement became one of E's most important rational responses, and he continued to use it throughout the rest of treatment and during the follow-up period. This discussion also revealed that E's anxiety decreased—instead of increasing, as E had expected—when the role player mentioned his perspiration. E reported that he had felt less pressured to perform once the symptom was acknowledged.

In discussing potential homework assignments, E indicated that he had a party to attend during the upcoming week but did not anticipate experiencing significant anxiety given his success in previous weeks. Brainstorming revealed two ways to make this situation more likely to include his worst fear (sweating): drinking a cup of tea immediately before the party and wearing a pink Oxford-style shirt, which would be most likely to reveal any perspiration he did experience. E readily agreed to the cup of tea but was more hesitant about wearing the shirt because he anticipated a hot, humid summer evening for the party. His concern revealed the fact that his progress to date had been based mostly on his discovery that the probability of his feared event was much lower than he had anticipated. However, the following dialogue reveals that E continued to believe that it would be disastrous if the feared event (excessive sweating visible to others) occurred:

THERAPIST:  So what would happen if other people at the party did notice you were sweating?

E:  They would think something was wrong with me and probably be disgusted.

THERAPIST:  How would you know if that happened? Would they say something or do something?

E:  Most people are too polite to say something. Probably no one would talk with me.

THERAPIST:  It sounds like you can imagine yourself standing at the party with no one talking to you.

E:  Exactly.

THERAPIST:  Has this ever happened to you before?

E:  Not really. If I am not talking to people, it is usually because I walked away from them when I was worried about sweating.

THERAPIST:  So what do you think about wearing a pink shirt to the party?

E:  You want me to do this because you think I won't sweat. But I will and it will show a lot.

THERAPIST:  No, I don't know whether you will perspire enough for it to show or not. What I'm saying is that it doesn't make a difference if your entire shirt is dripping wet. It is important for you to face your worst fears and realize you can live through them.

E:  That makes sense. But no one would want to be at a party with a disgusting shirt on.

THERAPIST:  I agree. However, we would like you to trust us enough to take the risk that if your worst fears happen, you can handle it. If you don't try, you will always be worried about it.

With some continued discussion E reluctantly agreed to drink the tea and wear the pink shirt. In order to determine at the following session whether E's fears had been realized, the therapists further explored his description of the disastrous consequences that might occur. The next week E reported that he had completed the homework assignment and had perspired to the extent that he felt it was clearly noticeable on his shirt. However, he had used his rational responses to help him stay in the situation and attend to whether anyone else seemed to notice his sweating. Much to his surprise, no one appeared concerned and other partygoers continued to be willing to converse with him.

*Exposure #4.* As noted earlier, the situation for E's last exposure involved another conversation with a high-status individual (the female attorney who had graduated from an Ivy League school). The role player was instructed not to comment on E's perspiration. He reported no new automatic thoughts and continued to use the same rational responses. His SUDS remained at 25 throughout the 5-minute conversation.

*Summary of other homework assignments.* A number of other anxiety-provoking situations were given as homework assignments for those sessions in which E was not scheduled for a role-played exposure. These included a series of graduated exposures to paying by check or credit card for purchases at increasingly more difficult (i.e., high-status) stores. Several assignments centered around scheduling meals with coworkers, friends, and his girlfriend's parents to address his fears about eating with others. Starting at Session 7, E and his fellow group members all had standing homework assignments to enter at least one anxiety-provoking situation every day. For E these tasks often included having conversations with supervisory personnel with whom he felt uncomfortable or shopping at a mall in which he might unexpectedly encounter someone he knew (particularly his ex-wife and her new partner).

## TERMINATION AND FOLLOW-UP

As part of the research program, E completed the same assessment at the end of treatment and 6 months posttreatment as he had completed before treatment. As can be seen in Table 2, E demonstrated substantial improvement on all measures and continued to make gains during the follow-up period. These measures and the clinical interview indicated that his only significant remaining fears involved giving presentations at work. He had had little opportunity to confront this fear, since the situation rarely arose in his current

Table 2
Posttreatment and 6-Month Follow-up Measures for E

|  | Score | |
| --- | --- | --- |
| Measure | Posttreatment | Follow-up |
| Social Avoidance and Distress Scale | 11 | 3 |
| Fear of Negative Evaluation Scale | 9 | 6 |
| Peak anxiety during behavioral test | 30 | 20 |
| Self-rated performance in behavioral test | 90 | 100 |

Fear-and-avoidance hierarchy

|  | Posttreatment | | Follow-up | |
| --- | --- | --- | --- | --- |
|  | Fear | Avoidance | Fear | Avoidance |
| 1. Dinner with strangers or people of a higher social status | 30 | 30 | 20 | 10 |
| 2. Formal presentation | 40 | 55 | 55 | 65 |
| 3. Parties (do not know everyone) | 30 | 10 | 25 | 20 |
| 4. Dinner with friends or equal-status acquaintances | 15 | 5 | 10 | 10 |
| 5. Meetings at work with more than one person | 30 | 25 | 25 | 25 |

Note. For all measures except the self-rated performance in the behavioral test (where higher ratings on the 0–100 scale indicate better performance), higher numbers indicate greater distress or avoidance. The minimum score on all measures is 0. Maximum scores are as follows: Social Avoidance and Distress Scale, 28; Fear of Negative Evaluation Scale, 30; all other measures, 100.

job. However, he anticipated seeking a promotion in the near future to a position in which such presentations would be routine. At the 6-month follow-up assessment, E indicated that he had felt confident enough to apply for the promotion and felt able to cope with his anxiety until it decreased with repeated exposure.

By the end of treatment and continuing at the time of follow-up, E had reduced his exercise regimen to a level that he felt would maintain his physical condition and had eliminated all exercise intended to reduce anxiety. He drank coffee and tea as desired, even before meetings at work when warm beverages had been previously avoided.

## OVERALL EVALUATION

As illustrated by this case, social phobia often responds well to relatively short-term cognitive behavioral intervention. Although E was treated in a group, these interventions are easily translated into individual sessions with the therapist, clerical staff, and fellow professionals serving as role-play partners as needed (Hope, 1993). Furthermore, homework assignments for *in vivo* exposure represent a key aspect of the treatment. Undoubtedly, some of E's positive response to therapy can be attributed to his willingness to enter more and more feared situations.

More treatment may be required for social phobics with more generalized fears. However, once a client gains the basic cognitive skills and is able to construct his or her own exposures, treatment may be less intensive. Significant comorbid depression is associated with poorer outcome and may require additional treatment. However, mildly depressed social phobics usually experience a decrease in depressive symptoms as their social isolation decreases.

### ACKNOWLEDGMENT

This chapter was supported in part by grant number 44119 awarded to the second author by the National Institute of Mental Health. The authors express their appreciation to David L. Penn for his comments on an earlier draft of the manuscript.

## REFERENCES

American Psychiatric Association (1985). *Diagnostic and statistical manual of mental disorders* (3rd ed.). Washington, DC: Author.
American Psychiatric Association (1987). *Diagnostic and statistical manual of mental disorders* (3rd ed., rev.). Washington, DC: Author.
Burns, D. D. (1980). *Feeling good: The new mood therapy.* New York: Morrow.

DiNardo, P. A., & Barlow, D. H. (1988). *The Anxiety Disorders Interview Schedule-Revised.* Albany, NY: Graywind Publications.

Heimberg, R. G. (1990). Cognitive behavior therapy for social phobia. In A. S. Bellack & M. Hersen (Eds.), *Comparative handbook of treatments for adult disorders* (pp. 203–218). New York: Wiley.

Heimberg, R. G., Dodge, C. S., Hope, D. A., Kennedy, C. R., Zollo, L., & Becker, R. E. (1990). Cognitive–behavioral treatment of social phobia: Comparison to a credible placebo control. *Cognitive Therapy and Research, 14,* 1–23.

Holt, C. S., Heimberg, R. G., Hope, D. A., & Liebowitz, M. R. (1992). Situational domains of social phobia. *Journal of Anxiety Disorders, 6,* 63–77.

Hope, D. A. (1993). Exposure and social phobia: Assessment and treatment considerations. *The Behavior Therapist, 16,* 7–12.

Myers, J. K., Weissman, M. M., Tischler, G. L., Holzer, C. E. III, Leaf, P. J., Orvaschel, H., Anthony, J. C., Boyd, J. H., Burke, J. D., Jr., Kramer, M., & Stoltzman, R. (1984). Six-month prevalence of psychiatric disorders in three communities. *Archives of General Psychiatry, 41,* 959–967.

Sank, L. I., & Shaffer, C. S. (1984). *A therapist's manual for cognitive behavior therapy in groups.* New York: Plenum.

Turner, S. M., & Beidel, D. C. (1989). Social phobia: Clinical syndrome, diagnosis and comorbidity. *Clinical Psychology Review, 9,* 3–18.

Watson, D., & Friend, R. (1969). Measurement of social-evaluative anxiety. *Journal of Consulting and Clinical Psychology, 33,* 448–457.

CHAPTER 10

# Simple Phobia

## F. DUDLEY McGLYNN and THOMAS VOPAT

## DESCRIPTION OF THE DISORDER

The term *simple phobia* refers to a large but clinically rare category of anxiety disorders characterized by peripherally cued anxiety behaviors. The diagnosis of simple phobia is applicable when the anxiety behaviors are significantly maladaptive and when other diagnoses (e.g., social phobia, post-traumatic stress disorder, obsessive–compulsive disorder) have been ruled out (American Psychiatric Association, 1987).

In principle, virtually any object or situation can become a peripheral cue stimulus for phobic anxiety behaviors. In the general population the most common phobia cues are illness or injury, violent weather, and animals. Among phobia-clinic patients the most common phobia cues are closed spaces, blood or injury, injections, dental procedures, and animals. Owing to methodological problems, the prevalence of simple phobia is unknown. Reich (1986) reviewed the epidemiological literature and concluded that 2.5% of U.S. residents display a lifetime prevalence of simple phobia.

The anxiety behaviors observed in simple phobia are best viewed as *patterns* of private/cognitive, physiological, and overt behavioral responses (Lang, 1978). The private/cognitive responses that are present before and during (and sometimes without) phobic encounters are characterized by exaggerated estimates of danger and by adverse performance-outcome expecta-

F. DUDLEY McGLYNN • Department of Psychology, Auburn University, Alabama 36849-5214
THOMAS VOPAT • Department of Hospital Dentistry, University of Missouri–Kansas City School of Dentistry, Kansas City, Missouri 64108-2795.

*Adult Behavior Therapy Casebook,* edited by Cynthia G. Last and Michel Hersen. Plenum Press, New York, 1994.

tions. The physiological responses that are seen can include changed cardiac function, increased blood flow to the skeletal muscles, increased or decreased blood pressure, increased respiration rate, and elevated levels and fluctuations of electrodermal flow. These changes are idiosyncratic and reflect metabolic support for cognitive and motor behavior as well as sympathetic activation. The motor behaviors seen in simple phobia can range from freezing to head-long flight and can include decrements in performance quality. Skillful and steadfast avoidance of phobia cue stimuli is prominent. The patterning of private/cognitive, physiological, and motor behaviors varies markedly as phobic individuals interface with their diverse environments. Various measures of phobic anxiety behaviors show low and often nonsignificant intercorrelations both within and between the three measurement domains.

Early behaviorists viewed phobias as the result of aversive respondent conditioning experiences. Over the years behavioral formulations have been broadened to include wider arrays of aversive unconditional stimuli and to add vicarious experiences and misinformation as etiologic "pathways" (see Delprato & McGlynn, 1984). The argument has been offered that some stimuli acquire phobia cue properties more readily than do others. It has been suggested also that genetic factors, biological vulnerability, and personality traits produce differential risks for phobia acquisition. These arguments are controversial. Hekmat (1987) has argued that private/cognitive behaviors strongly influence the course of phobia development quite apart from the circumstances of initial acquisition. Barlow (1988) has provided an interesting and potentially heuristic etiologic model of simple phobia that takes into account most of these complexities.

## CASE IDENTIFICATION

Kathy was an attractive 28-year-old mother of two who lived alone and supported her family by doing piecework in her modest home. She left an alcoholic-dysfunctional family environment to live independently at age 15, finished high school, and is progressing well in undergraduate studies at a state university.

## PRESENTING COMPLAINTS

Kathy initially presented to a clinic for the diagnosis and treatment of chronic head and neck pain. During the course of treatment (with medications, an oral appliance, and supportive counseling) it became apparent that part of her pain originated in dental problems. When Kathy was informed of the need for dental treatment, she revealed a dental phobia of long standing. She told us also that it took "all the courage [she] could muster" to come to the pain clinic initially even though a friend had told her that treatment of her pain problem would not involve injections or drilling. Prior to these revelations Kathy's idiosyncratic behavior in the clinic had been wrongly ascribed to shyness and/or deficient social skills. After the revelations dental phobia became a major focus of treatment.

## HISTORY

As noted, Kathy was reared in a family disrupted by alcoholism until her departure at age 15. When she was 11 years of age, she discovered that her mother was having an affair with the family physician. At age 12 she was raped by the physician on an examining table, apparently while her mother stood guard outside. After the rape Kathy became phobic for a variety of medical settings and activities. During the ensuing years numerous personal health problems and the births of two children forced Kathy into palliative contacts with physicians and medical settings. Consequently, many of her phobic behaviors were replaced by adaptive ones. However, Kathy had been to a dentist only once, at age 17. At that dental visit she experienced a painful injection into the palate, harsh treatment by the dentist, and oral penetration fantasies during drilling. Kathy had fearfully avoided dental settings from that time on.

## ASSESSMENT

There are three more or less distinct behavioral orientations to behavioral assessment and treatment of simple phobia. One is an orthodox behavior therapy orientation (e.g., Wolpe, 1973), in which clinical assessment of private/cognitive, motoric, and physiological anxiety behaviors serves to guide the use of systematic desensitization, modeling, flooding, and correcting misconceptions as treatment modes. A second is a monolithic exposure orientation (e.g., Marks, 1975), in which naturalistic assessment of anxiety behavior serves to guide the details of exposure therapy, which involves doing whatever it takes to expose the patient to feared stimulation. A third is a cognitive behavior therapy orientation (e.g., Bandura, 1977), in which assessment of theoretical constructs such as performance–outcome expectations and self-efficacy expectations serve to guide such therapy tactics as self-directed mastery trials and rational restructuring.

Clearly, the monolithic exposure orientation is dominant among contemporary behavioral practitioners (cf. Barlow, 1988). However, orthodox behavior therapy incorporates exposure-based approaches and has the additional advantages of prompting individualized assessment and treatment, as well as systematic thinking about behaviors that compete with fearful ones (Wolpe, 1986). The assessment and treatment used in Kathy's case reflect orthodox behavior therapy principles.

One goal of assessment in phobic disorders is differential diagnosis using the *DSM-III-R* categories of mental disorders (American Psychiatric Association, 1987). Fear of the dentist can be diagnosed as *simple phobia* (fear of pain or claustrophobia), as *social phobia* (fear of negative evaluation by the dentist), or as panic disorder (fear of panic in the dental office). In addition, fear of the dentist can be a constituent of *generalized anxiety disorder.*

Once the diagnosis of simple phobia is made, continuing assessment is guided by two major goals: First, the controlling stimuli for anxiety behaviors must be identified; this involves specifying exhaustively the exact stimuli (e.g., stairways, elevators, vehicles, animals, themes) that pose adaptive hazards. Second, the specific forms and instrumental properties of the anxiety behaviors must be spelled out. This involves three sets of determinations, which can be conceived as responses to the following questions: (1) To what extent does the client suffer *subjectively* from fear, terror, dread, and the like? (2) In what ways does the client *behaviorally* escape or avoid feared stimuli or otherwise allow his or her lifestyle to be compromised? (3) To what extent does the client respond *physiologically* during real and/or visualized encounters with phobic stimuli?

In Kathy's case the differential diagnosis of simple phobia was made tentatively after the first in-depth interview about her fear of dentists. During the interview she said, "I am terrified by needles and by the thought of the drill. I just can't stand pain." She also told of her rape at age 12, saying that at the time she was "completely unable to move, frozen with terror . . . not able to get away anyhow because [her] mom was guarding the door." She added, "Now I can't stand to be anywhere I can't get out of, and I am sure I would feel that way about a dentist leaning over me and touching me." Kathy denied fear of ridicule or criticism from a dentist and denied any history of panic episodes.

The tentative diagnosis of simple phobia was confirmed psychometrically and with an informal behavioral test immediately after the initial interview was over. First Kathy was asked to respond to a 60-item questionnaire about the events involved in seeking and receiving dental care. Her answers were scored on the basis of four factor-analytically derived subscales: fear of pain and its precursors, claustrophobia, social phobia, and fear of loss of control. The subscale raw scores showed clearly that fear of pain and claustrophobia were her paramount concerns. Next Kathy was escorted around the varying operatories in a dental school building and asked simply to pick out the most and least preferred spaces to receive dental treatment. The most preferred operatory was one of 12 examination and/or treatment areas that were housed in a large room, and were separated by chest-high partitions. This one was located nearest the door. The least preferred was a single operatory in a small room.

After the assessments just described the diagnosis of simple phobia (reflecting fear of pain and claustrophobia) was assigned. From an orthodox behavior therapy perspective, however, more information was needed for initial treatment planning. At the second session Kathy was asked to sit quietly and look into the most preferred (but empty) operatory for 8 minutes then to watch while a routine dental examination was done. Kathy's heart rate decelerated from 95 beats per minute to stabilize at around 80 beats per minute during the last 3 minutes of the 8-minute habituation period. It hovered around 100 beats per minute during the first 3 minutes of the dental examination and decelerated to an average of 88 beats per minute by the time the examination was over. Functionally equivalent results were found for skin-conductance levels.

Next Kathy was assured that nothing would actually be done if she sat in the dental chair and allowed the dentist to *act like* he was performing an oral examination of her. She did so and psychophysiological data acquired during the mock examination were somewhat lower than those recorded during her observation of the real examination. The second session continued with 16-muscle–group progressive relaxation training and ended with instructions to practice relaxation at home and to keep a diary of the time and locations of home practice.

At the third session Kathy's diary was checked, and she was again instructed in 16-muscle–group progressive relaxation. Afterward she was asked to maintain the state of relaxation and was instructed in various imaging exercises while heart rate and electrodermal flow were recorded. There were three types of imagery instructions: six dental treatments, six beauty-shop treatments, and six idyllic scenes, e.g., pastures, wooded streams, grazing cattle. The instructions for dental and beauty treatments were written so as to equate for factors such as room dimensions and activity levels. The various scenarios were imagined in randomized blocks of three for 30 seconds each, with each scene separated from the others by a 30-second period of "rest with a clear mind."

As expected, both heart rate and skin-conductance levels habituated non-linearly over the imaging period. However, when examined within blocks of three scenarios, mean skin-conductance levels were highest six out of six times and mean heart rates were highest five out of six times following instructions to imagine dental treatment.

## SELECTION OF TREATMENT

Given the presence of anxiety behaviors in all three response channels and of physiological arousal during imaging, virtually any orthodox behavior therapy intervention was considered potentially applicable. It was decided to deal with Kathy's fear of pain and claustrophobia separately. Fear of pain would be treated by correcting Kathy's misconceptions about the level of pain she would likely encounter. For claustrophobia in the dental office Kathy would be given some options and allowed to choose. Detailed assessment of the dental stimuli and themes controlling Kathy's claustrophobia was postponed, pending her choice of therapy.

The options described to Kathy were as follows: She could receive six to ten sessions of continued relaxation training and a complete regimen of systematic desensitization (which was explained to her) and could "track" her imaginal hierarchy *in vivo,* lagging several items behind. The therapist would accompany her to and during the dental visits but would gradually ease out of the process as she overcame her fear and grew to trust the dentist. Alternatively, Kathy could have a fearless partner, one who would receive a dental examination and treatment similar to her own while she watched and learned what to do; she could then be premedicated and could receive nitrous oxide during her own subsequent treatment after each observation period, but the premedication and nitrous oxide would gradually be reduced. The therapist would participate in her dental treatment as in the first option. After the nature of the nitrous oxide experience was described to her, Kathy chose the second alternative but indicated that premedication would not be necessary. She added that the therapist's presence during treatment was important.

## COURSE OF TREATMENT

### Fear of Pain

Kathy's fear of pain in the dental office was rooted in a misconception, albeit a very widespread one. As noted, this part of her problem was treated by correcting her misconception and providing information about nitrous oxide. The following conversation took place:

THERAPIST: Kathy, there are only three things about restorative dentistry that are truly painful. One is injections into the roof of your mouth, like you experienced before. In fact, the one time you went to the dentist you had the worst experience possible.

KATHY: It was awful. It hurt so much I cried, and the dentist got mad.

THERAPIST: I know it must have been painful. I've had that shot a few times, and I don't like it either. Another painful part of dentistry is an injection way back in the corner of your jaw. Now, Kathy, I don't know how bad your dental condition is or if you will elect to carry on with dental treatment after your pain problem is taken care of, but I am fairly sure you won't have to have an injection in the roof of your mouth or in the back of your jaw to solve the immediate problem.

KATHY:   Fairly sure?

THERAPIST:   Well, I'm virtually certain. I just didn't want to speak too strongly because I'm not a dentist.

KATHY:   You said there are three painful things.

THERAPIST:   Well, the other is an injection just above the front teeth. We don't have to worry about that either.

KATHY:   I *will* have to have some shots, though, won't I? They *will* hurt *some* won't they?

THERAPIST:   I am not so sure I would say they would hurt. They will be uncomfortable for you, something like an insect bite. Before the injection the dentist will put some anesthetic on your gums that will help. The nitrous oxide will really help.

KATHY:   Well, if you say so.

THERAPIST:   It is important for you to understand this, Kathy. Part of the problem is that you have exaggerated the amount of pain you will experience. You are afraid of something that won't happen. Now, I want you to tell yourself over and over again that the dentistry you need is not all that painful. I want you to say that to yourself whenever you think about going to the dentist.

KATHY:   I believe you, Dr. McGlynn, but what are you going to do about my fear of being closed up?

THERAPIST:   Well, it's not a matter of what I'm going to do as much as a matter of us working together on that. As I see it, we have two ways to go about it.

## Claustrophobia

The behavioral treatment for Kathy's dental claustrophobia included observation of a fearless model and graduated exposure to dental events under conditions designed to attenuate anxiety behaviors (i.e., nitrous oxide, the presence of a trusted therapist, an open dental setting). The plan also included gradual fading of the above anxiety attenuators. Few details were specified in advance because little was known about Kathy's dental condition or the amount of dental treatment she would need or elect.

As noted, Kathy observed the dentist perform a routine dental examination on a fearless partner, and she had already sat for a mock examination as part of her assessment. She agreed that she did not need to observe a fearless partner again before undergoing a dental examination herself. An appointment for her examination was made at the close of the second assessment session. The events to expect during the examination were reviewed. Kathy was told how to control the nitrous oxide experience by nose versus mouth breathing, by closing versus opening her eyes, and by varying the depth of breathing. She was reassured that there would be no injection or drilling during the purely diagnostic visit. Finally, she was told that the therapist would remain with her throughout the appointment.

Kathy arrived 30 minutes early for her dental appointment the following week. The available time was used to reassure her about the pain-free nature of the upcoming events and to review the events of the nitrous oxide experience and the techniques for controlling it. During this time Kathy alternated between anxiety, grim determination, and a dissociated state. The episodic trance behavior was no surprise in view of her traumatic history.

It was decided before she arrived that everything possible would be done to minimize Kathy's anxiety behaviors during the first dental visit. For example, the nitrous oxide would not be faded out and the therapist would remain clearly visible in the room. Kathy and the therapist walked together to her preferred examination area, where the dentist was waiting. He greeted Kathy in a very friendly way, reassured her about the absence of pain, showed her the nose piece used for nitrous oxide, and invited her to be seated. The chair was located next to an open door. The dentist, his assistant, and the therapist were seated so as to not block this escape route. At this point Kathy seemed frightened but grimly determined to proceed.

Nitrous oxide was administered according to a standard protocol. It was begun at 25% concentration and increased by 5% after 2, 4, and 6 minutes. Once the desired sedation was apparent, the dentist completed a routine head, neck, and oral examination while speaking softly to his assistant and from time to time asking Kathy how she was doing. Kathy opened her eyes several times, apparently to confirm that the therapist was still there. On completing the examination the dentist replaced the 40% nitrous oxide with 100% oxygen while Kathy sat for 5 minutes. On hearing that the dentist was finished Kathy said, "I can't believe it. I didn't think you had even started."

The dentist discovered teeth with atypical enamel that could very well be responsible for referring pain to the identified facial regions. He identified bruxism as the probable cause (this was not surprising because Kathy had presented with hyperactivity in the jaw elevator muscles at rest). The dentist also observed a number of carious lesions. He recommended that the two atypical teeth be crowned and that the cavities be filled. Kathy was told that placing the crowns would require injections and grinding on the teeth but that the injections were relatively painless ones. She was also told that several appointments would be needed to restore her dental health and that the crowns could be placed first in order to evaluate their effect on her remaining facial pain. Kathy said, "I will try to let you do the crowns."

Kathy telephoned a day in advance to cancel her next two appointments.

Therefore, it was decided that if and when she did make it to an appointment, the experience should again be completely pain free. The dentist suggested that he clean her teeth at the next visit. This suggestion was followed because it provided for nearly painless exposure to most of the cues involved in receiving dental care. When Kathy appeared for her next appointment, she was, as before, alternately frightened, dissociated, and grimly determined.

Kathy and the therapist again went to the dentist's office together. Kathy was introduced to a female model who was going to participate in Kathy's treatment by allowing her own dental treatment to be observed. Kathy was seated so as to be close to the door but still able to view the dental procedure performed on the model. The dentist then cleaned and polished the model's teeth. He explained his various activities and showed his instruments to everyone at each step of the procedure. Kathy wrung her hands, rocked back and forth, and gazed at the floor from time to time, but she watched most of the procedure and made no effort to leave.

After the modeling session the dentist cleaned and polished Kathy's teeth in the usual way while she inhaled 40% nitrous oxide. Again, Kathy opened her eyes from time to time to see if the therapist was still in the room. At the end of the session she again voiced surprise that it was over. The following conversation occured later that day:

THERAPIST: Would you like to talk about the appointments that you canceled?

KATHY: My daughter was sick one time and the other time I couldn't get a ride.

THERAPIST: Have you been reminding yourself that the treatment you need isn't all that painful?

KATHY: Yes, but I'm having trouble believing it.

THERAPIST: Well, keep reminding yourself that way, and you will come to believe it. How did you feel today?

KATHY: I was scared from the time I got up until I got into the nitrous. I didn't want to come in, but I didn't have a good excuse and didn't want you to give up on me.

THERAPIST: I don't give up easily. Did you experience any pain today?

KATHY: No, but I didn't get a shot or get drilled on.

THERAPIST: How about the feeling of being closed in or trapped?

KATHY: I felt that way when he laid me back in the chair and when he put the thing over my nose, but I was okay when I got into the nitrous.

THERAPIST: Would you like for me to ask Dr. Vopat about working on you without reclining the chair?

KATHY: Yes.

THERAPIST: Is there anything else I need to talk to Dr. Vopat about?

KATHY: Yes. Tell him to stop asking me how I am doing. I have to come out of the nitrous to answer him, then I have to get into it all over again.

THERAPIST: I'll tell him that. Now, Kathy, Dr. Vopat will locate a partner for you to watch and follow for a crown placement. So when he has found one, we would like to schedule your next visit. It's important for you to not give in to your fear and cancel out on us. Come in to see *me* even if you don't think you can go through with it. And keep telling yourself the discomfort won't be all that bad, especially with the nitrous.

KATHY: I don't think I need to watch someone else anymore.

THERAPIST: Okay.

Kathy arrived early for her next appointment. She wrung her hands, rocked back and forth, and talked rapidly, but she was not visibly dissociating and voiced her determination to "give it a try." The following exchange took place:

KATHY: I guess I'll find out today.

THERAPIST: What will you find out today, Kathy?

KATHY: If you were telling me the truth about pain.

THERAPIST: Well, I am confident that you will pull it off, Kathy. Remember that you are not tied down, that the door is open if you must leave, and that I'll be there with you hoping that you succeed.

KATHY: That's the most important, Dr. McGlynn. I couldn't be doing any of this without you.

THERAPIST: Well, Kathy, I will be happy when you *can* do things like this without me. That *will* happen if you hang tough for the next few weeks.

Kathy blanched white and reported that her heart was racing just after she was seated. The dentist encouraged her to get into the nitrous oxide, and he reclined the dental chair just enough to do his work. As the nitrous oxide inhalation was proceeding, Kathy looked at the open door twice but did not move. Once the desired sedation had been achieved, the dentist crowned her tooth without incident. Kathy exhibited virtually no pain behaviors during the injection and no fear behaviors other than vigilance. When the nose piece for the nitrous oxide was removed after the procedure, she said, "Is it over? Really, is it over? I can't believe it. I didn't feel a thing. Dr. McGlynn, you *were* telling the truth." The therapist replied, "I'm thrilled for you, Kathy. Now I *know* you are going to overcome the problem." The dentist commented that he was pleased also.

Kathy arrived early for the second crown-placement appointment. She did not appear to be anxious at all. She said she was looking forward to having the other crown on because her face had been hurting. She said also that if the upcoming procedure was like the last one, she would probably have the dentist fix her other teeth. Kathy was told that we wanted to cut back on the nitrous oxide except during the injection and that the therapist wanted to remain in the operating area but out of her view. Kathy said, "It's okay if you want to sit where I can't see you, but why do you want to cut back on the nitrous?" The therapist explained as follows: "It's like this, Kathy. You can't overcome your fear by completely tuning out what's going on. We're beginning a phase of your treatment where we want the nitrous to relax you while you pay attention to what's going on. The nitrous is to help *teach* you to relax while Dr. Vopat does his work. We *will* do the full dose of nitrous during the injection, and if we cut it back too far, you can signal to Dr. Vopat by lifting your left hand. Okay?" Kathy agreed but appeared to be more tense than before the exchange.

Kathy and the therapist again went together to the dentist's office. While being seated Kathy told the dentist she was less frightened than the week before. He responded ideally, saying, "If you keep coming to see me, you will be less fearful every time." The session proceeded as in the week before, except that the therapist sat out of Kathy's view and the dentist cut the nitrous oxide to 20% when he was finished preparing the tooth. Again, Kathy voiced surprise when the session was over. The dentist encouraged her to continue with the restorative dentistry. She agreed to do so and made appointments for the subsequent 7 weeks.

After the second crown had been placed, Kathy indicated that no model would be needed for any of the remaining appointments. For the next four appointments Dr. Vopat used 30% nitrous oxide during injections, 15% during cavity preparations, and 10% while filling the cavities. For the fifth and sixth appointments he used 20% nitrous oxide during injections, 10% during cavity preparations, and none while filling the cavities. At the final appointment 20% nitrous oxide was used during the injections only. For all appointments the dentist was encouraged to avoid the most painful injections even if the resulting anesthesia might be incomplete.

After the second appointment to fill cavities the therapist stopped sitting in. He escorted Kathy to the third and fourth appointments and continued to see her briefly before and after the remaining visits in order to provide encouragement and praise. Kathy appeared promptly for each of the seven appointments.

## TERMINATION

Treatment for Kathy's dental anxiety ended when her dental treatment was complete, and coincided with Dr. McGlynn's relocation away from the area in which Kathy lived. Ordinarily, attempts would have been made to achieve a more generalized reduction in dental fear, for example, by using more than one dentist and more than one setting. However, achieving the goal of generalized fear reduction would probably have required more extensive treatment, as well as transfer of the client to another therapist at the time of Dr. McGlynn's move. Because both the dentist and Kathy voiced long-term plans to remain in the area, the goal of being free of fear during appointments with one particular dentist was viewed as realistic and satisfactory.

## FOLLOW-UP

Eight months have elapsed since Kathy's last dental appointment. She is scheduled to have an examination and cleaning in 4 months. During a telephone interview she expressed no fear of Dr. Vopat and declared her intention to keep the upcoming appointment. She reported also that her facial pain problem has been manageable without further intervention. Personnel at the pain clinic confirmed that they had not seen Kathy for the past 8 months.

## OVERALL EVALUATION

Simple phobia is one of the behavioral disorders for which behavior therapy provides unambiguous benefit in the great majority of patients. The specific therapeutic tactics that were responsible for success here are unknown, but the array of tactics included observation of a fearless model, direct exposure to feared events, anxiety attenuation during the exposure, fading of anxiety attenuators during continued exposure, and the provision of corrective information. Similarly, the therapeutic mechanism cannot be pinpointed but probably includes some admixture of vicarious fear extinction, direct fear extinction, habituation and/or inhibition, and modification of schematic thinking.

The rapport with her therapist that was established during earlier supportive therapy for facial pain probably had much to do with Kathy's willingness to undergo the therapeutic exposure to dental procedures. Clearly, such an inference is supported by Kathy's spontaneous remarks. The role of the therapeutic relationship in behavior therapy has received far too little research and conceptual attention.

Ideally, behavioral practitioners will acquire better follow-up data than are reported here and will acquire them over a longer period of time. In the contemporary professional climate serious attention should be paid to documenting treatment outcomes. Furthermore, careful monitoring of intervention effects is part and parcel of behavior therapy.

Simple phobia is rarely encountered apart from other anxiety and mood disorders. In that sense, the case described here is deceptively simple. It is an instructive case, however, because it shows how treatment can be guided by orthodox behavior therapy principles without the piecemeal use of prototypical behavior therapy methods.

# REFERENCES

American Psychiatric Association. (1987). *Diagnostic and statistical manual of mental disorders* (3rd ed., rev.). Washington, DC: Author.

Bandura, A. (1977). Self-efficacy: Toward a unifying theory of behavioral change. *Psychological Review, 84,* 191–215.

Barlow, D. H. (1988). *Anxiety and its disorders: The nature and treatment of anxiety.* New York: Guilford Press.

Delprato, D. J., & McGlynn, F. D. (1984). Behavioral theories of anxiety disorders. In S. M. Turner (Ed.), *Behavioral theories and treatment of anxiety* (pp. 1–49). New York: Plenum Press.

Hekmat, H. (1987). Origins and development of human fear reactions. *Journal of Anxiety Disorders, 1,* 197–218.

Lang, P. J. (1978). Anxiety: Toward a psychophysiological definition. In H. S. Akiskal & W. L. Webb (Eds.), *Psychiatric diagnosis: Exploration of biological predictions* (pp. 365–389). New York: Spectrum.

Marks, I. M. (1975). Behavioral treatments of phobic and obsessive–compulsive disorders: A critical appraisal. In M. Hersen, R. M. Eisler, & P. M. Miller (Eds.), *Progress in behavior modification* (Vol. 1, pp. 65–158). New York: Academic Press.

Reich, J. (1986). The epidemiology of anxiety. *Journal of Nervous and Mental Disease, 174,* 129–136.

Wolpe, J. (1973). *The practice of behavior therapy.* Elmsford, NY: Pergamon Press.

Wolpe, J. (1986). Individualization: The categorical imperative of behavior therapy practice. *Journal of Behavior Therapy and Experimental Psychiatry, 17,* 145–154.

# CHAPTER 11

# Generalized Anxiety Disorder
## Combined Behavior Therapy and Cognitive Therapy

### GILLIAN BUTLER

### DESCRIPTION OF THE DISORDER

As its name implies, generalized anxiety disorder (GAD) is a general form of anxiety that ranges over a number of concerns. Because the definition of GAD was changed, and greatly improved, in *DSM-III-R* (American Psychiatric Association, 1987), the disorder, despite its general nature, can no longer be used, and vilified, as a ragbag category. It has a specific, identifiable nature that greatly influences response to treatment. The defining feature of GAD is "apprehensive expectation about two or more life circumstances" (or, in layman's terms, worry) that has lasted for at least 6 months. For people with GAD the world appears threatening or risky, and this perception may overwhelm their ability to cope. The essence of the problem is captured by the question often asked by patients with GAD—"What if?"—a question that reflects an alarming degree of uncertainty about the future and often followed by a list of distressing possibilities that may or may not be easily verbalized.

The precise form of the anxiety experienced in GAD varies. Some people complain most of physical tension and of being unable to relax whereas others may be mostly distressed by more specific physiological symptoms (e.g.,

GILLIAN BUTLER • Department of Clinical Psychology, Warneford Hospital, Headington, Oxford, United Kingdom OX3 7JX.

*Adult Behavior Therapy Casebook,* edited by Cynthia G. Last and Michel Hersen. Plenum Press, New York, 1994.

sweating, palpitations, trembling), by behavioral symptoms (e.g., restlessness, rushing about, avoidance) or by cognitive symptoms (e.g., poor concentration, hypervigilance, self-monitoring, and all manner of negative cognitions). The unifying feature of GAD is "apprehensive expectation" or worry, and the precise form it takes varies according to characteristics of the person and his or her circumstances.

Although this definition of GAD is helpful, it needs supplementing when describing what a clinician would expect to find in a particular case. People with GAD rarely worry about only two things. Although a limited number of concerns may predominate at any one time, the focus changes and worries tend to spread, especially at night or when distractions are hard to come by. People with GAD worry extensively, and the pervasiveness and/or intensity of their worry interferes with normal functioning. At the same time, anxious mood, unlike depressed mood, tends to fluctuate and therefore may not be present or obvious during an interview.

Since GAD is, by definition, persistent, secondary problems are also likely. In some cases there may be a high degree of hopelessness and depression; in other cases worry about negative evaluation from others may contribute to social anxiety, and loss of faith in oneself or in one's abilities may lower confidence. Most people who have been anxious for a long time become easily fatigued and then withdraw by degrees from demanding but pleasurable activities. This withdrawal, which differs from avoidance in that is is not motivated by fear, can leave the person with GAD feeling restricted, trapped, and demoralized. In addition, such people often mention spontaneously that they "have always been worriers" and raise the question themselves as to whether they were "born that way." The distinction between dysfunctional habitual reactions to the world, or personality types, and personality disorders is debatable. Obviously, recognized personality disorders may or may not coincide with GAD, but as the problem is *by definition* long-standing, it is likely to involve habitual patterns of responding to perceived threats.

GAD is arguably the most complex of the anxiety disorders and one of the hardest to treat. The revised definition has focused attention on cognitive processes, on worry in particular. What is worry? Everyone seems to know how to do it. If you ask people to "worry in their usual way," they set about it without query or difficulty and often report that initially it feels like a way of solving problems. Indeed, the activity may have short-term advantages and may even be a way of avoiding something worse (such as frightening images). However, in the longer term it appears not to lead to solutions and increases rather than reduces anxiety. The problem is therefore that its apparent short-term usefulness may make it hard to give up.

It can be difficult to make a definite diagnosis of GAD, and the following guidelines help to distinguish the disorder from others with which it is easily confused. Avoidance in GAD is less consistent than in phobias and is not provoked solely by specific circumstances, such as being criticized. Panic attacks often occur, sometimes with sufficient frequency to fulfill criteria for panic disorder, but the anxiety in panic disorder is directly related to panic symptoms and to the fear of having another attack; in GAD the episodes of high anxiety are usually provoked by the predominant worry at the time. When health anxiety is the main concern, anxiety is triggered by perceived signs of (serious) illness, dominated by the apparent need to prove that illness is absent and by persistent reassurance seeking. Moderate depression is common in GAD, and anxiety often occurs during recovery from depression; this distinction is most easily made by determining the order of onset. Other confounding problems include caffeine addiction and abuse of alcohol or other substances.

The person described in this chapter fulfilled *DSM-III-R* criteria for GAD. This case was selected to illustrate the multidimensional nature of GAD and the need for clarity and creativity from the therapist during treatment. Details that could identify the person described have been changed. Two common problems, which will not be discussed here, are how to deal with panic attacks and how to reduce dependence on anxiolytic medication. Concurrent treatment involving either of these symptoms is possible (see also chapter 8).

## CASE IDENTIFICATION AND PRESENTING COMPLAINTS

Nell, age 26 and unmarried, worked for a telephone company. At the time of referral she had recently started a 6-month training course in operating a new system. She was living in a town at some distance from her home, which she was able to visit on some but not all weekends. She found the work very demanding but was honored to have been chosen to take the course, in which she was the only woman.

During the first interview Nell was tearful, tense, and worried. Her main complaints were of being "wound up" and frightened. Physical symptoms included unpredictable episodes of high anxiety, possibly bordering on panic attacks, with heart pounding, sweating, and trembling; physical tension, which was present most of the time; insomnia; fatigue; and repeated bouts of a minor physical ailment such as a sore throat or cough. Behavioral symptoms and situational determinants were not so easy to elicit. When asked if there were things that she avoided, Nell could think of nothing but claimed always to push herself into difficult situations. Further questioning revealed that she dreaded meeting new people, had given up going to the local social club, and kept a low profile when in the vicinity of her supervisor. She could not bring herself to read the details of course requirements or to start work on a diffi-

cult written assignment. Cognitive symptoms included poor concentration and
many negative thoughts, such as "I don't want to upset people," "I never seem
to do things right," and "I can't stand this much longer."

Secondary aspects of the problem included marked loss of pleasure, low
self-confidence, loss of social confidence, dropping her fitness class, and increased self-doubt. Nell had previously succeeded by working hard, but now
she said, "I'm trying so hard there's nothing else I can do." She had developed
a striking habit of solving this problem by meeting it halfway and apologizing
for possible failures in advance. The word most frequently heard during our
first meeting was "sorry."

## HISTORY

Without prompting Nell confided that she had always been like this.
What she meant was that she had worried about the possibility of "doing
badly" or of failure for as long as she could remember. She had once had to
drop out of college for 6 weeks with a similar problem; she thought that it
arose because she was oversensitive. She had not previously received psychological or psychiatric advice.

Nell was the only child of hardworking parents who ran their own small
business. As a youngster she had frequently helped in the business, whose
fortunes were variable. She had learned to turn her hand to anything that was
needed and was critical of women who rely on men to do certain things,
including those demanding physical strength. Although Nell was under no
pressure to continue to work in the family business, she felt that she carried
the burden of the family's hopes. Relations with her parents seemed to be
warm and supportive: despite living away from home for some years she still
visited her parents weekly and confided her troubles to them. Thus, it was not
surprising to hear that she worried about "letting them down."

At school Nell had been a low-average student at first. However, in high
school she discovered that she could do better than this if she worked hard,
and her teachers, friends, and parents had been agreeably surprised by her
subsequent success. During the first interview she said, "I know that I have to
work hard to do well," and followed this up with the statement "If I don't try
my best, everything will go wrong." She started working for the telephone
company immediately after leaving college, without any specific training. She
took a long time to settle into the job, and 2 to 3 years ago had another period
of stress when moving into her own apartment, after which time her worries
never completely subsided. She tended to make few but very good friends, of
both sexes, both at college and at work and had had one close relationship,

which ended after a year when Tom was moved by his employers to another part of the country.

Against this background it seemed understandable that Nell's present situation should provoke an exacerbation of a relatively long-standing problem. She was isolated from the support system of friends and family, unconfident (lacking in confidence) about her ability to learn unless she worked very hard, distracted from learning by worries about her ability to cope, and shaken to find that her preferred method of solving problems, pushing herself as hard as she could, did not seem to be working.

## ASSESSMENT

Assessment is an ongoing process. It does not cease after the initial interview but continues in an interactive way throughout treatment. As questions arise, the therapist and client together work out how to test hypotheses, what information should be collected, and what action to take in order to address difficulties. Aspects of assessment that illustrate this process of continuous assessment are presented here. Discovery of the symptomatology and history described earlier formed part of the whole process.

### Rating Scales

Before the first interview Nell completed the Beck Anxiety Inventory (BAI; Beck, Brown, Epstein, & Steer, 1988) and the Beck Depression Inventory (BDI; Beck, Ward, Mendelson, Mock, & Erbaugh, 1961), and a measure of relatively stable patterns of responding, the Trait scale of the State–Trait Anxiety Inventory (STAI-Trait Scale; Spielberger, Gorsuch, & Lushene, 1970). Her mood scores were typical of a patient with moderate to severe GAD (BAI, 42; BDI, 19); a score of 63 on the STAI-Trait scale suggests that her distress was not likely to be transitory. Nell completed the BAI and BDI on every subsequent session.

When asked about her main difficulty, Nell said that she was most distressed by feeling "continuously wound up," mentally as well as physically. Although she was used to feeling like this, the problem was both more intense and less variable than it had previously been. It was necessary to exclude other possible disorders after gathering the details of her symptoms and history. It was relatively easy to determine that Nell was not phobic, even in the context of social avoidance, since she was unable to name any situation that always provoked anxiety and was clear that she would still be anxious even if she were able to avoid most immediate provocations. Nell's history provided *prima facie* reason to suppose that the depression was a secondary problem also. The BDI scores showed that she was mainly distressed by feelings of failure, guilt, self-blame, and sadness. This hypothesis was checked by asking Nell about her high rating of sad mood; she ascribed it to the worry that it was inevitable that she would fail and thus let other people down.

## Treatment Goals

Nell was quite clear about her goal: "I want to get the best out of myself." This goal provided a useful clue as to what was going to be important to her to achieve during treatment, but it was not helpful in the sense that it would be impossible to know exactly when it was achieved. More specific goals were sought, such as reducing her level of tension, learning how to deal with her numerous worries, and sleeping better. This wider assessment of her goals led Nell to admit that she was also troubled by the fear that she was losing control. While reassuring her that the purpose of treatment would be to help her manage the problem and thereby gain control, further discussion of treatment was postponed until her current self-management skills could be ascertained.

## Previous Coping

Recently Nell had put much energy into trying to relax. She had tried a variety of methods, including watching TV, listening to music, writing letters to friends, telephoning her parents (usually late at night), and telling herself to stop being so silly or to stop worrying. She had also tried to reduce the time she spent worrying about what to do at work ("Shall I do this or shall I do that?"). Worrying made her nervous, which led to making mistakes for which she was publicly admonished. However, even when she did not worry, she still made mistakes, and so far the strategy had only reduced her confidence further.

Nell shared lodgings with Jim, a colleague who spent most of his spare time with his girlfriend, was openly critical of Nell, and did none of the supposedly shared household chores. Instead of fighting with Jim about the chores, a strategy she had tried and found wanting, Nell had decided to take responsibility herself for the home. However, she now felt exploited, and relations with Jim, who neither acknowledged nor appeared to notice her efforts, were no better. This part of the assessment suggested that she might generally be a timid or unassertive person, a hypothesis that was not supported by her behavior during the interview or by her descriptions of her other social relationships. It seemed, rather, that she was motivated by a desire to do well and by the fear of letting people down and that she had selected a coping strategy that aimed to please someone other than herself.

## Sharing a Formulation of the Problem

The information collected so far, in its simplified and structured form, suggested a definite, coherent way of understanding the problem. The next step involved sharing this understanding with Nell so as to gauge her reactions to it; to modify it, if necessary; and to start thinking about its implications for treatment. This process provides a basis for developing a collaborative working relationship with the client, for explaining how treatment can help, and for assessing the client's hopes and expectations about treatment.

One way of introducing a formulation to a client is to say something like "Let me see if I've got that right" and then present the information in terms of predisposing, precipitating, and maintaining factors while using a dialogue format so that the patient can take part rather than giving a speech. Our first formulation of Nell's problem included the following points: She was the sort of person who wants to do well and who sets high standards for herself. Her parents were pleased when she did well, and at school she learned that if she worked hard she could certainly succeed. Sometimes the strain this caused led to difficulties, as she had found at college and when she moved into her apartment. Given this background, it was understandable that she should feel distressed right now. She was slected to attend a training course at work because she had done well there and was conscientious, but she was uncertain of her abilities and far away from her friends and family. Her worries made it hard for her to concentrate or to think clearly, so she was apt to make mistakes, to worry about doing well, and to become increasingly tense and wound up. This vicious circle made it even harder for her to think straight or to stop worrying, especially at night when she should have been sleeping. She was lonely away from home and felt sad because her failure to solve the problem despite great effort meant that she had let people down.

The outline of this formulation was written down, and diagrams were used to illustrate the vicious circles maintaining tension and worry. The therapist then asked Nell, "Does that make sense? Have I left anything out?" Nell replied that it did make sense and that it was helpful to feel that somebody understood the problem since she herself had become so confused by it. She added, thereby demonstrating a degree of assertiveness, that the formulation had left out many of her worries, such as those concerning her parents' business, her worry about being a worry to her parents, her financial worries, and her concerns about the difficulties that she faced working and living in a male environment, which tended to exclude her or to make her feel judged by her sexual, rather than personal, identity.

## Expectations

Nell's expectations were partly revealed by her attempts to control her symptoms and showed that she was already using a problem-solving approach. Even if her attempts had not so far been successful, they were an encouraging sign because she had tried at least two sensible strategies: trying to relax and saying something to herself to make herself feel better. Pointing this out was intended to endorse these sensible attempts to control her anxiety, to increase her confidence, and to encourage her to develop these methods during treatment. Nell clearly was not expecting to play a passive part in the process, and her active participation was encouraged by explaining that she would need to set aside time for homework assignments, and could expect during treatment to learn how to manage, rather than remove, symptoms of anxiety—an unrealistic expectation that would have led to disappointment if left unchanged.

## SELECTION OF TREATMENT

The revised definition of GAD, emphasizing the cognitive aspects of the disorder, together with the results of various research trials (e.g., Butler, Fennell, Robson, & Gelder, 1991) lent weight to the view that a cognitive-behavioral treatment was likely to be helpful in this case. Nell's cognitions reflected a stream of negative automatic thoughts, such as "I should be able to do this better by now" or "I'll never get through the day." She also described frightening images and spontaneously used many metaphors. For example, she described her efforts to overcome the problem as "trying to get through a thick, heavy hedge," adding, "All I do is pull off a few leaves." She readily verbalized some of the rules or beliefs that were important to her, such as "If I do something for someone, they should be pleased." (Thus, she had been surprised by criticisms from Jim after she had cleaned up their kitchen. She said, "He's always picking on me; he treats me like a slave.") This is not to say that cognitive-behavioral treatment is unsuited to people who verbalize less readily, only that its appropriateness is obvious in this case.

Selection of specific treatment strategies within a cognitive-behavioral framework was not so straightforward. Nell said she would like to learn relaxation, which seemed sensible, and asked whether she should take anxiolytic medication, for instance at night. After discussion she decided to keep this as a last resort in case the treatment should fail. Furthermore, she readily accepted the argument that when two treatments are started at once, it is impossible to determine which one is responsible for the outcome. Traditional graded exposure was not appropriate for Nell, given her inconsistent avoidance, but other behavioral methods such as time management, graded task assignment, and scheduling pleasurable activities were all potentially valuable considering the degree to which she felt overburdened and had become socially isolated. Thus, having discussed an outline formulation and its treatment implications, the assessment stage was completed by asking Nell, for her first homework assignment, to read a booklet describing the nature of anxiety and its treatment (available on request).

## COURSE OF TREATMENT

Nell had 15 sessions of treatment, including the assessment, the last two being "boosters" at intervals of 3 and 6 weeks. A follow-up appointment was made after 6 months and follow-up letters were exchanged a year later. Weekly sessions were structured in a standard way and planned jointly. Regular items on the agenda included reviews of the week and of homework assignments, reactions to the last session, discussion of one or more major topics, the assignment of new homework tasks, and, finally, brief summaries and comments about the session. Nell was encouraged to listen to recordings of therapy sessions and to note down useful ideas, both during the session and subsequently. This structured approach to treatment was intended to model a method of problem solving and to increase her sense of control.

### Sessions 2 to 5

The goals in the first stage of therapy were primarily to start reducing Nell's tension and anxiety, but they were also to ensure that the treatment rationale was properly understood, to continue the process of assessment and formulation, and to mobilize the client's own coping resources more effectively. The main strategies employed were behavioral ones, namely, self-monitoring using the Weekly Activity Schedule (WAS) described by Beck, Rush, Shaw, and Emery (1979; see also Fennell, 1989); relaxation; and breaking the habit of apologizing.

*Self-monitoring.* The purpose of using the WAS was twofold: (1) to find out more details of Nell's daily routine, and the associated variations in tension, and of her social and recreational activities and (2) to help her stand back from her problems so as to take a more objective look at them. Both objectives were explained; surprisingly perhaps, the second proved easier to achieve than the first. Nell reported that expressing herself "instead of bottling it up" was helpful, and after one week she abandoned the WAS in favor of a diary written in the form of a letter. She brought sheaves of paper with her, and a glance at them suggested that she might merely be translating her ruminations about particular worries onto paper, thus repeating the vicious circle in written form.

THERAPIST:   Can you explain how you are using your new diaries?

NELL:   I write about things that happened in the day and I sit and think "Well, today was quite a good day" or "Today was a bad day." Never mind . . .

THERAPIST:   What effect does writing the diary have on you?

NELL:   It puts things in perspective. Before I was running away from it. Now I'm standing up to it. It makes me think and look back over the day and think, "I didn't have a very good day, but I didn't do too much wrong."

THERAPIST:   In the bits I have been able to read you seemed sometimes to get trapped into the vicious circle on paper, and I wondered whether writing it made you remember all the bad things.

NELL:   It did, but it got them out of the way—out of my system too.

THERAPIST:   Good.

NELL:   So although it doesn't always look very good, it is helping.

Nell had understood the original rationale for self-monitoring with the WAS well and had adapted this technique to counteract her wish to avoid thinking about distressing events. Writing the more lengthy diary in the form of a letter got these events off her chest before going to bed and thus helped her to sleep better. Later, when discussing how to build on the freer diary form that she preferred she agreed to use it also as a way of "picking up the good points" about each day. She found in the end that it prompted her to "look back and see how far [she had] come, rather than trying to push on without stopping to think." The original WAS had also revealed that her time was almost completely filled with work or unrewarding chores. Without realizing it Nell had allowed her working day to lengthen by degrees. The new diary was then also used to reduce her fatigue and withdrawal by helping her plan more leisure and social activities, from small things like taking a hot shower after work to more complex ones such as joining an aerobics class and engaging in social activities at weekends.

*Relaxation.* Nell was taught progressive muscular relaxation using both guided instructions during therapy sessions and a recorded tape at home.

As soon as she was able to relax using the tape, she practiced increasingly short forms of the exercise and then used these to reduce tension at work. She liked to listen to the tape "as a comforter" but found it only moderately helpful, as she was able to relax physically but not mentally. Relaxation became more useful after she had learned the cognitive method of treatment (to be described) and had developed the new form of diary already mentioned.

*Breaking the habit of apologizing.* Nell's habit of apologizing was both striking and irritating. If others were finding it so, it is possible that their responses were contributing to her distress and to the maintenance of her anxiety. She was puzzled by being asked to describe what happened when she said, "Sorry," but after some thought she said that people appeared not to notice. She said that her supervisor at work shouted at her and blamed her even for mistakes for which she was not responsible and that Jim, too, was frequently angry with her even after she had made efforts to please him. She thought they dismissed her apologies as a sort of irrelevant female politeness. In either case the habit seemed counterproductive, so she was asked first to monitor the number of times a day she apologized (19 in the first few workdays) and then to try to reduce this number. This strategy was not discussed in more detail at this stage as there was no time. The idea was that if it were successful she could, with help, draw her own conclusions, and if it were not, further discussion could be based on her observations of others' reactions.

Results supported the original hypothesis and confirmed that Nell's habit was indeed provoking. Having been alerted to look out for others' reactions, she came to the following conclusions: "It's as if I'm asking to be told off"; "People think I have done something wrong and then blame me"; and "I'm hanging myself before I've committed the crime." Nell found it difficult to break this habit, sometimes substituting inappropriate gratitude for inappropriate apology, and was helped by role-playing and reverse-roleplaying of some of the relevant situations.

*Reactions to Sessions 2 to 5.* By Session 5 Nell's symptoms had started to improve (BAI, 33; BDI, 13), and she commented that treatment was "like planting a seed instead of a cut flower to make the garden pretty. It lasts longer." She was, however, still worried about her ability to cope: "I've pushed myself off into the swimming pool. I'm at the deep end and just about to let go of the side. . . . Maybe I still won't be able to handle a telling off. It's as if the first page is in English, but all the rest is in French. I'm scared I won't understand it and won't be able to go on because it's difficult." The predominantly, but not purely, behavioral strategies used so far were developed throughout therapy and were supplemented in subsequent sessions with conventional cognitive ones such as identifying, examining, and testing relevant thoughts and beliefs (see, e.g., Beck, Emery, & Greenberg, 1985; Hawton, Salkovskis, Kirk, & Clark, 1989).

## Sessions 6 to 12

As treatment progressed, patterns in Nell's thinking became clearer. For instance, she thought "It must be my fault" and "I'm going to be punished" when a machine that she regularly used at work broke down when being used by someone else. This incident was used as a basis for further discussion of the idea of themes, starting from the thoughts she had identified when this event occurred:

THERAPIST: Where do you want to begin? Which thought shall we pick up?

NELL: The ones about failure . . . and feeling disgusted with muself.

THERAPIST: And you just said it related to something else . . .

NELL: The feeling that I'd done something wrong. And confidence.

THERAPIST: Let's see how that fits together. You're disgusted and disappointed with yourself because you feel you've done something wrong, and then you think you're going to be punished . . .

NELL: And confidence as well.

THERAPIST: How does it relate to confidence? Can you explain a bit?

NELL: Because I haven't got much confidence in myself, I think I mustn't do things wrong . . . so that . . . Whereas someone doing a job would think "I'll have a good go at it," I think, "Oh crikey, I'm going to muck it up and everything and cause a lot of hassles." So it's negative thinking right from the start.

THERAPIST: That's a really good example. It's a typical thought that undermines your confidence, and you get disappointed and expect to be punished . . .

NELL: Yes, they all go round together.

THERAPIST: Okay, so is that a theme to work on? My idea was that this was like a sort of pattern of what's happening to you.

NELL: It's like a basic bed of things I'm worried about and they all shoot up together. One pulls another one with it. At the bottom it's about letting people down, doing things wrong, upsetting someone, not doing my best. Things like that. So a lot of it all stems from a couple of things.

THERAPIST: Yes, that's right. And I know when you first came you said there were so many things bothering you that it was really confusing. It was difficult to see that only a couple of things might be central.

NELL: Like a stem with lots of leaves. There's only one trunk, and they all come off the same one.

This dialogue marked a change of focus in Nell's treatment. From then on relatively little time was spent discussing details of the diary, relaxation exercises, her habit of saying "Sorry," or time management; attention was focused instead on defining and re-examining her beliefs, predominantly those concerned with pleasing others and with perfectionism.

*Perfectionism.* Nell readily put this belief into her own words: "I must always do my best in everything I do." A whole session was devoted to examining this rule and its advantages or disadvantages, during which time Nell became aware of its costs to her, namely, increased pressure and reduced flexibility. These disadvantages are reflected in the extreme words in which the belief was phrased: "I *must always* do my *best* in *everything* I do." She was then asked what the rule was for, what it was designed to achieve. She found this question helpful. She could readily redefine her goal as "To do as well as I can" and agreed that it would be nice, rather than essential, to do something especially well. After modifying the old rule in this way, she commented that it felt once again as if the instructions were written in French. When looking at the statement "I would like to do well" she said, "I want to cross out the *would* and put in a *must*," thus revealing the strength of the old belief and the difference that the new wording had made to it. Her homework task after this session was to summarize the discussion in her own words, using the session tape as a prompt, and to watch out for extreme words such as *must, should,* and *always.*

As would be expected, Nell had difficulty challenging this firmly held belief. Having examined it thoroughly and identified its origins in the attitudes of her parents, who "treat a small mistake as a disaster," she recognized its deleterious daily effect on her, in particular, when starting her written assignment for the training course at work. It takes courage to try changing entrenched beliefs in such circumstances, and Nell needed frequent reminders and support while completing this training course assignment, which she did with far less distress than usual and about the same degree of success. At this point she also found conventional behavioral strategies, such as goal setting and time management, helpful once again. By session 12 her BAI and BDI scores had fallen to 21 and 9, and her STAI-Trait score to 40.

This detailed work was followed by sessions in which Nell consolidated the gains already made. This entailed clarifying the methods used so far so that she could apply them in new situations and challenging other thoughts and beliefs, such as "I should have more ability than I have got at present" and "I let other people down by not doing my best."

## TERMINATION

The process of ending treatment was set in motion during the assessment when Nell was told that treatment would be brief (about 3 months) and that she could expect to learn how to manage, rather than eliminate, her anxiety, a skill that she could continue to perfect after therapy was over. All along Nell made notes of those things that she found helpful, and every time she successfully handled a difficult situation or succeeded in reducing her anxiety, she worked out what she had done that made the difference and formulated the successful strategy in terms intended to make it generally applicable. During the last of the weekly meetings these notes were drawn together into a summary or "blueprint for the future." First Nell made a draft from her own notes; then this was expanded using the therapist's notes, and the phrasing was checked to ensure that she would be able to understand the guidelines when referring to them in the future. Her final blueprint is shown in Table 1.

No new material was introduced during Sessions 13 and 14, which were spaced at intervals of 3 and 6 weeks. By the end of these sessions Nell's BAI and BDI scores had fallen to 16 and 5. She had, in fact, experienced a major setback about a month before the last of these sessions: Jim had asked her to leave the apartment she shared with him so that his girlfriend could move in instead. Although she knew she could contact me if necessary, she tried, as she had been advised, to apply relevant strategies from the blueprint to this new situation. This was difficult but eventually successful, and the process greatly strengthened her confidence. During Session 14 the strategies that she had used were summarized for future reference.

## FOLLOW-UP

Six months after treatment had ended Nell's mood ratings showed that she had maintained the gains made earlier: BAI, 17; BDI, 6; STAI-Trait = 38. She had by this time returned to her hometown and to her own apartment and was pleased to report that she was coping well despite considerable pressure at work. Since completing the training course she had been asked to lead a team of people learning how to use the new system and was in charge of a purely male team. She recognized the difficulties she faced; she said that when the pressure at work built up it was "like a train stopping. All the carriages

Table 1
Blueprint for the Future

1. Look to the future. Plant the seed and wait for the flowers to grow. Don't just cut the flowers. Look forward rather than back. You can't change the past, but you may be able to influence the future.
2. Keep things in perspective. Talk to people. Write things down in a diary. Writing them down gets them out of the head and helps to get them straight. Think of all the points of view and not just mine, and look for the evidence for and against them.
3. Defuse the worries that niggle; otherwise, they only grow.
4. Decide on goals before making rules. Then look to see whether the rule helps to achieve the goal.
5. Concentrate on the thoughts behind the feelings, and don't get sidetracked by feelings.
6. "Softer approach"; i.e., don't be prickly. Let things flow over your head rather than grabbing everything that's thrown at you.
7. Keep in contact with friends and family. Don't fall into the isolation trap, and remember it happens before you realize it.
8. Learn from mistakes, and don't treat them as disasters. Remember the family will still love me however I do. They only want me to be happy.
9. Don't go to extremes. Find the grey areas between the black and the white and work at filling them in.
10. Disarm any critic. Don't get on the offensive. Agree, keep calm, and tell the truth.
11. Stop and think things out. It prevents some of the tangles.
12. Take a wider look. Don't get narrowed vision.
13. Don't say "Sorry" just to please people or they will assume I have done something wrong.
N.B.: "If you act like a doormat, don't be surprised if people walk on you."

*In general, watch out for:*

- Accepting blame
- Accepting responsibility for disasters
- Accepting criticism
- Setting impossible standards

Remember: "A journey of a thousand miles begins with the first step."

bump into each other and everything seems to go wrong at once." On one such occasion her tension had increased and she had developed a stomachache and a throat infection. Nevertheless, she handled the difficulty without panicking; when she was ill she worked out a method of sharing responsibility with her team, a method that proved valuable subsequently. Her blueprint from her therapy continued to be relevant and useful. A year later she was still well, had had no major relapses, and was planning to marry Tom and move with him to another part of the country. She wrote an optimistic, happy, and confident letter that made it clear that she was not expecting to live happily ever after, and she enclosed a badge on which the following words were written: IF ALL ELSE FAILS, LOWER YOUR STANDARDS.

## OVERALL EVALUATION

Nell may sound unlike the typical GAD patient. She certainly had an unusual ability to express herself in metaphorical terms and to use analogies. This, however, was one reason for selecting her as an illustrative case; her expressions seem to represent what many others think but are unable to verbalize so well. Nor was she, as might be expected, of more than average intellectual ability, judging informally. Her best school attainments were still very average.

In fact, Nell both fulfilled the *DSM-III-R* criteria for GAD and suffered from a typical set of secondary problems, including depression, social anxiety, fatigue, loss of confidence and demoralization; moreover, she described herself as having always been a worrier. She had withdrawn from former sources of pleasure and reward until her life seemed to revolve around her problem and her perceived inability to cope with it. She was confused, was not at first able to use her own coping resources effectively, and blamed herself for all and any failures. Nell's case illustrates well the apparently unpredictable nature of generalized anxiety and the undermining effect it has on otherwise resourceful people. Nell was at first convinced that her bouts of high anxiety came "out of the blue." At one moment she might be feeling well and the next she would be on the verge of panic. However, further exploration in the context of a cognitive–behavioral formulation identified clear cognitive precipitants of anxiety, including thoughts, attitudes, beliefs, and unverbalized assumptions. So to say that anxiety is general is not to say that it cannot be explained.

The behavioral strategies used first helped Nell gain a degree of control over her symptoms. The cognitive strategies used subsequently played a larger part in preparing her to deal adequately with a future in which stress is endemic. The two sorts of strategies were closely coordinated, and it is possible that this combination is particularly effective in the case of GAD (see Butler & Booth, 1991, for a discussion of this).

## REFERENCES

American Psychiatric Association. (1987). *Diagnostic and statistical manual of mental disorders* (3rd Ed., rev.). Washington, DC: Author.

Beck, A. T., Brown, G., Epstein, N., & Steer, R. A. (1988). An inventory for measuring clinical anxiety: Psychometric properties. *Journal of Consulting and Clinical Psychology, 56,* 893–897.

Beck, A. T., Emery, G., & Greenberg, R. (1985). *Anxiety disorders and phobias: A cognitive perspective.* New York: Basic Books.

Beck, A. T., Rush, A. J., Shaw, B. F., & Emery, G. (1979). *Cognitive therapy of depression.* New York: Guilford Press.

Beck, A. T., Ward, C. H., Mendelson, M., Mock, J., & Erbaugh, J. (1961). An inventory for measuring depression. *Archives of General Psychiatry, 4,* 561–571.

Butler, G., & Booth, R. G. (1991). Developing psychological treatments for generalized anxiety disorder. In R. M. Rapee and D. H. Barlow (Eds.), *Chronic and generalized anxiety disorder* (pp. 157–209). New York: Guilford Press.

Butler, G., Fennell, M., Robson, P., & Gelder, M. 1991. A comparison of behavior therapy and cognitive behavior therapy in the treatment of generalized anxiety disorder. *Journal of Consulting and Clinical Psychology, 59,* 167–175.

Fennell, M. J. V. (1989). Depression. In K. Hawton, P. M. Salkovskis, J. Kirk, & D. M. Clark (Eds.), *Cognitive behaviour therapy for psychiatric problems: A practical guide* (pp. 169–234). Oxford: Oxford University Press.

Hawton, K., Salkovskis, P., Kirk, J., & Clark, D. (1989). *Cognitive behavioural therapy for psychiatric problems: A practical guide.* Oxford: Oxford University Press.

Spielberger, C. D., Gorsuch, R. L., & Lushene, R. E. (1970). *Manual of the State–Trait Anxiety Inventory.* Palo Alto, CA: Consulting Psychologists Press.

# CHAPTER 12

# Obsessive–Compulsive Disorder

## HELLA HISS and EDNA B. FOA

### DESCRIPTION OF THE DISORDER

The diagnostic manual of the American Psychiatric Association (1987), *DSM-III-R,* classifies obsessive–compulsive disorder (OCD) as an anxiety disorder. OCD involves persistent, disturbing, unwanted thoughts, images, or impulses that are generally experienced as intrusive and senseless (obsessions) and are often accompanied by repetitive ritualistic thoughts or actions (compulsions) that the patient feels driven to perform.

In the three American surveys reported by Weissman (1985), the pooled 6-month prevalence rate for OCD was 1.6% (58% higher in women than in men), with no strong relationship to age. OCD is usually chronic if left untreated and can be highly disruptive to one's social and occupational functioning. It is often accompanied by depression, which may be a consequence of the obsessive–compulsive symptoms (Foa, Steketee, Kozak, & Dugger, 1987). Until recently, the prognosis of OCD was considered bleak, if not hopeless. Psychodynamic therapy has been found to be ineffective for the majority of obsessive–compulsive patients. Innovations in behavioral and pharmacological treatment, however, have improved the prognostic picture for the majority of these patients. The efficacy of behavioral treatment by exposure and response

HELLA HISS and EDNA B. FOA • Center for Treatment and Study of Anxiety, Medical College of Pennsylvania at Eastern Pennsylvania Psychiatric Institute, Philadelphia, Pennsylvania 19129.

*Adult Behavior Therapy Casebook,* edited by Cynthia G. Last and Michel Hersen. Plenum Press, New York, 1994.

prevention has been demonstrated in controlled studies conducted in several countries with hundreds of OC patients. Reports of success range from 65% to 80% (for a review, see Marks, 1987, and McCarthy & Foa, 1990).

In this chapter, we describe the treatment by exposure and response prevention of a patient who manifested compulsive checking.

## CASE IDENTIFICATION

John, a 35-year-old Caucasian male, performed checking rituals that were precipitated by a fear of harming other people. While driving, he repeatedly had to stop the car in order to retrace his route. At home, he repeatedly checked the doors and electrical appliances (stove, lights, TV, washing machine) to ensure that they were shut or turned off so that no harm, such as burglary or fire, would come to his family owing to his negligence. At work, which consisted of repairing pipes, he felt extremely fearful that he would be responsible for some harm and, consequently, spent a lot of time checking and mentally reviewing to avoid making a mistake that would result in serious injury to other people. His extremely high standards caused him to feel inadequate. When interrupted in the middle of a task, John had to start over again to ensure that the task would be performed perfectly. While engaging in ritualistic checking he experienced an increase in anxiety (rather than the characteristic decrease in other OC's), which was prompted by thoughts of uncertainty that the ritualistic efforts would succeed in preventing him from making mistakes (e.g., "Was I paying enough attention? Did I do it right?"). Like other checkers, John reported poor memory for his checking actions. The uncertainty of whether or not he had checked adequately further increased his ritualistic behavior.

John recognized that his compulsive behavior was excessive and unreasonable but was unable to dismiss the intrusive thoughts and to resist the urge to perform the rituals. He devoted between 3 to 5 hours a day to obsessive–compulsive behavior.

## PRESENTING COMPLAINTS

John's major complaint was checking excessively—electrical appliances to prevent fire, windows and door locks to prevent burglary, and activities at work to prevent mistakes and criticism. He remained stuck for hours in a frustrating vicious cycle of checking, doubting whether he had completed the check sufficiently and checking again. The OC symptoms had caused a substantial impairment of his social and professional functioning and severely interfered with home management (e.g., making repairs, looking after the children, paying bills, filling out important forms such as income tax returns) and with satisfactory family relationships. In an attempt to reduce distress, John avoided many situations that triggered his symptoms. Because of this extended avoidance, he could not disconfirm his belief that without repeated checking, serious damage would occur at home or at work. Although John was a good driver, he avoided driving in crowded places (city streets or around schools and supermarkets). He quit his job in spite of being successful in accomplishing his duties. At home he had his wife involved in carrying out rituals on his behalf and continuously asked her for reassurance despite her reluctance to give it and her critical attitude toward his OC problems. John became severely depressed as a result of the discomfort and limitations that stemmed from the OC symptoms and perceived himself as a failure.

## HISTORY

John's OC behavior started after he finished high school at age 18. At that time he felt insecure, was indecisive about his future plans, and believed that he had to "be the best" ("Otherwise, I won't make it in life"). He went over his work repeatedly in search of mistakes, reviewed every detail many times before moving to the next task, and was obsessed with doing things perfectly. Despite his good grades, John believed that he was a failure and therefore would be incapable of pleasing those whose opinions he respected. He described himself as an unassertive, timid, and submissive person since early adulthood.

Between the ages of 20 and 25 John developed a strong habit of checking and mentally reviewing important tasks (e.g., taking tests). The OC symptoms were relatively contained until he became employed as a plumber in the city water department. When moved to a night shift, his sense of responsibility increased and his obsessional fears of making a mistake mounted. During that period John's OC symptoms increased but did not severely debilitate him, nor did they interfere seriously with his performance on the job. Indeed, he was highly regarded by his supervisors. At age 30 John began to complain about depression and anxiety and was placed on anxiolytic and antidepressant medication (Prozac); there was no significant relief of symptoms. The addition of psychotherapy was unsuccessful. Two years later John was hospitalized for depression, at which time all of his OC symptoms remitted. However, upon returning to work, these symptoms recurred immediately, reaching the prehospitalization level concomitantly with intense fear of failure and punishment.

In social situations, John was reluctant to actively participate in conversations because of his fear of saying something wrong or behaving foolishly. John's relationship with his wife was satisfactory until they bought a house. His checking rituals began to spread from work to home and became more severe. Owning a home increased his sense of responsibility and, consequently, the fear of failing to meet the new challenges adequately. John felt overwhelmed by even the most mundane responsibilities. He was afraid the house would burn down or a burglar would break in if he did not successfully complete all of his checking rituals. Over time he developed additional fears and rituals. The fear of harming others infiltrated almost every action he took. While driving he was afraid he had unknowingly hit a pedestrian; he would recheck his route and was unable to drive alone, constantly seeking reassurance from passengers that nothing disastrous had happened.

John's fear of appearing irresponsible had led him to delegate important decisions to his wife. This passive attitude generated criticism and disapproval from her and her family. Although he was hurt by her criticism, John continued to be passive because he was more motivated to reduce his OC distress than to behave in ways that would gain him his wife's respect.

John sought behavior therapy because he was afraid that his symptoms would render him increasingly more dysfunctional.

## ASSESSMENT

The structured clinical interviews for *DSM-III-R,* SCID I and II, and symptom rating scales were used to clinically evaluate the severity of John's OC symptoms. Assessment was directed at identifying elements of John's obsessive fears: (1) the thoughts, objects, and situations that provoked his distress; (2) his obsessive–compulsive behaviors, including avoidance and rituals; and (3) relationships between feared situations, his responses, and feared harm.

The assessment of obsessions (anxiety or discomfort-evoking thoughts) involves the identification of three components. (In the following discussion John's symptoms are given as examples and appear in parentheses.) *External cues* are objects or situations that are sources of high anxiety or discomfort (e.g., locking a door, driving in crowded places). *Internal cues* are thoughts, images, or impulses that provoke anxiety (e.g., thoughts of negligence about leaving the stove on or failing to lock the door). *Feared consequences* may be from external or internal sources (e.g., burglary if a door is not locked; punishment for making mistakes; loss of bodily control; functional impairment from continuous high anxiety).

The assessment of John's avoidance behavior involved the identification of two components: *passive avoidance,* which refers to situations or objects that are avoided (e.g., driving alone, bumping into people), and *rituals,* which are active attempts to escape from anxiety-evoking cues (e.g., checking and requesting reassurance).

John's fear, avoidance, and rituals were rated on 8-point Likert scales on which 0 represents no symptoms and 8 represents extreme severity of symptoms. They were rated by an independent assessor, by the therapist, and by the client himself. Three main fears (in terms of both the specific feared situation and the feared consequences—e.g., driving through crowded city streets and hitting pedestrians) were identified in order to design exposure tasks for the treatment. For the same reason, the situations most often avoided by John were also identified (e.g., driving in crowded areas without extensive use of mirrors) and were rated with regard to the degree of avoidance (0 = never; 8 = always). The rating (also on a scale from 0 to 8) of symptom severity of John's rituals was determined by the time and frequency he engaged in them.

The rating scales used for assessing John's obsessive–compulsive behavior were found to have good psychometric properties (.92 to .97 [$N = 72$]; Foa et al., 1983). These rating scales were found to be sensitive to treatment effects (e.g., Foa, Steketee, Grayson, Turner, & Latimer, 1984).

John's obsessive–compulsive symptoms were assessed through use of the Yale–Brown Obsessive–Compulsive Scale (Y-BOCS; Goodman, Price & Rasmussen, 1989), which contains ten items rated by a clinician on a 0 to 4 scale, five items referring to severity of obsessions and five items referring to severity of compulsions. John's compulsions were assessed on the *Compulsive Activity Checklist* (CAC; Freund, Steketee, & Foa, 1987), which contains 46 items. A factor analysis ($N = 99$) revealed two main factors: one for washing rituals (60% of variance) and one for checking compulsions (40% of variance). The CAC has been shown to be sensitive to change in obsessive–compulsive symptoms following behavioral treatment (Marks, Stern, Mawson, Cobb, & McDonald, 1980).

John's mood state was evaluated by means of the Beck Depression Inventory (BDI; Beck, Ward, Mendelsohn, Mock, & Erbaugh, 1961), a 21-item inventory for which its authors reported a split-half reliability of .93 and correlations ranging from .62 to .66, and the *State-Trait Anxiety Inventory* (STAI; Spielberger, Gorsuch, & Lushene, 1970), which contains 20 items for state anxiety and 20 items for trait anxiety and for which its authors reported a test–retest reliability for trait anxiety of .81, a test–retest reliability for state anxiety of .40, and internal consistency correlations ranging from .83 to .92.

John's pretreatment scores are presented in Table 1. They indicate severe obsessive–compulsive symptoms, limited functioning, and extensive avoidance. His scores also indicate marked depression (BDI) and high general anxiety (STAI). According to the SCID I and II, John met the *DSM-III-R* criteria for obsessive–compulsive disorder and avoidant personality disorder.

Table 1
John's Scores on Independent Assessor Ratings and Self-Report Instruments

|  | Pretreatment | Posttreatment |
|---|---|---|
| Assessor ratings | | |
| Y-BOCS | | |
|   obsessions | 11 | 4 |
|   compulsions | 12 | 4 |
|   total | 23 | 8 |
| Fear 1 | 5 | 2 |
| Fear 2 | 5 | 1 |
| Fear 3 | 4 | 1 |
| Avoidance 1 | 8 | 1 |
| Avoidance 2 | 7 | 0 |
| Avoidance 3 | 8 | 0 |
| Ritual 1 | 8 | 1 |
| Ritual 2 | 3 | 1 |
| Ritual 3 | 8 | 1 |
| Interference with OC symptoms: | | |
|   at home | 6 | 1 |
|   at work | N/A | N/A |
|   family relationships | 4 | 2 |
|   social activities | 3 | 1 |
|   private leisure activities | 4 | 0 |
|   sexual activities | 1 | 1 |
| Self-ratings | | |
| CAC | 39 | 14 |
| BDI | 22 | 0 |
| STAI-State | 69 | 34 |
| STAI-Trait | 68 | 38 |

## SELECTION OF TREATMENT

As noted earlier, traditional psychotherapy has not proved effective in ameliorating obsessive–compulsive symptoms. In a sample of 90 patients Kringlen (1965) found that only 20% had improved at 13 to 20 years post-treatment. Nor did the application of early behavioral techniques, such as systematic desensitization and aversion therapy, improve the prognostic picture by much (for a review see McCarthy & Foa, 1990). In 1966 Victor Meyer introduced a treatment for OCD called apotrepic therapy, which consisted of a combination of exposure with response prevention (which are described below). The success of this treatment generated much interest and stimulated studies, both controlled and uncontrolled, that have provided information on the efficacy of these procedures and the processes involved in them. These studies (see Marks, 1987) have led to the conclusion that, at present, exposure and response prevention is the psychosocial treatment of choice for OCD. Therefore, this program was selected for John's treatment.

At the Center for the Treatment and Study of Anxiety in the Medical College of Pennsylvania, treatment for OCD consists of three procedures: imaginal exposure, *in vivo* exposure, and response prevention. Treatment includes 15 daily sessions of exposure with 45 minutes devoted to imaginal exposure and 45 minutes to *in vivo* exposure. In the remaining time homework assignments are discussed. During the last week of therapy, home visits on two consecutive days are carried out to promote generalization of treatment gains from the clinic to the patient's home and work environment. This is especially important for checkers who feel less responsible (and have less of an urge to ritualize) for events outside their natural environment.

*Imaginal exposure* involves directing the client's attention to scenes of gradually increasing anxiety-evoking themes. The more detailed these images are, the more effective they are in reducing obsessional anxiety. The scenes typically include descriptions of external situations that cause distressing thoughts and physiological responses, such as heart palpitation and sweating. All scenes are tape-recorded and clients are asked to listen to the tape and imagine the scenes as vividly as possible as part of their daily homework assignment.

*Exposure in vivo* refers to confrontation with situations or objects that generate anxiety or discomfort. Prolonged exposure is graded so that moderately disturbing thoughts or situations precede more upsetting ones. Exposure to each situation is repeated until distress decreased considerably. Clients are asked to expose themselves as closely as possible to the situations they fear during each treatment session for a period of 2 hours.

*Response prevention* consists of instructing the patient to refrain from engaging in any ritualistic behavior. For checkers, only normal checking (one check) is permitted. For items ordinarily not checked (e.g., empty envelopes to be discarded), checking is prohibited. At home, response prevention is conducted under the supervision of previously designated relatives or friends who monitor compliance and help the client remain in the fear-evoking situation until the urge to perform a ritual decreases to a manageable level. With highly motivated patients, supervision is not required.

Foa and Goldstein (1978), for example, treated 21 patients with ten daily 2-hour sessions of imaginal and *in vivo* exposure and supervised response prevention. At posttreatment, 18 patients were much improved on measures of rituals and obsessions. At follow-up, only 20% of patients were unimproved. A later study compared the use of imaginal exposure with that of combined imaginal and *in vivo* exposure. Half of the patients receiving exposure *in vivo* only had relapsed to various degrees at 9-month follow-up whereas patients receiving both imaginal and *in vivo* exposure had maintained their gains. Thus, at least some patients benefit from the addition of imaginal exposure. Foa *et al.* (1984) examined the separate and combined effects of exposure and response prevention both immediately after treatment and at follow-up. They found that exposure alone and response prevention alone were not as effective as the combined treatment. Therefore, an effective treatment should include both procedures.

## COURSE OF TREATMENT

As described earlier, John's treatment was preceded by an extensive assessment of his OC symptoms. During the information-gathering phase, the exposure treatment program was described to John. He was trained to monitor activities or thoughts that evoke an urge to ritualize and to note the time spent on his two major rituals, checking and seeking reassurance. Exposure exercises were determined on the basis of John's report about situations and thoughts that caused him distress and evoked an urge to ritualize. He was instructed in the use of a scale of Subjective Units of Discomfort (SUDs), which ranges from 0 to 100, with 0 meaning no distress and 100 indicating extreme distress. John was asked to rate each situation or thought using the SUDs scale.

On the basis of John's scores, the following hierarchy was constructed:

- making mistakes (doing things wrong; e.g., income tax return)                                                          100 SUDS
- driving in crowded areas without retracing route          100 SUDS
- losing money or credit cards                                          100 SUDS
- leaving the stove on                                                      100 SUDS
- leaving electrical appliances plugged in                         90 SUDS
- leaving the water and lights on                                      90 SUDS
- leaving doors unlocked                                                 90 SUDS
- leaving things lying around where someone could trip and fall                                                                      80 SUDS
- using electrical appliances and checking them only once    60 SUDS
- checking the door only once and leaving the house          60 SUDS

In the beginning of each session a Self-Monitoring of Rituals Form and a Homework Form were examined and John's difficulties in following the program were discussed. As described earlier, John tried to prevent disastrous consequences that he felt would result from his being neglectful. The core of his concern was the image of the disaster he might cause. Since such disasters cannot be enacted in reality (e.g., seriously injuring someone while backing up the car), imaginal exposure is especially important for checkers. The imaginal exposure scenes included situations, thoughts and images, bodily reactions, and feared consequences. To increase the vividness of the image threat, specific thoughts (e.g., "Did I pay enough attention?"; "Did I make a mistake?") and words, such as *fire, accident, flood, screaming, hurt, blood, helpless, siren, yelling, failing,* were included. John was asked to describe his imagery aloud and to note his level of discomfort (SUDs) periodically. During *in vivo* exposure, his most distressing concerns were addressed: making mistakes, harming someone, being less than perfect.

In the beginning of John's treatment, imaginal exposure was focused on disastrous consequences due to John's negligence. In the first session John was asked to imagine the following scene: He leaves his workshop door open inadvertently and his infant son enters the workshop and is seriously hurt when he stumbles over the tools. John feels terribly guilty because he knows he could have prevented this accident. His wife blames him and calls him an irresponsible father.

During *in-vivo exposure,* John was required to turn the lights on and off once, to turn the microwave on and off once, and to open and close doors and windows once. After each action he was required to leave the room immediately and focus his attention on his failure to check these objects. This procedure was repeated throughout the session with different switches and windows.

During the following five sessions John was asked to imagine the following scenes: In the first scene he forgets to unplug his new television and his stereo during a thunderstorm, and they are damaged by lightning. Because they were not covered by insurance, he has to use his savings in order to repair the TV set and therefore he cannot afford to buy a new bike for his son's birthday. In another scene he neglects to check the stove, which remains on after he goes to sleep, and consequently his kitchen catches fire during the night and the house is destroyed. In a further scene he leaves the entrance door to his house unlocked and burglars vandalize his home while he is away.

After these imagery sessions John became more comfortable with the idea of damage to his belongings, and the therapy shifted to his fear of harming people while driving a car. Here is an example of the therapist's instructions to John during this phase:

> I would like you to imagine the following scene as vividly as you can, as if it is actually happening now and to experience the feelings as you imagine it.
>
> You are going to a supermarket to buy some groceries. You are rushing to your car. When you start backing up, in your mirror you catch a glimpse of an elderly lady walking toward her car. You continue backing up slowly without looking in your mirror. When you are ready to leave the parking lot you notice a bag of groceries on the ground, and as you are driving away you start thinking about the lady's groceries. Thoughts are running through your mind: "Did I cause

her to drop the groceries? Did I bump into her? Did I knock her down?" You feel compelled to go back and circle around the parking lot to make sure she is all right. But you resist doing so and you keep driving home.

You are at home, your children ask you to help them with homework, and you don't think any longer about the lady. Two hours later the doorbell is ringing, and two policemen are standing there. They are asking you if you are the owner of the truck, and you say yes. They have an eyewitness who says that you hit an elderly lady in front of a grocery store and drove away, leaving the scene of the crime. The policemen put you under arrest and take you to the police department. You cannot believe it, you are overwhelmed. Your worst fear just came true. You feel weak, you want to throw up, you want to faint. As you are taken in the police car, you notice all the neighbors are looking out of the windows. They see you in the back of the police car, and you feel ashamed. Everybody knows about it now.

At the police station you are treated as a criminal. They take your fingerprints and lock you up with muggers, robbers, and drug dealers. They give you a chance to call your wife. She yells at you: "You are a reckless driver. How am I going to explain it to my parents? Our life is ruined. How could I ever marry this bum? I am leaving you and taking the children with me. You are an irresponsible person and not worthy to live with us."

You are alone and still nobody from your family has come to help you get out of the detention. Thoughts are racing through your head: "I am a failure. I am no good. I will go to jail and never see my family again."

How do you feel right now? What is your level of anxiety?

Each of the scenes was 10 to 15 minutes long and was repeated three times in a 45-minute session. John was asked to dwell on every distressing detail in each image, including how guilty he feels about his negligence and how rejected he feels for being irresponsible. Simultaneously with imaginal exposure, John was asked to confront actual situations that triggered his urge to check. This included turning lights on and off once, opening and closing windows once, leaving his car unlocked in a parking lot, lighting candles, building a fire in the yard and checking only once, making mistakes (signing his checks with a wrong name, buying things without checking the price, underpaying a bill). After each action John was required to focus his attention on his failure to check these objects and thus on being held responsible for any harm caused by his negligence.

The following scenario illustrates the process of *in vivo* exposure:

THERAPIST: John, before we leave the office, I want you to turn the lights on and off. [*John performs the task.*] How distressed are you right now?

JOHN: Pretty anxious, about 50 SUDs.

THERAPIST: I want you to lock the workshop room without checking and take the key with you.

JOHN: Just thinking about it makes me more anxious. What if the door would not be locked and somebody would steal the lab equipment? It would be my fault.

THERAPIST: Well, this is the chance we all take. You need to learn to live with this kind of uncertainty. Should we go ahead and just do it?

JOHN:  Yes.

[*After John came back with the key, he and the therapist went out.*]

THERAPIST:  John, let's drive to the supermarket. When you drive, make sure that you do not check the rearview mirror. [*While John was driving, the therapist was not watching the traffic in order to counteract John's attempt to assign mental responsibility to the therapist.*]

JOHN [while in car with therapist]:  I am always afraid when I am backing up my car.

THERAPIST:  How likely are you to run over a person if you back up the car now?

JOHN:  Not very, because there are no people in the parking lot. You know, I am still thinking about the light. I am not sure that I turned off the light in your office.

THERAPIST:  Do you think it is safe, or shall we go and check? Suppose the light is still on. What is the worst that could happen?

JOHN:  It may cause fire, and I will be responsible for burning down the hospital.

THERAPIST:  How upsetting is this thought?

JOHN:  Very upsetting, about 90 SUDs.

THERAPIST:  How likely is it that the light on would result in burning down a hospital?

JOHN:  I know it is not likely, but it still could happen.

THERAPIST:  How long will it take for a light?

JOHN:  Maybe an hour.

THERAPIST:  Well, because it is unlikely, why don't we go ahead and go to the supermarket and find out later. You will get used to uncertainty. This is what the treatment is about.

In Sessions 6 through 15 exposure to similar situations was continued in various places until John's anxiety decreased substantially.

John's fear of making a fool of himself was also addressed during treatment by creating situations in which he acted "inappropriately," such as giving a tip to a cashier in a supermarket or paying for a pack of chewing gum with a hundred-dollar bill. In the beginning John opposed this instruction. He argued that paying a small amount of money with a hundred-dollar bill was an insult to the cashier and would result in her or his retaliation. After *in vivo* exposure John realized that he had exaggerated the risk of being criticized for doing something unusual. Over the course of treatment his fear of behaving foolishly decreased and the situations avoided decreased as well.

Treatment progressed in a satisfactory manner. John was compliant with exposure homework assignments and with response prevention. He showed habituation within and between exposure sessions. His subjective anxiety for feared situations decreased from 80–100 SUDs to 5–15 SUDs. His fear of being responsible for harm also decreased through his realization that performing tasks that he had previously avoided (e.g., checking only once) did not lead to disasters. Supported by the following statements, John was able to dismiss his obsessional thoughts: "I am only responsible for the work I per-

form, not the work of others" and "If I make a mistake, it is not the end of the
world, it is simply a mistake I can learn from." After 3 weeks of intense
behavior therapy, John's OC symptoms were mild. His obsessions and compulsions occupied less than 30 minutes per day.

The residual symptoms interfered only mildly with John's social activities and caused only occasional distress. He was able to resist his obsessive
thoughts and reported much control over his urges to perform rituals. His
scores on instruments measuring anxiety and depression decreased to normal
levels (see Table 1). At the end of treatment John no longer met *DSM-III-R*
criteria for obsessive–compulsive disorder.

## TERMINATION

During the last five sessions John was given the rules of normal checking. Response prevention requirements were relaxed to enable him to return to
what we consider to be a normal routine. In the final session John was
instructed to continue self-exposure to ensure periodic contact with previously
avoided situations and to prevent a relapse into his former avoidance patterns.
Part of John's maintenance regimen, for example, was to do the weekly shopping, in order to be exposed to his fear of buying the wrong things and his
fear of harming people while driving in crowded places. John was told that
whenever distressing thoughts entered his mind, he should dwell on them for
as long and as vividly as possible instead of pushing them away. He was
further encouraged not to engage in passive avoidance behavior, such as allowing his wife to make decisions in money matters or staying at home
instead of going out and making new friends.

For years John's wife was very frustrated because of his OC symptoms.
It was not surprising that she was impatient, expecting treatment to result in
complete symptom remission. John felt that his wife had set standards for his
functioning after treatment that he could not meet (e.g., applying for a higher-
paying position) and was distressed by the thought that his wife would not
accept him unless he became highly successful. To correct her unrealistic
expectations, John's wife was invited to participate in the last therapy session, during which the impact of her demands was discussed. This discussion
helped John and his wife redefine terms for living together (they decided, for
example, that John would look for a job with limited responsibility, that his
wife would maintain her part-time position, and that both would take care of
the children). This significantly reduced John's fear of being regarded as a
failure. The therapist explained to John and his wife that anxiety reactions
under stress are to be expected and do not reflect failure or relapse. His wife
was instructed not to protect John from upsetting situations but to encourage

him to reexpose himself immediately to the situation or thought that generated anxiety and the urge to ritualize.

## FOLLOW-UP

Before treatment John's work and leisure activities were severely curtailed by his OC symptoms and by his tendency to avoid situations that would distress him. As his symptoms decreased, John started to engage in social activities and was able to develop new interests to replace the ritualistic activities. It was especially important that John go back to work, but he was reluctant to do so. He avoided applying for a new job because he was afraid of inquiries as to the reasons for being out of work for a year. (Before treatment he had refused to apply for a job because of his fear of failing.) Four weeks after termination he had a partial setback, spending 60 minutes a day checking and obsessing about being rejected. Two telephone booster sessions helped John to overcome his fear of being a failure, and he finally went to a job interview (in which he found out that the interviewer was more interested in his previous job experiences than in the fact that he was absent from work for a year). He finally got a job, which entailed less responsibility than his former one. A telephone call 3 months later revealed that John was continuing to improve.

## OVERALL EVALUATION

John's case illustrates typical obsessive–compulsive behavior and concomitant psychopathology as well as a treatment with the aim of reducing symptoms. Exposure and response prevention were effective in reducing the severity of the OC behavior, depression, and general anxiety (see Table 1). The posttreatment depression scores support the hypothesis that depression in many OC patients is secondary to their OC symptoms and ameliorates with diminution of those symptoms.

A problem specific to treatment of patients with checking rituals arises when the urge to check is limited to the environment in which they feel especially responsible (e.g., at home, at work). This was also a problem in John's case. He lived 500 miles away from Philadelphia, where the treatment was conducted. Home visits are especially important in these cases in order to help clients generalize treatment effects to their natural environment.

Years of accommodation by family members to an obsessive–compulsive's symptoms (e.g., acquiescing to daily demands to participate in rituals or honoring requests for reassurance) establish maladaptive patterns of interaction that take time to change. Such patterns may interfere with maintenance of treatment gains and should be addressed in treatment when the OC symptoms decrease.

It is especially important to help OC clients adjust to their improvement and to function in their natural environment in the absence of OC symptoms. Patients who had become dysfunctional as a result of OCD need assistance in acquiring social skills in order to fill the vacuum that has been caused by the decrease in OC symptoms. Therefore, a follow-up program should include helping clients modify their lifestyle.

## REFERENCES

American Psychiatric Association. (1987). *Diagnostic and Statistical Manual of Mental Disorders* (3rd ed., rev.). Washington, DC: Author.

Beck, A. T., Ward, C. H., Mendelsohn, M., Mock, J., & Erbaugh, J. (1961). An inventory for measuring depression. *Archives of General Psychiatry, 4,* 561–571.

Foa, E. B., & Goldstein, A. (1978). Continuous exposure and complete response prevention of obsessive–compulsive neurosis. *Behavior Therapy, 9,* 821–829.

Foa, E. B., Grayson, J. B., Steketee, G. S., Doppelt, H. G., Turner, R. M., & Latimer, P. R. (1983). Success and failure in the behavioral treatment of obsessive–compulsives. *Journal of Consulting and Clinical Psychology, 51,* 287–297.

Foa, E. B., Steketee, G., Grayson, J. B., Turner, R. M., & Latimer, P. (1984). Deliberate exposure and blocking of obsessive–compulsive rituals: Immediate and long-term effects. *Behavior Therapy, 15,* 450–472.

Foa, E. B., Steketee, G., Kozak, M., & Dugger, D. (1987). Effects of imipramine on depression and obsessive–compulsive symptoms. *Psychiatry Research, 21,* 123–126.

Freund, B., Steketee, G. S., & Foa, E. B. (1987). Compulsive activity checklist (CAC): Psychometric analysis with obsessive–compulsive disorder. *Behavioral Assessment, 9,* 67–79.

Goodman, W. K., Price, L., & Rasmussen, S. (1989). The Yale-Brown Obsessive-compulsive Scale (Y-BOCS): Past development, use, and reliability. *Archives of General Psychiatry, 46,* 1006–1016.

Kringlen, E. (1965). Obsessional neurotics, a long-term follow-up. *British Journal of Psychiatry, 111,* 709–722.

Marks, I. (1987). *Fears, phobias, and rituals: Panic, anxiety, and their disorders.* Oxford: Oxford University Press.

Marks, I. M., Stern, R. S., Mawson, D., Cobb, J., & McDonald, R. (1980). Clomipramine and exposure for obsessive–compulsive rituals. -I. *British Journal of Psychiatry, 136,* 1–25.

McCarthy, P., & Foa, E. B. (1990). Treatment interventions for obsessive–compulsive disorder. In M. Thase, B. Edelstein, & M. Herson (Eds.), *Handbook of outpatient treatment of adults* (pp. 209–234). New York: Plenum.

Meyer, V. (1966). Modification of expectations in cases with obsessional rituals. *Behaviour Research and Therapy, 4,* 273–280.

Spielberger, C.D., Gorsuch, R. L., & Lushene, R. E. (1970). *Manual for the State-Trait Anxiety Inventory (self-evaluation questionnaire).* Palo Alto, CA: Consulting Psychologists Press.

Weissman, M. M. (1985). The epidemiology of anxiety disorders: Rates, risks, and familial patterns. In A. H. Tuma & J. D. Maser (Eds.), *Anxiety and the anxiety disorders* (pp. 275–296). Hillsdale, NJ: Erlbaum.

CHAPTER 13

# Posttraumatic Stress Disorder

## FRANK W. WEATHERS and TERENCE M. KEANE

### DESCRIPTION OF THE DISORDER

Posttraumatic stress disorder (PTSD), which develops following exposure to horrifying or life-threatening events, is a complex, debilitating disorder that can affect virtually every aspect of psychological functioning. Traumatic events that trigger PTSD include physical or sexual assault, combat, accidents (e.g., serious automobile or industrial accidents), and natural disasters such as earthquakes and floods.

The characteristic clinical presentation of PTSD includes three different groups of symptoms: First, individuals with PTSD reexperience the traumatic event through nightmares, flashbacks, or disturbing recollections. Reexperiencing symptoms, the hallmark of PTSD, often are provoked by some reminder of the trauma, but they can also occur in the absence of any obvious precipitant. These episodes involve replaying at least some of the sensory details of the trauma, and they are typically accompanied by the painful emotions elicited during the original event. Second, individuals with PTSD typically avoid reminders of the trauma and experience numbing of responsivity through loss of interest in important activities, social isolation or withdrawal, or emotional constriction. Third, those with PTSD experience increased physiological arousal, manifested in sleep disturbance, excessive irritability, exaggerated startle response, hypervigilance, or arousal in response to reminders of the trauma.

FRANK W. WEATHERS and TERENCE M. KEANE • Boston Department of Veterans Affairs Medical Center, Boston, Massachusetts 02130.

*Adult Behavior Therapy Casebook,* edited by Cynthia G. Last and Michel Hersen. Plenum Press, New York, 1994.

185

In addition to problems in each of these three core symptom clusters, individuals with PTSD often concurrently experience the symptoms of major depression, substance abuse, panic disorder, and other anxiety disorders. When evaluating and treating someone with PTSD, a systematic assessment for the presence of comorbid disorders is imperative, as these additional problems can complicate clinical decision making and can undermine progress in therapy if they are not identified and appropriately addressed.

The natural course of PTSD appears to be quite variable. Onset can occur immediately after the trauma or can be delayed for months or even years, when symptoms may surface unexpectedly, possibly in response to a stressful life event. Although symptoms can diminish over time, PTSD symptoms can be remarkably intractable and may persist for decades. It is common for World War II veterans, now 50 years posttrauma, to seek treatment for significant symptoms of PTSD. Although some have proposed that PTSD is a phasic disorder (e.g., Horowitz, 1986) with alternations of intrusive and avoidant/numbing periods, PTSD in combat veterans generally is characterized by a simultaneous mix of reexperiencing, arousal, and numbing and avoidance symptoms.

PTSD is not a rare disorder. In the Epidemiologic Catchment Area Survey (Helzer, Robins, & McEvoy, 1987) the lifetime prevalence of PTSD was found to be 1% in the general population, 3.5% for those who had suffered a physical attack (including rape), and 20% for Vietnam veterans who had been wounded. Other reports have found even higher prevalence rates. Kilpatrick et al., 1989, found that of 294 female crime victims 28% had a lifetime diagnosis of PTSD and 7% had a current diagnosis of PTSD. The National Vietnam Veterans Readjustment Study (NVVRS; Kulka et al., 1988) found that nearly 31% of male Vietnam veterans and 27% of female Vietnam veterans had a lifetime diagnosis of PTSD. The NVVRS also found that 15% of male veterans and nearly 9% of female veterans had a current diagnosis of PTSD.

Several broad conclusions can be drawn from these and similar studies: First, PTSD is at least as common in the general population as other kinds of psychopathology, such as schizophrenia and bipolar disorder.

Second, those who experience intense or prolonged traumatic events are much more likely to develop PTSD. For example, Kilpatrick et al. (1989) found that rape victims who had sustained an injury during the attack and who perceived their lives to have been endangered were more than eight times as likely to develop PTSD as victims who did not suffer a completed rape, sustain an injury, or perceive a life threat. Similarly, Kulka et al. (1988) found that the current prevalence of PTSD in Vietnam veterans who were exposed to very high levels of war-zone stress was more than double the current prevalence for the total sample.

Third, even though prevalence estimates vary widely, the prevalence of

PTSD is always less than 100%; that is, not everyone who is exposed to a traumatic life event develops PTSD. This suggests that PTSD results from a complex interaction between aspects of the trauma (e.g., severity of the traumatic event, degrees of life threat) and aspects of the trauma victim (e.g., biological vulnerability; prior exposure to trauma; presence of coping strategies for handling strong aversive emotions; availability of social support). When assessing and treating trauma victims who do develop PTSD, it is essential to consider both the objective features of the trauma and the individual's appraisal of the event.

## CASE IDENTIFICATION

John was a 42-year-old white Vietnam combat veteran referred to our PTSD clinic while he was an inpatient on a psychiatric unit. He had been admitted to the hospital during a severe depression, but his psychiatrist suspected that he also suffered from PTSD related to his combat experiences.

John lived with Beth, his wife of 20 years, and their three teenage children in a middle-class suburb of a large northeastern city. He grew up in the city, the third of seven children in an Irish Catholic family. Most of his siblings still lived in the area and continued to get together as a family, but John did not feel particularly close to them. Although he was raised as a Catholic, he described himself as not being very religious. John completed high school before the military, and he had an associate's degree in business management. He was the assistant general manager at a wholesale plumbing supply company in the city, where he had worked since his discharge from the military in 1988.

## PRESENTING COMPLAINTS

This was John's first admission to a psychiatric unit. The hospitalization was ordered by a psychiatrist who had been treating John for depression for 18 months. Over the 2 months prior to admission John had become severely depressed and had contemplated suicide. He complained of most of the typical symptoms of depression, including dysphoria, anhedonia, poor appetite and sleep, and impaired concentration. In addition, John reported a number of symptoms of PTSD: He was having nightmares about his combat experiences nightly, as well as daily intrusive thoughts of Vietnam that left him unable to work. He was socially withdrawn, and the only emotion he could feel was intense anger. He was alarmed about his potential for violence: He was furious with Beth, who had been accusing him of being emotionally unavailable, and he was afraid that he might lose control and hurt her.

## HISTORY

In the 2 years prior to hospitalization John had endured a series of events involving death and illness. He had been treated for cancer twice and had worried through a third episode, which turned out to be a false alarm. Four months prior to hospitalization one of his closest friends died unexpectedly. Two months later his mother suffered a stroke and was left confined to a wheelchair, unable to speak. Finally, a month before John came to the hospital, a neighbor's son died of the same cancer to which John's son had lost a leg as a five-year-old.

As these stressful events accumulated, John felt increasingly saddened, frightened, and worried. However, rather than seeking support from family or friends, he became increasingly withdrawn as he struggled stoically to maintain control over his emotions. Beth was sensitive to John's distress and tried to reach out to him, but he was uncommunicative. She became increasingly frustrated with him, partly because she felt he was unresponsive and unappreciative of her efforts to help him and partly because he was not meeting her own emotional needs. She began to confront him and in her desperation even threatened to leave him. On the day John was hospitalized a heated argument with Beth had left him feeling suicidal and homicidal and had precipitated his admission to the psychiatric unit.

Although the events of John's past 3 years would have strained anyone's emotional resources, they were especially taxing to him for two reasons: First, his upbringing had left him poorly equipped to cope with painful emotions. John developed an impassive style at an early age. In his family strong emotions were neither displayed nor discussed. Although John felt loved, his parents weren't openly affectionate with the children or with each other. Resentments went unexpressed and unresolved, and open displays of anger were explicitly discouraged. John learned to keep his feelings to himself—and eventually to keep his feelings from himself. Second, he had encountered much illness and death throughout his life, both as a child and in Vietnam, and these new stressors stirred up painful memories he had struggled to avoid.

Significantly, John's mother was ill during much of his childhood, and when he was 10 she was in bed much of the time during a difficult pregnancy. John was resentful that she wasn't available to take care of him, but because she was ailing he felt guilty for having these feelings. He had no one with whom he could talk openly about these feelings, and he resolved the conflict by suppressing his anger and hurt. He learned to manage all strong negative emotions by minimizing them or suppressing them, and he became emotionally self-reliant, believing that asking for help was at best an imposition on others and at worst a sign of weakness.

Growing up, John experienced two traumatic events related to illness and sudden, unexpected loss. When he was 8 years old he stayed overnight in the hospital for the first of three mastoid operations. His parents stayed with him as long as they were allowed, but they had to leave when visiting hours ended. John was terrified. He felt his parents had deserted him, and he felt helpless and alone. These feelings of vulnerability and apprehension would be recapitulated in Vietnam and during his bouts with cancer

A more tragic incident occurred when John was 15. His beloved older sister, who in many ways was a mother figure for the other children, died abruptly of scarlet fever. John was devastated by her unforeseen death, but he only openly grieved her loss once, at her funeral. In the more than 25 years since her death he had avoided her grave, even though she was buried a short distance from where he worked. In his typical fashion, he refused to allow himself to think about his sister, keeping his grief hidden from others and from himself.

John joined the Army in 1965 at the age of 19 and served one 12-month tour in Vietnam. He saw heavy combat action as a door gunner on a helicopter for nearly 6 months of his tour, and his unit served in and around Hue during the Tet Offensive of 1968. His combat experiences were harrowing: He was appalled by the death that surrounded him, and he lived in constant dread of being injured or killed himself.

After he left the military, John tried to put Vietnam behind him. He refused to talk about it with anyone, and he struggled to push the terror, horror, and sadness he had felt out of his mind forever. Initially, he was successful at suppressing memories of Vietnam while he became absorbed with working, starting a family, and buying a home. In the early 1970s the only conscious legacy of the war for him was a new seriousness and aloofness, and occasional nightmares and intrusive thoughts.

In the years that followed, John would endure two more events involving unexpected, life-threatening illness. His oldest son was diagnosed with cancer at the age of five. Although the boy was treated successfully and the cancer went into remission, John and Beth were distraught. Incredibly, this tragedy was repeated a few years later when their second son also was diagnosed with cancer and had to have his leg amputated. This second cancer was a devastating blow for the family. Beth sought treatment for depression, and John fought to control his own anguish, which was exacerbated by painful memories and emotions related to his combat experiences and to the loss of his sister. He became increasingly unable to contain his emotions, and when he himself was diagnosed with cancer, he decided to seek psychiatric help.

John worked with one therapist for 6 months, then was transferred to the psychiatrist who eventually would order his hospitalization. Throughout these 2 years John increasingly experienced intrusive memories and terrifying nightmares of Vietnam. He would wake from these nightmares trembling and sweating profusely; sometimes the dream state persisted as he awoke, and he would assume combat postures, such as firing a gun at an imaginary enemy. On many nights his screams during nightmares would wake the entire household. Despite these symptoms, he steadfastly refused to talk about Vietnam in his therapy sessions, always managing to divert the discussion to a recent crisis. Thus, it can be said that prior to coming to the hospital John had never spoken to anyone in depth about the traumatic events to which he had been exposed in Vietnam.

## ASSESSMENT

When the clinician first greeted him on the ward John appeared haggard and sullen and his mental state appeared to be a complex blend of bitterness, exhaustion, and desperation. He spoke slowly and deliberately, and though he conveyed an urgency to deal with Vietnam, he was reluctant to tackle the subject directly. The clinician worked to establish rapport by being empathic and nonjudgmental and by allowing John to set the pace of the interview.

It was clear by the end of the first session that John had become so distraught that he could no longer avoid talking about what had happened to him in Vietnam. He had struggled for 20 years to keep his emotions in check, but now he was unable to maintain his previous level of self-control and it frightened him. As he put it, "I've had a lot of bad things happen and I've always held it together, but now it's getting to me. I'm so depressed. It got to the point that two weeks ago I wanted to kill myself. I get so mad that I'm going around punching holes in walls. I've held it all in and it's about to explode." When the clinician outlined the evaluation procedure to John and asked him what he wanted to get out of it, he explained, "I just want to know if Vietnam has anything to do with how bad I feel, and if so I want to know what I can do about it."

John was given a comprehensive evaluation for PTSD, following a standard protocol. Because of the complexities of the typical clinical picture in PTSD, and because of the inherent limitations of any single assessment method or instrument, we advocate a multimethod assessment procedure in which converging evidence from interviews, questionnaires, and a physiological assessment are combined to yield a detailed description of the client's current functioning (see Keane, Wolfe, & Taylor, 1987, for a complete description of the evaluation procedures).

In John's case each component of the assessment provided strong evidence for a diagnosis of PTSD. On interview John clearly met the diagnostic criteria for PTSD: First, his combat experiences clearly qualified as a stressor outside the range of normal human experience. Although his entire 12-month tour was harrowing, several incidents were particularly traumatic. On his very first day in Vietnam, just as John disembarked from the plane, Viet Cong snipers opened fire on the landing strip, killing a number of troops on the runway. John was stunned and horrified at this initiation into the war. On another occasion his helicopter was involved in a firefight with a group of Viet Cong. During this engagement he witnessed the other door gunner, a close friend, get shot through the head by an enemy bullet. He also recalled an incident in which his unit was driving in a convoy through a supposedly safe village when grenades were thrown at them. They opened fire on the villagers, killing many of them. Later that night they were trapped on a beach waiting for a boat to transport them, and they were terrified that they would be attacked in retaliation for killing the villagers.

Second, John reported reexperiencing these and other traumatic events. During the day he would spend several hours ruminating over his combat experiences, unable to control the images. He had nightmares almost every night. During his hospitalization he once awoke from a nightmare thinking his two roommates were Viet Cong; he was terrified as he tried to figure out which one of them he should shoot first. He also described having occasional dissociative episodes during the day in which he would go into a daze and hear sounds and see images from Vietnam.

Third, John described a numbing of responsiveness that had developed subsequent to Vietnam. He felt detached from other people, even from his family and closest friends. Beth corroborated this, saying that she had noticed a dramatic change in John when he returned from Vietnam. It was an old sore point between them that when John first got back he completely withdrew socially and refused to see Beth for 6 months, even though they had dated for several years, had planned to get married, and had corresponded nearly every day while he was in Vietnam.

Over the years John had actively avoided all reminders of Vietnam, including veterans' activities and movies, books, or television shows on the war. In addition, it appeared that he had psychogenic amnesia for some of his combat experiences. For example, he referred to an extended search-and-destroy mission, in which his unit was sent out to locate and engage Viet Cong forces, as "the 42 missing days." He said that he could recall being sent out in the choppers and dropped off and he could recall coming back to base having lost a number of men, but he could not recall what happened in the interim.

Finally, John reported many symptoms of hyperarousal. He had considerable difficulty sleeping almost every night, and his concentration during the day was so poor that his job performance had declined precipitously. He was extremely irritable and would act out his anger by yelling and punching holes in walls. Beth said his anger was so intense she was frightened of him at times. In addition, John reported that a variety of external stimuli, such as helicopters, tree lines, and Asian people, could trigger intrusive thoughts or flashbacks.

Psychometric data confirmed the diagnosis of PTSD. John scored a 133 on the Mississippi Scale for Combat-Related PTSD (Keane, Caddell, & Taylor, 1988), which placed him well above the suggested cutoff of 107. In addition, he obtained an 8-2-7 profile on the MMPI, which was quite similar to the modal 2-8/8-2 profile that has been identified in other veterans with PTSD (Keane, Malloy, & Fairbank, 1984), and he scored exactly at the suggested cutoff of 30 on the MMPI PTSD scale (Keane et al., 1984).

Perhaps the most compelling evidence for a diagnosis of PTSD came from John's reaction to the physiological assessment. He was apprehensive at the outset and appeared extremely tense throughout the neutral slides and the first few combat slides, as if he were determined to physically restrain his emotional responses. He began to tremble, his face turned ashen, and he began to mutter indistinctly, yet he insisted on continuing with the assessment. However, the clinician terminated the procedure after the seventh of nine combat slides. The image on this particular slide, which had been photographed in the air from the perspective of a door gunner on a helicopter, proved to be a powerful idiographic retrieval cue for John. He began to shake, partly from the force with which he was contracting all his muscles, and he gripped his fists tightly in front of him as if he were firing a machine gun. His muttering grew louder, and he began to thrash about in the chair. He dissociated to the point that he was completely unaware of his surroundings, and he was unable to respond to the clinician for several minutes.

As he began to recover, John described the scene that he had relived and explained why that particular slide had triggered such a powerful reaction. When his physiological record was examined later, it revealed a dramatic increase over baseline heart rate during the combat slides, in particular during the slide that triggered the flashback.

In sum, the assessment data confirmed that John suffered from both PTSD and major depression, and the clinician recommended that the various symptoms of these syndromes be the primary targets of treatment. The clinician also recommended that other closely related problems be addressed, including the marital discord between John and Beth; John's difficulty in expressing his emotions, particularly his difficulty modulating anger; and his unresolved grief over the loss of his sister.

## SELECTION OF TREATMENT

Our treatment approach to PTSD is based on a learning model of psychopathology proposed by Levis and his colleagues (e.g., Levis, 1985; Levis &

Hare, 1977; Stampfl & Levis, 1967) and extended to PTSD by Keane, Zimering, & Caddell (1985). According to this model, the aversive emotions that are elicited during combat become associated with a range of previously non-feared stimuli, including external cues (e.g., helicopters, tree lines, smell of diesel fuel) and internal cues (thoughts, images, mood states). The traumatic conditioning events are stored in memory and can be reactivated not only by the conditioned cues originally present during the trauma but, through the processes of generalization and higher-order conditioning, by cues that only resemble in some way the original conditioned cues.

When memories of the trauma are reactivated by conditioned cues, trauma victims experience painful emotions similar to the emotions experienced during the trauma. They attempt to reduce or terminate these feelings by avoiding both the memories and the conditioned cues that may reactivate the memories. Avoidance may involve a variety of behaviors (avoiding war movies, fireworks, and veterans' activities, and using drugs or alcohol to block out memories) and cognitive strategies (distraction, suppression, psychogenic amnesia).

Avoidance may be so extensive that it interferes with work or social functioning. Also, avoidance is rarely completely successful, and trauma victims are unable to eliminate reactivation of the traumatic memories. We view as symptoms both the restrictions on lifestyle choices that avoidance may cause and the reactivation of the traumatic memories with the concomitant painful emotions. From our perspective the therapeutic task is to determine the external and internal conditioned cues that are being avoided and then expose the client to those cues until the conditioned emotional responses to those cues extinguish.

The client can be exposed to conditioned cues either in the environment (*in vivo* exposure) or in imagery (imaginal exposure). We employ a version of imaginal exposure known as implosive therapy (see Levis & Hare, 1977; Lyons & Keane, 1989), in which the client is exposed to a range of conditioned cues in imagery in a deliberate effort to elicit the aversive emotions while preventing the usual avoidance strategies. When exposure in imagery is sustained for a sufficiently long period and avoidance is prevented, the conditioned cues lose their power to elicit the aversive emotions (see Levis & Hare, 1977, for a detailed classification scheme for conditioned cues).

The efficacy of implosive therapy for PTSD has been documented in case study reports and controlled clinical trials (Fairbank & Keane, 1982; Keane, Fairbank, Caddell, & Zimering, 1989; Keane & Kaloupek, 1982). It appears to be particularly effective in reducing such positive symptoms of PTSD as reexperiencing symptoms and conditioned fear responses. We typically use implosive therapy in conjunction with skills-training interventions designed to address such negative symptoms as social withdrawal and communication deficits. In John's case two adjunct skills-training interventions were used: First, in marital therapy sessions the clinician provided training in communication skills through instruction, modeling, and encouragement. Second, throughout the course of therapy the clinician used cognitive restructuring to challenge John's irrational beliefs regarding issues such as asking others for help or expressing feelings.

## COURSE OF TREATMENT

Following completion of the assessment the clinician outlined the conditioning model conceptualization of PTSD and described how repeated, prolonged exposure to feared and avoided cues leads to extinction of the conditioned emotional responses to those cues. This rationale made sense to John and he volunteered, "It's just like when my son lost his leg to cancer. At first I kept crying and I could hardly stand to even think about it, but then as I had to explain the story over and over to different people it got easier and easier to deal with." The clinician also predicted to John that he actually might feel somewhat worse initially as painful buried memories and feelings began to surface and explained that this was a normal and positive indicator that he was working effectively in treatment.

The clinician explained that treatment would consist primarily of imaginal exposure but also might include *in vivo* exposure to feared situations, such as visiting his sister's grave, visiting the Vietnam Memorial in Washington, D.C., and watching Vietnam movies. The clinician helped John develop a list of traumatic scenes and informed him that exposure would be both graded (in the sense that he didn't have to start with the most upsetting scene) and ungraded (in that once a scene had been selected for exposure, the idea was to maximize anxiety and arousal in order to maximize extinction).

In the first treatment session the clinician led John through a relaxation induction and then through a guided imagery exercise using a neutral scene. Within a therapy session, relaxation allows the client to concentrate more fully on imagery and facilitates a return to a comfortable baseline after an arduous exposure session. Outside of therapy, relaxation provides the client with a coping strategy for dealing with unpleasant arousal. Training in guided imagery enhances the clarity of feared cues, which boosts the effectiveness of imaginal exposure. The clinician also explained to John several guidelines for participating in implosive therapy, as follows:

> John, as we start to do this work there are several things to keep in mind. First, it's important to make these scenes as realistic as possible by putting yourself right into them as if they actually were happening to you. We'll start a scene by having you describe an event in as much detail as possible, and then I'll start to work with you to help you stay with the scene and explore it more fully. Sometimes I may ask you to imagine things that never really happened, but that you might be afraid

could happen, and I want you to make those things as realistic as possible too. You're like an actor getting into a role, putting yourself fully into a scene and feeling all the emotions, and I'm like the director helping you with your part.

John had excellent imagery skills and found it easy to put himself completely into scenes. He quickly developed a knack for incorporating hypothesized cues into the realistic aspects of a scene, and he displayed numerous overt signs of anxiety, making it relatively easy for the clinician to test the impact of exposure to various cues.

An early session included the following exchange. In the first presentation the therapist has John "walk through" the scene with minimal prompts in order to elicit reportable cues and information relevant to hypothesized cues. In the second presentation the therapist becomes much more active and directive. He elaborates the reportable cues, embellishes the scene with additional cues, and directs John to maintain focus on the most anxiety-arousing aspects of the scene. The therapist focuses on four themes in the second presentation: (a) horror and fear; (b) physical pain and suffering; (c) helplessness and loss of control, predictability, and safety; and (d) existential fear and grief over loss of a loved one (the cues related to mourning were particularly powerful for John and were probably related to existential fear and to his unresolved grief related to the deaths of his sister and his buddies in Vietnam).

THERAPIST: You are going back to 1968. It's your first day in the country, and you're on the plane approaching the airstrip. Put yourself there now. What's going on?

JOHN: [calmly] Okay, I'm on the plane, no problem, no sweat. Everyone's fine. We're all loose, joking around. We're flying into a secure area, so no big deal. The plane lands and everyone starts to get ready to get off. They open up the ramp on the plane.

THERAPIST: What do you notice around you?

JOHN: When they open the ramp, I hear it hit the pavement. [pause] Bam! The heat hits you like a wave. God it's hot, and all the smells . . . [breathes in] Now the guys in back start to unload out of the plane. I'm about a third of the way back, so some of them are ahead of me and they're going down the ramp. I get up and start to head down and . . . [pauses; grimaces and clenches fists tightly]

THERAPIST: Go on.

JOHN: [in loud, anguished voice; rushing] All of a sudden we get hit! There's gun fire coming from somewhere, and everyone's confused and they just start running, and guys are getting hit and falling down on the runway and oh God, I don't know where to run and someone's yelling at me, "Over here, over here," and I start running toward some shelters. [visibly anxious] I'm so scared and they said this place was safe . . . we don't even have weapons yet! [long pause; appears fully engaged in scene; trembling] And then it's all over and we get out of the shelters and go back out on the runway to try to help the guys who are down. [pause; begins to sob; talking through tears] Jesus, they're screaming for help and some of them are dead. I go out to help this one guy, try to tie something around his leg to keep it from bleeding, and he's screaming for help. [*long pause; moaning*] And then they open up the plane again, and I look back at the rest of the guys coming down the ramp, and some of them start throwing up, and I realize I feel like a veteran already . . . I can take this stuff and they can't, and they seem so young to me. Ten minutes ago I probably looked the same as them, and now I'm a veteran.

THERAPIST: [*long pause; gently*] Okay, let yourself come back into the room now. [*pause*] What did that scene bring up for you?

JOHN: [*opens his eyes; looks drained*] It was scary. I remember it like it was yesterday.

THERAPIST: What other feelings came up for you? What do you make out of that scene?

JOHN: I didn't want to die. I felt helpless, scared. None of us knew what to do. We didn't have any weapons. We were so unprepared; they told us it was safe and I believed them.

THERAPIST: Anything else?

JOHN: I felt angry. I felt angry that they told us it was safe when it wasn't. I felt angry at the sniper. I was there maybe 15 minutes and I already hated the whole country. I wanted some payback. I felt so sorry for those guys who died. They barely even got off the plane . . . think of their families and girlfriends who'll never see them again.

THERAPIST: How anxious or upset did you get during the worst part of the scene, if 0 means not at all and 10 means extremely anxious or upset.

JOHN: I would say about a 6 or 7.

THERAPIST: And how about right now?

JOHN: Probably about a 3.

THERAPIST: Okay, we're going to go back through the scene, and this time I'll be more involved. I'll ask you to focus on certain parts of the scene, and I'll ask you to imagine some things that didn't actually happen. So go ahead, close your eyes, and put yourself back into the scene. It's 1968, it's your first day in the country, and you're on the plane approaching the airstrip.

JOHN: Yeah, I'm on the plane, I'm feeling fine. Everything's all right. They told us we're flying into a secure area. So the plane lands and rolls to a stop. They open up the ramp and I hear it hit the ground. [*clearly visualizing the scene; slight body jerk when ramp hits the ground*] The heat is unbelievable, and there's all these smells— diesel fuel, jungle smells.

THERAPIST: Feel the heat wash over you. You break into a sweat and you feel the beads of sweat start to run down your face. Breathe in all those smells. [*pause as John responds to suggestions*] Go on.

JOHN: The guys in back start to unload, and then I get up and head to the top of the ramp. I go down the ramp, and just as I get to the runway I hear gunfire coming from somewhere. We're being attacked! [*appears less anxious than in first presentation*] I don't know what to do, and then I hear somebody yelling, "Over here, over here," and I start running.

THERAPIST: Slow it down. Everything's in slow motion. Focus on the gunfire. [*speak-

*ing very deliberately*] Listen very carefully so you can hear every shot. Where is the gunfire coming from?

JOHN: It's . . . I think it's coming from the right, from the jungle up that hill.

THERAPIST: Hear the shots coming from that hill. Hear each one ring out very clearly. Slow it all down, feel it all in slow motion. Feel yourself frozen in place as your mind is racing and you're trying to run for cover and you realize you're being shot at. This isn't make-believe, this isn't practice. This is for real! These are real bullets and you could easily be killed and you don't know what to do or where to run to save yourself. You think about running for cover, but you're stuck and can't move. You're a sitting duck out here on the runway. A minute ago you were SAFE and everything was FINE, and now all of a sudden you're about to be killed and you're COMPLETELY AND UTTERLY HELPLESS to do anything about it. [*John groans; his fists are clenched and he looks highly distressed.*] Look up at the hill and see the sniper up in the trees. See yourself in the sights of his rifle; see your head right in his sights. He's got a bead on you, and the bullet in the chamber has your name on it.

JOHN: [*loud voice; tormented*] I'm going to die! God, I don't know where to run! I don't want to die!

THERAPIST: Yes, you're going to die and you NEVER EXPECTED TO DIE and there's NOTHING YOU CAN DO. See the sniper squeeze the trigger, slowly, deliberately. You're an easy target, and now the bullet is coming straight at your head, slowly, slowly. It's the bullet meant just for you, and there's nothing you can do to stop it . . . or maybe he'll just toy with you a little. You're a sitting duck, and he can pick you off whenever he wants. Maybe he'll shoot your legs first and then your arms and watch you writhing in agony, bleeding, suffering unbelievable pain. See his face leering at you, mocking your helplessness. He's completely in control, and there's nothing you can do. He's got your number, he's completely in control, he can blow you away whenever he feels like it.

JOHN: [*fully engaged in the scene; shaking*] No! I can run away, I can get away! I'm not going to die here, I'm not! I can make it!

THERAPIST: Stay with the fear. You can't get away and you know it. You're going to die here. THERE'S NOTHING YOU CAN DO TO ESCAPE. Look around at the other bodies on the runway—twisted, mangled, bleeding all over the ground. Some of them aren't dead yet. They're suffering, they hurt so much, and one of them reaches up to you with a bloody hand. Listen to them screaming, "Help me, Help me," but there's no help for them . . . See yourself as one of them. Feel yourself in total agony and there's no one to help you—you hurt so much and you scream so loud and you CAN'T GET THE HELP YOU NEED! You're going to die. You're going to be dead just like the lumps of flesh lying all around you. Someone will be coming along to scrape you up into a body bag . . . Imagine yourself in that body bag. Just another bag of bones and flesh, and they zip it around you tight. Nothing left but darkness. Nothing left.

JOHN: [*moans; looks horrified*]

THERAPIST: You're dead. Really dead now . . . How will your family react? Johnny's never coming back. How will Beth take it? You're never coming back, they'll never see you again. It's over, just like that. One minute you're here, the next minute you're gone. Death can happen that quick. And how will they hear about it? A telegram maybe: "YOUR SON IS DEAD." And imagine your mother's reaction, how hurt she will be at losing her son. See her face as she reads the news . . . No more get-togethers, no more Christmases with everyone there, and everyone happy. Just death. Nothing left at all. Nothing.

JOHN:    [*sobs but appears less anxious than earlier in the scene*]

THERAPIST:    [*long pause*] Okay, when you're ready, let yourself come back into the room.

Following this exchange John indicated his peak SUDS during the second presentation reached a 9 and declined to a 3 by the end of the scene. The clinician encouraged him to talk about any new memories and feelings that emerged for him during the session, and the session concluded with a brief relaxation induction with pleasant imagery. Although the session had been emotionally taxing, John felt sufficiently comfortable to drive home.

John was seen over an 18-month period. Sessions were held once or twice a week for the first 6 months and focused primarily on imploding three traumatic scenes. John remained extremely depressed throughout this period, and he also experienced a marked increase in intrusive thoughts and nightmares of his combat experiences. This is a common result of imaginal exposure and indicates that the associative networks of trauma memories are being accessed rather than repressed. The clinician framed this result as an indicator of progress and explained that John was beginning to allow himself to experience these painful memories and affects that previously he had worked so hard to avoid.

After 6 months sessions were reduced to two or three times a month, and John began to focus less on fearful memories and more on loss experiences and grief. The clinician encouraged him to visit his sister's grave, and in one session John and the clinician met in a cemetery for *in vivo* exposure to cues related to death. Soon after, Beth accompanied John to his sister's grave. Two subsequent sessions involved imaginal exposure to his sister's death, and John began to allow himself to experience genuine grief over her death. A few weeks after visiting his sister's grave John went to the Vietnam Memorial in Washington, D.C., for the first time, and he began to explore the sadness related to his losses in Vietnam.

In the second 6-month period John began to try new interpersonal behaviors. He tried being more open with Beth and his children about his feelings, and he began to be more assertive about his needs. Beth was responsive to these changes, but she continued to feel frustrated with his depression, his focus on Vietnam, and his medical problems, including recurrences of cancer. John was sensitive to her exasperation with him, and he would get angry and withdraw, feeling that his needs were not being met. They continued to struggle with these issues, but they made progress and the relationship remained solid.

In the last 6 months John appeared to have reached a plateau in terms of accessing and habituating to traumatic memories, and he showed considerably less arousal during imaginal exposure. He also reported a decrease in nightmares and intrusive thoughts, although he continued to experience them periodically. The clinician suggested that he and John watch the movie *Platoon* to test John's extinction to trauma-related stimuli. For two sessions John controlled his exposure to the movie with a remote control and watched the first third of the movie. This was a very powerful retrieval cue for him and brought up several new memories, which were discussed in session. Finally, he rented the movie by himself and watched it in its entirety at home. He was pleased with being able to watch the whole movie and took this to be a tangible indicator of progress.

## TERMINATION

Over the course of treatment John had become involved with a number of different caregivers. He remained in therapy with his psychiatrist, he began attending individual and marital sessions at a Vet Center, and he joined a cancer support group. He went from being unable to ask for help to trying to get as much help as he could. Beth felt that he was too involved in the various therapies, and as he began to improve she urged him to limit his therapy to his sessions at the Vet Center, which was near their home. At Beth's insistence John terminated his work at our clinic somewhat abruptly. The clinician had been encouraging John to consider terminating because he seemed to have made some significant gains and his progress seemed to have leveled off. When he left treatment, John agreed to contact the clinician if he felt he needed more help.

## FOLLOW-UP

The clinician contacted John 6 months after termination and invited him to come in for a follow-up discussion. He completed an abbreviated version of the standard assessment, including a structured interview to assess PTSD symptoms, questionnaires, and the physiological assessment procedure. The interview revealed that John was experiencing substantially fewer intrusive thoughts, that these were greatly reduced in intensity, and that he was experiencing fewer nightmares. He continued to feel some detachment from others and continued to avoid some reminders of Vietnam, although he said that he was fascinated by the Persian Gulf conflict and watched the television coverage almost nonstop, with no apparent increase in symptoms. He reported a marked reduction in irritability and denied any reactivity to reminders of Vietnam or any strong startle reactions. He did complain of continued difficulty concentrating at work, and he said he still had some difficulty with sleep disturbance.

The questionnaire data revealed mixed results. John continued to report very high levels of depression and anxiety, and his follow-up MMPI suggested that he was actually having more difficulties, not fewer. However, on other measures he showed significant reductions in symptomatology. This mixed pattern may in part be attributable to the stressors he had encountered since leaving therapy: His mother had passed away, one of his sons had experienced a recurrence of cancer, and he himself was experiencing continued medical problems.

The physiological assessment provided solid evidence of improvement. First, John was able to watch all the combat slides without terminating the session or having a dissociative reaction. Second, although he still showed some heart rate responsivity to the slides, it was considerably less than on his original assessment.

The most compelling evidence that treatment had been effective came from John's and Beth's subjective, global evaluation of his current functioning. John felt that although he was still symptomatic, the symptoms had decreased to the point that they were tolerable and no longer significantly disrupted his daily life. Beth was more emphatic about his progress:

> He can talk about Vietnam easier and he doesn't sit around and brood the way he used to. He's consistently in a better mood. He doesn't have nightmares anymore, or maybe just once a month. I think he's made some peace with Vietnam, and made some peace with himself. He's able to say how he feels about things, and he feels that our relationship is secure. He's even getting involved in more outside activities. It's like the old John is back again. The kids have noticed it too.

## OVERALL EVALUATION

Taken together, all the evidence indicates that John made considerable gains in the 2 years since he was referred to our clinic. He was not completely symptom free at follow-up, but it may be that there is no cure for chronic combat-related PTSD and that the most that can be accomplished is an alleviation of the most disruptive symptoms. The new stressors he had experienced over these two years may also have helped maintain or even exacerbate some symptoms. Perhaps the most important measure of the impact of treatment was that both John and Beth were pleased with the progress John had made.

In particular, they both reported feeling increased satisfaction with their marital and family life.

John received a number of different interventions, as is typical in Veterans Affairs Medical Centers, over the 2 years, and thus it is difficult to make causal statements regarding the efficacy of implosive therapy from these data. However, he showed a remarkable reduction in reexperiencing and hyperarousal symptoms, and the implosive therapy was the only intervention that systematically targeted his traumatic memories.

Clearly, the treatment of traumatized patients requires complex and multidimensional interventions. In its most severe forms, PTSD is a debilitating and persistent disorder with multiple social, psychological, and biological components. While psychoeducation, stress management, relapse prevention, cognitive therapy, and social skills training all are a part of the comprehensive approach to PTSD treatment, the foundation of clinical care for this disorder appears to be direct therapeutic exposure to traumatic memories.

## REFERENCES

Fairbank, J. A., & Keane, T. M. (1982). Flooding for combat-related stress disorders: Assessment of anxiety reduction across traumatic memories. *Behavior Therapy, 13*, 499–510.

Helzer, J. E., Robins, L. N., & McEvoy, L. (1987). Post-traumatic stress disorder in the general population: Findings of the Epidemiological Catchment Area Survey. *The New England Journal of Medicine, 317*, 1630–1634.

Horowitz, M J. (1986). Stress response syndromes (2nd ed.). Northvale, NJ: Aronson.

Keane, T. M., Caddell, J. M., & Taylor, K. L. (1988). Mississippi scale for combat-related posttraumatic stress disorder: Three studies in reliability and validity. *Journal of Consulting and Clinical Psychology, 56*, 85–90.

Keane, T. M., Fairbank, J. A., Caddell, J. M., & Zimering, R. T. (1989). Implosive (flooding) therapy reduces symptoms of PTSD in Vietnam combat veterans. *Behavior Therapy, 20*, 245–260.

Keane, T.M., & Kaloupek, D. G. (1982). Imaginal flooding in the treatment of a posttraumatic stress disorder. *Journal of Consulting and Clinical Psychology, 50*, 138–40.

Keane, T.M., Malloy, P. F., & Fairbank, J. A. (1984). Empirical development of an MMPI subscale for the assessment of combat-related posttraumatic stress disorder. *Journal of Consulting and Clinical Psychology, 52*, 888–891.

Keane, T. M., Wolfe, J., & Taylor, K. L. (1987). Post-traumatic stress disorder: Evidence for the diagnostic validity and methods of psychological assessment. *Journal of Clinical Psychology, 43*, 32–43.

Keane, T. M., Zimering, R. T., & Caddell, J. M. (1985). A behavioral formulation of posttraumatic stress disorder in Vietnam veterans. *The Behavior Therapist, 8*, 9–12.

Kilpatrick, D. G., Saunders, B. E., Amick-McMullen, A., Best, C. L., Veronen, L. J., & Resnick, H. S. (1989). Victim and crime factors associated with the development of crime-related post-traumatic stress disorder. *Behavior Therapy, 20*, 199–214.

Kulka, R. A., Schlenger, W. E., Fairbank, J. A., Hough, R. L., Jordan, B. K., Marmar, C. R., & Weiss, D. S. (1988). *Contractual report of findings from the National Vietnam Veterans*

*Readjustment Study (NVVRS): Executive summary, description of findings, and technical appendices.* Research Triangle Park, NC: Research Triangle Institute.

Levis, D. J. (1985). Implosive theory: A comprehensive extension of conditioning theory of fear/anxiety to psychopathology. In S. Reiss & R. R. Bootzin (Eds.), *Theoretical issues in behavioral therapy* (pp. 49–82). New York: Academic Press.

Levis, D. J., & Hare, N. A. (1977). A review of the theoretical rationale and empirical support for the extinction approach of implosive (flooding) therapy. In M. Hersen, R. M. Eisler, & P. M. Miller (Eds.), *Progress in behavior modification* (Vol. 4, pp. 299–376). New York: Academic Press.

Lyons, J. A., & Keane, T. M. (1989). Implosive therapy for the treatment of combat-related PTSD. *Journal of Traumatic Stress, 2,* 137–152.

Stampfl, T.G., & Levis, D. J. (1967). Essentials of implosive therapy: A learning-theory-based psychodynamic behavioral therapy. *Journal of Abnormal Psychology, 72,* 157–163.

# CHAPTER 14

# Bulimia Nervosa

## DAVID M. GARNER

## DESCRIPTION OF THE DISORDER

Bulimia nervosa is characterized by morbid overconcern with weight and shape leading to extreme and often dangerous weight-controlling behaviors. This eating disorder is generally conceptualized as a final common pathway, with symptoms resulting from the interplay of biological, psychological, familial, and sociocultural etiological factors. The clinical features and related psychopathology in bulimia nervosa are well documented and widely accepted. The essential features required for a diagnosis of this disorder are (1) recurrent episodes of binge eating (rapid consumption of a large amount of food in a discrete period of time) occurring at least twice a week for the past 3 months; (2) a feeling of lack of control over eating behavior during these binges; (3) self-induced vomiting, use of laxatives or diuretics, strict dieting or fasting, or vigorous exercising in order to prevent weight gain; and (4) persistent overconcern with body weight and shape (APA, 1993). There are various associated psychological symptoms, such as depression, anxiety, poor self-esteem, hostility, somatization, social maladjustment, confused sex-role identity, and borderline personality features, that may or may not have etiological significance in bulimia nervosa but, in any case, contribute to the heterogeneity in the disorder on presentation. Finally, bulimia nervosa results in potentially serious physical and psychological

DAVID M. GARNER • Department of Psychiatry, Michigan State University, East Lansing, Michigan 48824-1316.

*Adult Behavior Therapy Casebook,* edited by Cynthia G. Last and Michel Hersen. Plenum Press, New York, 1994.

sequelae that may not only perpetuate the eating disorder but may also cloud the assessment picture.

Although binge eating is considered the key symptom in identifying bulimia nervosa, agreement has not been achieved about the definition, measurement, or relative significance of this behavior in the disorder. There is relatively little empirical justification for the requirement that the episodes must be "rapid" and "discrete." Similarly, specifying that binges must be "large" is inconsistent with research indicating that a significant proportion of binges reported by bulimia nervosa patients involve small amounts of food (cf. Garner et al., 1992). There are many similarities between the clinical features of bulimia nervosa and the related disorder, anorexia nervosa. Both disorders are characterized by determined efforts to control body weight within certain limits, with body weight becoming the main or even sole gauge for self-evaluation. Binge-eating and recurrent inappropriate compensatory behavior in order to control body weight (i.e. self-induced vomiting, misuse of laxatives or diuretics) are required for a diagnosis of bulimia nervosa; however, these symptoms are present in about 50% of those cases diagnosed as anorexia nervosa. The main difference between the disorders is that anorexia nervosa patients must weigh 85% of body weight expected using norms for age and height. It is generally agreed that bulimia nervosa patients tend to have a more favorable response to treatment.

There are limitations to estimates of the incidence and prevalence of bulimia nervosa, since most estimates have been derived from methods that have not been well validated. However, it has been suggested that serious cases occur in as many as 1% to 4% of female high school and college students. Suspected cases of clinical eating disorders or subclinical variants are even more common among groups exposed to heightened pressures to diet or maintain a thin shape, such as ballet students, professional dancers, wrestlers, swimmers, skaters, and gymnasts. While there have been case reports of bulimia nervosa in young children and geriatric adults, the consensus is that it is rare in these age groups. Bulimia nervosa is less common in men than in women, but when it occurs it has a similar clinical picture.

## CASE IDENTIFICATION

At the time of the initial assessment Jane was a 24-year-old full-time university student, 5 feet 4 inches tall and weighing 110 pounds. Her highest adult weight, approximately 130 pounds, had been reached 8 years earlier, and her weight had fluctuated between 110 and 120 pounds since she achieved her lowest adult weight shortly thereafter, when she lost weight to 90 pounds. When her weight fell below 105 pounds, she reported, her menstrual periods ceased for approximately 6 months; thus, she met diagnostic criteria for anorexia nervosa at that time. The return of her periods, her weight at the time of assessment, and her binge eating patterns gave her a current diagnosis of bulimia nervosa. Jane was referred by her family physician, who had been aware of her eating disorder for the previous 3 years and had repeatedly attempted to refer her for treatment. Jane had resisted these attempts at referral since she felt that acknowledging a "psychiatric problem" would be humiliating to her and to her family. At the time of the initial assessment Jane lived alone in an apartment near the university and was working and attending a college of education, as she had for the previous 2 years. She had a steady boyfriend of four years, who was also working and attending college. Before enrolling in the university, Jane had lived at home with her family: her mother, a 46-year-old full-time homemaker; her father, then age 52 and a prominent radiologist in the city; and a brother, then age 17 and living at home.

## PRESENTING COMPLAINTS

Jane typically binged and vomited between one and ten times a day and had consciously attempted to restrict her food intake over the previous 6 years. She reported that she did not remember any days in the past 6 months in which she had not binged and vomited at least once. She indicated that bingeing and vomiting episodes would often last for 3 hours or more. The types of foods consumed on a binge typically consisted of those items prohibited from her diet, such as desserts and other sweet foods that were high in fat content. However, she would also binge on other foods that were not proscribed from her daily diet. Eating behavior during a binge was often frenzied and bizarre. A typical bout involved the impulsive purchasing of two to three dozen doughnuts; Jane would eat the top icing layer of each doughnut and then throw the remainder of it off the balcony of her apartment in order to avoid consuming it. Eating binges were followed by intense guilt, depression, and self-induced vomiting. Jane also reported abusing laxatives, taking between five and ten Ex-Lax tablets several times a week. There was no reported history of diuretic, alcohol, or drug abuse. Although binge eating episodes usually involved consuming more than one thousand calories of food before vomiting, Jane also described vomiting after eating small amounts because she felt guilty or bloated. The degree of disparagement and revulsion related to her body was striking, even for someone with a diagnosis of bulimia nervosa. Jane experienced her body as "disgustingly fat" and burst into tears several times during the initial interview because of thoughts of it. Her distress about her shape and weight was compounded by a marked cyclical edema related to vomiting and abuse of laxatives. Jane described feeling highly anxious about losing control over her eating, and she experienced severe depression on most days. She admitted that she had contemplated suicide many times but had not made any suicide attempts. She indicated that one of the major factors that prohibited her from committing suicide was the fact that she could not tolerate others seeing her body, which she viewed as grotesque.

## HISTORY

Jane described herself as being very concerned about her weight for as long as she could remember and stated that she was "chubby" as a child and adolescent. She indicated that her episodic bingeing began when she was about 17 years old following a period of intense dieting, which had resulted in about a 25-pound weight loss. Vomiting and laxative abuse began about 1 year later. At first, vomiting was infrequent, occurring usually less than once a month and following a particularly large binge eating episode. It progressed over the next year to its current level of one to ten times a day, with laxative abuse several times a week.

Jane described her early childhood in very positive terms. She indicated that her relationships with her mother, father, and brother were extremely close and supportive until she reached adolescence. Although there had always been pressure for academic achievement in the family, Jane had been a model student and had conformed to the expectations for superior performance without difficulties until she reached adolescence. She described her relationships with her parents as extraordinarily close and sometimes even "smothering." Both Jane's mother and father were extremely concerned about diet and weight. Her father was described as highly obsessional and preoccupied with keeping detailed records of family events. He was concerned about diet and health, which was later determined to be related to his own father's death from cardiac disease at a young age. Jane's mother apparently had developed anorexia nervosa during her own adolescence, and although her eating disorder improved without treatment, she remained extremely diet, fashion, and youth conscious.

Jane described being concerned about her own weight throughout her childhood; this was intensified markedly when she gained approximately 15 pounds at a summer camp at the age of 16. Mother became distressed at her daughter's weight gain and insisted that corrective action be taken. Jane made diligent efforts to restrict her intake, and, as indicated earlier, she gradually lost weight to about 90 pounds. However, she resented her mother's hypervigilance at mealtimes and the intensity of her mother's efforts to control food intake. Jane began having bouts of overeating, which she described as being disturbing but at the same time satisfying since she felt that it allowed her to discharge anger that had been building toward her mother. The binge eating escalated over time, and her weight increased to between 110 and 120 pounds. Jane continued to maintain excellent academic standing despite her depression and her eating disorder.

## ASSESSMENT

As with other eating-disordered clients, Jane's initial and ongoing assessment may be divided into two broad areas: The first includes the client's attitudes toward weight and shape as well as symptoms fundamental to the eating disorder. The second concerns the various psychological and social factors that are not specific to bulimia nervosa but that may predispose toward or maintain the eating disorder. Accordingly, the initial assessment of Jane's disorder covered several key areas, including the following: (1) weight history; (2) attitudes toward weight and shape; (3) presence, frequency, and duration of bingeing and vomiting; 4) details of weight-losing behaviors such as dieting, exercise, abuse of laxatives, diuretics, and appetite suppressants; (5) complications (self-induced vomiting, purgative abuse, and resulting electrolyte disturbances may cause various symptoms or abnormalities—such as general weakness, muscle cramping, edema, swollen salivary glands, erosion of dental enamel, paresthesia, various neurological abnormalities, kidney and cardiac disturbances, and finger clubbing or swelling—which should be evaluated by a physician familiar with the complications of eating disorders); (6) psychological state, with particular reference to depression, anxiety, and personality features; (7) impulse-related behaviors; (8) social and family functioning; (9) reasons for seeking treatment; and (10) motivation for change. The relevance of each of these areas is discussed in detail in the articles referenced at the end of this chapter. Clinicians should be familiar with specific questions or probes aimed as assessing eating disorder symptoms (Garner & Parker, 1993).

The increasing recognition that eating disorders are heterogeneous along various psychological dimensions provides the rationale for the assessment of the type, depth, and severity of associated symptomatology. The clinical features and background information that guide the approach to treatment are best derived from a clinical interview; however, psychometric evaluation with standardized psychological tests is also recommended. The Eating Disorder Inventory (EDI) is an instrument specifically developed to assess a range of psychological characteristics clinically relevant to eating disorders (Garner, 1991). The EDI is a standardized, multiscale measure composed of three subscales (Drive for Thinness, Bulimia, Body Dissatisfaction) assessing attitudes and behaviors concerning eating, weight, and shape. It also includes subscales that tap more general organizing constructs or psychological traits clinically relevant to eating disorders (Ineffectiveness, Perfectionism, Interpersonal Distrust, Interoceptive Awareness, and Maturity Fears). The EDI-2 adds three new constructs—Asceticism, Impulse Regulation, and Social Insecurity—to the original instrument.

Jane had markedly elevated EDI subscale scores on Drive for Thinness, Body Dissatisfaction, Bulimia, Ineffectiveness, Perfectionism, Asceticism, and Social Insecurity. Other self-report instruments indicated that she was experiencing severe depression, anxiety, poor self-esteem, and interpersonal sensitivity. Personality testing indicated that Jane had an obsessional style, and there was some evidence of poor impulse regulation, suggestive of a possible borderline personality disorder.

Much of the initial assessment interview with Jane was devoted to obtaining detailed information related to attitudes and behaviors pertaining to eating habits, dieting, and weight control practices. It was learned that Jane spent most weekends with her family but would not eat in front of any family member. Her level of depression and possible suicide risk presented a serious concern. Through detailed questioning, it was determined that much of her depressive thought content emanated from a sense of hopelessness about her condition. She was reassured to learn that treatment for her condition had a good likelihood of success, and it was determined that the current risk of suicide was low. Arrangements were made for Jane to contact either the primary therapist or a crisis center if she felt like harming herself.

After Jane was interviewed alone, she, her brother, and her parents were interviewed together. Jane's mother was an attractive women who appeared considerably younger than her stated age. She was tearful during the interview and blamed herself for her daughter's eating disorder. She described herself as an extremely insecure individual who avoided virtually all interpersonal contact outside the family. She confirmed that she suffered from anorexia nervosa as an adolescent and also admitted to marked concerns about her own weight as well as strict control over her own eating ever since. Battles over food intake were common in the family. Jane described her mother as continually trying to overfeed others in the family while she restricted her own food intake. Jane's mother would provide others in the family with prodigious amounts of food at mealtime, and Jane would either try to surreptitiously dispose of food or vomit after eating. The father was highly involved in his professional life and tended to leave all family matters in the hands of his spouse. He avoided eating foods served to the other members of the family by rigidly adhering to a low-cholesterol diet. Since his own father had died of a heart attack (at the age of 46), Jane's father described being preoccupied with his own diet and health. He failed to confront his wife or daughter about their odd eating behaviors since he basically accepted and shared their preoccupations about weight. Both parents had become quite concerned about Jane's weight gain in adolescence and had even suggested that she consider breast reduction surgery at the peak of her weight gain. Jane was unable to openly express any anger toward her parents related to their concerns about her weight. She idealized both parents and believed that the family environment had little to do with her eating disorder. Jane's brother was shy and withdrawn in the interview. He stated that he did not understand his sister's eating disorder and felt that it must be related to academic pressures.

## SELECTION OF TREATMENT

The treatment chosen was individual cognitive–behavioral therapy for Jane in addition to separate cognitive family therapy meetings for Jane and her family. Treatment reviews indicate that cognitive therapy is particularly effective for bulimia nervosa (Garner, Fairburn, & Davis, 1987). Many of the cognitive–behavioral techniques originally developed by Aaron Beck and colleagues for the treatment of depressive and anxiety disorders are directly applicable to bulimia nervosa. However, other methods have been developed or adapted to address those features that distinguish eating disorders from other diagnostic groups (Fairburn, 1985; Garner & Bemis, 1982, 1985). For example, much of the behavior of eating-disordered patients can be understood as a direct consequence of the firm conviction that weight or body shape is of the utmost importance in their overall self-evaluation. Because the cognitive–behavioral theory of eating disorders has generally not focused on early historical antecedents of symptomatic behavior, it has been described as a proximal or abbreviated model of pathogenesis (Garner & Bemis, 1982). The primary point of emphasis of the cognitive–behavioral view has been the analysis of functional relationships between current distorted beliefs and symptomatic behaviors related to eating, weight, and body shape.

Nevertheless, the cognitive–behavioral model is well suited for examining historical, developmental, or family interactional themes identified with some eating-disordered patients, although these themes have been described best by psychodynamic and family theorists. Such themes as fear of separation, engulfment or abandonment; failures in the separation–individuation process; false-self adaptation; transference; overprotectiveness; enmeshment; conflict avoidance; inappropriate involvement of the child in parental conflicts; and symptoms as mediators of family stability all involve distorted meaning on the part of the individual or the family, or both. Although the language, style, and specific interpretations may differ sharply between the cognitive–behavioral model and the dynamic model that has generated these respective formulations, it is notable that both orientations are specifically concerned with meaning and meaning systems. Moreover, the respective therapies are aimed at identifying and correcting misconceptions presumed to have developmental antecedents (Garner & Bemis, 1985). The advantage of the cognitive–behavioral approach is that it allows the incorporation of developmental themes when they apply to a particular client but does not compel all cases to fit into one restrictive explanatory system.

The cognitive–behavioral model of eating disorders also emphasizes the interplay between current cultural pressures on women to diet and the untoward consequences of dietary restraint. Given the current cultural pressures for thinness, it is not hard to understand how women, particularly those with persistent self-doubts, could arrive at the conclusion that personal failings are to some degree related to weight or that the attainment of slenderness would measurably improve self-estimation. It has been asserted that for some who develop eating disorders, the motivating factor does not seem to go beyond a literal or extreme interpretation of the prevailing cultural doctrine glorifying thinness (Garner, Rockert, Olmsted, Johnson, & Coscina, 1985; Garner & Wooley, 1991). However, for others the impetus is more complicated, with a range of psychological and interactional factors playing a role (Garner, 1993).

There are a number of general treatment principles and issues considered central to the cognitive–behavioral model, and these include the following: (1) giving special attention to the therapeutic relationship, (2) enhancing motivation for change, (3) using a directive style, (4) following a "two-track approach" (the first track pertains to issues related to weight, bingeing, and vomiting, and the second track addresses beliefs and thematic underlying assumptions that are relevant to the development and maintenance of the eating disorder), (5) recognizing and addressing ego-syntonic symptoms, (6) differentiating starvation symptoms from primary psychopathology, and (7) enlisting special strategies to normalize eating and weight. Since these have been described fully in previous publications (see references), they will be only briefly touched upon here to the extent that they pertain to the case material being presented.

## COURSE OF TREATMENT

After a complete individual and family assessment Jane's therapist provided an initial formulation of psychological and family factors that may have contributed to the development and/or the maintenance of her eating disorder and then reviewed psychoeducational material aimed at managing the eating disorder symptoms (Garner et al., 1985).

In cases where there is obvious family psychopathology, it is critical to recognize and counter any attempts to vilify family members as "the cause" of the eating disorder. Moreover, it is often difficult, particularly early in treatment, to differentiate primary psychopathology or family dysfunction from behaviors that are secondary to the eating disorder. In this case, the mother's unresolved eating disorder and the father's dread of physical illness needed to be addressed with the same sensitivity and compassion as Jane's eating disorder. That the therapist succeeded in doing so is evident in the following excerpt of the transcript of the first cognitive family therapy session:

THERAPIST [*to family*]: It is important to emphasize that it would be wrong to blame anyone for Jane's eating disorder. Rather, it is the goal of treatment to understand the values, beliefs, underlying assumptions, and feelings of each member of the family so that Jane can overcome her eating problems and also to provide the opportunity for other people to address difficulties they may identify as sources of concern.

MOTHER: But I feel like my own eating disorder and my pressuring Jane about weight is the cause of her current problems.

THERAPIST: Clearly, the concerns you and your husband have had about weight have had an impact, but I don't think that you planned to have an eating disorder yourself or that your husband had any malicious intent in his weight concerns. In fact, you have both suffered for many years without adequate help.

THERAPIST [*to Jane after family leaves the room*]: You and your family have been extremely helpful in giving me some idea of the evolution of your eating disorder. I think the factors that have probably contributed to your disorder can be divided into two broad areas. The first relates to things in your background that we have only touched upon now or that have not been discussed but need to be understood in order to help you recover from your eating disorder. Also, there may have been other things that have gone on in your past that may not even be related to your eating disorder but turn out to be important issues to address in treatment. The second relates to the fact that there is good evidence that many eating disorder symptoms are the direct result of dieting and weight suppression. Clearly, your extreme concerns about your weight and the pressures from other's to control weight have been prominent for almost ten years. This has occurred against the backdrop of a culture totally fixated on thinness as an ideal for feminine beauty, supported by a multibillion-dollar-a-year diet industry that profits on the insecurity that it breeds in women regarding their shape. This has been further reinforced by the strong and consistent messages from the health professions warning of the risks associated with obesity. I want to take a few minutes to review some specific points.

The therapist then reviewed some of the psychoeducational material about social pressures on women to diet, the biological resistance to weight change, and the range of "starvation" symptoms (including binge eating) that result from weight loss (Garner et al., 1985; Garner & Wooley, 1991). These points have to be covered carefully, with sensitivity to the resistance or fear they might generate. Periodic questions such as "Does this make sense so far?" and

"How do you feel so far about what I have said?" and awareness of nonverbal signs in the client of anger, fear, anxiety, and withdrawal are particularly important in pacing the presentation of the educational material. If the client balks at any point, the source of concern should be identified and explored. It may be necessary to proceed more slowly or to temporarily curtail the educational mode of discussion while attempts are made to deal with emergent issues.

The use of an educational approach has several major advantages: First, there is intrinsic value in clarifying misunderstandings related to bodily functioning and weight control. Second, the suggestion that certain symptoms and behaviors may be logically derived from cultural pressures on women to diet and from biological reactions to dieting, rather than being purely psychogenic in nature, may diminish potential untoward effects associated with psychiatric labeling. Third, sometimes educational material can provide the basis for testing and refining beliefs that drive symptomatic behavior. For example, Jane weighed herself at least 20 times each day and assumed that the dramatic daily shifts in her body weight reflected changes in actual body fat levels rather than changes in fluid retention due to edema. This assumption caused Jane to panic and to institute drastic weight control methods whenever her weight appeared to increase. By linking the weight changes to water retention rather than fat buildup, it was possible to reduce Jane's panic and also convince her that weighing herself less often was justified. At the same time, it was helpful to illustrate how closely tied her intense affect was to numbers on the scale, irrespective of their true meaning. This was underscored in a simple experiment:

THERAPIST: When you step on the scale, how do you feel?

JANE: I feel extremely apprehensive beforehand, and then I completely panic when I step on the scale and my weight has gone up.

THERAPIST: Do you feel elated when your weight goes down?

JANE: Sometimes I feel good, but usually I feel upset because I know it will just go up later.

THERAPIST: What does it mean when the numbers go up?

JANE: It means that I have gained weight and I am fat and I am disgusting.

THERAPIST: I wonder if the scale has become an independent barometer for your feelings regardless of what the numbers really mean. Let's try an experiment. We have discussed the issue of water balance and the scale. I am going to ask you to stand on the scale while I gently step on the back and change the numbers. [*The numbers slowly increase.*] How do you feel as the numbers go up?

JANE: [*visibly distressed*] I am really frightened when I see the numbers go up.

THERAPIST: How do you feel about yourself when you look at the scale now [*up 15 pounds from her actual weight*]?

JANE: I feel like a disgusting pig. I hate myself. I can't stand this.

THERAPIST: And this is true when you know that I am making the numbers increase on the scale. You can see that your feelings and what it means when the numbers go up have become almost automatic. The feedback is distressing and destructive even when you know that it has nothing to do with actual changes in body fat. This is why it would be good for you to avoid weighing yourself daily, and we can begin just weighing you once a week here to make sure that your weight is not out of control.

The more fundamental therapeutic issue in this case, as with virtually all eating-disordered patients, relates to the degree to which weight or shape has become the sole or predominant yardstick for determining or modulating self-worth (Garner & Bemis, 1982). This key issue had to be addressed repeatedly and from many different vantage points throughout the course of therapy with Jane and her family. In challenging such a value system and in the absence of a "replacement system" for regulating self-concept, particular care must be taken to guard against a frontal attack that could strip the individual or the family of the core marker being used for personal identity. Initially, Jane's feelings about weight and her self-definition were so strong that simply saying the word "fat" would result in her bursting into tears. Later in therapy, her feelings about herself were tied more to relationships with others whom she valued and to doing certain things that she enjoyed, rather than strictly to performance and evaluation of outcome.

During initial sessions Jane was encouraged to monitor her eating, bingeing, vomiting, laxative abuse, mood, and the circumstances surrounding eating and eating symptoms (Fairburn, 1985). Later sessions of the individual therapy focused on helping Jane decouple self-esteem from weight while developing problem-solving skills to deal with family problems. Jane's mother was referred to another therapist for help with her own eating problems. The family meetings lasted for 2 months and focused on "consciousness raising" regarding the prejudice that family members shared about obesity (Garner & Wooley, 1991). In family meetings Jane was able to express her competitive feelings toward her mother and to see how the competition had extended to food and weight. The family meetings also allowed Jane's father to articulate his ongoing distress regarding his father's death, and the family was able to support his attempts to challenge his unrealistic view of his heightened health risks. It also became evident that he suffered from chronic depression, and some time was spent in the family meetings focusing on cognitive–behavioral techniques to address his mood. In the course of family meetings Jane's brother revealed that he was angry at the family for what he perceived to be undue pressure to follow a program of studies that would lead to a career in medicine rather than follow his own interests in art.

## TERMINATION

Jane was seen in therapy for about 1 year. Although many reports of cognitive–behavioral treatment for bulimia nervosa describe a relatively brief course of treatment, it is important to emphasize that there are patients who may be recalcitrant in the short-term but who benefit with extended treatment. Jane's fears related to maintaining a normal body weight were extreme, and she required longer-term cognitive–behavioral treatment in order to consolidate her more accepting attitudes regarding her body weight and to decouple her self-esteem from her weight (Garner & Bemis, 1985). She had numerous relapses that led to the reemergence of weight suppression attempts; however, she gradually became more consistent in resisting urges to diet and increasingly aware of how her concern over her weight interfered with other life goals that she valued deeply. She was able to keep her competitive feelings toward her mother from translating into weight control; however, her mother's continued symptoms around eating and weight were a source of distress to Jane. She spent less time with her parents and focused increasing energy on her relationship with her boyfriend. She was able to see how her early family environment had provided a lens through which cultural values toward weight and achievement had been magnified.

At termination Jane's eating symptoms were completely under control and she had not binged or vomited for 3 months. She was able to (1) increase her caloric intake to an appropriate "nondieting" level without anxiety, (2) space meals so that food was consumed throughout the day rather than just in the evening, (3) gradually incorporate "forbidden foods" into her diet, and (4) inhibit urges to diet or engage in weight-controlling behaviors. More emphasis was placed on controlling dieting rather than controlling bingeing, since the dieting efforts were conceptualized as the primary cause of the urge to binge eat (Garner et al., 1985). Challenging underlying assumptions related to dieting and obesity was the primary focus early in treatment. Later, more general themes were explored: family relationships, how they related to self-definition, and feelings of insecurity in current relationships. Jane was able to address her negative feelings about obesity and to recognize that her disparagement of her shape was based on assumptions about obesity in general that were inaccurate and inconsistent with her other principles for viewing human worth. She expressed considerable anger toward the fashion and dieting industries for promoting the superficial standard of judging women's self-worth exclusively in terms of physical appearance.

## FOLLOW-UP

At the 1-year follow-up, Jane reported no disturbed eating patterns, and the improvements in general psychological functioning had been maintained.

## OVERALL EVALUATION

Illustrating cognitive–behavioral therapy for eating disorders with the case study format has the primary advantage of providing concrete examples of actual interventions, thus giving life to otherwise sterile theoretical accounts of treatment. Unfortunately, the case study format also has a number of disadvantages that are of particular concern in illustrating the treatment of eating disorders, for these disorder, it has repeatedly been emphasized, are multi-determined and present with a myriad of associated forms of psychopathology. The case presented here demonstrates only one set, among a wide array of possibilities, of presenting problems, underlying assumptions, and applications of the method; format for delivery, duration of treatment, and resolution. Jane did present with other primary psychopathology in addition to her eating disorder, although much of her initial psychological distress was secondary to her chaotic eating pattern (Garner et al., 1990). There are many clients with bulimia nervosa whose presentation and course of treatment are more straight-forward and who respond favorably to brief cognitive–behavioral or educational techniques.

This case illustration could inadvertently convey the impression that simply recognizing a flawed underlying assumption is sufficient for change whereas in most instances there is a tremendous amount of creative repetition required to essentially "relearn" a more accurate or adaptive system of thinking. Effective cognitive interventions can be brief in some cases, but for others they assume a lengthy course. A particular therapy format—individual, group, or family—may be advantageous for a particular client (or they may be combined in some instances). For some clients, even inpatient treatment may be necessary to normalize eating and weight; to interrupt bingeing, vomiting, or laxative abuse; to treat complications; and to occasionally disengage the family from destructive interactional patterns. Many of the nuances of treatment go well beyond the scope of the case study presented here but have been described in detail elsewhere (see references).

## REFERENCES

American Psychiatric Association (1993). *Diagnostic and statistical manual of mental disorders* (4th ed.). Washington, DC: Author.

Fairburn, C. G. (1985). Cognitive–behavioral treatment for bulimia. In D. M. Garner & P. E. Garfinkel (Eds.), *Handbook of psychotherapy for anorexia nervosa and bulimia* (pp. 160–192). New York: Guilford Press.

Garner, D. M. (1991). *Eating Disorder Inventory-2 Professional Manual*. Odessa, FL: Psychological Assessment Resources.

Garner, D. M. (1993). Pathogenesis of anorexia nervosa. *Lancet, 341,* 1631–1635.

Garner, D. M., & Bemis, K. M. (1982). A cognitive–behavioral approach to anorexia nervosa. *Cognitive Therapy and Research, 6,* 123–150.

Garner, D. M., & Bemis, K. M. (1985). Cognitive therapy for anorexia nervosa. In D. M. Garner & P. E. Garfinkel (Eds.), *Handbook of psychotherapy for anorexia nervosa and bulimia* (pp. 107–146). New York: Guilford Press.

Garner, D. M., Fairburn, C. G., Davis, R. (1987). Cognitive–behavioral treatment of bulimia nervosa: A critical appraisal. *Behavior Modification, 11,* 398–431.

Garner, D. M., Olmsted, M. P., Davis, R., Rockert, W., Goldbloom, D., & Eagle, M. (1990). The association between bulimic symptoms and reported psychopathology. *International Journal of Eating Disorders, 9,* 1–15.

Garner, D. M., & Parker, P. (1993). Multimodal assessment of eating disorders. In T. H. Ollendick & M. Hersen (Eds.), *Handbook of child and adolescent assessment* (pp. 384–399). New York: Pergamon Press.

Garner, D. M., Rockert, W., Olmstead, M. P., Johnson, C. L., & Coscina, D. V. (1985). Psychoeducational principles in the treatment of bulimia and anorexia nervosa. In D. M. Garner & P. E. Garfinkel (Eds.), *Handbook of psychotherapy for anorexia nervosa and bulimia* (pp. 513–572). New York: Guilford Press.

Garner, D. M., Shafer, C. L., & Rosen, L. W. (1992). Critical appraisal of the *DSM-III-R* diagnostic criteria for eating disorders. In S. R. Hooper, G. W. Hynd, & R. E. Mattison (Eds.), *Child psychopathology: Diagnostic criteria and clinical assessment* (pp 261–303). Hillsdale, NJ: Erlbaum.

Garner, D. M., & Wooley, S. C. (1991). Confronting the failure of behavioral and dietary treatments for obesity. *Clinical Psychology Review, 11,* 1–52.

# CHAPTER 15

# Low Sexual Desire Disorder

## J. GAYLE BECK

### DESCRIPTION OF THE DISORDER

A quick reading of most descriptions of sex therapy would lead one to believe that many cases of sexual dysfunction are simple, straightforward, and readily resolved with behavioral and cognitive–behavioral techniques. Nowhere is this impression less true than in the case of low sexual desire disorder. As has been recognized with increasing clarity (e.g., Leiblum & Rosen, 1988), presentation of low sexual desire often masks a complex clinical picture involving sexual arousal difficulties, interactional problems within the couple, and, occasionally, secrets held by one partner. The present chapter will illustrate the treatment of such a case, using a combination of intervention modalities.

Although early descriptions emphasized the etiologic roles of unconscious emotional conflicts (Kaplan, 1979) or biological factors, such as low androgen levels, in disorders of sexual desire, current formulations are more descriptive and reflect our appreciation of the multiple causes of this problem. According to current definition, low sexual desire disorder (LSDD) is characterized by a persistent or recurrent absence of sexual fantasies and motivation for sexual activity. Within *DSM-III-R* (American Psychiatric Association, 1987), this disorder is termed *hypoactive sexual desire disorder*. In diagnosing LDSS, most clinicians do not rely on the client's frequency of sexual partner contacts since this seems to reflect traditional prescriptions concerning initiation and acquiescence with sexual requests rather than a patient's level of

J. GAYLE BECK • Department of Psychology, State University of New York at Buffalo, Buffalo, New York 14260.

*Adult Behavior Therapy Casebook*, edited by Cynthia G. Last and Michel Hersen. Plenum Press, New York, 1994.

sexual motivation per se (Beck, 1992). It is not unusual for both men and women with LSDD to report fewer sexual fantasies and less sexual daydreaming relative to sexually functional individuals. Oddly, one available empirical study of LSDD suggests that men with this disorder masturbate more frequently than do men in normal samples whereas there was no difference in the frequency of masturbation between women with LSDD and female controls (see Leiblum & Rosen, 1988, and Beck, 1992, for a review of the available empirical literature on LSDD).

LSDD must be distinguished from sexual aversion, which is characterized by repugnance, fear, or disgust associated with sexual activity. Sexual aversion is often associated with a sexual trauma, such as rape or incest, and these clients report extreme emotional reactions and active avoidance of sexual situations. In contrast, LSDD is characterized by apathy, a lack of motivation, and passive avoidance of sexual contact. This distinction is central in case formulation. For example, sexual aversion disorders frequently coexist with posttraumatic stress disorder, while LSDD may co-occur with an affective disorder (Schreiner-Engel & Schiavi, 1986) or with premenstrual distress syndrome.

At present, the diagnosis of LSDD is highly controversial, and no consensus exists regarding the operational criteria for classification. In particular, experts disagree about the utility of the diagnosis, with one extreme maintaining that this may be a "catch-all diagnosis with blurred boundaries and symptoms distributed on a normal curve in the 'normal' population" (Clearing-Sky & Thornton, 1987, cited in Leiblum & Rosen, 1988, p. 9). Despite this scholarly debate, there has been a marked increase in the prevalence of LSDD in sex therapy practice (Leiblum & Rosen, 1988), suggesting the need for systematic examination of the psychopathological features and treatment of this syndrome. Currently, sexual desire problems are managed with a variety of clinical approaches, including psychodynamic, Gestalt, cognitive–behavioral, family systems, and drug therapies. As exemplified in the following case, versatility and flexibility are essential in treating these cases, given the strong possibility for surprises in the process of treatment.

## CASE IDENTIFICATION

Judy and Richard had been living together 15 years at the time of initial contact. Judy was a poised, attractive 40-year-old who was employed as a senior partner in a large law firm. Despite the fact that he was 43, Richard appeared younger than his wife and was noticeably more concerned with his looks. He was employed as a junior vice president for a major company. The couple did not have children, having decided when they married that their careers would preclude raising a family.

Both Judy and Richard had obtained graduate degrees (a J.D. and a Ph.D., respectively) and described themselves as hardworking and achievement-oriented. Several years prior to seeking treatment, they had purchased their "dream house," which was located in an affluent section of town. Despite the effort involved in acquiring this house, neither spent much time at home. Judy's job required extensive travel, and Richard reported a wide variety of hobbies, such as golf, swimming, and skydiving, that filled his time. Whenever possible, the couple socialized with colleagues, in addition to entertaining for business purposes.

Judy and Richard had met one another during graduate school. Despite a stormy relationship, when Richard relocated to take a job the couple maintained close contact, phoning and visiting each other frequently. When Judy completed law school a year later, she joined Richard in a city where, she said, "I knew no one, didn't have a job, and had no means to support myself emotionally or financially." After cohabiting for a year, the couple married— only to legally divorce a month later because of the tax benefits. At the point of initial contact, neither found this arrangement unusual.

## PRESENTING COMPLAINTS

The chief complaint, according to both Judy and Richard, was infrequent sexual contact stemming from Judy's apparent lack of sexual interest. The problem was long-standing, although there were discrepancies in identifying the date when the problem began. Judy stated that the problem had begun 5 years earlier, while Richard noticed a change 2 years prior to seeking professional help. Their frequency of sexual contact averaged once every 2 months, with Judy refusing Richard's overtures on other occasions because she wasn't "in the mood." Judy described their sexual interactions as mechanical and emotionally unsatisfying, although she experienced adequate lubrication, subjective arousal, and orgasm. Richard was distressed solely by the infrequency of sexual contact, stating that he enjoyed intercourse and wished that it occurred more often. Neither reported problems with pain during or after intercourse or inadequate arousal. Judy masturbated once per week, while Richard stated that he did not masturbate.

## HISTORY

Judy was the eldest daughter in a large family. She described her mother as stern, strong willed, and loving. Her parents had divorced when she was 12, owing to her father's alcoholism. Judy described her childhood as a quest for her father's approval; in her memory, nothing was ever adequate by his standards. She secretly believed that he wished she were a boy. As a result, Judy had excelled in mathematics and science courses throughout prep school, earning her high praise from her father. After her parents' divorce, Judy remained in contact with her father while living with her mother and five sisters. She recalled that her father never approved of her steady boyfriend during college. By the time she was in law school, her father's drinking had progressed to the point that he needed to be involuntarily hospitalized, which Judy organized and financed using a family trust fund. Her father died shortly after Judy married Richard; his death was felt to be a release from years of trouble caused by his uncontrolled drinking.

Judy's sexual history was unremarkable. Her first sexual relationship occurred in college with a steady boyfriend. She described this relationship as "terrific" and stated that they are still friends. She experienced no difficulties with sexual desire, arousal, or orgasm at this time. She met Richard at a party when she was in law school and found him charming, funny, and elusive. The relationship was characterized as difficult from the beginning: Judy would pursue Richard who withdrew and often dated other women in the interim; then when Judy would withdraw from the relationship, Richard would court her and seek to reestablish intimacy. This pattern continued for the 2 years prior to Richard's relocation to start his first job.

Richard was an only child; his mother died of cancer when he was 10, and he was sent to a boy's military school for the duration of his schooling. Two years after his mother's death, his father married a woman who had two daughters and who did not welcome Richard in "her" house. Subsequently, visits at home were shortened, and many school holidays were spent with friends' families or alone in the dorm. Richard confided that between the ages of 14 and 18, he had maintained a sexual relationship with one of his stepsisters on those rare occasions when he went home. This was his first sexual experience. Although never discovered by other family members, Richard recalled considerable apprehension surrounding these contacts. During college Richard dated many women and derived a sense of self-esteem from being pursued by them when he would distance himself. He was an above-average student but never put full effort into his studies. After college he worked for two years prior to entering a Ph.D. program. He dated many women during this interval and usually would end a relationship after sexual contact was initiated. Given his high level of sexual activity, he never masturbated, although he fantasized about being emotionally close with a woman. Upon entering a Ph.D. program, Richard became more serious about his career and focused his attention on studying. He excelled in his classes and enjoyed a reputation as one of the brightest students in the program.

Richard described the beginning of his relationship with Judy as pleasant; although he wasn't looking for a steady girlfriend, he found Judy interesting, pretty, and very intelligent. He recalled that he felt pressured by her for emotional closeness and that at times he would distance himself. Their sexual relationship followed the course of this emotional tango, with problems arising whenever the tension of prolonged emotional intimacy became too great for Richard. At these points Richard would date other women. When he would attempt to reestablish the relationship with Judy, she would lose her interest in sex, which was frustrating for Richard. This pattern was repeated no fewer than six times during the 2 years that they dated. Despite recounting their history together, neither Judy nor Richard saw the parallel with their current situation.

Three years prior to entering therapy, Richard had confided to Judy that he had had an affair with a woman at work. He revealed this information because he felt burdened by guilt and wished to reconcile with Judy. After a brief interval of pastoral counseling with their minister, Judy and Richard reported an interval of closeness and marital satisfaction, including sexual satisfaction. This was their only other contact with the mental health profession.

## ASSESSMENT

Prior to selection of an assessment battery, both Richard and Judy were interviewed individually, as it appeared that the presenting problem was maintained by an amalgamation of individual and dyadic factors. Given the couple's history of ambivalent attachment to one another, disturbed communication, and somewhat discrepant accounts of the onset of their problem, the aim of these individual interviews was to determine each partner's perspective on the problem in order to develop a series of treatment goals. In light of the long-standing history of the problem, to focus solely on sexual desire appeared misguided.

During her interview Judy indicated that she had never felt that Richard wanted or approved of her. Much like her childhood experience with her father, Judy continually felt pressured to prove herself to Richard in order to be accepted and loved by him. She reported considerable depression, with disturbed sleep, apathy, and feelings of sadness, and indicated that she only rarely gained Richard's approval. When queried about the possibility that her frequent travel might be relevant in maintaining the emotional distance between them, Judy expressed surprise, stating that she "didn't see how that could be relevant." She did acknowledge feeling angry at Richard for his past affair but felt that this was not a major consideration in her current sexual apathy. Judy believed that if she could feel that Richard wanted to be emotionally close on a consistent basis, her sex drive would be normal. Her sexual fantasies revolved around romantic themes, often including her husband. Judy tearfully acknowledged that she was afraid that therapy would reveal that Richard did not want to be her partner and that this would be the medium for a long-overdue decision to separate.

During his interview Richard was guarded and inappropriately cheerful. He stated that he did not understand his wife's sexual apathy but that he wished it would stop, "as if a switch could be thrown" to achieve this end. Although he acknowledged that this was a problem that involved both of them, he appeared to hold his wife responsible for their infrequent sexual contact. When asked about his sexual history—including his past incestuous relationship with his stepsister, his high level of sexual activity with many different partners preceding marriage, and his past affair—he indicated that he had a strong sex drive and that he perceived these activities as part of normal male development. When informed that incest was not usually considered normal, he expressed remorse and revealed that he found "forbidden" and illicit sexual contact extremely arousing. He reported fantasies involving anonymous partners in illicit sexual liaisons (e.g., sex with a flight attendant on an airplane) but denied acting on these fantasies. Richard expressed feeling alone in his marriage; he, like his wife, feared that separation was a realistic, albeit undesired, possibility.

Following these individual interviews, Richard and Judy completed a questionnaire battery selected to assess both individual and dyadic factors. This included the Dyadic Adjustment Scale (Spanier, 1976); Derogatis Sexual Functioning Inventory (DSFI; Derogatis, 1979), an omnibus instrument that assesses ten areas of responding, including sexual fantasies, satisfaction, and attitudes, and includes the Brief Symptom Index (BSI) as a measure of general psychological status; Beck Depression Inventory (BDI; Beck, Ward, Mendelson, Mock, & Erbaugh, 1961); and Sexual Arousal Inventory (SAI; Hoon & Chambless, 1986). Table 1 lists relevant pretreatment scores and the interpretation of these values relative to available norms. As can be seen, both Richard and Judy reported extreme marital unhappiness, particularly around the issues of demonstration of affection, use of leisure time, and sex. On the DSFI Judy reported average levels of sexual drive (her ideal frequency of sexual contact was once a week) and typical sexual fantasies (e.g., fantasies involving oral–genital sex, intercourse). Judy scored in the clinical range on the BDI and reported distress from depressive and anxiety symptoms on the BSI. In contrast, Richard's scores on the BDI and BSI were within the normal range. On the DSFI he reported a high level of sexual drive, indicating that ideally he would prefer to have sexual contact several times a day. On the fantasy subscale he endorsed such items as sex with multiple partners, having a

Table 1
Questionnaire Assessment Battery: Pretreatment Scores and Norms

| Scale | Richard | Judy | Norm for nondistressed individuals |
|---|---|---|---|
| Dyadic Adjustment Scale | 71 | 63 | 115 |
| Derogatis Sexual Functioning Inventory (DSFI) | | | |
| Information | 70 | 61 | 50 |
| Experience | 70 | 49 | 50 |
| Drive | 81 | 52 | 50 |
| Attitude | 48 | 53 | 50 |
| Symptoms (Brief Symptom Index; BSI) | see text | | |
| Affects | not administered | | |
| Gender role | 56 | 53 | 50 |
| Fantasy | see text | | |
| Beck Depression Inventory (BDI) | 5 | 18 | 0–10 |
| Sexual Arousal Inventory (SAI) | 90 | 83 | 80–91 |

forbidden lover, and watching others engaged in intercourse as arousing images, in addition to fantasies involving sex with his spouse. Both Richard and Judy reported adequate levels of arousal to a wide variety of sexual activities on the SAI.

In addition to this questionnaire battery, both Judy and Richard were asked to maintain daily self-monitoring records of their sexual urges, fantasies, and activity. Included on these records were ratings of subjective sexual desire, feelings of sexual arousal, genital response, and sexual activity (masturbation, contact with a partner). Both individuals were asked to maintain private records in order to reduce bias. Richard was asked to record his complete range of sexual fantasies, including fantasies involving illicit or anonymous sexual contact.

## SELECTION OF TREATMENT

On the basis of the results of the pretreatment assessment, including both interview and self-report sources, several treatment goals were articulated. Specifically, it appeared that Richard had poor tolerance for emotional closeness and tended to interpret Judy's requests for intimacy as sexual overtures, although most often Judy was seeking support and comfort. When rebuffed, he would withdraw, which would lead to Judy's pursuit and eventual anger at her husband. Judy, for her part, appeared to lack the communication skills for direct expression of her emotional needs and would mask her needs by attempting to excel (at work and hobbies) so that she could win Richard's approval and love. When this was not forthcoming, she would withdraw, which often was perceived by Richard as a preoccupation with her work. Additionally, Richard appeared to live much of his sexual life alone in fantasies that focused around taboo images. These fantasies were quite arousing, although he denied acting on them. It was felt, however, that the presence of these fantasies distracted Richard from engaging emotionally with his wife.

Thus, on the basis of this analysis, four treatment goals were planned, as follows:

1. To alter the couple's pattern of sexual initiation and interaction, which consisted of Richard pressuring Judy for intercourse and, if she consented, repetition of a sexual pattern that included minimal involvement on Judy's part and was primarily oriented around intercourse.
2. To stop the emotional pursuit between Judy and Richard. In particular, the issue of emotional intimacy appeared unresolved, with Judy seeking closeness and approval and Richard distancing himself when this became overwhelming.
3. To strengthen communication between the partners so that they could express emotional needs and desires directly and honestly. In particular, the development of negotiation skills was desired by both individuals.
4. To monitor Richard's use of taboo sexual fantasies. Although he denied masturbation involving these fantasies, it was felt that his nearly constant sexual fantasies detracted from attention to and interaction with his wife.

The intervention strategies selected to address these goals included exercises derived from the Gestalt tradition designed to heighten sensory and experiential awareness. These were used in order to teach both Richard and Judy to differentiate sensual and sexual feelings. Intervention strategies also included communication skill enhancement (e.g., negotiation skills); exploration of the couple's differences regarding emotional closeness through cognitive restructuring and role-playing; and the assignment of behavioral homework designed to expand the couple's sexual repertoire, beginning with sensate focus. These interventions were selected following guidelines provided by Friedman and Hogan (1985). These guidelines emphasize the importance of including interventions designed to help clients become aware of the physical responses associated with their emotional responses and to gain insight into the nature of the problem. Additionally, Friedman and Hogan suggest a dyadic treatment format, including a series of graded sexual tasks designed to elicit emotional responses during the course of treatment as well as to provide the couple with self-help skills regarding sexual functioning. Although not strictly behavioral in focus, broad-spectrum treatment of LSDD currently is recognized as necessary to address the complex web of affective, cognitive, and behavioral factors that operate between sexual partners. Both individuals were instructed to continue self-monitoring throughout the course of treatment.

## COURSE OF TREATMENT

The course of treatment with Richard and Judy was divided into several phases. In the first phase experiential and sensory awareness were heightened through body awareness exercises, including sensate focus exercises. The purpose of these exercises was to teach Richard and Judy to attend to bodily cues of emotion, to recognize and label feelings, and to verbally share these emotions with each other. Emphasis was placed on both pleasant and unpleasant feelings, as it was noted that neither Judy nor Richard attended to or articulated emotions well. Given the long-standing pattern of distancing and pursuit that had been noted, these exercises were also intended to help each individual learn to respond verbally to the partner's feelings instead of resorting to the entrenched interaction pattern. Although a ban was placed on intercourse, nongenital sensate focus exercises were included in order to increase sensual contact and to help this couple differentiate sensual touch from requests for sexual activity. As communication is an intrinsic part of sensate focus, the inclusion of this exercise set the stage for later communication training.

This first treatment phase was greeted enthusiastically by Judy, who reported enjoying the opportunity to express herself emotionally to Richard. In contrast, Richard stated that he found the awareness exercises "odd" and wasn't quite sure what to say. Although Richard did not avoid participating in these exercises, it was clear that it was Judy who took the initiative in scheduling and organizing these activities. She reported feeling closer to Richard following each exercise but indicated that Richard had not reciprocated in emotional expression. In Session 3 Judy expressed anger at this imbalance and stated that she felt as if Richard was blaming the problem on her. Although Richard enjoyed sensate contact, he expressed frustration with the ban on intercourse and wished for the therapist to remove this restriction. Despite the therapist's restatement of the necessity to avoid repetition of their dysfunctional sexual pattern, Richard continued to push for sexual contact. A glance at his self-report records indicated an increase in taboo sexual fantasies during the 3-week interval in which the awareness exercises were practiced. It appeared that Richard was responding to these exercises with an increase in sexual desire but was avoiding emotional contact with Judy in spite of the therapist's instructions.

This development led to an individual session with Richard, to explore the issue of taboo fantasies further. During this session, Richard revealed that he had a long-standing masturbatory pattern involving fantasies of sex with strangers. He admitted to masturbating one or two times a day using these fantasies and felt quite ashamed of this. In his opinion this pattern was deviant, and he had tried unsuccessfully on many occasions to stop himself. He stated that he had acted upon these fantasies only twice, in situations where he felt that this behavior would not be detected (e.g., at conferences). His wife was uninformed of the nature and frequency of his masturbatory activities and of his prior sexual contact with strangers. Richard was understandably apprehensive about her reaction and revealed that he had not disclosed this information at the outset of treatment since he believed that if sex with Judy occurred more frequently, his masturbatory pattern would be easier to control.

This new information necessitated a revised formulation of the maintaining factors for LSDD in this couple. In many respects, Richard's masturbatory pattern resembled that seen in sexual deviants, namely, a high daily frequency of fantasies and infrequent performance of the behavior. A major difference, however, was the nature of the "deviant" behavior; in this case, it did not involve illegal sexual contact, as rape or voyeurism do. However, given Richard's preoccupation with these taboo fantasies and the extent to which this superseded sexual and emotional contact with Judy, it was felt that it was necessary to decrease such masturbatory urges with a separate treatment component, with the aim of reducing the arousal produced by the taboo fantasies. On the basis of available literature on sexual deviation (e.g., Quinsey & Earls, 1990), a treatment combining masturbatory satiation and covert sensitization was selected and described to Richard. Although he consented to these procedures, Richard was reluctant to inform Judy of the true nature of his arousal pattern. In-session role-playing with Richard facilitated this process, which was scheduled for the next conjoint session.

Session 5 involved Richard's revealing his masturbatory pattern to Judy and discussion of this pattern as it related to the couple's ongoing marital distress. Judy was extremely upset to hear of Richard's sexual contact with strangers, particularly given concerns about AIDS. Additionally, this information confirmed her belief that Richard did not want to be her partner, and she expressed ambivalence about her ability to remain committed to him. Judy agreed to stay in treatment for a 3-month trial to help strengthen their communication skills, as this would be helpful irrespective of whether the partnership was to continue or not. Individual treatment with Richard was scheduled to occur during this interval. Judy also requested that Richard undergo AIDS testing. The ban on intercourse remained in place, but the couple was encouraged to continue with the experiential and sensory awareness exercises on a twice per week basis.

The second phase of treatment with Richard and Judy involved eight sessions of structured communication training scheduled over a 3-month interval. Emphasis was placed on understanding how specific irrational beliefs impeded clear communication between the partners. For example, Judy's be-lief that Richard was not interested in her needs and desires were explored, as can be seen from the following transcript excerpt:

JUDY:   It just seems that every time I express my feelings, he either changes the topic or walks away. It's hard enough to share my feelings but when that happens [*tear-fully*] I just feel like giving up . . . I think he doesn't care about me.

RICHARD:   That's not true. I don't walk away from you. I just don't know what to say sometimes.

THERAPIST:   This is a good example of a time when active listening skills are called for, Richard. See if you can paraphrase the feelings that Judy is expressing right now, instead of defending yourself.

RICHARD:   Well, Judy is saying that I don't listen to her, that I just leave the room.

THERAPIST:   And is she saying anything else?

RICHARD:   I guess she's saying that she thinks that I don't love her.

JUDY:   [*sobbing*] Exactly.

THERAPIST:   Judy, how would you like Richard to respond at those times?

JUDY:   I just want him to listen to me, not to give advice or leave me alone or talk about what he had for lunch.

THERAPIST:   Do you want to role-play this, to make sure that both of you know how to listen and communicate with each other at these times?

Communication training included the techniques of reverse role-playing, active listening (as illustrated in this excerpt), problem-solving, and anger management. Richard and Judy both noted a significant decrease in marital conflict during this interval. During the sixth session of this phase, Judy expressed renewed interest in maintaining the relationship, although her spon-taneous sexual interest did not increase appreciably.

Simultaneously with these conjoint sessions, Richard was seen individu-ally on a weekly basis for 3 months. These meetings involved covert sensiti-zation scenes, which paired auditory fantasies of taboo sexual activities with aversive outcomes. An example of a typical covert sensitization scene is pro-vided in Table 2, in abbreviated form. This procedure was implemented in a two-room chamber with intercom communication in order to provide privacy for Richard. Masturbatory satiation was practiced as homework during this 3-month interval. This technique asks the patient first to masturbate using normal sexual fantasies (in this case, fantasies involving consensual sexual contact with Judy). Following ejaculation, Richard was asked to masturbate for an additional 15 minutes using taboo fantasies in order to associate deviant fantasies with the period of time when sexual arousal and interest are at their lowest. Richard was asked to perform satiation homework daily and was instructed to state his fantasies aloud and to audiotape each practice occasion.

## Table 2
## An Example of a Typical (Abbreviated) Covert Sensitization Scene
## Used with Richard to Decrease Arousal to Taboo Fantasies

You're in a restaurant in New Orleans, where you've been attending a conference. It's been a rough week, and you're feeling relaxed and happy to be away from it all. You notice one of the waitresses—she's about 5 feet 3 inches and shapely, with beautiful red hair. You begin to watch her as she moves around the tables near to you; her movements are sexy and you can't help but stare at her large breasts. She can tell that you're watching her; she looks back and smiles every time she passes you. You start to think about how you can talk to her when all of a sudden she's standing next to you. She says, "I'm sure glad that this place isn't crowded. It makes everything so much easier, and I get a chance to know the customers. Is everything allright?" You can feel yourself getting aroused, and you hope that she doesn't notice the bulge in your pants. You start to talk to her, asking her about herself: Does she like her job? How long has she been working here? All you can think about is how much you'd like to undress her, to fondle those large firm breasts. You can almost hear her moan with pleasure as you talk to her, fantasizing about having sex with her. She excuses herself and moves away to serve another customer. You decide to ask her to go out for a drink, thinking how much you'd like to get her into bed tonight. As you are paying your check, she comes by you and you grab her hand, asking her if she'd like to go for a drink later. She smiles, teasingly, and says, "Sure. I'm finished here now." You wait outside for her. When she comes out, she's wearing a tight pair of slacks that reveals an incredible body. She walks you to her car and says, "I know just the place where we can go." Driving to the bar, all you can think of is her naked body—ripe, full breasts, her great legs. You walk into the bar with your arm around her; she is giggling and teasing you. As you sit in the dark bar, you start to fondle her, slowly touching her body over her clothes—her firm breasts, her legs, her crotch. She is responsive and begins to kiss you—slow, passionate kisses. Although the bar is dark, you notice some people standing several feet away, watching you. You look up and it's your boss, your wife, and your best friend. They are watching in horror as you fondle this woman and seduce her. They have seen everything and know what a sickie you are, how you just can't stop thinking about seducing every woman you see, how you can't think of anything else. You've been caught red-handed, and everyone is glaring at you. You start to mumble an excuse, but you feel sick and embarrassed; you can feel your dinner churning in your stomach. Your wife removes her wedding ring and throws it at you as she walks away. Your boss says, "Richard, we don't appreciate this type of behavior from one of our executives." You are so humiliated as you sit there, halfway undressed by this strange woman, embarrassed in front of the people you care about most. You know that you're sick and disgusting to these people, that you've lost their trust and respect. They know that you're a chronic womanizer. You feel like you're going to throw up. But suddenly you get away—it was only a dream. You wake up and you can relax, your stomach doesn't hurt, and you're glad that you're away from womanizing, free from seducing strange women. You relax again.

This permitted the therapist to assess his compliance with the satiation home-work and to spot-check that he was following instructions accurately. Richard reported that the taboo fantasies gradually became less arousing during this interval and occurred less frequently. In the final 3 weeks of this treatment phase, Richard began to experience spontaneous fantasies involving Judy for the first time in many years.

The third phase of treatment involved several techniques designed to address the issue of emotional intimacy and to develop this couple's sexual repertoire to include greater flexibility in initiation and interaction. Ten conjoint sessions, spaced over a 4-month interval, were involved in this phase. Treatment discussions focused on the implications of intimacy; that is, what it would mean if they got closer to one another and how this change would impact their current priorities for time management. In this context Richard expressed fears that he would be overwhelmed by Judy if emotional intimacy were to last for too long. Exploration of these feelings revealed that Richard feared that he would lose his independence and would end up like his father, that is, "smothered and controlled," as his father had been by his stepmother. Cognitive restructuring techniques were employed to change these self-statements and to help Richard perceive Judy's requests for emotional closeness as an affirmation of her love and commitment to him. Judy was taught to identify pursuit behaviors and to replace these with verbal requests for support and intimacy in order to interrupt their dysfunctional distancing-and-pursuit pattern. The couple was given the assignment to date one another at least weekly, alternating responsibility for arranging the date and inviting one another out.

During this treatment phase sensate focus exercises were used as the starting point for building this couple's sexual repertoire. Given that Richard and Judy had been practicing sensate focus for 3 months, their communication of sexual likes and dislikes was good. In order to expand their range of sexual behaviors, they were asked to read and discuss together several popular sex manuals (e.g., *The Joy of Sex* by Comfort, 1972). This generated a collection of sexual behaviors that both found appealing and were interested in exploring. Although the ban on intercourse was still in place, Richard and Judy were instructed to experiment with genital pleasuring and to incorporate these new activities into their sexual repertoire while communicating and sharing these novel experiences with each other. Responsibility for initiating these sexual contacts was alternated between Judy and Richard. Judy reported an increase in sexual desire shortly after this phase of treatment began, which facilitated this treatment strategy. The couple reported mutually satisfying sexual interactions within 1 month of beginning this treatment phase, at which point the ban on intercourse was lifted.

Figure 1 illustrates the changes in sexual desire reported by Judy and Richard during the course of treatment. These ratings were derived from self-monitoring records, which were maintained throughout the 8 months of treatment.

## TERMINATION

The final three treatment sessions were devoted to termination. This involved fading out the therapist's influence by loosening the structure of treat-

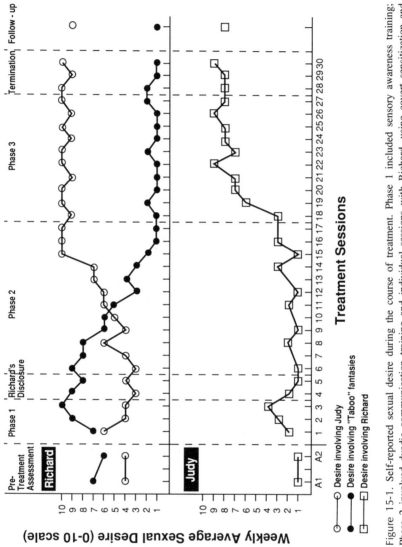

Figure 15-1. Self-reported sexual desire during the course of treatment. Phase 1 included sensory awareness training; Phase 2 involved dyadic communication training and individual sessions with Richard, using covert sensitization and masturbatory satiation; Phase 3 addressed emotional intimacy issue and expansion of sexual repertoire. (Data are average ratings of strength of subjective sexual desire and urges for sexual contact; 1 to 10 scale where 1 = none, 10 = maximum.)

ment in order to facilitate the couple's ability to independently address relationship issues as they arose. During one of these sessions Richard asked Judy for forgiveness for neglecting her and for his past transgressions with other women. Judy stated that her forgiveness was expressed by her actions, by the fact that she had agreed to remain committed to Richard and to work through the barriers that had separated them emotionally. The couple decided to continue their regular dates and to schedule "talk times" in order to maintain their level of communication and to focus on their relationship. Judy also informed Richard that she had requested a reduction in her job-related travel since she felt that this disrupted the continuity of their marriage. While this reduction was not scheduled to occur for several months, Richard expressed relief and appreciation.

Prior to the final session the couple completed the battery of self-report questionnaires for posttreatment assessment. These scores are reported in Table 3; as can be seen, both Richard and Judy reported significant increases in marital and sexual satisfaction. Judy no longer experienced depression, and she reported adequate levels of sexual interest. Although Richard's level of sexual interest remained higher than Judy's, this was noted by the therapist as a desire discrepancy (Zilbergeld & Ellison, 1980) rather than a problem area. The couple reported satisfaction with the frequency and variety of their sexual contacts and indicated that they planned to continue their sex education reading. Richard reported that occasionally he would have a taboo fantasy but that he was careful to mentally switch the partner in this fantasy to Judy when this occurred.

## FOLLOW-UP

At the last session, a follow-up meeting was scheduled for 3 months later. This session was termed a "booster" session and was designed to as-

Table 3
Posttreatment Questionnaire Scores

| Scale | Richard | Judy |
| --- | --- | --- |
| Dyadic Adjustment Scale | 120 | 110 |
| Derogatis Sexual Functioning Inventory (DSFI)[a] | | |
| Information | 75 | 73 |
| Experience | 70 | 65 |
| Drive | 81 | 59 |
| Attitude | 54 | 56 |
| Gender role | 55 | 54 |
| Beck Depression Inventory (BDI) | 5 | 8 |
| Sexual Arousal Inventory (SAI) | 90 | 95 |

[a]Other subscales from this instrument were not administered.

sess this couple's maintenance of treatment gains. When Richard and Judy arrived for this session, they announced that they had decided to get legally married, and Judy proudly displayed her engagement ring. Although the regularity of their dates and "talk times" had been somewhat inconsistent, both partners were content with their marital communication. They denied any instances of the distancing-and-pursuit pattern that had characterized their pretreatment interactions.

During the follow-up interval sexual interactions had continued with the same frequency as was noted at termination, and both partners were satisfied with the quality of their sexual contact. Richard revealed that he had experienced a burst of taboo fantasies during an interval of work-related stress. He had handled this by returning to daily masturbatory satiation exercises for a 3-week period, which reduced the frequency and intensity of these images. Although it is unusual for a patient to reinstate this aversive procedure voluntarily, Richard was extremely motivated to keep himself from "getting off the track." His long struggle with these intense urges apparently was sufficiently unpleasant to motivate him, particularly because of the extreme marital problems that had resulted when these taboo fantasies were present. Richard's commitment to Judy was noticeably stronger and his willingness to be legally married to her (in spite of the loss of tax benefits) stood as firm evidence to Judy that he indeed wanted to be with her. Judy reported experiencing sexual desire three to four times per week, which appears average for women in light of available data (Beck, Bozman, & Qualtrough, 1991). Overall, the couple was confident in their ability to handle sexual and relationship issues as they arose.

## OVERALL EVALUATION

Although this case is not necessarily typical of most LSDD couples presenting for sex therapy, we currently do not have a clinical picture of the modal LSDD patient and his or her partner. As illustrated, the use of a variety of therapeutic techniques, including treatment strategies designed to heighten sensory awareness and to expose long-standing relationship patterns, was important in the successful resolution of low sexual desire. To have treated this problem in a vacuum, without consideration of the marital system, would have been a mistake since a powerful synergy of sexual and relationship issues often combine to produce inadequate levels of sexual desire in one partner. In this instance, one partner reported excessive sexual interest, albeit of an unusual form, while the other reported hypoactive levels of desire. Inclusion of strategies borrowed from the treatment of sexual deviation was necessary to reduce one partner's excessive sexual interest while procedures designed to address the sexual and marital problems that reduced sexual desire in the other partner were instituted.

Fortunately, neither partner was resistant to change. Although Richard initially withheld important information from the therapist, this is not unusual in cases where atypical arousal patterns are present. Once this secret was revealed, treatment proceeded with the full cooperation of both partners. For those cases where more extreme resistance is observed, the reader is referred to relevant chapters of Leiblum and Rosen (1988) for a discussion of intervention strategies, such as paradoxical and antisabotage procedures, that address this process issue. In many respects, a common denominator in the successful treatment of most cases of LSDD is therapeutic flexibility. As illustrated in the case of Richard and Judy, the initial formulation often captures only part of the picture in this clinical disorder. With careful probing and continuous assessment, the mystery of low sexual desire sometimes unfolds further. One asset of using a behavioral approach to LSDD is the use of thorough, ongoing assessment, which can assist the therapist in detecting secrets, revising treatment plans, and, ultimately, helping patients to lead satisfying sexual lives.

## REFERENCES

American Psychiatric Association. (1987). *Diagnostic and statistical manual of mental disorders.* (3rd ed., rev.) Washington, DC: Author.

Beck, A. T., Ward, C. H., Mendelsohn, M., Mock, J., & Erbaugh, J. (1961). An inventory for measuring depression. *Archives of General Psychiatry, 4,* 561–571.

Beck, J. G. (1992). Behavioral approaches to sexual dysfunction. In S. M. Turner, K. S. Calhoun, & H. E. Adams (Eds.), *Handbook of clinical behavior therapy* (2nd ed.), (pp. 155–173). New York: Wiley.

Beck, J. G., Bozman, A. W., & Qualtrough, T. (1991). The experience of sexual desire: Psychological correlates in a college sample. *Journal of Sex Research, 28,* 443–456.

Comfort, A. (1972). *The Joy of Sex.* New York: Crown.

Derogatis, L. R. (1978). *Derogatis Sexual Functioning Inventory* (rev. ed.). Baltimore, MD: Clinical Psychometrics Research.

Friedman, J. M., & Hogan, D. R. (1985). Sexual dysfunction: Low sexual desire. In D. H. Barlow (Ed.), *Clinical handbook of psychological disorders* (pp. 417–461). New York: Guilford Press.

Hoon, E. F., & Chambless, D. (1986). Sexual Arousability Inventory (SAI) and Sexual Arousability Inventory-Expanded (SAI-E). In C. M. Davis and W. L. Yarber (Eds.), *Sexuality-related measures: A compendium* (pp. 21–24). Syracuse: Graphic Publishing.

Kaplan, H. S. (1979). *Disorders of sexual desire.* New York: Brunner/Mazel.

Leiblum, S. R., & Rosen, R. C. (Eds.). (1988). *Sexual desire disorders.* New York: Guilford Press.

Quinsey, V. L., & Earls, C. M. (1990). The modification of sexual preferences. In W. L. Marshall, D. R. Laws, & H. E. Barbaree (Eds.), *Handbook of sexual assault* (pp. 279–296). New York: Plenum.

Schreiner-Engel, P., & Schiavi, R. C. (1986). Lifetime psychopathology in individuals with low sexual desire. *Journal of Nervous and Mental Disease, 174,* 646–651.

Spanier, G. B. (1976). Measuring dyadic adjustment: New scales for assessing the quality of marriage and similar dyads. *Journal of Marriage and the Family, 38,* 15–28.

Zilbergeld, B., & Ellison, C. R. (1980). Desire discrepancies and arousal problems in sex therapy. In S. R. Leiblum & L. A. Pervin (Eds.), *Principles and practice of sex therapy* (pp. 65–101). New York: Guilford Press.

# CHAPTER 16

# Exhibitionism

## BARRY M. MALETZKY

### DESCRIPTION OF THE DISORDER

Against the background of the maladaptive sexual approach disorders, exhibitionism stands out as unusual in several respects. As opposed to pedophiles, exhibitionists commit a significantly greater number of deviant acts and are apprehended more often, yet they are jailed less often as well (Maletzky, 1991). Perhaps this is a result of society's view that the victims of exhibitionism are less seriously affected than victims of other sexual crimes, such as child molestation and rape. Indeed, exposure of the genitals is, by and large, a misdemeanor rather than a felony; even the judicial nomenclature sounds mild: *public indecency* or *indecent exposure*. Since these charges can stem from accidental acts—such as failure to take adequate precaution against exposure (e.g., urinating in public)—society may believe that exhibitionism is less serious than other sexual crimes and that, along with fetishism, transvestism, and bestiality, it is largely a victimless act.

Investigations of exhibitionists and their victims, however, provide evidence that the effects of exhibitionism can be devastating to both its practitioners and its victims. Exhibitionists often choose victims who are unusually sensitive, such as children, the elderly, or the disadvantaged (Langevin, 1983). Even when victims are not particularly vulnerable, exhibitionism can leave its mark: many girls and women exposed to are subsequently shy, mistrusting, and afraid to venture far from safety. A surprising number rate the experience

---

BARRY M. MALETZKY • Oregon Health Sciences University, Portland, Oregon 97202.

*Adult Behavior Therapy Casebook,* edited by Cynthia G. Last and Michel Hersen. Plenum Press, New York, 1994.

as upsetting long after its occurrence, though very long-term studies are as yet pending (Cox & Maletzky, 1980).

Moreover, exhibitionism often does not exist alone. Of 500 exhibitionists in a recent sample almost half (47%) engaged in other sexual crimes as well, most frequently voyeurism, 27% of the entire sample, and pedophilia, 17% (Maletzky, in press). Although the case to be described is one of "pure exhibitionism" for ease of presentation, clinicians are well advised to suspect, and search for, hidden paraphilias among cases presenting as exhibitionism alone.

Is exhibitionism a precursor to more serious sexual crimes? Most often it is not. In a review of descriptive studies investigating the course of untreated exhibitionism, just 14% of exhibitionists progressed from exposing to crimes of physical contact, such as the pedophilias or rape (Maletzky, 1980). Viewed another way, however, over one in ten exhibitionists will eventually proceed to inappropriate physical contact with a victim, contact with well-documented and severe consequences. Because it is currently difficult to specify which offenders will follow that course, it is crucial to employ effective treatment modalities for exhibitionists as soon as they are apprehended.

Fortunately, successful treatment programs for exhibitionists have been extensively described. Although earlier, largely psychodynamic, approaches were ineffective (Bastani, 1976), more recent therapies springing from the behavioral and cognitive literature have achieved documented success, both in short- and longer-term follow-ups. Employing these techniques has led to success rates in excess of 85% in the treatment literature (Maletzky, 1991; Maletzky & George, 1974). Lest we become complacent, however, it is best to recall that most of these studies have had follow-up periods of less than 2 years and that even in the most successful programs approximately one in ten exhibitionists will continue to accumulate victims.

Moreover, the relative success of behavioral and cognitive approaches does not inform us about the genesis of this disorder. The etiology of the maladaptive sexual approach disorders continues to be clouded in mist and controversy. Many theorists have pointed to an association between exhibitionism and an avoidant or schizoid personality pattern; exposing may represent frustrated and transposed sexual desires. Although it makes some intuitive sense that men who are inadequate socially would insert a sexual behavior (exposing) inappropriately early in the heterosocial-heterosexual chain, this hypothesis as stated does not lend itself to experimental verification. In addition, large clinics share the experience of treating a number of exhibitionists who have adequate social and sexual outlets.

The role of early childhood experiences, especially at critical stages of brain development, is also uncertain. Some, but not most, exhibitionists recall childhood sexual games in which the act of exposing played a prominent role (Maletzky, 1980). Also of interest may be an example of exhibitionism in infrahuman species: in many primate species, a male initiates sexual activity by exposing his erect penis to a female (Maletzky, 1980). Whether an evolutionary mechanism gone awry results in human exhibitionism, however, is at this time purely speculative.

While the origins of exhibitionism remain obscure, effective treatments exist. In the opinion of most researchers and clinicians in this field, almost every exhibitionist should be afforded access to behavioral and cognitive therapies.

## CASE IDENTIFICATION

B was a 29-year-old single white male referred by his attorney following charges of indecent exposure. This arrest was B's third for exposing himself. He had served no time and had previously been treated by a counselor specializing in assertiveness training and the acquisition of social skills.

## PRESENTING COMPLAINTS

B believed he would never expose again, and perhaps was sincere in that belief. Nevertheless, he seemed quite willing to enter a treatment program, although his cooperation appeared to be partly for the benefit of the court. At his first therapy session he entered no complaints spontaneously but admitted he had lost control of his urge to expose.

## HISTORY

Although there was little of dramatic interest in B's upbringing, he was always noted to be shy and introspective. He lacked social confidence, often believed he was different from others, and rarely dated as a teenager. He described his parents as strict and cold; affection was rarely shared at home. He rarely perceived parental support or praise.

Following graduation from high school, B attempted to go to a community college but had to drop out after 6 months due to financial constraints. He began to work in his father's metal shop, but arguments between him and his father led to his quitting. He had worked at a variety of shop and mechanic's jobs since and had been working as a mechanic at the same place of employment for 3 years at the time of his referral for treatment.

B had never been molested as a child. He recalled two experiences possibly related to subsequent sexual development, however: At the age of 5 or 6 he inadvertently entered his parents' bedroom when they were engaged in foreplay; saw and was baffled by his father's erect penis. When he was 10, B and a female

cousin 1 year older exposed their genitals to each other. He began to masturbate shortly thereafter, using images of this event to fuel his fantasies.

As he developed, B began to stare at attractive females and fantasized
about sexual acts with them. He engaged in this activity very much from afar,
believing no desirable female would pay him any heed. When he was old
enough to drive, he would cruise about town looking for attractive females,
then masturbate about them at home. At community college he encountered
many young women his age and incorporated some of them into his fantasies.
He began to park in various spots on campus so that he could see these
women. He would usually stimulate himself while staring at them. This progressed to masturbating by taking his erect penis out of his pants.

At first B had only the urge to satisfy himself while looking at women.
On one occasion, however, a woman walked by his vehicle and saw his erect
penis. She seemed both shocked and amused and lingered a bit before moving
on. B almost immediately reached orgasm. Although masturbating in his car
continued, from that point forward B began more and more to arrange events
so that he would be seen. His typical pattern was to park on campus or in
parking lots of shopping centers, masturbate while watching women, and then
call attention to himself by motioning for a woman to come over to his car,
ostensibly so he could ask her for directions or the time. In trying to analyze
his actions, B said that he was hoping to see a shocked and/or amused
reaction; however, the victim's response was not essential for sexual pleasure.
B also reported that he would sometimes arrange for a woman to see him
exposed without calling attention to himself. He would then feign embarrass-
ment at being so discovered. He would usually reach orgasm during or immediately after the exposing acts.

Even though B appeared socially and sexually handicapped, he had enjoyed two relatively long-term relationships with girlfriends. However, he had
continued to expose even during his relationships with these girlfriends. He
never told them of his exhibitionism. He recalled that he first experienced
sexual relations with a woman when he was 22—somewhat late in life given
present social customs. He reported no problems with obtaining or maintaining an erection during sexual activity or with premature ejaculation. He denied
any sexual interest in children or in homosexuality, sadomasochism, bondage,
or humiliation. He similarly denied any interest in, or activities connected
with, voyeurism, fetishism, transvestism, or bestiality. However, he did admit
to an increase in frequency of masturbation fantasies of exposing, with reactions of surprise and approval.

B estimated that he had exposed over 200 times. He was apprehended three
times, even though often he took no precautions to camouflage himself; indeed,
exposing from his vehicle provided immediate identification. Following his first
arrest at the age of 20, he received a 2-year probation without treatment.

When arrested a second time 3 years later, he was mandated into a treatment program, but the nature and qualifications of the program were left to his selection. He began treatment by seeing a pastoral counselor, who then referred him to a therapist, mentioned earlier, who specialized in assertiveness and social skills training. Following 6 months of such therapy, B was released with the recommendation that "probation can be terminated early, as the chance of exposing again is infinitesimal." Unfortunately, B was continuing to expose during treatment.

When evaluated following his third arrest, B appeared contrite, claiming, "I have learned my lesson." He minimized his exposing at first, saying that it only happened "occasionally," and most victims probably were amused, and that little damage could have been done. At this evaluation B was slightly overweight and had paid poor attention to his appearance. He manifested a slumped posture and stared at the floor, avoiding direct eye contact. He answered with short latencies but with long durations of utterance as well. Mental status findings indicate that B's cognitive functions were intact, though at times he appeared verbally slow. He showed a relatively flattened affective range with a depressed mood. There was no loosening of associations nor other evidence of a thought disorder and no suicidal ideation.

B's attorney referred him to a sexual abuse clinic prior to sentencing after he pled guilty to charges of indecent exposure. B believed his cooperation with evaluation and treatment procedures could lessen the severity of his sentence. He was seen for two evaluation sessions prior to sentencing, at which he received 30 days in a work release center and was mandated into an outpatient sexual offender treatment program.

## ASSESSMENT

The assessment of the sexual offender poses several problems peculiar to this population. Often a therapist will not be able to obtain an accurate history; it is very much to the offender's benefit to camouflage his complicity in prior deviant behaviors. Moreover, deviant sexual acts are often private, such as masturbation to deviant fantasies, and hence not accessible to a therapist. Even overt acts, as in exposing incidents, are generally not consistently reported by victims. A number of assessment techniques for the offender have been designed (and many were used in B's case), but it is necessary to keep the aforementioned caveats in mind.

### Frequency Records

B was asked to keep a sexual log and to note (1) covert exhibitionist behaviors (i.e., fantasies, urges, and dreams related to exhibitionism) and (2) overt exhibitionist acts (i.e., masturbation to exhibitionist fantasies or actual exposing in a real-life situation).

## "Significant Other" Data

B lived with his mother and 19-year-old sister. Despite her youth, B's sister functioned almost as a parent at home because the mother was chronically ill. She agreed to become involved in the treatment by meeting with B's therapist every 4 weeks to learn about his treatment program and to answer, on a 0 to 4+ scale, the following three questions: How well is B doing in treatment? How well is B completing homework assignments? Do you see any evidence that B is continuing to expose? Data were collected throughout treatment and at 1-, 3-, 5-, and 10-year follow-up periods.

## The Penile Plethysmograph

A penile plethysmograph is simply a device to measure and record expansion of the penis (Pithers & Laws, 1988). An offender places a thin mercury-in-rubber strain gauge on the midshaft of his penis. Figure 1 depicts the

Figure 16-1. The penile plethysmograph.

plethysmograph and Figure 2 the gauge. (Together they are termed the "penile plethysmograph.") The gauge registers expansion, which is taken to signify sexual arousal; such expansion is charted on a continuous strip of graph paper to form an ongoing record of penile tumescence under a variety of conditions. As commonly employed, excitation is recorded while the offender is exposed to sexually stimulating material, such as slides, movies, videotapes, and descriptions of graphic, hard-core pornography. Stimuli commonly presented to an offender in plethysmograph evaluations depict a wide variety of deviant situations, including heterosexual and homosexual pedophilia, exhibitionism, and aggressive sexuality. In almost all males with even minimal sexual arousal, blood is shunted to the penis, increasing its diameter and length (Pithers & Laws, 1988). The strain gauge registers the resulting increase in circumference with exquisite sensitivity: at times, even slight increases in tumescence too low for the offender himself to recognize are reflected in the plethysmograph tracings. Figure 3 depicts B's plethysmograph tracing during his initial evaluation, taken on the third clinic visit. Tracings of arousal are most commonly expressed in terms of percentage of full tumescence. The offender is shown a variety of pornographic materials and asked to signal when he believes he has attained a full erection. In some cases (but not in B's), the offender must masturbate with the gauge on to attain full erection. In common practice,

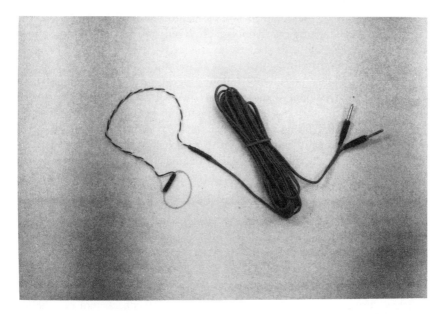

Figure 16-2. A mercury-in-rubber strain gauge.

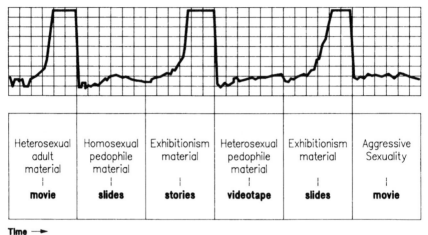

| Heterosexual adult material | Homosexual pedophile material | Exhibitionism material | Heterosexual pedophile material | Exhibitionism material | Aggressive Sexuality |
|---|---|---|---|---|---|
| ¦ | ¦ | ¦ | ¦ | ¦ | ¦ |
| **movie** | **slides** | **stories** | **videotape** | **slides** | **movie** |

Time →

Figure 16-3. The initial penile plethysmograph for B, taken during his third session.

arousal levels below 20% of full erection are considered to be below the level of sensitivity of error for the instrument and are interpreted as nonarousal.

As seen in Figure 3, B demonstrated full erection to a number of sexual stimuli, including consenting adult heterosexual behavior and scenes of exposing. The latter were presented mostly as auditory stimuli (story lines), since visual materials depicting exhibitionism are often ambiguous and arouse many males who do not expose. B showed no arousal to heterosexual and homosexual pedophile stimuli or to aggressive sexual stimuli.

In order to more objectively follow progress in treatment, three stimuli that elicited high deviant sexual arousal (two slides and one story line on initial testing) were excluded from all subsequent treatment sessions and then used every 3 months during treatment and at 1-, 3-, 5-, and 10-year follow-ups to measure arousal while eliminating effects of habituation.

The penile plethysmograph is not a phallic lie detector. It merely demonstrates arousal under the conditions of the test. It can never be employed to prove that an act did or did not occur. Indeed, approximately 30% of admitted sexual offenders demonstrate either normal plethysmograph tracings, that is, showing appropriate arousal to nondeviant stimuli and nonarousal to deviant stimuli, or a flat line of no arousal to any stimuli. Although B demonstrated deviant arousal at the 70% level, his arousal to nondeviant stimuli was even higher, approaching 100%, a not uncommon finding in exhibitionists. The abnormal arousal for B led his therapist to use the plethysmograph to monitor progress during treatment and to function as a biofeedback tool (see below), two of its most useful qualities. Indeed, under the sterile laboratory conditions of the test, it is surprising that the majority of offenders *do* demonstrate arousal and that the instrument itself has proven to be valid and reliable (Frenzel & Lang, 1989). For example, B showed no deviant sexual arousal to stimuli associated with young boys or girls or to aggressive sexuality.

B's therapist administered plethysmograph tests throughout the course of treatment and at 1-, 3-, 5-, and 10-year follow-ups.

## The Polygraph

Despite the uncertainty about the validity of lie detector tests as legally and scientifically significant, these tests have often proven helpful in the assessment and treatment of the sexual offender. B was tested at intervals of 3 months throughout his treatment course and at 1-, 3-, 5-, and 10-year follow-ups.

## Criminal Records

In cooperation with local law enforcement officials, charges and arrest records were computer-scanned during treatment, and at 1-, 3-, 5-, and 10-year follow-ups for any evidence that B had become involved with the law again. While these computerized files are reasonably complete, occasionally a charge is not documented (e.g., if an offender has successfully used an alias). Nonetheless, such records have proven helpful in the past in identifying any potential legal problems an offender might be having.

## Psychological Testing

Psychological testing is conspicuously absent in the evaluation of B's progress in treatment. Such testing was not requested even at initial evaluation, except for a WAIS (Wechsler Adult Intelligence Scale), which showed a Full Scale IQ of 97. This test was completed because the question of dulled intellect was raised during the mental status evaluation. A full psychologic assessment was not completed because (1) there is, as yet, no empirical evidence that a sexual offender fits any particular psychologic profile and (2) results of testing would not have changed the treatment recommendations. Hence, such testing was believed in B's case to add only cost to the assessment. Certainly an opposite view is tenable: testing before treatment might have illuminated corners of B's personality hidden from full view, while pre- and posttreatment testing might have indicated whether positive personality change had occurred during treatment. In the final analysis, such testing of B was thought to represent a triumph of technique over purpose and was omitted.

## SELECTION OF TREATMENT

At the beginning of this last decade of the millennium, the diverse treatment approaches commonly employed for the sexual offender have coalesced into two groups, the behavioral and the cognitive approaches, which are usually combined in the treatment of any offender. Most clinicians in this field have foregone the psychodynamic therapies, while medical approaches such as the use of anti-androgenic medications are generally viewed as necessary only in those offenders at large in the community who pose an immediate physical risk to others.

### Behavioral Approaches

*Covert sensitization.* The pairing in imagination of covert deviant sexual stimuli, such as fantasies, with negative consequences is termed covert sensitization (CS). CS was initially employed as the sole technique for sexual offenders but is now generally reserved for homework assignments.

*Assisted covert sensitization (ACS).* Another technique, variously termed aversive imagery or aversive conditioning, adds an extra punch to the aforementioned covert technique by introducing a noxious odor (usually rotting tissue[1]) during scene presentations and coincident with the imaginary adverse consequences.

*Foul taste aversion.* The offender is asked to thoroughly chew a bitter pill (Pro-Banthine is commonly used) when in a situation previously eliciting exposing behavior.

*Penile plethysmograph biofeedback.* During biofeedback the plethysmograph is connected to a column of multicolored biofeedback lights (see Figure 4). The offender, while viewing or listening to stimulus material, is variably asked to increase arousal to normal stimuli or decrease it to deviant stimuli, thus gaining both immediate feedback about his arousal state and practice in modifying, and hence controlling, sexual responses.

*Aversive behavior rehearsal (ABR).* The offender is asked to duplicate deviant sexual acts in the presence of others, usually clinic staff. For example,

---

[1] Contact the Sexual Abuse Clinic, 8332 SE 13th Avenue, Portland, Oregon 97202, for details.

Figure 16-4. Penile plethysmograph biofeedback lights.

a pedophile might be asked to demonstrate, using a life-size anatomically correct doll, how he molested a child or an exhibitionist might be asked to expose (e.g., from his car) to clinic staff, who would make no response. This technique generates a great deal of anxiety in the offender and must be applied with much explanation and support.

*Masturbation techniques.* Two quite different techniques for the sexual offender utilize the powerful images generated during masturbation. In both of these techniques, the offender is asked to masturbate privately at home but to tape-record his spoken fantasies so that the therapist can check compliance.

In the "masturbatory fantasy change" procedure the offender masturbates to deviant fantasies or materials until the point of ejaculatory inevitability, at which time he switches to nondeviant fantasies or materials. With each subsequent episode of masturbation, he is asked to make his shift earlier and earlier in the masturbatory chain until he is eventually masturbating to nondeviant fantasies from the beginning of self-stimulation.

In the "masturbatory satiation" procedure the offender is asked to masturbate to nondeviant fantasies or materials until climax and then to continue masturbating, but to deviant fantasies and materials, for 30 to 60 minutes thereafter. This technique combines deviant fantasies with the time of lowest sexual arousal. In addition, it is perceived as an aversive act since the offender generally will not be able to obtain an erection during this time and often notes irritation to the penis with continued self-stimulation. Moreover, masturbation at this time becomes boring because of the instruction to use the same fantasies repeatedly.

## Cognitive Approaches

*Relapse prevention.* The therapist works with the offender to define the set of environmental configurations eliciting deviant sexual arousal and deviant sexual acts and then constructs with him a program of behaviors designed to prevent encountering these situations. Relapse prevention includes examining cognitive distortions that frequently accompany and justify the offender's deviant behavior.

*Cycle definition and awareness.* In a related approach the therapist reviews in fine detail the welter of emotions and situations that lead to offending and helps the offender to become keenly aware of situations and emotional states that begin the cascade of responses ultimately leading to an offense. The offender is then taught alternatives to block the earliest steps in this chain, since early competing responses are the most effective in diverting deviant sexual behavior.

*Empathy training.* Many offenders are remarkably unaware of the harm to victims their behavior can cause. Others attempt to block out such awareness. In empathy training the therapist utilizes a variety of materials and techniques to enhance awareness of the victimization process, including books describing the bitter trauma that sexual abuse causes, letters and videotapes of actual victims' descriptions of the impact victimization has created in their lives, and face-to-face meetings with victims, often accomplished through group therapy. Moreover, most offenders are asked to write letters of clarification to their victims, acknowledging their responsibility (however, such letters are rarely employed in exhibitionism owing to the transient, nonpersonal nature of the contact).

*Adjunctive cognitive techniques.* Although not easily classified, a number of adjunctive approaches have been of value in the treatment of offenders, some particularly so for exhibitionists. These include assertive training; social skills training, often utilizing psychodramatic methods and employing a female therapist; desensitization to heterosocially/heterosexually appropriate behaviors; group therapy, which is often used for support but also for chipping away at the veneer of denial; and family/marital therapy, a method generally necessary in cases where a family has been involved.

## COURSE OF TREATMENT

B was assessed and treated in a large sexual abuse clinic in Portland, Oregon. The clinic has treated over five thousand sexual offenders in 18 years. Treatment was carried out in an office/laboratory similar to the one pictured in Figure 5. The setting is rather formal and pedestrian, but it has yielded good clinical results while retaining the equipment necessary to treat sexual offenders in the present day.

B was initially evaluated by the clinic director, a psychiatrist, and then referred to a psychologist for treatment. The director and psychologist met monthly to discuss the case. While B's treatment course was typical, any single offender may have a somewhat different course based on individual variations.

In accord with the clinic's emphasis on the problem-oriented medical record, the following problem list was initially generated for B: (1) exhibitionism, (2) deficient social skills, and (3) obesity, mild. Note was made of the following assets as well: (1) acceptance of treatment, (2) stable job, (3) supportive family, and (4) good physical health.

B's primary therapist was a male psychologist with 7 years' experience in treating sexual offenders. All treatment sessions except two aversive behavior rehearsal (ABR) sessions were conducted in the office/laboratory pictured in Figure 5. Following his accommodation to the laboratory during the first two treatment sessions, B underwent a penile plethysmograph evaluation, which revealed absence of arousal for all but two categories: heterosexual consenting adult activity and activities connected with exposing.

### Phase I

Phase I consisted of weekly sessions of 1 hour each for 4½ months that included covert sensitization (CS), assisted covert sensitization (ACS), and foul taste conditioning. Following B's accommodation to the laboratory and to plethysmograph testing, the therapist held two sessions with him to review scenes. Fortunately, B admitted rather openly to all of his charges and even divulged numerous earlier exposing incidents not known to the authorities. The majority of offenders, while admitting to doing something wrong, will usually minimize their crimes; exhibitionists appear more willing to divulge their true history, perhaps owing in part to the perceived lack of physical contact and harm done to a victim.

Table 1 presents in an abbreviated form representative scenes from B's treatment course. Each scene was presented to B, with embellishment and additions of details, for 1 to 3 minutes three times per session. (The asterisks mark the points of addition and removal of foul odor.)

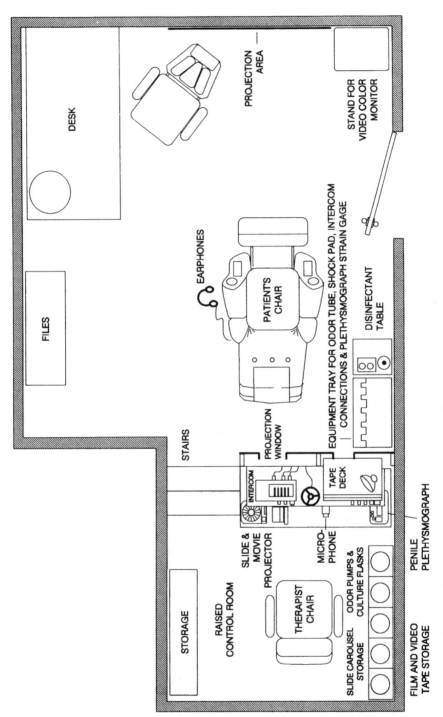

Figure 16-5. Typical office/laboratory for treatment of the sexual offender.

Table 1

Abbreviated Representative Scenes for Assisted Covert Sensitization (ACS) for B

*Scene 1*—You've been crusing around your neighborhood late at night when you suddenly see a young woman just leaving a grocery store. It's dark and no one else is around. You circle the block and start to drive by slowly as you fondle yourself. You're getting hard, and as you pull up to her you pull your stiff penis out and start to really jerk off. You can see her body but not her face yet. She's really built, though. You pull up and call her over to ask for directions. You've got your prick out and are really pumping it. She bends down as you lower the window,* but suddenly you see her face and it's your sister! She's staring right at your penis with a hurt and angry look as she yells at you, "You're sick!" You're starting to get sick to your stomach as you look at her. You're going soft. You start to puke. Chunks of vomit catch in your throat; you try to gulp them down, but you can't. You're throwing up chunks of vomit; vomit dribbles off your chin and onto your penis. You've got to get out of there. You drive away and clean yourself off.* You can breathe the fresh night air, now that you got away from exposing.

*Scene 2*—You've been parked on campus, watching the girls, when all at once a beautiful red-haired girl starts to walk toward your car. You start to fondle yourself, and as she approaches you pull your penis out and start to jerk off. You really want to show it to her. As she passes by, you roll down the window and pretend to ask for the time. She bends down and you follow her eyes as she starts to realize you're exposed. She's surprised and just stares at it, but suddenly* there's a sharp pain in your groin—you've caught your prick in your zipper. You're starting to bleed, and your penis really hurts. Blood's everywhere and the redhead is just laughing at you. You're getting sick to your stomach. You quickly drive away* and get your penis unstuck. The pain is easing up as you get away from exposing and can breathe the fresh air as your stomach calms down.

*Points at which foul odor was introduced and/or removed.

These scenes carry obvious cognitive messages and suggestions, particularly relief associated with escape from exposing. At present it appears that the olfactory conditioning component is the crucial element in this treatment, since many scenes lack suggestive wording and often nausea does not obviously result naturally from the circumstances presented. Scenes were recorded and B was asked to listen to his tape (four were eventually made) four times each week and to smell his own supply of foul odor at appropriate times in the scenes. He was also asked to imagine such scenes with adverse consequences, but without odor, on alternate nights prior to going to sleep.

To accomplish aversive olfactory conditioning, an odor-presentation apparatus was used that delivered any one of four odors, three foul and one pleasant (fresh air, cedar, or perfume), to B's nostrils via a catheter and nasal cannula.[2] The odor delivery system is depicted in Figure 6. B was connected to the plethysmograph and odor-delivery device while wearing earphones and watching scenes on videotape or slides. He often complained that he felt like

[2] Contact the Sexual Abuse Clinic, 8332 SE 13th Avenue, Portland, Oregon 97202, for details.

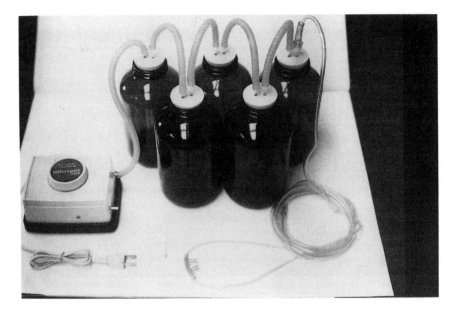

Figure 16-6. An odor-delivery apparatus for treating the sexual offender.

a terminally ill hospital patient being connected to a variety of machines! Nonetheless, he appeared to accommodate well to this intrusion of instruments, which did not preclude good sexual arousal or prevent establishment of a trusting therapeutic relationship.

Twelve of the first sixteen clinic visits included aversive odor conditioning; however, some time was taken in these contacts to review homework assignments. These included use of the tapes and odor, foul taste (B was asked to chew a foul-tasting tablet of Pro-Banthine whenever he encountered a tempting situation), and CS assignments, mentioned earlier. In addition, B was asked to keep a sexual log, to write a sexual autobiography, and to read a variety of handouts on sexual abuse and male sexuality and make notes on how this material applied to him or how he could apply it to his own life. During parts of some Phase I sessions, time was taken by B's therapist to review homework assignments and to select new tasks. In addition, time was allowed for ventilation and support and to discuss referrals for social skills training and group therapy.

During the weekly sessions of CS, ACS, and foul taste conditioning, B's therapist employed a wide range of stimuli in random order, including appropriate sexual material and deviant material associated with exposing. Visual stimuli have proven more useful for pedophiles and rapists than for exhibitionists, for whom story lines appear to yield the highest arousal. Scenes in a story are surprisingly powerful in eliciting arousal, perhaps because the offender can fantasize ideal faces, postures, and situations instead of being presented with visual images already chosen by treatment personnel.

*Penile plethysmographic biofeedback.* During seven of the first sixteen sessions, B was given feedback from the vertical array of lights depicted in Figure 4. He was asked to keep the red lights (over 50% arousal) off for deviant stimuli and the green lights (under 20% arousal) off for nondeviant stimuli. After the first two such sessions B was able to comply with these measures of sexual control in over 80% of trials.

*Masturbation techniques.* B was asked, beginning at the fifth session, to masturbate to exhibitionist fantasies until the point of ejaculatory inevitability and then to switch immediately to nondeviant fantasies. He then was asked to make this switch earlier and earlier in the masturbation chain. By the tenth session, he was asked to masturbate to climax with normal fantasies, then to continue masturbating for 30 more minutes to deviant fantasies. He made tape recordings of both techniques.

*Cognitive therapy.* During the five of the first sixteen sessions, B's therapist introduced elements of cognitive therapy. B was asked to keep a log of urges to expose and to note under what circumstances they occurred. He learned that most exposing situations occurred on his way home from work on weekends. He was asked to construct a relapse prevention plan and was encouraged to have his family participate in this task with him. B devised the following rules, applied on weekdays and weekends: (1) he was to call his sister just prior to leaving work (since she knew how long the drive home would take, it would automatically mean he exposed if he was late); (2) he was never to go driving alone on weekends; and (3) he had to switch vehicles with a brother who owned a pickup truck, since he could not be seen exposing as readily in the truck.

In addition, during these sessions B's therapist explored the concept of a chain or cycle of behaviors leading to exposures. To facilitate this part of therapy, B completed several workbooks prepared specifically for sexual offenders (Bays, Freeman-Longo, & Hildebran, 1990). Several additional stimuli were uncovered that increased the risk of deviant behavior in B, including feeling frustration secondary to imagined rejections by women. Figure 7 presents an abbreviated reproduction of one deviant chain of behaviors leading to exposing, with examples of possible interventions. (A cycle was not the fittest metaphor for B's deviant behavior; in many offenders, however, it is.)

By exploring these chains of behaviors, the therapist was able to elicit

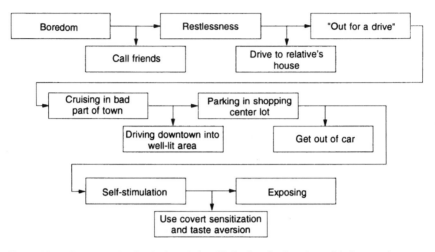

Figure 16-7. One example of a deviant chain of behaviors for B and possible interventions.

B's help in planning intervention strategies. For example, B elected to telephone one of three friends whenever he noticed an increase in restless behavior in order to join him in some activity. At another point in a different chain (increased smoking) he decided to either go swimming or play basketball at the local YMCA. In general, interventions early in a chain were more successful than those attempted later and closer to actually exposing.

## Phase II

Sessions 17 to 25, spaced at twice-monthly intervals, consisted of assisted covert sensitization (ACS) for part of each session and aversive behavior rehearsal (ABR) during sessions 18, 20, and 23. Following an explanation of the latter technique, B's therapist asked him to carefully consider whether to accept the recommendation for its inclusion in his therapy regimen. B assented and signed a consent form for the procedure. At the designated sessions four clinic staff, two men, one of whom was B's therapist, and two women, observed him expose for 3 minutes from his car in a secluded parking lot blocked off from the street. Staff made no response but simply observed.

B manifested extreme anxiety (and no arousal) before, during, and after these AGR sessions. The therapist supported him at all points in time. Following the second session, B confided that he "could never feel aroused when exposing again."

Sessions in Phase II also included a review of homework and extension and refinement of intervention strategies intended to prevent relapse. Empathy training also took place during sessions of this phase of treatment. B was asked to read several journal articles and chapters about the victims of exhibitionism. (Cox & Maletzky, 1980). He expressed surprise at the psychologic harm victims described, and his justifications for exposing began to increasingly erode. The therapist then asked B to engage in an unusual but often helpful task: lecturing at a local high school program on sexual abuse. B presented himself there honestly as an exhibitionist and received a positive response for his courage in becoming thus unmasked.

During this intermediate phase B agreed to five sessions with a female therapist for social skills training and assertiveness training. Using these newly learned approaches, B was able to ask for several dates and began relationships with two women.

Also during this phase B was enrolled in closed-end group therapy format (of eight sessions) designed to facilitate disclosure and improve confidence in group situations. His participation was marginal, however, and it was debatable whether any benefit occurred.

## Phase III

B had additional "booster" sessions 1, 2, and 3 months after termination. These sessions consisted of (1) a review of any urges to expose and of behavioral and cognitive techniques used to interrupt chains of behavior leading to such urges, (2) plethysmograph testing with the three test stimuli never associated with aversion, and three scenes of ACS.

## Summary of Treatment Approach

The following considerations were taken into account in planning B's treatment course: (1) It was deemed important to reduce B's deviant sexual arousal quickly so as to prevent further victimization; thus, the aversive behavioral techniques were employed early in the treatment course. (2) Cognitive techniques were slightly delayed in order to build better rapport and yield improved disclosure.

Although the phases of treatment presented in this case have been described as sharply defined, in many such cases the margins are blurred by clinical exigencies. Nonetheless, B's treatment is representative of that of many exhibitionists and of most other sexual offenders as well.

## TERMINATION

The decision to terminate B's treatment was based on self-reports, "significant other" reports, results of use of the penile plethysmograph and the polygraph, and B's clean criminal record update. From a review of all assessment indicators it appeared that B was, at least at the end of active treatment, a clinical success. Overconfidence was avoided by the realization that long-term follow-ups of sexual offenders are rare and that these assessment techniques would likely be viewed 5 to 10 years hence as clumsy and primitive.

### Self-Reports

Although generally regarded as biased, self-reports provide a source of data and can be correlated with more objective methods of assessment. B claimed no persistent arousal to stimuli associated with exposing. In addition, his sexual logs detailed situations he encountered that previously had prompted exposing behaviors but were no longer arousing to him, such as noticing an attractive woman walking alone in a secluded area.

### "Significant Other" Reports

B's sister had supplied answers to the three questions asked of her (described in the Assessment section) every 4 weeks. Her reports over the final 4 months of active treatment were in a decidedly positive direction:

- How well is B doing in treatment? (Response = 3.5+ on a 0 to 4+ scale)
- How well is B completing homework assignments? (Response = 3.0+)
- Do you see any evidence that B is continuing to expose? (Response = no)

### The Penile Plethysmograph

Figure 8 presents B's final plethysmograph recording at his last "booster" session. His deviant sexual arousal was under 20% on all exposing items, but B showed normal arousal to consenting adult heterosexual stimuli. How can we be sure, however, that these findings do not represent accommodation or improving skill in controlling erections?

Unfortunately, we cannot be absolutely certain. However, these results include exposure to the three test stimuli never associated with aversion and presented only rarely during the course of treatment. Moreover, diminished erectile responses would represent an increasing skill in sexual control, which

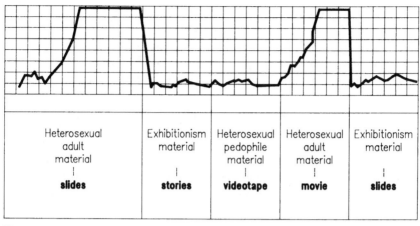

| Heterosexual adult material | Exhibitionism material | Heterosexual pedophile material | Heterosexual adult material | Exhibitionism material |
|---|---|---|---|---|
| ⦙ | ⦙ | ⦙ | ⦙ | ⦙ |
| **slides** | **stories** | **videotape** | **movie** | **slides** |

Time ━▶

Figure 16-8. The final penile plethysmograph recorded for B, taken during his 30th session.

is itself a not unhealthy response to treatment. Nonetheless, we cannot state with certainty that plethysmograph results on their own are indicative of success; it is their correlation with other data that prompts some measure of confidence in these results.

## The Polygraph

B was required to undergo lie detector tests every 3 months during active treatment. His responses to critical questions (e.g., Have you exposed yourself to any women in the past 3 months?) were indicative of honesty. While not usually admissible in court, the polygraph has been helpful in therapy: approximately 1 week prior to the test B was reminded that a polygraph was upcoming and he was encouraged to divest himself of any secrets so that he could be certain of "passing," a strategy that produced some important disclosures during treatment, as when B, early in the treatment course, admitted he was leaving work early to cruise about town.

## Criminal Records

A check of computerized police files on a monthly basis during treatment revealed no evidence of charges nor of any legal actions taken involving B.

Fortunately, B was, in the main, a fairly stable individual and agreed to our invitation to be reassessed at increasing intervals after the termination of active treatment. By clinic policy, follow-ups are attempted for all sexual offenders at 1, 3, 5, and 10 years. While follow-ups as long as 18 years have been reported in this clinic, B's most recent assessment was conducted 10 years following termination of active treatment. The policy of reinitiating (without charge) active therapy for any offender found to have recurrent deviant sexual arousal on follow-up was not necessary in B's case owing to continuing evidence of the persistence of treatment effects.

During follow-up evaluations, B completed a log of sexual activities for the month prior to the assessment, and attempts were made unsuccessfully to contact his sister for her report. (She had moved several months after active treatment ended.) Plethysmograph data were obtained to a variety of novel stimuli and to the three test stimuli at each follow-up session. A polygraph was also completed, and clinical personnel searched police files for any mention of charges and convictions against B.

B continued to demonstrate the absence of exposing behaviors and showed no deviant sexual arousal on the plethysmograph during the follow-up period. Polygraph appraisals and police file searches did not yield any suspicious data at any of the follow-up sessions. Although B had transferred to a neighboring state, he indicated agreement to return to the clinic periodically to undergo further checkups.

## OVERALL EVALUATION

Certainly, any clinical author is eager to share therapeutic triumphs rather than dismal failures. Any clinic would be happy to treat a coterie of clients like B, given the ease with which he apparently progressed through his course of treatment. Such sanguine reports should not blur the other end of the spectrum. Treatment failures are not uncommon in any sexual abuse clinic. While therapy success rates in excess of 90% are often quoted for exhibitionists and pedophiles (Maletzky & George, 1974), more difficult patients, such as rapists, predatory offenders, and those with multiple paraphilias, often are not treated with such facility. Even though many clinics report success rates in these cases of 75% to 80% (Maletzky & George, 1974), this still results in the potential for one out of every four offenders to create additional victims. Clinical research is needed to document the factors associated with treatment failure and repeated offending. Small, cogent double-blind studies are often called for but may not be feasible, given the dangers of offering placebo or no treatment conditions for this population. Therefore, even retrospective data reviews involving large numbers of offenders would help to pinpoint the assessment and treatment strategies most likely to yield benefit, especially in offenders still difficult to treat, such as rapists and those with a combination of heterosexual and homosexual pedophilia. Seminal efforts in this regard are being mounted (Marques, 1990).

Nonetheless, the success reported here is not atypical, especially in a single, relatively uncomplicated case of exhibitionism. The use of behavioral and cognitive treatment approaches in such cases has yielded apparent clinical success maintained over a number of years following the termination of active therapy. Chapters in books not yet published will hopefully document the persistence of treatment gains over future decades in the treatment of these disorders of desire.

## REFERENCES

Bastani, J. B. (1976). Treatment of male genital exhibitionism. *Comprehensive Psychiatry, 17,* 769–774.

Bays, L., Freeman-Longo, R., & Hildebran, D. D. (1990). *Guided workbooks for clients in evaluation and treatment.* Orwell, VT: The Safer Society Press.

Cox, D. J., & Maletzky, B. M. (1980). Victims of exhibitionism. In D. J. Cox & R. J. Daitzman (Eds.), *Exhibitionism: Description, assessment, and treatment* (pp. 179–189). New York: Garland Press.

Frenzel, R. R., & Lang, R. H. (1989). Identifying sexual preferences in intrafamilial and extrafamilial child sexual abusers. *Annals of Sex Research, 2,* 255–275.

Langevin, R. (1983). *Sexual strands: Understanding and treating sexual anomalies in men.* Hillsdale, NJ: Erlbaum.

Maletzky, B. M. (1980). Assisted covert sensitization. In D. J. Cox & R. J. Daitzman (Eds.), *Exhibitionism: Description, assessment, and treatment* (pp. 122–155). New York: Garland Press.

Maletzky, B. M. (1991). *Treating the sexual offender.* Newbury Park, CA: Sage.

Maletzky, B. M. (in press). The prediction of dangerousness in male sexual offenders. *Annals of Sex Research.*

Maletzky, B. M. & George, F. S. (1974). "Assisted covert sensitization" in the treatment of exhibitionism. *Journal of Consulting and Clinical Psychology, 42,* 38–40.

Marques, J. (1990, November). *The SOTEP program in California.* Presented to the Association for the Treatment of Sexual Abusers, Annual Conference on the Treatment of Sexual Offenders. Toronto.

Pithers, W. E., & Laws, D. R. (1988). The penile plethysmograph: Uses and abuses in assessment and treatment of sexual aggressors. In B. Schwartz (Ed.), *A practitioner's guide to the treatment of the incarcerated male sex offender* (pp. 37–49). Washington, DC: National Institute of Corrections.

CHAPTER 17

# Pedophilia

## A. ECCLES and W. L. MARSHALL

## DESCRIPTION OF THE DISORDER

According to *DSM-III-R* (American Psychiatric Association, 1987) the criteria for a diagnosis of pedophilia is the presence of urges and fantasies to be sexually involved with a prepubescent child or children, whether or not these urges are acted upon. These urges or acts must be present for at least 6 months, and the patient must be at least 16 years old, with the child or children in question at least 5 years younger.

We have argued elsewhere that *DSM-III-R* is not a particularly useful tool for the clinician who assesses and treats sex offenders (Marshall & Eccles, 1991). The most salient problem with its use is that very few offenders can actually be classified because of the reliance on the identification of sexually deviant thoughts and practices. The diagnosis requires either an acknowledgment by the offender of deviant fantasies and urges or the establishment of the existence of deviant sexual preferences by plethysmography. Both of these requirements can be difficult to satisfy. Note that the commission of a sexual offense against a child does not in and of itself warrant a diagnosis of pedophilia. The diagnosis is only appropriate when these offenses are motivated by persistent and deviant sexual fantasies of children. This is a characteristic which is not a feature of many men, particularly intrafamilial offenders, who sexually abuse children.

While most clinicians who work with other client populations can reason-

A. ECCLES and W. L. MARSHALL • Kingston Sexual Behaviour Clinic, and Department of Psychology, Queens University, Kingston, Ontario, Canada K7L 3N6.

*Adult Behavior Therapy Casebook,* edited by Cynthia G. Last and Michel Hersen. Plenum Press, New York, 1994.

ably expect their clients to assist the therapeutic process by being truthful and sincere, these assumptions cannot be made about sex offenders. This is particularly true if an assessment of an offender has been requested to facilitate sentencing, parole, or family reintegration decisions. The situational demands of these assessments make it quite likely that an offender will present a substantially sanitized version of his behavior and difficulties. In fact, there is growing recognition among those who assess sexual offenders that most of these men are going to be untruthful at least to some degree (Salter, 1988). Indeed, assessments conducted at our clinic routinely assess the degree to which an offender is denying or minimizing his behavior. While this is more readily achieved with regard to external events such as the specifics of an offense, it is not so easily done with internal events such as fantasies and urges.

Some researchers have championed the use of phallometric techniques in the objective determination of sexual preferences (e.g., Freund, 1987; McConaghy, 1991). While phallometry is most useful in the assessment of nonfamilial child molesters, 20% to 30% of men do not respond sufficiently to permit profile interpretation (Barbaree & Marshall, 1989). Furthermore, we have found that less than 50% of nonfamilial child molesters and less than 30% of incest offenders display deviant profiles at phallometric evaluation (Marshall & Eccles, 1991). Combined with the problem of attempts by offenders to fake their responses (Rosen & Beck, 1988), phallometry is clearly somewhat limited in the role it can play.

While *DSM-III-R* is of limited utility, at least in relation to the sexual disorders, the reality is such that behavior therapists and others must be familiar with it if we are to communicate effectively with the many professionals who do use it. The case that follows describes the assessment and treatment of an offender who meets the criteria set by *DSM-III-R* for the diagnosis of pedophilia. Since there is no such thing as a typical pedophile, we have chosen a case that illustrates some unusual features that might not ordinarily be brought to the readers's attention.

## CASE IDENTIFICATION

Bob, a 30-year-old man, was referred to the Kingston Sexual Behaviour Clinic by the staff at the emergency department of a local general hospital. Bob had gone there after prompting from his wife following her discovery that he had been sexually abusing her 11-year-old daughter from her previous marriage. Bob was clearly depressed and emotional about the prospect of losing his family and facing criminal charges, although the hospital staff determined that he was not suicidal. Bob was further distressed to learn that the attending physician had to inform the Children's Aid Society (CAS) about the abuse, although he was placated somewhat when appointments were made for him to be seen at our clinic later that same day. He was then released by the hospital, which later contacted the clinic to confirm his attendance here.

## PRESENTING COMPLAINTS

Bob stated at the outset that some difficulties had surfaced recently and were contributing to "major intermarital problems." He stated that he had attempted to touch his stepdaughter on three occasions while she slept. He had been discovered on his last attempt when he inadvertently woke the girl up. While he recognized this as being inappropriate, he felt that it was secondary to his deteriorating relationship with his wife over the last 18 months. Amelioration of the couple's marital difficulties would, he felt, resolve the problem he had with his stepdaughter.

## HISTORY

Bob reported an unremarkable childhood and upbringing. There was no emotional, physical or sexual abuse within the family, nor was he abused by others. Overall, he described his childhood as "happy." His education was likewise unremarkable. He had been a slightly above average student academically and had pursued some university training before switching to a community college to train as an electrician. At the time of assessment he was working as the chief technician at the laboratories of a local research center. He had no previous charges for any sexual or nonsexual offenses.

## ASSESSMENT

Bob was seen on several occasions for his assessment. This included an interview, the completion of a number of questionnaires, and a laboratory assessment of his sexual preferences. The following account describes these procedures and the results derived from them. It should be noted, however, that the distinction between assessment and treatment is not one that in practice is always clearly defined. For example, an offender's denial and minimization of his abusive behavior are important targets of treatment, but even during an assessment we will typically challenge an offender's denials and distortions. Not only does this give a more detailed picture of the offender's conceptualization of his offense, but it also helps to provide an indication of his motivation for treatment. Similarly, during treatment sexual offenders frequently reveal more information relevant to the description of their problem than they were willing to report before establishing rapport with the therapist.

## Cognitive Factors

The cognitive factors that we assess are those that have been found to facilitate sexually abusive behavior. While denial can clearly be determined in a straightforward manner, the assessment of qualified admissions is more difficult. In our interviews we look for evidence that the offender is

1. Minimizing his responsibility for his actions by blaming the child (e.g., "She walked around the house in her underwear like she was saying 'Take me, I'm yours' ")
2. Minimizing his responsibility by blaming external factors (e.g., alcohol)
3. Minimizing his responsibility by blaming internal factors that he says are beyond his control (e.g., an "uncontrollable" sex drive)
4. Minimizing the frequency of the assaults
5. Minimizing the severity and intrusiveness of the assaults
6. Minimizing by distorting his intent (e.g., "I thought it was the best way to find out if someone was abusing her")

In addition to these cognitive factors, a number of other distorted attitudes and myths about child sexuality are assessed. These are determined through interviews and through questionnaires, such as *The Sex with Children Scale* (Marshall & Hodkinson, 1988) and the *Multiphasic Sex Inventory* (Nichols & Molinder, 1984). These assessment procedures are as yet in their infancy (Murphy, 1990; Stermac, Segal, & Gillis, 1990), and their transparency probably means that many inappropriate attitudes remain undetected. However, they at least permit identification of the more blatant distortions of attitude that the offender endorses.

During our interviews we also look for information about how the offender has talked himself into doing something he clearly knows is wrong. In addition to their efforts to minimize the seriousness or severity of the abusive behavior, offenders typically rationalize their behavior as they set up opportunities to offend (e.g., "The kids have been on their mother's back all day; I'll tell her to visit her friend Laura so she can get a break, and I'll look after the kids tonight"). Information so derived provides the basis for further interviews and for questioning the offender during treatment.

In Bob's case, there was considerable evidence that he both minimized and rationalized his behavior and that these distortions served to maintain his offending. Initially, he admitted to three incidents, which he said were isolated in nature and nonintrusive. Furthermore, Bob made it quite clear that he did not consider these incidents to be the primary problem. He believed that improving his marriage would eliminate the thoughts of touching his step-daughter as his "sexual needs" would be met. Bob added that he hadn't been himself when he committed the acts because all three had followed alcohol consumption. He was confident, however, that his stepdaughter would suffer no ill effects, as he had gone into her room when she was asleep and she had awakened only during the most recent incident.

Bob denied any fantasies or urges of having sex with any young girls, including his stepdaughter, and could not explain why these three incidents had occurred. While he admitted that he had entered his stepdaughter's room late at night on these three occasions, Bob insisted that he never went into her room with the intent of abusing her. On each occasion, Bob said he was the last person to go to bed and had simply entered her room "to see that she was covered up." He stated that "something came over" him when he was in the room.

Bob said he did nothing the first night but probably would have if the girl had not suddenly stirred in her sleep. Bob stated that he got "scared" and left the room. The next evening he again entered her room. Again Bob was insistent that he initially went in to cover her but said that as he pulled the sheet up over her, he took the opportunity to look up between her legs at her genital area. He claimed that he then got up and left the room quickly, shocked by what he had just done. He calmed down by reassuring himself that because she had not awakened "it couldn't have hurt her" and that nobody would ever know. Bob promised himself he would never do anything like that again. Despite this pledge to himself, he entered his stepdaughter's room again the very next evening. This time he touched her vagina, waking the girl, who then screamed, alerting her mother.

In our first interview Bob denied that he had ever done anything like this before or that he had ever thought about doing it. He reported sexual interests and fantasies that exclusively involved sexual acts with consenting adult fe-males. Moreover, he could recall no other incidents in the past that were at all suggestive of sexual behavior problems.

## Social Factors

The deterioration that Bob reported in his marriage was manifested by an increased emotional distance between husband and wife. In his view, both of them were dissatisfied but their earlier attempts to deal with these problems had led to fruitless angry exchanges, accusation, and counteraccusations. These discussions had been so unpleasant that the couple stopped trying to resolve conflicts and settled into a relationship characterized by progressive emotional distance and loss of intimacy. They rarely did things together and even took their holidays at different times. They socialized very rarely, making an exception only when they "had to" for such events as office Christmas parties. Sexual contact also diminished in frequency to about once every 2 months.

Overall, Bob described the relationship as a "marriage of convenience." He added that the sense of loneliness that this produced was augmented by his not having any close male or female friends. Bob was discouraged because he felt that he had now lost confidence in his ability to socialize effectively with others. Not surprisingly, his scores on questionnaires such as the *Social Self-Esteem Inventory* (Lawson, Marshall, & McGrath, 1979) and the *Social Avoidance and Distress Scale* (Watson & Friend, 1969) reflected an individual who believed himself to be socially inept, lacking in confidence, and rarely at ease with people he did not know well. His responses on the *Fear of Negative Evaluations* questionnaire (Watson & Friend, 1969) were consistent with someone who is concerned about the opinions others have of him, with the expectation that these opinions would be negative.

Bob also described a troubled work environment. He stated that he felt completely overwhelmed at work. While he took great pride in his work, so much was demanded of him that he occasionally rushed some jobs because he had stretched himself too thinly. He had received some strong criticism for the poor quality of his work recently from some of the research staff at the laboratories where he was employed. This distressed Bob greatly, as he felt that his job was one area of his life in which he performed well.

## Sexual Preferences

Bob's sexual preferences were assessed using penile plethysmography. The procedure is described summarily here as it has been described in detail in several earlier articles (for a summary of these, see Marshall & Eccles, 1991). During this assessment Bob was exposed to a series of colored slides of naked individuals in sexually provocative poses (child and adult males and females); a set of videotapes depicting an adult male sexually interacting with both males and females (child and adult); and a set of audiotapes describing consenting and coercive acts between an adult male and children of both genders. Typically, we expose child molesters to sets of stimuli involving both females and males and depicting consenting and coercive acts. While he watched these stimuli his penile responses were recorded by a device attached to his penis. Bob showed no arousal to males or to coercive sexual acts. (At our outpatient clinic only a small, but nevertheless significant, percentage of child molesters display a bisexual profile or arousal to coercive acts. In evaluating incarcerated child molesters in Canada, we find that this proportion has increased over the years from 1975 to the present but nevertheless remains relatively small.) However, Bob did show a clearly deviant response to female children. As Figure 1 shows, his responses were a decreasing function of age, with his highest responses being to prepubescent females and his lowest responses being to adult females.

We confronted Bob with these results, which we told him were inconsistent with what he had told us about his exclusive interest in adult women. While he at first tried to suggest that our results must be mistaken, when we showed him the computer printout he became very tearful and admitted to having a long-standing sexual interest in young females. He stated that he could remember developing these deviant sexual interests at the age of 10 or 11 years. Bob remembered that as he got older he started to develop some interest in adult females; however, his sexual interest in young girls never seemed to go away. While Bob reported being sufficiently interested in adult females to fantasize and be aroused by them, he agreed that he had always had

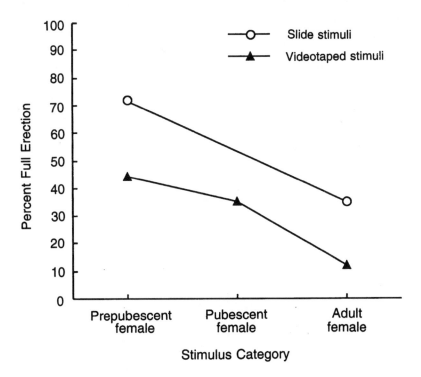

Figure 17-1. Bob's sexual responses to different age categories, expressed as a percentage of full erection.

sexual thoughts of children, which he had successfully controlled until these three recent incidents.

## SELECTION OF TREATMENT

We recommended that Bob participate in both group and individual treatment. Our group treatment sessions are specifically designed to address the offenders' cognitive distortions about their sexually abusive behavior, in addition to addressing victim impact issues. Each group member is also instructed and guided in the development of a relapse prevention plan, something we believed to be critical in Bob's case (as his deviant sexual arousal put him at a moderate-high risk of reoffending). Concurrent with the development of a relapse prevention plan, we train offenders in the group in the skills necessary to avoid risks and to deal with those factors that put them at risk when avoidance is not possible. The goals selected for Bob's treatment were the supervision of the implementation of his relapse prevention plan and the development of self-control over his deviant sexual arousal.

Bob's treatment plan was devised to address directly the antecedents functionally related to his deviant sexual behavior. The successful completion of each phase of treatment was considered to be Bob's best hope of coping with his deviant proclivities. In orienting him to treatment we encouraged Bob to adopt the view that treatment would result in increased control rather than a cure. We told him that he could realistically expect to develop a framework and some tools in treatment that would help him to better control his behavior. Moreover, we informed him that he should see relapse or reoffense prevention as a long-term behavior management strategy.

## COURSE OF TREATMENT
### Cognitive Distortions

As a first step, Bob, along with all other group members, was required to present an offense biography, in which he was to list all his offenses past and present. In our groups members are told that they should include all offenses whether or not they have been charged with them. In cases where acts of sexual abuse have not come to the attention of the authorities, the group members are asked not to identify their victims nor to say exactly where and when they occurred. In addition to his biography, each person is asked to give his understanding of why he did what he did. Group members then question the person who is presenting his offense biography, keeping alert as they do this for evidence of distortions.

The therapist does the same, although he or she will have access to more information than will the other group members. To be effective the therapist must garner as much information as possible regarding the offense history of each offender by consulting files of correctional officers, child protection agencies, and the like. Of particular importance are independent accounts, preferably by the victim, of the nature, extent, and severity of the abuse. Moreover, an offender's spouse and other family members frequently volunteer information about acts of abuse that did not result in charges being filed and that, consequently, may not appear on any official files. While this may appear to some as though we are trying to "catch" our clients, our view is that this enables us to ask each group member about some things he may do routinely but not construe as being sexually motivated or abusive (e.g., pinching his stepdaughter's breasts or commenting on how she's "growing"), but which comments or actions may, in the context of ongoing abuse, be seen by the victim as sexual.

Bob presented his offense biography, which was limited to outlining the three incidents described earlier. While in Bob's case we had little independent information, we had no reason to believe that his description of what he did was in error. However, his description of the process was vigorously challenged by others. The following is an abridged version of the discussion that followed between the therapist, the various group members, and Bob.

THERAPIST: Thanks, Bob. Does anybody have any comments they would like to make or questions they would like to ask Bob about his biography?

GROUP MEMBER: I have a question. You said that you touched your daughter "impulsively." What does that mean?

BOB: Yeah, it was like I'd go into her room, and when I got in there something would come over me and . . . I don't know, I just did it without thinking.

GROUP MEMBER: So, how come you went into her room in the first place?

BOB: Well . . . like I said, I was the last person up, my wife was in bed, and I was just checking to make sure my daughter was covered up. I didn't mean to do anything when I went in there.

GROUP MEMBER: I don't understand. I mean maybe the first night you went in there to cover her up, but the next night when you went in there you could remember what you did the last time, right?

BOB: Well . . . sure but . . .

GROUP MEMBER: But what? I mean how can you say that you just went to her room to cover her up knowing what had happened the night before?

BOB: I don't know . . .

THERAPIST: I guess what people are saying to you is that maybe going to your daughter's room to see if she was covered up was a ruse, a way of deceiving yourself to make it easier for you to go in there. What would it mean, after all, if you went in there deliberately to abuse her?

BOB:   Well . . . that would be planned . . .

GROUP MEMBER:   And that would make it worse?

BOB:   I guess so.

THERAPIST [*to the group*]:   So how does Bob, who sees himself as a generally nice guy, arrange things to give himself the opportunity to do something which, let's be honest, was sexually exciting on the one hand, but something he knew was very wrong on the other hand?

BOB:   You are saying I set myself up, right?

THERAPIST:   I think so.

GROUP MEMBER:   Look, Bob. I have had a drinking problem for a long time, though I've not had a drink now for seven months. But suppose I came in next week and said, "Gee guys, I don't know how it happened, but I just started drinking again." Then I tell you it happened when I went to the bar on Friday night to join some friends I knew would be there. I tell you as well that I had absolutely no intention of drinking at all, I was just going to drink Coke. Then I figured I could handle just one drink if I sipped it really slowly. Before I knew it I lost control and was drunk again. Would you believe me?

BOB:   Well, I'd believe you but I know what you're saying. You deceived yourself so that you could have another drink, and you think maybe I'm doing the same thing?

GROUP MEMBER:   Right.

THERAPIST:   Whenever any of us want to do something that we really know we shouldn't, we often distort the world or make excuses and rationalizations for our behaviors to give ourselves "permission," in a sense, to do it. So, for example, the employee who wants to take a tool from work for his own use at home might say to himself something like, "A big company like this isn't going to miss one tool; besides, everyone else is doing it anyway." In reality, he is stealing just as much as if he picked it up off a store shelf, but he probably won't see it that way. Is it possible that what you were doing was deceiving yourself about your real reason for going to your daughter's room so that you could set up an opportunity for yourself?

BOB:   [*smiles*] When I think about it I guess it makes sense.

GROUP MEMBER:   Because if you were really honest about your promise not to do it again, you wouldn't have kept going to her room.

BOB:   Right. And now I think of it, I wouldn't have been up so late in the first place. I was never really interested in the TV. I think I only watched it so I would be the last person to go to bed.

THERAPIST:   Exactly. This is an important first step in developing a relapse prevention plan for yourself. You have to get used to the idea of always monitoring your behavior and your thoughts, when they have the potential to provide you with an opportunity to offend. So, for example, if you decide to sign your wife up for a night course as a birthday present, you must ask yourself whether you are really doing it because she's always wanted to go or whether you are really just engineering an opportunity to have unsupervised access to your daughter. Even if you decide that your motives are honest, it may still not be a wise thing to do if you have a habit of distorted thinking by which you might talk yourself into a relapse. You have to recognize how you did this in the past, the role that this distorted thinking played in your offense, and how to successfully challenge it. The better you become at recognizing these distortions and combating them, the better prepared you are to prevent their reoccurrence.

Bob's assertion that he had not done this before despite long-standing deviant arousal was also greeted with some skepticism. Bob eventually acknowledged, rather tearfully, that although he had not attempted to look at his daughter's genitals or to touch her at night before, he had gone into her room on several occasions and had become aroused just looking at her lying in bed. Typically, he would go to the bathroom afterward to masturbate to images of the girl. However, Bob adamantly denied any previous sexual contact with any other young girls.

## Victim Impact Issues

Once we were satisfied that Bob had a good understanding of his cognitive distortions, we began some exercises designed to increase his understanding of the effects of sexual abuse. He watched a number of videotapes of interviews with survivors of sexual abuse and read a series of handouts describing the effects of such abuse.

Along with other group members Bob was required to complete several assignments, such as writing a letter that his stepdaughter might send him if given the opportunity. These assignments are expected to reflect a true understanding of how the victim might respond, and the group provides feedback on each member's efforts. For example, Bob, like many other offenders, was rather optimistic in his opinion of what his stepdaughter's letter would contain. His first attempt contained expressions of concern by his daughter for his welfare, but little or no anger or animosity toward him, and references to her own difficulties were cursory. By reading several letters from victims of sexual abuse Bob became better able to understand the confusion, pain, and anger that his stepdaughter was likely to be feeling.

## Relapse Prevention

Relapse prevention has become an integral part of many contemporary sex offender treatment programs. A complete discussion of this methodology is beyond the scope of this chapter, but the reader is referred to Laws (1989) for a comprehensive review and for some excellent examples of clinical application.

In this part of group treatment we stress to the men that their offenses did not just happen spontaneously but were, instead, the final act in a chain of events over which they could have exercised control but that ultimately led to the abuse. While these chains are different for each offender, they typically start with some form of stress with which the offender copes poorly. What follows is a series of lapses into moods, attitudes, and behaviors during which the risk to reoffend escalates as the chain of events progresses. This risk becomes very high when the offender starts to masturbate to fantasies of deviant sex and starts to plan an assault. The men are taught how the return of cognitive distortions are central to the progression of lapses and the escalation of risk. Each man is told that while his risk increases the further he progresses down his reoffense chain, it is never too late to prevent the relapse, that at all times he has the ability to control his behavior, and that he can readily escape or avoid his high-risk factors if he decides to. If he does not avoid them, we stress that it is because he has made a purposeful and willful decision not to do so. Each offender is told that he can certainly increase his chances of avoiding a relapse if he has prepared and rehearsed ahead of time coping strategies for dealing with these lapses when they occur.

In compiling his relapse prevention plan, Bob was encouraged to look for patterns in his behavior. For example, what made those days when he offended different from the days he chose not to? Bob was able to discern that his offenses always happened on the days he was overwhelmed or criticized at work. Typically, he would come home and brood, unable or unwilling to talk to his wife about it. Bob would also drink during the evening and stay up until his wife had gone to bed. His visits to his stepdaughter's bedroom would typically take place on his way to bed later on.

Figure 2 summarizes Bob's relapse prevention plan. It outlines his likely reoffense sequence and gives some examples of what he can do to cope at each point. Bob was somewhat concerned about the proposed system of dealing with work orders and the requirement that he not rush a job or start the next one until the current one was completed. He felt that a backlog of jobs would build up, causing even more trouble, but he agreed to give it a try.

At this point Bob completed the requirements of group therapy and entered individual therapy. Here we followed up on the implementation of some of his relapse prevention strategies. He had special work orders printed up and got to them in the order in which they were received. While having people wait was initially stressful, he soon found that having a more formal work system made it easier for him to be assertive in making decisions about getting to certain jobs. (In fact, after several months it became apparent to the department that there was too much involved in Bob's job for one person, so they hired a junior technician to help him.)

We also interviewed Bob's wife and discussed with her the specifics of his relapse prevention plan. She was instructed in the nature of the signs indicating that Bob's risk to reoffend was escalating or that a child was being abused by him. She and Bob both signed a contract agreeing that she would call the clinic as soon as she saw any of these signs. In particular, she was to call if Bob ever drank alone, tried to stay up late alone, or tried to engineer any other situation that might give him an opportunity to abuse his stepdaughter or any other child. It was, however, made clear that inclusion of Bob's wife in treatment did not imply that she was in any way responsible for the abuse.

The couple were also referred to a marital therapist to improve the quality of their relationship. Both were keen to do this, as they each felt they had suffered from the emotional isolation that had developed between them.

Bob practiced and rehearsed responses to each of the distortions he felt he might try to use in the future. He also had to be able to respond immediately whenever questioned about how he would cope with various unpredictable high-risk situations that might arise (e.g., his wife suddenly having to stay in the hospital or be out of town overnight). He was also instructed to carry at all times a wallet-sized card we gave him with the telephone numbers of his therapist and various crisis lines.

These arrangements completed the specifics of Bob's relapse prevention plan, implementation of which was monitored on an ongoing basis during the next stage of treatment, which was designed to reduce Bob's deviant sexual arousal.

## Deviant Sexual Arousal

Reducing Bob's sexual interest in children was targeted by employing three different but complementary techniques: (1) orgasmic reconditioning, (2) aversive therapy, and (3) satiation. (See Marshall & Barbaree, 1988, for details of these procedures.) Bob had very little difficulty with the orgasmic reconditioning exercises. Because he was aroused by women, his task was to aggressively counter with fantasies of them whenever any sexual fantasies of children occurred during masturbation. He was warned against deluding himself that fantasizing about children while masturbating was a harmless way of relieving the urges to act deviantly and informed that doing so actually serves to strengthen these urges.

Bob also began a 3-month course of aversive therapy. He repeatedly paired sexual thoughts of children with the rapid inhalation of smelling salts,

**Relapse Prevention Plan**

NAME: _____

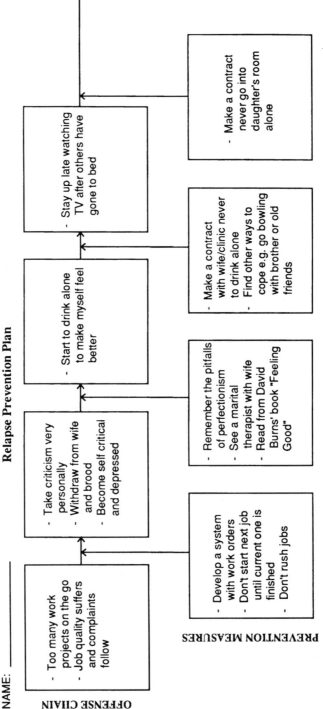

**OFFENSE CHAIN**

- Too many work projects on the go
- Job quality suffers and complaints follow

- Take criticism very personally
- Withdraw from wife and brood
- Become self critical and depressed

- Start to drink alone to make myself feel better

- Stay up late watching TV after others have gone to bed

- Make a contract never go into daughter's room alone

**PREVENTION MEASURES**

- Develop a system with work orders
- Don't start next job until current one is finished
- Don't rush jobs

- Remember the pitfalls of perfectionism
- See a marital therapist with wife
- Read from David Burns' book "Feeling Good"

- Make a contract with wife/clinic never to drink alone
- Find other ways to cope e.g. go bowling with brother or old friends

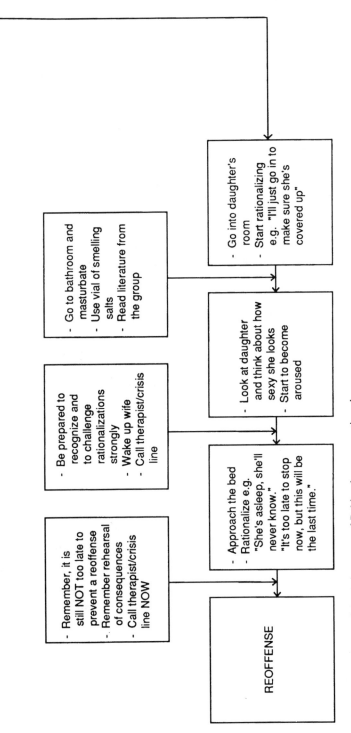

Figure 17-2. Summary of the main aspects of Bob's relapse prevention plan.

which are generally experienced as aversive and were so to Bob. However, initially Bob's response to children was maintained despite considerable use of the unpleasant fumes. Satiation exercises were then introduced; these required Bob to repeatedly rehearse his deviant fantasies immediately after orgasm and until boredom was achieved. He found these exercises very unpleasant, but by the end of 6 weeks a midtreatment assessment revealed considerable gains.

Figure 3 depicts the results of the phallometric assessments (Bob's responses are converted to a ratio, or deviance quotient, by dividing his arousal to sexual thoughts of children by his arousal to sexual fantasies of women). The changes evident in Figure 3 are due to the fact that Bob's response to fantasies of children had significantly reduced by midtreatment while his response to fantasies of women remained unchanged.

Having completed the six weeks of exercises described above, we began to reduce the frequency of the satiation exercises and to get Bob to the point where he no longer needed to use the smelling salts but was instead

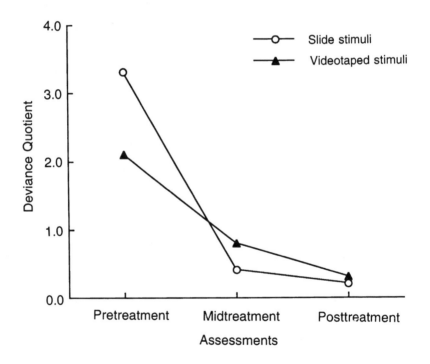

Figure 17-3. Bob's responses to sexual fantasies of females of different ages, expressed as deviance quotients (mean response to deviant stimuli divided by mean response to appropriate stimuli). Prepubescent and pubescent categories were combined for the slide data. Results are presented for pretreatment, midtreatment, and posttreatment assessments.

using exclusively cognitive strategies such as covert sensitization. In covert sensitization, Bob cognitively rehearsed his offense sequence and at varying points interrupted that sequence by imagining a realistic but catastrophic consequence.

A posttreatment assessment was conducted at the end of Bob's final treatment session. As shown in Figure 3, this revealed that Bob's midtreatment gains had been further enhanced. Bob reported a considerable increase in his sense of self-efficacy as he began to realize that he could exercise remarkable control over his thoughts and arousal and that they did not in fact control him.

## TERMINATION

Having completed the group and individual therapy as described, Bob was regarded as having completed the core requirements of his treatment. He and his wife had been referred for marital counseling and were due to start this soon. Bob was functioning much better at work and was taking more initiative socially, such as contacting old friends. Overall, he was assessed as having implemented his relapse prevention plan satisfactorily. His involvement in the program was then switched to follow-up supervision.

## FOLLOW-UP

Follow-up evaluations were conducted at 3 and 6 months. At the 3-month follow-up, all gains had been maintained and reports from the marital therapist indicated that she was satisfied with the couple's progress and was concluding her efforts. Six months later there were no significant difficulties or negative developments to report. We continue to remain available if Bob ever encounters future problems, but we will not see him again unless he or his wife request it. His wife will continue to be the person responsible for monitoring Bob's behavior, and she appears to us to fully appreciate the fact that he will need this for the foreseeable future. However, we typically attempt to appoint a relapse prevention supervisor who is likely to remain a bit more objective about the offender's risk. Unfortunately, since this case did not lead to any charges, no public official was available as a supervisor. External supervision, while a sensible practice, has not yet been demonstrated to decrease the likelihood of reoffending, and, to date, otherwise similar therapy programs have varied considerably in the type and extent of supervision they have provided (Marshall, Hudson, & Ward, 1992). We await an empirical evaluation, but until that is available our inclination is to maximize the extent of external supervision.

## OVERALL EVALUATION

In some respects Bob is not a typical pedophile. Many of the pedophiles we see have a more extensive history of offending than Bob did, and they have also characteristically been more sexually intrusive. There are, however, numerous accounts in the literature of these types of pedophiles. Bob represents a less frequently described, but often mentioned, pedophile. He was preoccupied by sexual thoughts of female children for many years, indeed, since his childhood days when he first became aware of sexual feelings. Yet he was able for many years to resist acting on these urges. Articles describing pedophilia frequently suggest that many men may be sexually attracted to children but refrain from actual molestation. Numerous researchers have found that some nonoffender men show strong sexual arousal to children in the laboratory, and yet there is little in the literature discussing these men. Bob's sexual history indicates that he too would have responded to children prior to his offenses (when he would have been classified as a nonoffender). Our report on Bob, then represents one of the few accounts of a pedophile who had a long history of feeling sexually attracted to children but who was able for many years to inhibit the overt expression of these feelings. The details of Bob's offenses suggest that ready opportunity combined with alcohol intoxication were the crucial factors in releasing his inhibitions, and this may be true of other such men.

While Bob has coped well to date with his difficulties, we have cautioned him against undue optimism regarding his sexual thoughts and fantasies. We have encouraged him not to consider them to be entirely eliminated, and we have told him that we predict that occasional urges will recur. The important point for him, and others in his position, to realize is that recurrences are to be expected. They should not be seen as a sign of failure but, rather, as a sign to initiate coping responses. We believe that it is advantageous for offenders to construe their future as being best characterized as an effort to cope effectively with occasional lapses. An offender who believes that he has entirely mastered his problems will have unrealistic expectations and he runs the risk of becoming overly discouraged when these are not realized. An approach which emphasizes coping inoculates offenders against this risk and more readily lends itself to responding to difficulties in an effective manner. Bob appears to be cognizant of these issues which augers well for an offense-free future.

## REFERENCES

American Psychiatric Association. (1987). *Diagnostic and statistic manual of mental disorders* (3rd ed., rev.). Washington, DC: Author.

Barbaree, H. E., & Marshall, W. L. (1989). Erectile responses amongst heterosexual child molesters, father–daughter incest offenders and matched non-offenders: Five distinct age preference profiles. *Canadian Journal of Behavioral Science, 21,* 70–82.

Freund, K. (1987). Erotic preference in pedophilia. *Behaviour Research and Therapy, 5,* 339–348.

Laws, D. R. (1989). *Relapse prevention with sex offenders.* New York: Guilford Press.

Lawson, J. S., Marshall, W. L., & McGrath, P. (1979). The Social Self-Esteem Inventory. *Educational and Psychological Measurement, 39,* 803–811.

Marshall, W. L., & Barbaree, H. E. (1988). *A Manual for the Treatment of Child Molesters.* Available from Dr. W. L. Marshall, Department of Psychology, Queen's University, Kingston, Ontario, Canada K7L 3N6.

Marshall, W. L., & Eccles, A. (1991). Issues in clinical practice with sex offenders. *Journal of Interpersonal Violence, 6,* 68–93.

Marshall, W. L., & Hodkinson, S. M. (1988). The Sex with Children Scale. Unpublished scale under development.

Marshall, W. L., Hudson, S. M. & Ward, T. (1992). Sexual deviance. In D. H. Wilson (Ed.), *Principles and practice of relapse prevention* (pp. 235–254). New York: Guilford.

McConaghy, N. (1991). Sexual disorders. In M. Hersen & S. M. Turner (Eds.), *Adult psychopathology and diagnosis* (pp. 323–359). New York: Wiley.

Murphy, W. D. (1990). Assessment and modification of cognitive distortions in sex offenders. In W. L. Marshall, D. R. Laws, & H. E. Barbaree (Eds.), *Handbook of sexual assault: Issues, theories and treatment of the offender* (pp. 331–342). New York: Plenum.

Nichols, H. R., & Molinder, I. L. (1984). The Multiphasic Sex Inventory. Available from Nichols & Molinder, 437 Bowes Drive, Tacoma, WA 98466.

Rosen, R. C., & Beck, J. G. (1988). *Patterns of sexual arousal: Psychophysiological processes and clinical applications.* New York: Guilford Press.

Salter, A. (1988). *Assessment and treatment of child sexual offenders: A practical guide.* Newbury Park, CA: Sage.

Stermac, L. E., Segal, Z. V., & Gillis, R. (1990). Social and cultural factors in sexual assault. In W. L. Marshall, D. R. Laws, & H. E. Barbaree (Eds.), *Handbook of sexual assault: Issues, theories and treatment of the offender* (pp. 143–159). New York: Plenum.

Watson, D., & Friend, R. (1969). Measure of social evaluative anxiety. *Journal of Consulting and Clinical Psychology, 33,* 448–457.

# CHAPTER 18

# Primary Insomnia

## MINDY ENGLE-FRIEDMAN

### DESCRIPTION OF THE DISORDER

When clients seek therapy for sleep problems, they generally are looking for an answer to what they feel is a clear-cut issue. Oftentimes, this problem is indeed straightforward and can be successfully treated with education about sleep hygiene. Other clients experience a multitude of additional problems whose significance is equal to or greater than that of the sleep issues for which they seek therapy. These clients require not only specific attention to the sleep problem but equal and separate attention to the additional problems, which might figure prominently in the person's life. Solving the sleep problems will not automatically solve the nonsleep problems, but improved sleep and less concern about sleep will have a marked effect on functioning in other areas of life. The attention to the nonsleep problems is necessary to relieve stress as well as strengthen treatment gains in sleep. The sleep problem, however, must be dealt with as a separate problem or group of habits to be changed.

### CASE IDENTIFICATION

This is a case study of Mario, a 29-year-old Italian male who sought help for his difficulty falling asleep and staying asleep. Our relationship in therapy

MINDY ENGLE-FRIEDMAN • Department of Psychology, Baruch College, City University of New York, New York, New York 10010.

*Adult Behavior Therapy Casebook,* edited by Cynthia G. Last and Michel Hersen. Plenum Press, New York, 1994.

lasted for approximately 2 years. We met once a week for 1-hour sessions. The sleep problems Mario experienced were largely under control within the first 4 months, with occasional increases in sleep disturbance in the remaining 1 year and 8 months.

## PRESENTING COMPLAINTS

Mario reported sleep difficulties throughout his life. When he was a child, his mother would give him sleeping pills to help him fall asleep. At the onset of our relationship, he averaged 2½ hours to fall asleep. In addition, he had at least three awakenings per night three or more nights per week. When I met him, Mario was working for a law firm. He had tried and failed to pass the bar two times. He reported that his lack of ability to sleep was the cause of his inability to pass the bar. He believed that if he slept well enough the night before the exam, he would be able to pass. He believed that he was so focused on the sleep loss that he couldn't take the exam or attend to the questions. At the time of the exams he was taking sleeping medication prescribed by his physician. Additionally, he was drinking approximately ten cups of coffee during the day and two to four cups of espresso in the evening hours.

## HISTORY

Mario grew up in an area of Boston that was not predominantly Italian, and he experienced racist remarks from some of the people in his neighborhood. In addition, he came from a very disrupted household: his father was an alcoholic, as was his mother, who died when he was 22 years old. The parents constantly fought with each other verbally as well as physically. Mario's brother was an alcoholic and a drug abuser. As a result of the repeated abuse, the brother suffered multiple medical problems, for which Mario became increasingly responsible.

Mario, a first-generation American, became proficient in the use of the English language. He served as a translator for his parents in many situations, including his own registration for school when he was 5 years old. In addition, he was relied upon to translate in situations involving his family's financial matters and in dealings with doctors who cared for his brother.

Mario experienced frequent criticism from his parents despite his superior performance in elementary and junior high school. His style of communication with his family was often argumentative. He firmly believed that they were trying to make his life difficult. He repeatedly told them that he thought they failed to take him seriously and were trying to undermine him. He also would berate his family members for their ideas and would not consider their feelings. He would often raise his voice and rarely took another person's perspective, whether within or outside the family.

Despite these difficulties, Mario graduated from high school and won a scholarship to a prestigious New England college. He experimented with recreational drugs in high school, including marijuana, cocaine, and barbiturates. He greatly increased his drug use in college. This increase in drug abuse and his anxiety that he did not belong in the college he had chosen increased the frequency with which he missed classes. He dropped out of college after 2 years and became a waiter. After a year of waiting tables, he enrolled in a Boston college. His grades improved sufficiently, and his drug abuse decreased substantially. He then was admitted to law school. Despite ongoing drug use in law school, Mario was able to graduate, and did so on time.

Mario's medical history indicated that he had been diagnosed as having irritable bowel syndrome, from which he intermittently experienced extreme stomach cramps, sometimes lasting for days. These exacerbations of his condition seemed to be related to unusual or spicy foods, increases in anxiety at work, difficulties with his father and brother, or troubles with finances.

## ASSESSMENT

The initial assessment consisted of a semistructured interview in which Mario's family, social, medical, and psychological history was discussed. Later, evaluation sessions involved information gathering that was more open-ended. In addition, the therapist evaluated sleep diaries that Mario completed each morning when he awakened. The sleep diary, seen in Figure 1, asks the client to think back to the day before and to indicate how many naps were taken during the day, the time he retired for the evening, and how long it took him to fall asleep. It also asks how many times he awakened during the night, how long he was awake at each awakening, at what time he awakened in the morning, how many hours of sleep he had, the extent to which he felt refreshed or exhausted, the extent to which he felt he had a restless or sound sleep, whether he felt the sleep was like or unlike his usual sleep, and the amount of medication, alcohol, or coffee he had taken before bed.

Mario completed the sleep diaries for two weeks prior to the start of treatment and throughout the entire treatment period. He was diligent at keeping the records and he relied on them to begin the discussion of sleep during the therapy session. He took pride in the changes he was able to observe on the records and was able to focus on areas that required additional attention.

The sleep information obtained from Mario's diaries was not always

Name: _____

Fill this out each morning when you get up

| | YESTERDAY | | | | | | THIS MORNING | | | | | | | | |
|---|---|---|---|---|---|---|---|---|---|---|---|---|---|---|---|
| | I took this many naps | I went to bed at this time | I fell asleep at this time | I had this many awakenings | I woke up at this time in the morning | I slept this many hours | When I got up this morning, I felt: | | | My sleep last night was: | | | Overall my sleep was: | | |
| | | | | | | | Very Tired | | Very Awake | Very Restless | | Very Sound | Worse than Usual | Same as Usual | Better than Usual |
| MONDAY | | | | | | | -1 | 0 | +1 | -1 | 0 | +1 | 1 | 2 | 3 |
| TUESDAY | | | | | | | -1 | 0 | +1 | -1 | 0 | +1 | 1 | 2 | 3 |
| WEDNESDAY | | | | | | | -1 | 0 | +1 | -1 | 0 | +1 | 1 | 2 | 3 |
| THURSDAY | | | | | | | -1 | 0 | +1 | -1 | 0 | +1 | 1 | 2 | 3 |
| FRIDAY | | | | | | | -1 | 0 | +1 | -1 | 0 | +1 | 1 | 2 | 3 |
| SATURDAY | | | | | | | -1 | 0 | +1 | -1 | 0 | +1 | 1 | 2 | 3 |
| SUNDAY | | | | | | | -1 | 0 | +1 | -1 | 0 | +1 | 1 | 2 | 3 |

Figure 18-1. Sleep diary.

consistent during the initial assessment and early weeks of treatment. He would go to bed at different hours, ranging from 9:30 P.M. to 2:00 A.M. The weekends were the times of his latest attempts to go to bed. Throughout the treatment period he awakened within 20 minutes of the designated sleep awakening time and took no naps during the day.

## SELECTION OF TREATMENT

After the evaluation was completed, it was apparent that there were many areas in which Mario was having difficulty in addition to his insomnia. These included family problems, difficulty communicating, lack of assertiveness skills and overuse of aggressive strategies, poor problem solving, and procrastination. It was decided that the therapy would focus first on the sleep problem and that once that was under control the focus would be shifted to the client's interpersonal problems and problem-solving behaviors.

## COURSE OF TREATMENT

Sleep diaries completed during the first 2 weeks after the first meeting with the client were used as the initial nontreatment evaluation of sleep. The initial treatment sessions focused on a reduction of sleep medication. Mario had been prescribed Dalmane (30 milligrams daily) by his physician and had been using this medication for approximately 2 years. Since Dalmane can have the effect of inducing an insomnia after prolonged use, as well as of causing side effects the next day, it was suggested to him that he contact his physician and, with the physician's guidance, slowly withdraw himself from this medication. Mario's medication was reduced by half the first week and was completely discontinued by the third week of therapy. At the same time, he was taught basic information concerning sleep hygiene. This information in abbreviated form is as follows:

1. Alcohol before bed may make one drowsy, but it will increase awakenings in the second half of the night.
2. Sleep medications can induce insomnia after repeated use and can increase drowsiness the next day and impair performance.
3. Naps during the day will begin the sleep period early and impair facility in falling asleep quickly at night. They will also increase awakenings and possibly result in early morning awakenings from which one is unable to return to sleep.
4. Leaving music or the television on while trying to fall asleep will

increase the time it will take to fall asleep and will increase awakenings. It will also decrease the amount of time spent in deeper stages of sleep (Stages 3 and 4).

5. Caffeine can have a half-life of 8 hours or more. Caffeine after noon can impair swift sleep onset. Caffeine is present in coffee, tea, colas, chocolate, and some medications.

6. Tobacco contains nicotine, which is a stimulant, and, consequently, will also impair sleep onset.

7. Sleep loss can have a minimal impact on reaction time. It does not impair higher cognitive functions. Humans can function without sleep and will not become psychotic with sleep loss.

8. Each person has a natural circadian rhythm. This means that there are regular daily fluctuations in mood, general activation, and alertness. These fluctuations are consistent with increases and decreases in normal body temperature and occur despite nights of insomnia. Therefore, a person experiencing fatigue after a sleepless night will feel an increase in energy as the day proceeds and then a decrease in energy in the late afternoon and into the evening.

Sleep hygiene information was given to Mario, and he was informed how it related to his own sleep experience. For example, in addition to recommending that he reduce his sleep medication intake, it was important to educate him as to why sleep medications were not to his advantage. Additionally, he commonly took a nap after work and would make dinner following his nap. This nap behavior had to be eliminated since it alone was capable of causing a significant increase in sleep latency. Similarly, Mario would wear his Walkman to sleep each night in the hope that the music would lull him to sleep, but this behavior can impair sleep onset and disturb sleep (Engle-Friedman, Bootzin, & Hazlewood, 1983). Furthermore, Mario drank approximately ten cups of regular coffee each day and two cups of espresso coffee in the evening after dinner. He drank approximately two glasses of wine with dinner at least three nights per week. He also drank approximately six cans of diet cola and smoked one pack of cigarettes each day. Thus, it was also necessary to point out to Mario the adverse effects on his sleep of these stimulants and behaviors.

As previously noted, Mario was able to achieve and maintain a gradual reduction in his sleep medication. He also eliminated naps from his routine, going for a walk instead before he made dinner. He stopped listening to the Walkman in bed and turned off all music and television each night when he decided to retire for the evening. He eliminated all caffeinated beverages from his diet and substituted decaffeinated ones in their place. He reduced his intake from approximately twelve glasses of wine per week to two glasses of wine on the weekends only and changed his brand of cigarettes to one with low levels of nicotine.

All of these changes did not occur at the same time; Mario did not feel that he could make such vast changes in his routine all at once. Approximately two new sleep hygiene suggestions were dealt with in each session. Since Mario's attempts were not always successful, reinforcement for any attempts at change was given and strategies to complete the change were discussed. Then Mario attempted the change again. Successive approximations of change were always reinforced. For example, reducing caffeinated beverages was extremely difficult for this client. He first made coffee with 80% caffeinated coffee and 20% decaffeinated coffee and then gradually continued to change the percentages so that by the end of 2 weeks the coffee he drank was completely decaffeinated. In the past the client had a regular regimen of exercise but had not continued his exercise routine with any consistency. The exercise that he did take was at a fitness club in the evening after late hours on the job; it was common under these circumstances for him to exercise at 10 or 11 in the evening. Hauri (1970) has shown that exercise prior to bedtime increases sleep latency. Therefore, a regimen was developed in which Mario would exercise three or four times per week on his lunch hour.

Each sleep hygiene suggestion was made with an understanding of the client's limits and abilities. He was not told that he had to carry out the suggestion in a specific way. Instead, the suggestion was given to him, he was asked if he felt he could follow through with it, and strategies were then discussed to help him implement the recommendations. He was asked to describe the recommendation in his own words so that any misunderstandings could be cleared up and any areas he had forgotten could be highlighted. Mario took notes on these, since they were to be his homework assignment for the week. Once he had used these suggestions for 1 week, he was to return to the therapy session to report on his progress and his difficulties accommodating the suggestion into his life. After he was able to fully incorporate the recommendation into his life, he was expected to continue using it as part of his sleep hygiene. Mario would occasionally ask when he would be able to stop certain aspects of the sleep hygiene or whether he could abandon some aspects once his insomnia totally disappeared. He was told that these suggestions were meant to be part of a new approach to sleeping, that if he kept to these, his sleep would for the most part be pleasant and comfortable, and that if he did not maintain the hygiene, his sleep might be negatively affected. He was also told that the reintroduction of sleep hygiene techniques would bring a reinstatement of good sleep and that the techniques were not to be viewed as a cure but as a new sleep regimen that would serve him well if he maintained it.

## Stimulus Control

Once the sleep hygiene techniques were in place and were being used on a regular basis, I introduced the stimulus control instructions as the next component of therapy (Bootzin, 1972). Stimulus control has been found to be effective in a variety of populations, including young adults (Bootzin, 1975), older adults (Engle-Friedman, Bootzin, Hazlewood, & Tsao, 1992), persons having difficulty falling asleep (Bootzin, 1970), and persons having difficulty staying asleep (Lacks, Bertelsen, Sugarman, & Kunkel, 1983). The purpose of the stimulus control instructions is to establish the bed as a cue for sleep onset and return to sleep after awakening during the night. For many people the bed is not a cue for sleep; it is a cue for anxiety. The anxiety around and near the bed can be so great that not only do such people have extreme difficulty sleeping there but they sometimes discard the bed in the belief that it is the bed itself that is prohibiting sleep. In other cases the bed is a cue for behaviors that interfere with sleep. In the case presented here, the client hated his bed and had purchased different beds in an attempt to solve his sleep problem. He had already had a water bed and a Japanese futon. He was currently sleeping on a firm conventional American mattress. Moreover, once in bed he would eat and talk on the phone. Thus, the bed became a cue for hunger and eating as well as for the negative affect that he experienced following phone calls with his father and brother.

Unlike the sleep hygiene recommendations, which were given a few at a time, the stimulus control instructions were given to the client as a set of instructions that had to be followed as specifically as possible. Each instruction was discussed at length with the client to ensure that he understood all aspects of it and could apply it to his sleep. The stimulus control instructions are as follows:

1. Lie down intending to go to sleep only when you are sleepy.
2. Do not use your bed for anything except sleep. Do not read, watch television, eat, or worry in bed. Sexual activity is the only exception to this rule. On such occasions the instructions are to be followed afterward, when you intend to go to sleep.
3. If you find yourself unable to fall asleep after 10 minutes, get up and go into another room. Stay as long as you wish and then return to the bedroom to sleep. Although we do not want you to watch the clock, we want you to get out of bed if you do not fall asleep immediately. Remember, the goal is to associate your bed with falling asleep quickly. If you are in bed more than 10 minutes without falling asleep and have not gotten out of bed, you are not following this instruction.

4. If you still cannot fall asleep, repeat Step 3. Do this as often as is necessary throughout the night.
5. Set your alarm and get up at the same time every morning regardless of how much sleep you had during the night. This will help your body acquire a consistent sleep rhythm.
6. Do not nap during the day.

Mario had some initial difficulty applying the first instruction to his nightly routine. Three days a week he had to awaken especially early for early office hours. He felt determined to go to bed early so that he could awaken early with a good night's sleep behind him. When he was told to go to sleep only when he was tired, regardless of the hour, he balked. He said that he wouldn't be tired until 1 in the morning and that he wouldn't be getting enough sleep to have an effective day at work. It was pointed out to him that tossing and turning in bed until 2 or 3 in the morning was not helping him, since he did not really rest during that time but had extreme anxiety about sleeping, which was then associated with the bed. It was explained to him that if he did not get the sleep he felt he needed, he would be able to function just as he had been for so long with insomnia, that good sleep would ultimately return using these instructions, and that it was a difficult but important investment that he would have to make in order to have good sleep. This instruction took several weeks before Mario agreed to fully follow it and not to automatically attempt to go to bed when the clock read 10.

The second instruction, which limits use of the bed only to sleeping and sex, also presented somewhat of a problem. Since Mario had developed so many routines in and on the bed, these routines had to be shifted to other times and other areas of his apartment. I taught him how to problem-solve by helping him list all the possible solutions to one problem at a time. After examining the entire list and evaluating the strengths and weaknesses of each solution, Mario was asked to select the best strategy for performing these behaviors out of bed. He initially moved his television out of his bedroom into the living room. He thereafter watched television only in the living room. He then reported falling asleep on the couch while watching late-night television. It is very common for people who have a sleep problem to fall asleep in a place other than the bed, for they have not developed negative associations to these other locations. It was helpful to show Mario that he could sleep in other locations and that this was an indication that he *could* sleep and *could learn* to sleep in the bed as well, but he had to be told that sleeping on the couch was off-limits—that if he felt sleepy at night, he had to go to bed. Mario contended that he would fall asleep on the couch without much warning. After problem-solving he decided that he would watch television in a hard-backed wooden chair so that he would be less likely to fall asleep but would be aware of his increasing sleepiness and could then go to the bedroom when those feelings came on.

The third instruction (he was to get out of bed if he was not asleep in 10 minutes and to stay out of bed until he was tired) was one that Mario thought would be no problem for him. However, this proved to be difficult for him in a number of ways: First, he spent the entire 10 minutes watching the clock. He had to be reminded not to look at the clock, and he learned to turn the clock away from his gaze unless he had trouble falling asleep, in which case he would check the time. In addition, when Mario got out of bed to wait until he became sleepy, he began to eat. This behavior had to be stopped early, since a repeated pattern, such as eating at a particular time of night, can cause a client to awaken from sleep in the future. Furthermore, Mario had a penchant for Stephen King novels and would read them while waiting to become tired. These novels would scare him when he read them late at night and would prevent him from becoming sleepy or from feeling like he wanted to go to bed.

The fourth instruction (to repeat Step 3 if sleeplessness persists) was even more difficult to follow than the third. At first Mario would get out of bed willingly, but after he had done this two or more times in one evening, he felt that the therapist was being unduly cruel to him. He would get out of bed twice, but on the third occasion he would say to himself, and later to the therapist, "I'm too tired to get out of bed. It's making me exhausted to get out of bed, and at least I'm resting while I'm in bed. I'll never be able to function the next day if I don't rest my body." I reminded him of all the important changes he had made so far and that each of these was a great change in his normal routine. He was told that he would gradually be able to get used to the new instruction. By staying in bed while awake he was teaching his body to make the association between bed and being-awake. Instead, he needed to reteach his body that the bed was only a place to sleep. By getting out of bed when he was awake and returning only when he was sleepy he was making that association stronger. By occasionally staying in bed when he was awake, he was reducing some of the gains he had made by getting out of bed earlier. If he followed this instruction, I told him, eventually he would not have to get out of bed repeatedly since he would have taught himself that the bed was a place for falling asleep quickly, staying asleep, and returning to sleep quickly once awakened. He was also told that staying in bed without sleeping was not going to help his body rest or help him function better the next day, and that since he spent much of the time awake in bed ruminating about his inability to fall asleep, staying in bed while awake only increased his anxiety and stress. Because Mario was given this instruction in the winter, when his apartment was typically colder than he would have liked, making compliance even more difficult, it was then necessary to problem-solve; Mario decided that he would have his bathrobe waiting at the end of his bed, his slippers at bedside, and a blanket waiting for him on the wooden chair in the living room.

The fifth instruction required Mario to get out of bed at the same time every morning regardless of the amount of sleep he had had the night before. He was asked to select a particular time at which he would arise each morning; he selected 7:30. He was told to set his alarm each weekday for that time and on weekends to sleep no later than 8. He was told to get out of bed as soon as the alarm went off, regardless of the amount of sleep he had that night. This would put pressure on his own circadian rhythm so that he would want to go to sleep earlier, the next night. Initially, Mario said that he thought that this was going to be an impossible instruction to follow. He said that since he often had as little as 2 hours of sleep a night, if he had extra time to sleep in the morning he was going to take advantage of it. Also, since this instruction is meant to be followed 7 days a week, he balked at the idea of not sleeping in on weekends. I pointed out to him that he often managed throughout the day with little or no sleep on the days he had to be at the office early. I agreed that this would be difficult to follow initially and told him that with creativity and determination he would be able to do it and that his sleep would improve greatly if he followed the instruction.

The sixth instruction asks the client not to nap during the day. Fortunately, Mario was no longer a napper and this was not a problem. (As previously mentioned, this problem was successfully dealt with in the sleep hygiene portion of his therapy). When this is a problem, the client is asked to identify alternative activities during the nap time, since napping has been shown to interfere with sleep onset and the initiation of deep sleep (Webb, 1975).

## FOLLOW-UP

All improvements in sleep problems were maintained at an 8-month follow-up (Figure 5). Mario reported problems in sleep and a return to poor sleep habits when he neglected the sleep hygiene and stimulus control instructions. However, as soon as he followed these instructions again, his normal sleep pattern returned. From these experiences he came to understand the importance of adhering to stimulus control and good sleep hygiene.

## OVERALL EVALUATION

In the first two sessions baseline data through sleep diaries were collected, but no treatment was initiated. Sleep hygiene education began in the third therapy week, and stimulus control instructions were initiated in the eighth week.

Mario's progress is graphed in Figures 2 to 4, which display three important parameters of sleep: latency to sleep onset, number of awakenings during the night, and feeling refreshed upon awakening in the morning. As can be seen in Figure 2, Mario's initial latency to sleep onset was well over 3 hours. With initiation of sleep hygiene, there was a gradual and persistent decrease in sleep latency after an initial lag phase. By the fifth week of sleep hygiene education (Week 7 of therapy), his latency was approximately 2½ hours. At Week 8 of therapy, stimulus control was instituted and Mario's progress in shortening the latency to sleep period continued and accelerated. By Week 13 he was well under 1 hour of sleep latency, and by the end of the treatment period (Week 16) he was falling asleep in about 10 minutes. The increased rate of drop in sleep latency after Week 9 can be attributed to the fact that both sleep hygiene and stimulus control were being utilized throughout this time.

We also see a similar pattern of improvement when the number of awakenings per night are evaluated. At initiation of the evaluation Mario was averaging approximately four awakenings per night. After sleep hygiene edu-

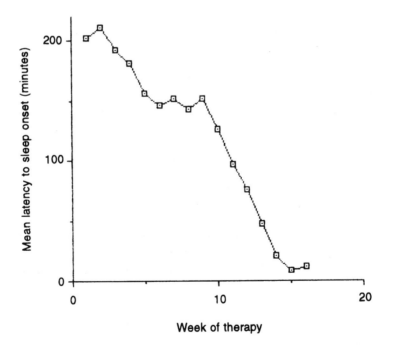

Figure 18-2. Mean latency to sleep onset (in minutes) for the two initial evaluation weeks and through the 14-week treatment period.

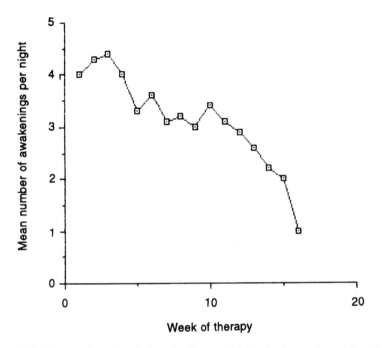

Figure 18-3. Mean number of awakenings for the two initial evaluation weeks and through the 14-week treatment period.

cation was completed, he was down to three per night, and at the end of therapy his average was about one awakening per night.

Similarly, the ratings Mario gave the feelings he experienced upon awakening in the morning dramatically improved in his sleep diary assessment. For the first 5 weeks he reported continuous exhaustion upon awakening. However, with sleep hygiene and stimulus control instructions firmly in hand, he experienced a refreshed feeling upon awakening for 5 of the last 6 weeks of the therapy period.

Following the noted improvement in sleep, other critical issues in this client's life became the focus of therapy. It is important to note that in a case where multiple problems exist, sleep problems can be evaluated and corrected apart from the other problems.

## TERMINATION

Mario felt that his sleep was greatly improved and he no longer described himself as an insomniac. He was able to maintain good sleep hygiene and to

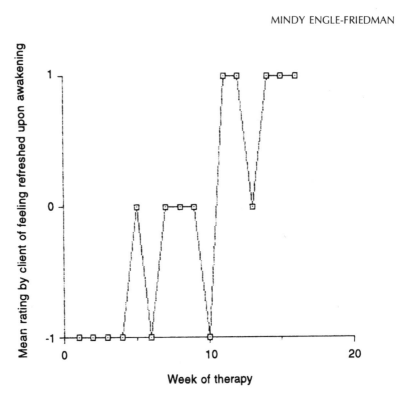

Figure 18-4. Mean rating by client of feeling refreshed upon awakening in the morning for the two initial evaluation weeks and through the 14-week treatment period (1 = very refreshed, 0 = neither refreshed nor exhausted, –1 = extremely exhausted).

follow the stimulus control instructions on his own without having to be reminded by me. He was able to take responsibility for his sleep and could point out how any problems sleeping he had were related to his presleep activities. He was also able to correct his presleep activities the next night, and thus experience an improvement in sleep. With his greatly improved sleep and his ability to control his sleep, he decided he no longer needed treatment for sleep and I fully agreed.

While Mario's improved sleep helped him feel more alert and relaxed at work, he was still having problems interpersonally, both at work and with his family. He asked for my support in these areas and we began addressing his social difficulties. Though we did not terminate fully at the end of his treatment for insomnia, we no longer discussed sleep problems. Mario no longer saw insomnia as his primary problem and, therefore, could focus on other areas in his life that were problematic.

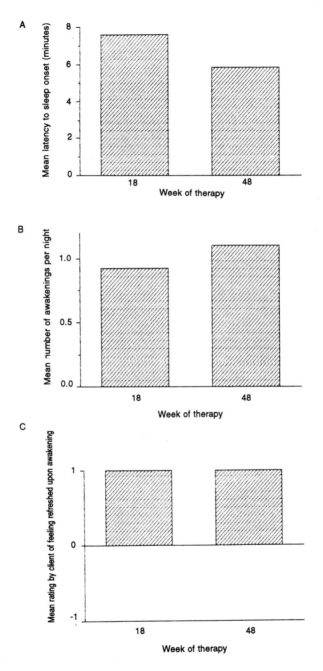

Figure 18-5. Follow-up data at 2 weeks following completion of therapy (Week 18) and at 8 months following completion of therapy (Week 48): *A*, Sleep latency follow-up data; *B*, Awakenings follow-up data; *C*, Feeling refreshed follow-up data.

# REFERENCES

Bootzin, R. R. (1972, September). *Stimulus control treatment of insomnia.* Paper presented at the meeting of the American Psychological Association, Honolulu, HI.

Bootzin, R. R. (1975). *A comparison of stimulus control instructions and progressive relaxation training in the treatment of sleep onset insomnia.* Unpublished manuscript, Department of Psychology, Northwestern University, Evanston, IL.

Engle-Friedman, M., Bootzin, R. R., & Hazlewood, L. (1983, November). *The effect of music and temporal cues on sleep: A test of the stimulus control theory.* Paper presented at meeting of the Association for the Advancement of Behavior Therapy, Washington, DC.

Engle-Friedman, M., Bootzin, R. R., Hazlewood, L., & Tsao, C. (1992). An evaluation of behavioral treatments for insomnia in the older adult. *Journal of Clinical Psychology, 48*(1): 77–90.

Hauri, P. (1970). Evening activity, sleep mentation and subjective sleep quality. *Journal of Abnormal Psychology, 76,* 270–275.

Lacks, P., Bertelsen, A. D., Sugarman, J., & Kunkel, J. (1983). The treatment of sleep maintenance insomnia with stimulus control techniques. *Behavior Research and Therapy, 21,* 291–295.

Webb, W. B. (1975). *Sleep: The gentle tyrant.* Englewood Cliffs, NJ: Spectrum.

# CHAPTER 19

# Pathological Gambling

## RICHARD A. McCORMICK

## DESCRIPTION OF THE DISORDER

Pathological gambling is a disorder that affects up to 1.1 million individuals in America alone (Commission on Review of the National Policy Toward Gambling, 1976). Opportunities for recreational gambling continue to increase: almost every state uses legal lotteries to generate revenue, casino gambling and sports betting are becoming legal in more jurisdictions, a volatile stock market is providing opportunities for the more affluent, and illegal gambling is continuing to thrive. It is estimated that over 10 billion dollars are wagered annually in state lotteries and over 70 billion dollars in legal and illegal sports betting. Despite the increase in gambling and the recent notoriety associated with pathological gambling by public figures, research into etiological factors and effective treatment interventions is very limited.

Pathological gambling is classified as a disorder of impulse control marked by the persistent inability to resist the urge to gamble despite the significant disruption of vocational, personal, and family functioning. There is considerable heterogeneity among pathological gamblers, and gamblers tend to present with complex problems and comorbidities, including significant depression, hypomania, suicidal tendencies, substance abuse, and cognitive impairments (McCormick, Russo, Ramirez, & Taber, 1984; Ramirez, McCormick, Russo, & Taber, 1983). Personality disorders are also common, most notably borderline personality disorder and narcissistic personality disorder.

RICHARD A. McCORMICK • Psychology Service, Cleveland Veterans Affairs Medical Center, Brecksville Division, Brecksville, Ohio 44141.

*Adult Behavior Therapy Casebook,* edited by Cynthia G. Last and Michel Hersen. Plenum Press, New York, 1994.

There have been a small number of reports on the utility of individual insight-oriented psychotherapy with pathological gamblers. The most common treatment approach has been that used by Gamblers Anonymous (GA), which is closely modeled after the Alcoholics Anonymous program. For more severe cases a limited number of inpatient programs are available; these tend to supplement a strong commitment to GA with group therapy, family therapy, individual counseling, and educational interventions. Formal reports on the use of behavioral techniques have been limited and have focused primarily on small samples in which aversive conditioning or desensitization was employed (Taber & McCormick, 1987).

It is important to recognize that not all behavioral treatments are field tested and refined by behaviorally oriented therapists who approach a particular problem from a theoretical perspective. Very often, people who would not label themselves behaviorists develop treatments through trial and error that are, in fact, behavioral interventions. Such is the case in the field of treatment for pathological gambling. The systematic structuring and repetitions of the GA model and the inculcation of positive self-statements, such as "I must deal with my gambling problem one day at a time" (an ideal alternative self-statement for the catastrophizing gambler overwhelmed by the enormity of his life problems), are examples of this phenomenon.

The heterogeneity and complexity of the problems presented by the pathological gambler require the therapist to thoroughly assess multiple variables and carefully match treatment to the particular case. Behavioral treatments can be an important part of the treatment plan. Behavioral treatments can blend well with more standard peer group approaches, particularly if therapists are able to recognize the behavioral principles underlying many of the GA approaches, redefine them in behavioral terms for themselves and their clients, and then build on them in developing the behavioral aspects of the treatment plan for a particular client.

## CASE IDENTIFICATION

The client to be presented was seen by me in a private practice setting. He had never been in inpatient treatment but had been active in GA for some years. An outpatient case has been deliberately chosen on the assumption that only a small percentage of readers will be operating from one of the few inpatient treatment centers for pathological gambling.

The client was a 37-year-old married male. He was living with his wife and three children, who ranged in age from 5 to 12 years. He was employed as a retail store manager on a full-time basis and also held a part-time job as a salesman in another retail establishment. He worked over 65 hours per week.

He was in good physical health, except for a history of ulcers, which continued to cause him distress. His wife worked part-time as a salesperson. He was referred by a GA colleague who was concerned about his recent deterioration.

## PRESENTING COMPLAINTS

The client presented as an articulate, sincere informant. He was notably anxious and had trouble sitting still during the initial interview. He sought treatment because he was experiencing a recurrence of pathological gambling after a 3-year period of abstinence. He had been gambling with progressively larger amounts of money for the past 7 months. His wife had become aware of his relapse and was responding with intense anger. She was attending gam-anon sessions and had been instrumental in his seeking help beyond his GA involvement. He had been abstinent for the 3 weeks prior to his appointment with me but was experiencing strong, constant urges to gamble. He reported feeling overwhelmed by the combination of his urges to gamble, the pressure from his wife, the anger and frustration of those around him about his relapse, and the need to work to ease financial pressures, which were chronic but were now severely exacerbated by his recent gambling cycle. He also reported increased emotionality, which was a new experience for him. He remembered having periods in the past when he felt anxious but reported that in the last few weeks he had been feeling severely anxious and overtly depressed, even to the point of tearfulness, which also was a totally novel experience for him.

## HISTORY

The client was the oldest of five children. His parents were both first-generation Americans for whom achieving financial success and stability and maintaining religious and moral values was very important. The father was a hardworking blue-collar worker who was described by the client as being emotionally distant and strict. The father was also depicted as a problem drinker who became loud and verbally abusive when drunk. The mother was a housewife who was nurturing to the children but relatively passive. The client's parents wanted very badly for their children to obtain a good education and surpass their own social and financial status. Special expectations were placed on the client in this regard since he was the oldest son and the father's namesake.

The client's relationship with his father was distant. He felt pressured to succeed and was the object of intense anger, particularly when his father had been drinking. He handled these outbursts by withdrawing as quickly as possible from the situation. While he felt that his mother loved him, she seemed preoccupied with caring for the younger children and coping with the family's financial and emotional struggles.

The client reported achieving average grades in school. He expended considerable energy into trying to excel at sports, particularly baseball and football. Because of his short stature and lack of natural speed he had to work especially hard. Nevertheless, he never felt he succeeded at the level expected by his father.

The client had good friendships but did not begin dating until his junior year in high school. His first, and only, serious relationship was with the girl he eventually married, whom he started dating in his senior year. He reported feeling unsure of himself in social situations but not letting his discomfort show externally.

The client attended a local community college for 2 years following graduation from high school and did moderately well. He was married at age 21, at which time he started working full-time and attending school on a part-time basis. He stopped attending school just prior to the birth of his first child, when he was 24 years old.

## ASSESSMENT

As noted earlier, pathological gamblers generally present with a complex set of problems. It is critical, therefore, that the assessment extend beyond the presenting problem (i.e., excessive gambling) and include at least the following: a comprehensive assessment of all disorders of impulse control and impulsive behaviors; a thorough assessment of how the client experiences and expresses his emotions; a history of significant life traumas; an assessment of the client's current repertoire of coping skills; an assessment of factors that led to prior relapses; and a history of prior attempts at treatment. These assessments need to be in sufficient detail to support the matching of explicit behavioral treatments to the patient's deficits.

Such an assessment was accomplished with this client through the use of several self-administered psychometric instruments and a written autobiography. All of these assessment procedures, which represented considerable work for the client, were assigned to be done at home. Homework increases the efficiency of the assessment and also emphasizes to the client from the beginning that what transpires in treatment sessions is merely a small part of the therapeutic work.

### The Written Autobiography

The client was given at the end of the initial interview a detailed outline for a written autobiography. The outline begins with a two-page listing of significant life events, which are categorized into subheadings (e.g., childhood events, physical problems). The client was instructed to circle any event that he had experienced and to note the age at which it occurred (for each subcategory the client was also asked to indicate and similarly identify any other applicable events). The remaining instructions required the client to write in a narrative format a personal autobiography addressing for each developmental period (childhood, adolescence, early adulthood, adulthood, the present) at least the following topics: gambling experiences; use of alcohol and other drugs; interpersonal relationships, including family relationships and intimate and sexual relationships; the manner in which he handled his emotional responses; significant events, including all the events circled on the first two pages; academic and vocational pursuits; successes and failures; and prior treatments for gambling or any other mental health condition. The client was given a self-addressed envelope in which to return the autobiography and psychometric instruments prior to the next session.

## Psychometric Instruments

The client completed the Minnesota Multiphasic Personality Inventory (MMPI), which was used to help assess personality structures and presence of comorbidities. The MMPI was chosen because of the relatively large body of literature citing use of this instrument with pathological gamblers (McCormick & Taber, 1987). The client also completed the California Personality Inventory (CPI), which was chosen because it is standardized to a normal population and has been found useful by our research group in assessing personality traits and coping strategies across the normal domain (McCormick, Taber, Kruedelbach, & Russo, 1987). Also used for assessment was the South Oaks Gambling Screen (SOGS; Lesieur & Blume, 1987), which provides a measure of severity of gambling normed against a population of pathological gamblers. The Barratt Impulsivity Scale (BIS) was used to help assess the client's degree of impulse control. This instrument measures three subtraits of impulsivity: motor impulsiveness, cognitive impulsiveness, and nonplanning impulsiveness (Barratt, 1987). We have found pathological gamblers, although clearly an impulsive group when gambling, to vary considerably on the degree to which impulsivity is pervasive in their lives. Understanding a client's capacity for impulse control in other areas of life is important in planning treatment strategies, for these can be aimed at either providing external structure and basic impulse control training (for the pervasively impulsive gambler) or helping the client to generalize relatively good impulse control skills to the area of gambling (for the less impulsive gambler).

## A Structured Interview for Impulsive Behaviors

The initial portion of the second session was spent administering a detailed structured interview designed to assess a broad range of disorders of impulse control and impulsive behaviors. The interview is designed to assess the following behaviors: gambling, substance abuse, impulsive eating, paraphilias, stealing, excessive spending, lying, excessive, compulsive sexual behavior, and firesetting. For each of these behaviors the following parameters are assessed: mode (e.g., sports betting vs. casino betting); intensity (e.g., amount of money wagered); frequency and pattern; context (e.g., where and with whom the person wagered); and the person's phenomenological experience (i.e., what the experience was like for the subject).

The information provided by this client in his autobiography and the results from the BIS served as the starting point for the interview. Since the patient presented for pathological gambling, the interview began by focusing on his gambling behavior. It then progressed to alcohol use and lying, both of which were mentioned by him in his autobiography. The remaining behavioral domains were then assessed in a standard progression.

## Assessment of Relapse Factors

The client also completed for his first homework assignment, as part of the assessment procedure, a modification of the Inventory of Drinking Situations and the companion instrument, Situational Confidence Questionnaire (Annis & Davis, 1988). The modification involved changing important terminology to refer to gambling situations rather than drinking situations. Together these instruments provided a self-report by the client of specific situations where he was prone to relapse; a means of grouping these situations into interpersonal, intrapersonal, and situational factors; and an indication of the degree of confidence (self-efficacy) the client felt in resisting the urge to gamble in each of these situations. The responses and scores of the client on the factors served as the starting point for the second part of the second interview: a detailed behavioral analysis of the situations and stimuli most closely associated with past relapses and with urges or cravings. The Situational Confidence Questionnaire, in conjunction with the phenomenological portion of the structured interview assessment of impulsive behavior, provided a broad analysis of the negative and positive expectations that the client associated with gambling.

## Assessment of Coping Skills

Included in the first homework assignment was the Ways of Coping Scale (Lazarus & Folkman, 1984), which assesses a broad range of coping behaviors and groups them into eight factors that represent general modes of coping. The Ways of Coping Scale, in conjunction with the CPI data, served as the starting point for the third portion of the second interview, which focused on the client's characteristic modes of coping with life stressors and difficult situations.

## View of Client's Problem as a Result of Assessment

The client began gambling in high school on a small scale. He began sports betting through a bookmaker at age 22, with the size of bets increasing steadily over the next 3 years. During this period he also began betting on horses at local race tracks and through the bookmaker. By age 26 he was gambling in a compulsive manner, wagering up to three thousand dollars per week and spending large portions of the day researching sports teams and handicapping horses. He financed his gambling initially through working overtime, which he concealed from his wife, and through personal loans. The intensity of his gambling continued to increase over time, and he began procuring funds through illegal means, including small embezzlement and small-scale bookmaking. At age 31 a series of events, including pressure from his family and employer, financial disasters, and hospitalization for his stomach condition, motivated the client to begin participation in GA. He continued to gamble in sporadic binges for the next 2 years and then entered a 3-year period of abstinence, which he maintained through GA participation. During the 7 months prior to his seeking individual treatment he had returned to sports gambling, wagering up to one thousand dollars per week. While his gambling was more sporadic than in the past, its frequency was steadily increasing.

The client's relapse triggers were largely of an intrapersonal nature. He experienced urges when he was anxious, depressed, or feeling bored. He had a strong need to be in constant action of some sort, whether action at work, playing sports competitively, or through gambling. When he was not consumed with some type of action, he felt severe negative emotions. He rationalized his gambling as an attempt to provide for his family the level of support that he saw them demanding and expecting of him. He perceived that he had a special skill and that he was capable of out-handicapping the odds makers. He responded to his wife's anger and the anger of others by being passive and avoiding or withdrawing, and then he would feel guilty and inadequate, His personality testing was consistent with this pattern of relapse triggers. His MMPI (code type 7213) and CPI suggested an unassertive individual with a poor self-concept who experienced frequent anxiety, sadness, and guilt and who tended to somaticize his emotions. He had been raped as a young teenager by a camp worker but had not sought support for the incident; in fact, he had not shared it with anyone prior to the assessment.

The client lied frequently, always in situations where the lie would prevent him from being confronted by the dissatisfaction of someone else. Such lying went beyond his gambling behavior and persisted during periods of abstinence. He also spent money impulsively, invariably to please others or to increase his external stature. Nevertheless, in general he scored lower than most gamblers on the measures of impulsivity, which was consistent with his successful retention of jobs despite his gambling and with his having kept his family intact. In areas other than his gambling, and the associated spending and lying, he tended to have adequate impulse control.

Gambling made the client feel more powerful and adequate. He also experienced the action of planning his bets as a relief from anxiety and boredom. At the time of assessment he had low self-efficacy expectations for being able to avoid relapse in response to a wide variety of trigger situations.

The client's primary modes of coping were escape/avoidance and problem solving. His problem-solving skills were quite good and accounted for much positive feedback at work. People often sought him out for advice on practical matters. In situations that had a strong emotional component, whether his own internal emotional reaction or the strong emotions of others, he utilized escape and avoidance strategies, even when he fully realized that the long-term results made them illogical choices. Notably absent from his repertoire of coping skills were the ability to seek emotional support from others (or to give it in a non-problem-solving context) and the ability to reframe events in a more positive manner.


## SELECTION OF TREATMENT

### External Structuring

The client was actively gambling at the point of entering treatment. The first concern needed to be strengthening and reinforcing of external structuring forces in his life. It was important to provide a daily schedule of specific activities that would fill all his time in a productive manner. Gambling compulsively is a time-consuming activity. Alternative activities are critical components in the treatment plan. Although he was still active in GA, the client

had decreased his attendance at meetings as his gambling increased. Moreover, his sponsor in GA was rather unassertive, and the client had only limited
contact with him. At the beginning of treatment a contract was developed that
specified that the client would attend regular GA meetings (two general meetings and one meeting which focused on the steps to recovery (step-work) per
week, would seek out and participate actively with a new sponsor, would
attend the scheduled sessions with his therapist regularly, and would call the
therapist or his sponsor when the urge to gamble became intense. He also
agreed to regularly scheduled marital counseling, which thus involved participation by his wife in providing additional external structure. The importance of the structure provided by his current regular work schedule was also
stressed. Leisure time activities with his children were planned to fill his
remaining available free time.

## Coping Skills Enhancement

While the structuring interventions were very useful in stopping the steady
increase in time and money spent in gambling, the primary goal of treatment
was to increase the client's ability to cope with the situations that were precipitants to his relapses. Coping skills training and enhancement interventions
therefore served as the core of the treatment strategy and are described in
detail in the following paragraphs.

Structured training in *relaxation strategies* was used to give the client the
skills necessary to decrease the physiological component of the arousal, which
invariably accompanied and helped to incite his urge to gamble. His gambling
most often began with a feeling of anxiety, which could at times be traced to
a proximal experience (e.g., a fight with his wife) but which also seemed at
times to be unrelated to any external precipitant. Such anxiety would escalate
as the client began to ponder and plan for his gambling experience.

Efforts were made to expand the client's *seeking of emotional support* as
a coping strategy, particularly for the emotion-laden problems that often precipitated his relapses. This was accomplished by training him to seek emotional support from his sponsor and wife.

*Reducing the use of escape/avoidance coping strategies* was an additional
focus of treatment. This included reducing not only the client's gambling but
also his lying and procrastination.

The client was given a course of *assertiveness training,* including role-
playing practice sessions around real-life situations that presented themselves
during therapy. In the marital counseling sessions both husband and wife were
instructed in techniques for more effective *conflict resolution.* The wife's sup-

port was enlisted to help the client tolerate her when upset and face anger-laden situations that arose in the relationship instead of avoiding them.

The urge to gamble often accelerated very quickly for this client in response to intrapersonal triggers. Customized *positive self-statements* were used to provide him with a quick and easily implemented strategy for managing a cycle in which he began feeling bad, immediately exaggerated in his mind the positive advantages of gambling, experienced low self-efficacy and powerlessness to refrain from gambling, and perceived no alternative coping options. Self-statements were designed to offset each phase of this recurring process.

## COURSE OF TREATMENT

### Session I

The first treatment session was devoted to negotiating an initial treatment plan. The session began with a short "lecture" on the relapse cycle in order to make explicit the steps involved in relapse. The cycle was presented as divided into three components. The first was a *trigger event,* which could be a hot tip on a horse given by an old betting buddy or an intrapersonal stimulus such as a guilt-provoking fight with his wife. The second was a *need state* that was aroused in the client and experienced by him as an urge to gamble or as an emotion such as anxiety or boredom. The third was the *choice point,* that is, the point in the cycle where the client had to decide how to cope with the need state, whether to use escape/avoidance mechanisms, such as gambling, or whether to cope in a more productive manner.

It was emphasized that if the client chose gambling, the short-term relief would rebound to a new, increased need state, thus accelerating the relapse cycle. It was important to demystify the relapse process in order to begin to enhance the client's confidence that he could solve this problem as he had previously successfully solved many problems in the workplace. The treatment plan was introduced as the means to short-circuit the cycle at a number of points.

During this session the portions of the plan dealing with providing external structure were developed in detail. The specific GA meetings to be attended were specified. A potential new sponsor was identified, and an action plan for contacting him and contracting with him about receiving telephone calls when the urge to gamble became intense was established (the therapist offered to be available for calls as a backup). The current positive structuring elements in the client's life, including his regular attendance at work, were reinforced and redefined as treatment elements.

The remaining portions of the treatment plan were delineated in a more general manner. Included were conjoint therapy with his wife and the learning of new methods to cope with stressful situations. As a homework assignment the client was instructed to share the initial treatment plan with his wife and to relate to her the importance of his having external structure at this point in his recovery. The client was then expected to "brainstorm" with his wife about strategies through which she could provide additional structure. The therapist described examples that other couples had developed to facilitate this assignment. This session set the tone for the overall structure for most subsequent sessions: the imparting of information necessary for the task or skill to be addressed in the session; experiential work on the task; and the assignment of an active homework project.

## Session II

The next session began with an immediate review of the homework. As his homework assignment, the client had asked his wife to be involved in the therapy process. She proposed a plan in which she would handle all the family finances and he would provide written verification of all pay he received. These suggestions were presented with anger, and the client agreed with reluctance and smoldering resentment. They also agreed that he would call her twice during the workday to "check in."

The client had followed through on the other structuring elements, including successfully engaging a new sponsor. He had remained abstinent since the last therapy session but had experienced significant urges, which he had handled without calling his sponsor or the therapist. During the session the self-statements he used to rationalize not calling someone were made explicit. The client agreed to the following alternative self-statement: "Having the urge to gamble is normal, expected, and serious. I have to take the insurance policy of calling someone." The statement was written by the client on a small index card, and he agreed to tell his sponsor and his wife about it, carry it in his shirt pocket, and read it to himself if he felt a strong urge to gamble prior to the next session. The remainder of the session was spent in training the client in brief relaxation skills. He was given a tape, which included progressive relaxation and imagery, to practice with at home. The therapist reviewed the relapse cycle with the client, emphasizing the point where relaxation training and positive self-statements intervened in the cycle.

## Session III

The client and his wife were seen together for the next session and for alternate sessions thereafter. The session began with a review of the concept of the relapse cycle, both as a review for the client and to help his wife understand the goals of the treatment process. The couple agreed to the initial marital goals of learning to give and receive emotional support and improving their interactions in emotional situations. The wife was able to easily resonate with the client's problems handling negative emotional situations. In an emotional manner she talked about her own frustration, fears of loss of security, and anger.

A structured exercise was used to help her be more explicit about what emotions she was experiencing and how they related to the client's behavior. She was asked to complete the sentence "When you do . . . , I feel . . . " A number of iterations were used to help her clarify her communications and to help the client differentiate the various emotions she felt, rather than assume that all her emotional responses were angry ones.

As is often the case with the partner of a gambler, the wife's level of trust had greatly deteriorated. The client's lying, particularly through lies of omission, was clearly the key behavior that perpetuated this lack of trust. The latter part of the session was spent in negotiating a "full disclosure" contract between husband and wife. The client agreed to spend time over the next week writing down all the lies of omission, major or trivial, of which he was currently aware. His wife agreed to try to respond with explicit statements of how she felt. The process was started in the session, with the client disclosing a two-thousand-dollar debt that he had incurred as part of his most recent gambling spree.

## Session IV

The next session began with a review of the homework on the disclosure contract. The client reported having a very difficult time with how emotional his wife had become. Role play was used to reveal self-statements evoked in the client by his wife's emotional response. The intensity of her emotion had made him feel guilty and had caused him to make negative self-statements about himself. The following alternative self-statement was added to his card: "Her intense emotional reaction is her way of dealing with things. It doesn't mean that I'm bad." He was instructed to say this to himself every time he felt uncomfortable when his wife became emotional.

## Later Sessions

In subsequent conjoint sessions further work was carried out to help both the client and his wife express their emotions more explicitly and tie them to specific behaviors. The client succeeded in being able to better tolerate his wife's emotional outbursts without resorting to escape/avoidance coping strategies. Both were also instructed on the importance of seeking emotional support as a valid coping mechanism for emotional situations. In an initial homework assignment they were able to recall a time early in their relationship when they would share with each other the mutual frustrations they felt with their parents and would provide support to each other. This recollection helped them to appreciate the power of such a coping mechanism. By using guided role play and interactions during the sessions, they were able to improve their skills in empathic listening and to reexperience the power of seeking emotional support.

Subsequent individual sessions with the client were used to further expand his alternative self-statements to those that portrayed more realistically the outcomes of gambling (e.g., "Succeeding at gambling will not make me a successful husband") and those that reinforced his ability to cope in other ways, (e.g., "I am a good problem solver, especially when I ask someone to listen to my problems first").

Three sessions were used to teach the client assertiveness skills. This flowed naturally from an incident that occurred at his work where he failed to confront an employee who was taking advantage of his aversion for conflictual interactions. Role play rehearsal was used to prepare the client for a planned confrontation with the employee about his behavior. The client followed through on the encounter and experienced his power to manage a conflictual situation. The last assertiveness session focused on expressing his wishes and needs to his wife. In the following conjoint session the client practiced such assertive responding with his wife.

The client's urges to gamble decreased over the course of treatment, as he was compliant with the structuring interventions. He gradually became more confident in his ability to cope in ways other than gambling or avoiding an unpleasant situation. During his therapy sessions he was strongly reinforced for using positive coping skills. For example, toward the end of treatment (Session 14), he related an incident in which his wife was complaining about their lack of funds and comparing their situation with her sister's family, which was more affluent. This evoked a series of negative thoughts in the client about his being an inadequate father and husband. He was able to first talk to himself, reinforcing the concept that his worth should be judged on more than a financial scale, and then was able to tell his wife how he felt in response to her complaints. The client was congratulated for his successful coping with what had formerly been a strong negative intrapersonal trigger (guilt over someone else's dissatisfaction with him). The event was discussed in detail, comparing it with the client's past behavior in such situations, in order to reinforce his power to implement an alternative coping response.

## TERMINATION

The length of time between sessions was increased to 2 weeks for a period of 2 months, while still alternating individual and conjoint sessions. This was explained to the client and his wife as a prelude to termination. Following a 6-week period during which the client was not seen for a combination of reasons, including a vacation by the therapist and two canceled appointments, the client terminated treatment. Thus, no formal termination session was conducted. Normally, a formal termination session is used to negotiate a written relapse prevention plan.

## FOLLOW-UP

Approximately 3 months after termination the client called to report a lapse. He had placed a four-hundred-dollar sports bet. He had shared the lapse with his sponsor but not with his wife. The client was counseled on the importance of keeping the lapse from cycling into a relapse. He was able to recognize that the thought of confronting his wife was making him extremely anxious, and he agreed to cope with the lapse by not avoiding the needed disclosure. He seemed to understand that the anxiety caused by avoiding the confrontation with his wife would only increase his urges to gamble. Approximately 6 months later the therapist received a report from a reliable fellow GA member that the client was remaining abstinent and maintaining active participation in GA.

## OVERALL EVALUATION

Pathological gambling, like all disorders of impulse control, is a condition that is prone to relapse. This case illustrates the important role of structuring interventions in establishing abstinence and the complementary role of enhancing coping skills in maintaining abstinence and reducing the likelihood of lapses degenerating into relapses. The client was able to quickly comply with structuring interventions, which helped reverse his gambling relapse. He made progress in increasing his awareness of the factors that often preceded such lapses. He subsequently was able to articulate the relapse cycle and personalize it to his life situation. He succeeded in expanding his repertoire of coping skills, including the utilization of positive alternative self-statements and assertiveness. However, he never succeeded in making practical use of the relaxation skills. His relationship with his wife improved, with both of them being able to provide more support to the other while improving their ability to manage conflicts when they occurred. Although the overt anger and lack of trust expressed by the client's wife diminished somewhat, they remained salient issues at termination.

The client still maintained deep-seated negative beliefs about his worth at the point of termination. He may well have benefited from additional cognitive therapy for this problem. His follow-up call, and the later information on his progress, indicated that he had increased his awareness of the relapse cycle and had improved his repertoire of coping skills sufficiently to maintain abstinence and prevent a lapse from developing into a full-blown relapse. The conjoint sessions, which forced the client to deal more explicitly with his wife's emotional reactions, including her anger and mistrust, were very difficult for him. This difficulty may have contributed to his abrupt termination of treatment as soon as he regained confidence in his ability to maintain abstinence.

## REFERENCES

Annis, H. M., & Davis, C. S. (1988). Assessment of expectancies. In D. M. Donovan & G. A. Marlatt (Eds.), *Assessment of addictive behaviors* (pp. 84–111). New York: Guilford Press.

Barratt, E. S. (1987). Impulsiveness and anxiety: Information processing and EEG topography. *Journal of Research in Personality, 21,* 453–463.

Commission on the Review of the National Policy Toward Gambling. (1976). *Gambling in America.* Washington, DC: U.S. Government Printing Office.

Lazarus, R. S., & Folkman, S. (1984). *Stress, appraisal and coping.* New York: Springer.

Lesieur, H. R., & Blume, S. B. (1987). The South Oaks Gambling Screen (SOGS): A new instrument for the identification of pathological gamblers. *American Journal of Psychiatry, 144,* 1184–1188.

McCormick, R. A., Russo, A. M., Ramirez, L. F., & Taber, J. I. (1984). Affective disorders among pathological gamblers seeking treatment. *American Journal of Psychiatry, 141,* 215–218.

McCormick, R. A., & Taber, J. I. (1987). The pathological gambler: Salient personality variables. In T. Galski (Ed.), *The handbook of pathological gambling* (pp. 9–40). Springfield, IL: Charles C. Thomas.

McCormick, R. A., Taber, J. I., Kruedelbach, N., & Russo, A. M. (1987). Personality profiles of hospitalized pathological gamblers: The California Personality Inventory. *Journal of Clinical Psychology, 43,* 521–527.

Ramirez, L. F., McCormick, R. A., Russo, A. M., & Taber, J. I. (1983). Patterns of substance abuse in pathological gamblers undergoing treatment. *Addictive Behavior, 8,* 425–428.

Taber, J. I., & McCormick, R. A. (1987). The pathological gambler in treatment. In T. Galski (Ed.), *The handbook of pathological gambling* (pp. 137–168). Springfield, IL: Charles C. Thomas.

# Index